A TEAM OF FIVE MILLION?

THE 2020 'COVID-19' NEW ZEALAND GENERAL ELECTION

A TEAM OF FIVE MILLION?

THE 2020 'COVID-19' NEW ZEALAND GENERAL ELECTION

EDITED BY JENNIFER CURTIN, LARA GREAVES AND JACK VOWLES

Australian
National
University

ANU PRESS

Australian
National
University

ANU PRESS

Published by ANU Press
The Australian National University
Canberra ACT 2600, Australia
Email: anupress@anu.edu.au

Available to download for free at press.anu.edu.au

ISBN (print): 9781760466473
ISBN (online): 9781760466480

WorldCat (print): 1434632028
WorldCat (online): 1434631708

DOI: 10.22459/TFM.2024

Cover design and layout by ANU Press.
Cover photograph: Hagen Hopkins, New Zealand Listener.

This book is published under the aegis of the Social Sciences editorial committee of ANU Press.

Contents

List of Figures

List of Tables

Abbreviations

GDP	gross domestic product
GFC	Global Financial Crisis
IMF	International Monetary Fund
MMP	mixed-member proportional
MP	Member of Parliament
NZES	New Zealand Election Study
NZSMS	New Zealand Social Media Study
OECD	Organisation for Economic Co-operation and Development
TOP	The Opportunities Party
UK	United Kingdom
UN	United Nations
US	United States

Acknowledgements

No study of New Zealand's 2020 general election could avoid the fallout from the Covid-19 pandemic. An effective response to the crisis presented a challenge both to the government and to civil society. The legal and administrative capacity of the New Zealand state was stretched to its limits. Of equal importance was the public response: the extent to which New Zealand civil society would accept the policies established to contain the virus—namely, lockdowns and border controls. The majority of New Zealanders accepted these restrictions—in most cases, willingly. That acceptance was greatly facilitated by the political communication skills of then prime minister Jacinda Ardern, their effectiveness summed up best by the concept of the 'Team of Five Million'. Not all were impressed and, arguably, some were left out. But the result of the election confirmed an overwhelmingly positive response. In this book, we examine the why and how of Labour's return as a majority government. We do this using data about public opinion and political behaviour that we collected immediately after the 2020 election.

This is the ninth in a series of books on New Zealand elections with sample survey data from the New Zealand Election Study (NZES), and marks 30 years since the first NZES survey, in 1990. The 2020 election study was led by Jack Vowles (Te Herenga Waka–Victoria University of Wellington), Lara Greaves (Te Herenga Waka–Victoria University of Wellington), and Jennifer Curtin (University of Auckland–Waipapa Taumata Rau)—the editors of this book—and was supported by a team of scholars from around New Zealand. It was funded by grants from several sources, including the New Zealand Electoral Commission, Te Herenga Waka–Victoria University of Wellington, the University of Auckland–Waipapa Taumata Rau, and the University of Otago. The survey was administered by the University of Auckland's Public Policy Institute. Lara Greaves and Luke Oldfield organised and coordinated the survey administration, under very difficult conditions due to Covid-19 restrictions. For most of 2021, they and their assistants, Frank Gore, Amanda Sesio, and Justin Wong, had no access to offices and equipment when collecting and capturing data. We also wish to acknowledge the efforts of Kiri Picard, who was supported by a Ngā Pae o te Māramatanga internship.

In 2020 the online survey was translated into te reo Māori and Chinese and for this we are grateful to Hēmi Kelly and Jie Huang, respectively. Additionally, several research assistants at the University of Auckland–Waipapa Taumata Rau helped with the envelope 'stuffing', including Jeevan Karki, Chrystal Thompson, Anthonia Uzoigwe, and Sinchana Appachoo. Kaylee Brink provided invaluable editorial assistance in preparing the final version of this manuscript. At Te Herenga Waka–Victoria University of Wellington, Matthew Gibbons matched the panellists and Ben Stubbing did the occupational coding. As always, our research and analysis would not be possible without our 3,730 participants, who generously shared with us their perspectives and preferences on politics, policy issues, Covid-19, and our electoral system. We appreciate being able to publish our findings with ANU Press because their open access download option enables our participants to read our analyses. For those who want to explore our data in more depth, you can visit our new website: www.nzes.net.

Finally, to our families and friends, who continue to support our endeavours during and after each election, know this volume would not have happened without you.

Jennifer, Lara, and Jack

Contributors

Fiona Barker is Senior Lecturer in Comparative Politics at Te Herenga Waka–Victoria University of Wellington. Her research interests include political representation, immigration and electoral politics, and nationalism. Recent publications have examined parliamentary representation of diversity in mixed electoral systems, immigrants' electoral participation, and governance of immigrant integration in multinational societies. Fiona is co-editor of the journal *Political Science*.

Sam Crawley is a Whitinga Postdoctoral Fellow in Political Science at Te Herenga Waka–Victoria University of Wellington. His research focuses on the politics of climate change and his current primary research project compares climate opinion in Aotearoa New Zealand and Australia. Sam also has ongoing research projects examining broader aspects of public opinion, political behaviour, and comparative politics.

Jennifer Curtin is Professor of Politics and Inaugural Director of the Public Policy Institute at the University of Auckland–Waipapa Taumata Rau. She researches New Zealand and Australian politics, and gender politics, policy analysis, and political leadership. She leads the Gender Responsive Analysis and Budgeting Project (available from: www.grab-nz.ac.nz) and her research features regularly in a range of media outlets.

Celestyna Galicki works in the public sector and is a Research Associate of the Public Policy Institute at the University of Auckland–Waipapa Taumata Rau. Her PhD at Auckland explored barriers to voting for young, migrant, and low socioeconomic voters in New Zealand and Sweden, with special focus on barriers created or exacerbated by election administration procedures.

Matthew Gibbons (Te Herenga Waka–Victoria University of Wellington) researches voting behaviour, including voting and nonvoting, and party policy. He has a PhD in politics from the University of Waikato. In 2023, he taught a course on New Zealand political parties at Victoria University.

Lara M. Greaves (Ngāpuhi/Pākehā/Tararā) is an Associate Professor in Politics at Te Herenga Waka–Victoria University of Wellington and a Senior Research Fellow in statistics at the University of Auckland–Waipapa Taumata Rau. Lara teaches and researches in the areas of New Zealand, Māori, and Indigenous politics. She is also working in the areas of Māori/Indigenous data sovereignty, electoral law, history, and political participation.

Janine Hayward is a Professor of Politics at the University of Otago. She researches Te Tiriti o Waitangi/Treaty of Waitangi politics and constitutional/electoral politics. She works with local government on issues relating to representation reviews, electoral systems, and Māori wards. She co-edits *Government and Politics in Aotearoa New Zealand* with Associate Professor Lara Greaves and Dr Claire Timperley.

Mona Krewel is a senior lecturer at Te Herenga Waka–Victoria University of Wellington and the Director of the Internet, Social Media, and Politics Research Lab, which publishes the New Zealand Social Media Study. Her research focuses on misinformation and disinformation on social media, as well as persuasive and mobilising campaign effects on voters in electoral contests.

Kate McMillan is an Associate Professor of Politics at Te Herenga Waka–Victoria University of Wellington. Her research examines the intersection of electoral and immigration politics in New Zealand, and the politics of forced migration in the Asia-Pacific. Recent publications have looked at the reporting of election campaigns in the Chinese-language media and the history of New Zealand's non-citizen voting rights.

Ella Morgan is a PhD student in politics and international relations at Te Herenga Waka–Victoria University of Wellington. Her research interests include Māori politics, Mana Wahine, and gender and politics.

Luke D. Oldfield is a lecturer of Politics at Te Herenga Waka–Victoria University of Wellington. He has a PhD in politics and international relations from the University of Auckland–Waipapa Taumata Rau.

Josh Van Veen received an MA with first-class honours from the University of Auckland–Waipapa Taumata Rau. His thesis examined labourism and class dealignment in the United Kingdom and New Zealand. He has experience as a researcher, analyst, and writer, and is a Research Associate at the Public Policy Institute.

Jack Vowles is a Professor at Te Herenga Waka–Victoria University of Wellington, has led the New Zealand Election Study since 1996, and is a Fellow of the Royal Society Te Apārangi. His research is mainly on New Zealand and comparative electoral behaviour. He is co-author of *Democracy Under Siege? Parties, Voters, and Elections After the Great Recession* (Oxford University Press, 2020).

V.K.G. Woodman is a lecturer in politics and international relations at the University of Auckland–Waipapa Taumata Rau. She was a research associate at the Public Policy Institute between 2019–2023. Her research and teaching interests are New Zealand and comparative politics, gender politics, and public policy.

1

A 'Team of Five Million'? Covid-19 and the 2020 New Zealand general election

Jennifer Curtin, Lara Greaves, and Jack Vowles

Introduction

On 11 March 2020, the World Health Organization announced that Covid-19 had proliferated widely around the world. A global pandemic was declared and, in the months that followed, almost everything changed. 'Normality', as defined by the immediate past, became a memory to be cherished. Everyday lives, societies, and economies were disrupted. Nowhere were the challenges faced more apparent than in the world of politics and government.

In this book, we examine electoral politics during the crisis in New Zealand—one of a handful of countries that held a national election amid the pandemic. It was also one of the few countries in which the policy response stood out and was remarkably successful. New Zealand's general election provides an opportunity to gauge the immediate impact of the Covid-19 crisis and the impact of the New Zealand Government's policy responses on electoral politics and public opinion. While New Zealanders were voting on 17 October 2020, their country had recorded only 25 confirmed Covid deaths in a population of five million people.

A crisis can bring people together or set them apart. By the time of the 2020 election, support for the government's crisis management was at its height. Labour, the leading party in the incumbent coalition government, secured a historic election victory. Prime Minister Jacinda Ardern had taken up the metaphor of the New Zealand people as a 'Team of Five Million' facing the Covid-19 threat together. It was an idea that resonated strongly in public opinion; it implied that, in solidarity and through a focus on community, New Zealand could compete successfully to beat the virus in the same vein as a sports team. In the chapters that follow, we seek to explain the success of the government's strategy through an analysis of the election campaign and outcome. We also address the limits of this approach and the extent to which some voters felt alienated from rather than connected with the 'team'.

Our inquiry focuses on those on the front line of the experience, the people of New Zealand, through sample survey research. We draw primarily on data from the 2020 New Zealand Election Study (NZES) to explore the extent to which the idea of a Team of Five Million might have represented a new, more inclusive New Zealand or whether it was a discursive reframing of business-as-usual politics (Vowles et al. 2022). By analysing the responses of 3,730 randomly selected participants, the chapters in this book seek to untangle the themes of collective solidarity and identity, exploring a series of questions in 10 chapters that reveal the value, complexity, but also fragility of notions of unity during a time of crisis. For example, Chapter 9 asks whether the calls for a united response under strong government leadership generated stronger support for greater government leadership and involvement in other policy areas such as climate change. Chapters 4 and 7 discuss how much Ardern's discourse of 'togetherness' and her personal popularity contributed to increased voter turnout and her party's stunning election victory. Indigenous Māori and other groups most vulnerable to Covid-19 were already marginalised by continuing inequality, poverty, and discrimination. Did their voting patterns follow the rest of the Team of Five Million? Chapter 7 discusses an undercurrent of polarisation despite the continued high levels of trust in the government and public institutions. Chapter 6 asks whether sentiments about immigration shifted with border closures and a focus on protecting the country from the world.

To place these questions in context, we use the remainder of this introductory chapter to outline the background to this Covid-19 election, including the main features of the government's policy response. We recap the story from the 2017 election, when Labour won a smaller share of the vote than the centre-right National Party but was able to form a coalition with the populist New Zealand First party. The appearance of Covid-19 drew a clear line between the government's polling performance before and after the crisis. Struggling to retain traction immediately before, Labour began to soar above its competitors in popularity and support in the months that followed the onset of the pandemic. The results of the election are then analysed. Vote shifts between 2017 and 2020 are highlighted, the net effect of which was the biggest in New Zealand's electoral history. We note the significant increase in turnout particularly among younger people. We review the demographic and social foundations of voter choice in 2020. We conclude that the election outcome is best seen as a big swing of New Zealand's electoral pendulum but it did not generate a reset of the party system. Indeed, three years on, the party system looked much as it did before the pandemic. The final section of this introductory chapter offers an overview of the chapters in the remainder of this book.

The background and the crisis

The Covid-19 pandemic is a perfect example of an exogenous shock—that is, an event that came from outside the parameters of normal domestic politics.[1] Covid-19 presented a dual challenge to public health services and the economy. It left many governments to assume initially that a trade-off between the two was required. New Zealand's centre-left coalition government led by Labour Party leader Jacinda Ardern rejected that trade-off, resolving that the best economic response was to protect public health. As Ardern put it in March 2022, looking back over the experience of the previous two years: '[P]utting people's health first was also the strongest economic response' (Ardern 2022). New Zealand pursued an effective 'go hard, go early' elimination strategy. The border was closed to all except citizens, residents, their families, and a few other exceptions and a mandatory two-week custodial quarantine period in a state-managed facility post-arrival was implemented. There was a six-week lockdown from late March into early May 2020—one of the strictest by world standards, as estimated by the Oxford *COVID-19 Government Response Tracker* (BSG 2020–23). Most people deemed the policy response decisive and necessary; others thought it extreme and unnecessary (Curtin and O'Sullivan 2023; Mitchell 2021).

---

1   By this we mean a shock exogenous to New Zealand's political and party systems, not to the global capitalist economy, within which 'crises' are generated internally from time to time.

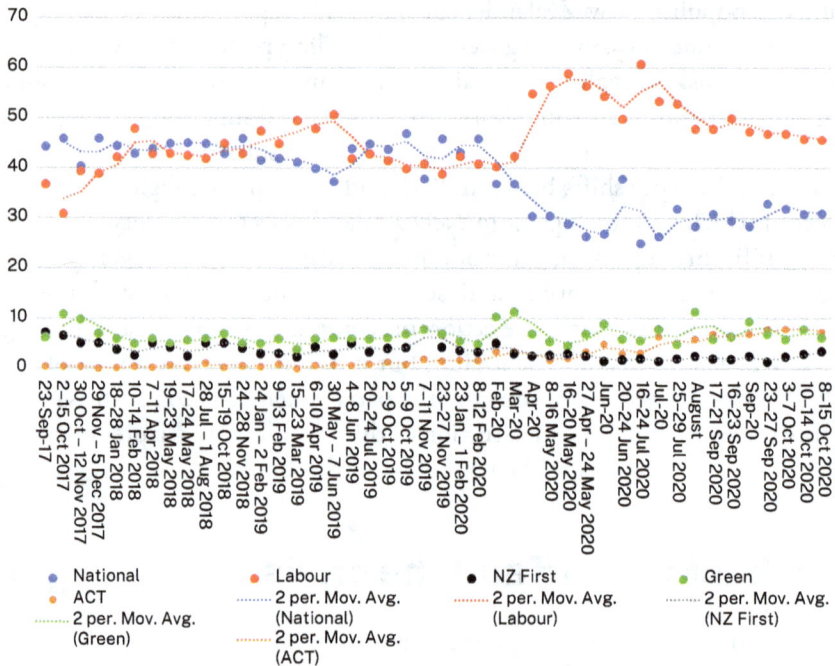

Figure 1.1 Public polling between the 2017 and 2020 elections
Sources: Colmar-Brunton Research (2017–20); Reid Research (2022); Roy Morgan (2022); Cooke (2019b).

Wide public acceptance of these lockdowns and later, less onerous restrictions were underpinned by effective communication on the part of Prime Minister Ardern and senior government officials. Ardern's description of New Zealand as a Team of Five Million—the entire population— encouraged a sense of collective purpose and identity. As a phrase, it soon became the go-to metaphor for news outlets around the world seeking to understand how Ardern had swayed a democratic nation to accept an elimination approach.

The onset of the pandemic crystalised a substantive reset of public opinion and voting intentions. The extent of Labour's victory in October 2020 could not have been predicted a year earlier. As Figure 1.1 shows, throughout the last half of 2019, the opposition National Party was outpolling Labour. While the combined left vote of Labour and the Green Party was usually sufficient to retain a margin over National, and National's ally ACT New Zealand, two polls—one in November 2019 and another in February 2020—put the combination of Labour plus Green and National on an equal footing. New Zealand First had given Labour the reins of government after the 2017 election. By 2020 it was consistently polling below the party vote threshold of 5 per cent necessary for representation under New Zealand's mixed-member proportional (MMP) electoral system. Even the Green Party was in danger of dropping below the crucial 5 per cent and out of parliament. National Party strategists hoped the 2020 election would see both of Labour's government allies banished from parliament and National winning the edge in a two-party race. This was more than just their hope; it was a real possibility.

The tight race expected for the forthcoming election was a consequence of the difficulties encountered by the coalition government. Most of those involved did not anticipate its formation. Before the 2017 election, Labour did not expect to be in a position to win or rule. Its appointment of Jacinda Ardern as leader only weeks before the election paid off in a poll surge that made it a feasible government *formateur* after the election, but National still gained more votes than Labour (Vowles and Curtin 2020).

While there were some policy synergies between New Zealand First and Labour, there were also big differences. The exclusion of the Green Party from Cabinet was at the behest of New Zealand First and reflected longstanding tensions between the two parties. Under-researched and overambitious Labour Party promises developed while in opposition meant there were inevitable difficulties in delivery. For example, Labour aimed to build 100,000 houses for sale over 10 years from 2018, but its program failed to take off and, by early 2020, the target was abandoned (Cooke 2019a; Church 2019; Small 2019). Labour also promised to set up light rail from central Auckland to the city's airport, but a combination of uncertainty about options and lukewarm support from New Zealand First meant there had been no progress at all by the 2020 election. That said, progress was made on the minimum wage, pay equity, and child poverty, with the last mandated as part of the budget process (Curtin 2020).

New Zealand First resistance also stood in the way of the stronger action on climate change and reform of employment law that the Labour and Green parties would have implemented if they had been able to govern without their more conservative partner. However, Jacinda Ardern's popularity remained the Labour Party's strongest grounds for hope of re-election in 2020. Her leadership and communication skills were further demonstrated by her response to an attack on Muslim worshippers in Christchurch. She coined the phrase 'they are us' to channel the country's support and sympathy for those who died or were injured and their families. Covid-19 and the government's response to it swung the balance of political preferences to Labour. Ardern and her government's handling of Covid-19 was adept. The evocative phrase the Team of Five Million underpinned the idea of a strong collective effort to fight the virus. Particularly during the lockdowns, her televised afternoon press conferences with the Director-General of Health were widely watched (Beattie and Priestly 2021; Grieve 2020). Valuable for mobilising the collective response, they had the effect of overshadowing whatever the National and ACT parties might do to attract public attention.

While not everyone was impressed, the dissenters formed a small minority. The government faced a huge challenge in setting up contact-tracing systems, effective enforcement of border controls, and the establishment of quarantine facilities in hotels not designed for the purpose. Implementation of government priorities was often slow to reach the front line. Journalists played a valuable role in drawing attention to flaws in the processes, but some ran the risk of damaging public confidence by excessive alarmism. While it concurred with the broad thrust of the response, the opposition National Party did not always play a constructive role, often setting itself apart from the mood of a collective effort.

Polling support for Labour soared after the lockdown and the near-normal conditions that followed the end of the first outbreak. National Party leader Simon Bridges was often strongly critical of the government (for example, Small 2020). He frequently struck sour notes and failed to gain his party any traction. In May 2020, Bridges's leadership was successfully challenged by his colleague Todd Muller, but Muller succumbed to the pressures of the job only 54 days later. The National Party caucus then elected Judith Collins— the third person to lead the party in less than a year. Meanwhile, a small fringe of the population challenged the severity of the crisis, questioned the need for lockdowns, and ignored social distancing where community cases had been detected. However, their occasional demonstrations and participation in the election campaign were but minor irritants.

After almost 100 days with no community cases during most of the crucial winter months, a community outbreak in August led to a second lockdown in Auckland and a four-week postponement of the scheduled general election. By 17 October, the day of the election, only a handful of community cases remained and, coupled with a high level of advance voting, the administration of the election proceeded smoothly under the required Covid-19 conditions.

The election results

As anticipated—at least by those following the polls since about May 2020—New Zealand voters delivered victory in October to the Labour Party. However, the extent of that victory was much greater than expected, in the form of a historic landslide. When the final count was announced on 6 November, Labour's share of the vote was 50 per cent, giving it 65 of the total 120 seats. The main opposition, the National Party, was decimated, with its vote share falling to 25.6 per cent. Table 1.1 displays the results in detail, comparing them with the previous two elections, in 2014 and 2017.

For several reasons, this outcome represented a significant win for the left in New Zealand. First, it was the largest share of the vote won by the Labour Party in 82 years, second only to its vote share of 55 per cent in 1938. It was the first time a party had won enough seats to form a government alone since New Zealand's first election using the MMP electoral system, in 1996. The trajectory of change is equally remarkable. Labour's 2020 party vote share was double that of its most recent low point in 2014.

Second, there were changes in the minor-party landscape. Labour's coalition partner, the populist New Zealand First party, failed to reach the 5 per cent threshold needed to enter parliament. Although the 7.6 per cent share of the vote for Green was lower than its heyday in 2011, it was a small increase from 2017. The party secured 10 list seats and, in a closely run contest, captured the inner-city electorate of Auckland Central. The latter was a rare win for the Greens, although the party had achieved a similar feat in 1999, narrowly taking the Coromandel electorate in its first attempt to contest an election independently. Very few minor parties can achieve sufficient geographical concentration of the vote to win an electorate seat without an explicit or implicit strategic deal with a major party.

Table 1.1 The 2020, 2017, and 2014 elections: Party votes and seats

	2014		2017		2020	
	Votes (%)	Seats	Votes (%)	Seats	Votes (%)	Seats
Labour Party	25.1	32	36.9	46	50.0	65
National Party	47.0	60*	44.4	56	25.6	33
Green Party	10.7	14	6.3	8	7.9	10
ACT New Zealand	0.7	1	0.5	1	7.6	10
New Zealand First (NZF)	8.7	11	7.2	9	2.6	0
(New) Conservative Party (CONS)**	4.0	0	0.2	0	1.5	0
The Opportunities Party (TOP)	n.a.	n.a.	2.4	0	1.5	0
Māori Party	1.3	2	1.2	0	1.2	2
Aotearoa Legalise Cannabis Party	0.5	0	0.3	0	0.5	0
Mana Party***	1.4	0	0.1	0	n.a.	n.a.
Ban1080	0.2	0	0.1	0	n.a.	n.a.
Advance NZ****	n.a.	n.a.	0.1	0	1.0	0
United Future (UF)	0.2	1	0.1	0	n.a.	n.a.
NZ Outdoors Party	n.a.	n.a.	0.1	0	0.1	0
(Democrats for) Social Credit	0.1	0	0	0	0.1	0
Others	n.a.	n.a.	n.a.	n.a.	0.6	0
Total		121		120		120
Left (Labour, Green, MANA, Māori [2020])	37.2	46	43.3	54	59.1	77
Right (National, ACT, CONS)	51.7	61	45.1	57	34.7	43
Centre (NZF, Māori [2014, 2017], TOP, UF)	10.2	14	10.9	9	4.1	0
Others	0.8	0	0.6	0	2.1	0

* National lost the Northland electorate seat to New Zealand First at a by-election early in 2015, bringing it down to 59 seats.

** The Conservative Party had added 'New' to its name by 2020.

*** Allied with the Internet Party in 2014.

**** The New Zealand People's Party contested the 2017 election and formed an alliance with Advance NZ in 2020 under the latter's name.

Note: n.a. not applicable.

Sources: Electoral Commission (2014, 2017, 2020).

Meanwhile, on the centre-right and right, National's decline was partly offset by the rise of ACT New Zealand, which won nearly 8 per cent of the party vote—its best performance in both seats and votes since its formation in 1994. Leader David Seymour had been its only MP since 2014, representing the Auckland blue-ribbon seat of Epsom, which was effectively gifted to him by an informal arrangement with the National Party. In recent elections, National has campaigned only for the party vote in the electorate, signalling its supporters to vote strategically for the local ACT candidate in the hope of boosting the centre-right seat count. But not since 2008 had ACT gained enough of the party vote to gain the extra seats beneath the party vote threshold that this electorate seat would have mandated. The 10 seats ACT won in 2020 put it back on the electoral map in its own right. Together, National and ACT won 35 per cent of the party votes—a low point for the centre-right in recent New Zealand politics, although not as low as the combined National and ACT New Zealand votes in 2002 (28 per cent).

Alongside this, the Māori Party made a comeback. An effective campaign from the Labour Party for the Māori electorates, paired with a gradual decline in support, had ousted the Māori Party from parliament in 2017. The Māori Party had provided support for the National government between 2008 and 2017—an arrangement of which many Māori increasingly had come to disapprove. In 2020, the party recovered by winning one of the seven Māori electorates from Labour. Its 1.2 per cent share of the party vote was almost the same as its party vote share in 2017—enough to give the Māori Party a second MP from its party list. Across the seven Māori electorates, the party's electorate vote performance was up by 6 per cent, but much of this increase came from the disappearance of the Mana Party that had run in Te Tai Tokerau in 2017, the Māori Party having then stood aside there. Indeed, the Māori Party electorate vote in 2020 was only a whisker more than the Māori Party/Mana combined vote in 2017. The Māori Party won Waiariki on much the same vote share it had in 2017. It was a 10 percentage point Labour vote collapse in that electorate that produced the Māori Party victory—an outcome that was labelled 'stunning' (Maxwell 2020). The two new MPs, Rawiri Waititi and Debbie Ngarewa-Packer, quickly went on to make their mark in parliament.

In summary, the magnitude of Labour's win cannot be underestimated. In addition, when combining the vote for the Labour, Green, and Māori parties, the result indicates that 59.1 per cent of voters opted for the 'left', translating to 64 per cent of parliamentary seats. The 2020 election recorded the biggest net vote shift in a New Zealand election for more than a century (Vowles 2020a).

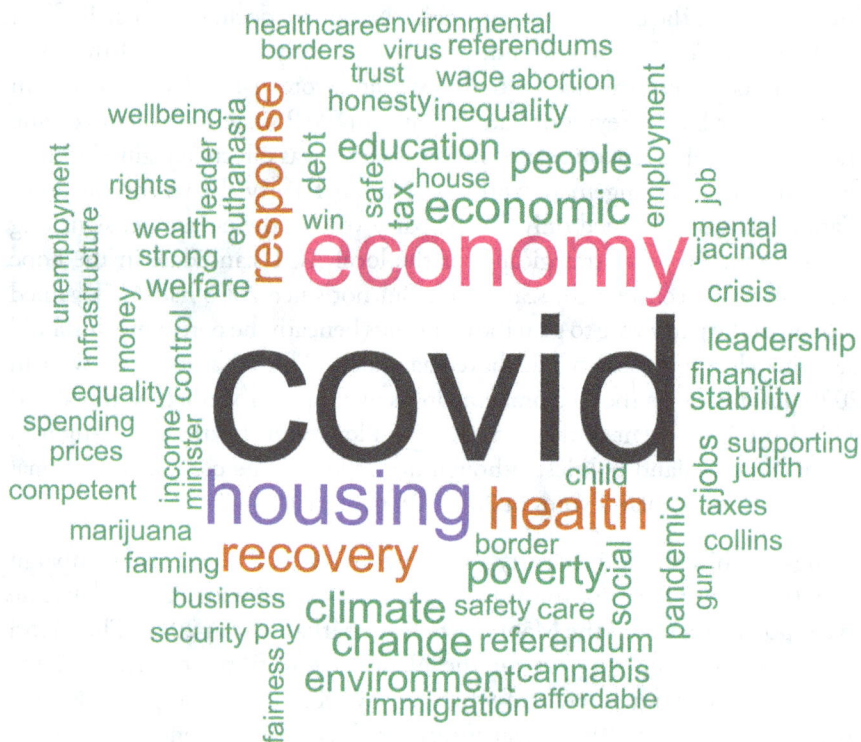

Figure 1.2 Word cloud of issues in the 2020 election
Source: 2020 NZES (Vowles et al. 2022).

Driven by its management of the pandemic, the related issues of health and wellbeing, and the economy, Labour had won a substantial victory. Analysis of the NZES shows Covid-19 loomed the largest in the open-ended responses to the question 'What is the most important issue for you in the 2020 Election?'. The word cloud in Figure 1.2 displays visually the distribution of responses.[2] Nearly 26 per cent of respondents named Covid-19 or an aspect of it, followed by just over 15 per cent mentioning the economy.

Traditional left–right issues, however, also mattered. In her campaign opening speech, Jacinda Ardern began and ended on the Covid-19 response. She also talked at length about a kind and empathetic government that

---

2   The word cloud in Figure 1.2 is evocative, but because it counts more than one word for each respondent it runs the risk of over-representing respondents who included more words than others. Appendix Table A1.2 is based on manual coding of the single most important issue and confirms little or no bias in the word cloud, and is the basis for the percentage responses reported here.

was responding to the needs of society according to traditional Labour Party values (Ardern 2020). Indeed, 8 per cent of NZES participants mentioned housing, and 5 per cent mentioned the environment. Health was surprisingly low, with only about 3 per cent of participants listing this as the most important issue. One or other of welfare, inequality, and poverty were mentioned by about 6 per cent in total, while 16 per cent did not state an issue of concern. Ardern's speech did not mention Te Tiriti o Waitangi (the Treaty of Waitangi), nor did issues specifically defined as Māori register among NZES respondents.

National Party leader Judith Collins's opening speech sought to emphasise the failure of the government to prevent the Auckland outbreak that had postponed the election (Collins 2020). Her narrative emphasised Labour's alleged and real failures to deliver on its promises. Traditional National Party values came to the fore in her support for business and her claims that Labour could not be trusted on tax policy nor in keeping the size and influence of government under control. Among those who identified the economy or taxes as the most important issue, National was still considered the best party to deal with them. But on almost every other issue, and particularly those that were most salient, Labour was well ahead.

Electoral turnout

Meanwhile, turnout among those qualified to vote[3] reached its highest in 20 years, and the biggest gains in voter turnout were among those aged under 30, at last bearing out hopes for a 'youthquake' (Edwards 2017; Hall 2018). Turnout had increased in 2017, but enrolment among those aged between 18 and 24 was down (Smith 2017). Thus, in 2017, an apparently healthy increase of 6 per cent of those aged under 30 was based on those who were already on the electoral roll, while the increase was only 2.6 per cent when

---

3   As the note to Figure 1.1 points out, the data are the percentages of valid votes cast on a base of all those qualified to be enrolled, rather than official turnout, which includes disallowed votes on a base of only those enrolled to vote. An enrolment base for turnout has the perverse effect of failing to acknowledge a turnout increase accompanied by a matching higher level of enrolment, to the point that a turnout increase could be entirely hidden or even estimated as an apparent decline. In the case of 2017, as explained above, the apparent increase for those aged 18–29 on a roll base was much smaller than it appeared after taking enrolment into account. By counting disallowed and informal votes as part of the numerator, persons disallowed because they are not on the roll and therefore not in the denominator distort the estimate, and those casting informal votes—which could have been a protest—are counted as having voted when their votes could not be counted.

based on the number of those eligible to vote by age. In sharp contrast, enrolment in 2020 was substantially higher among those aged under 30, and turnout was higher again.[4]

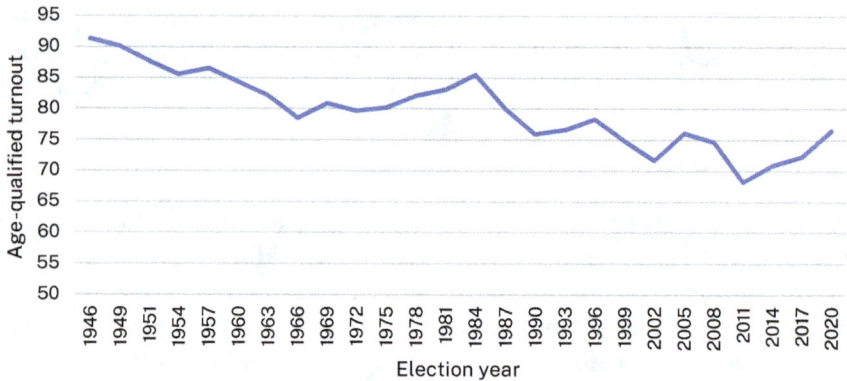

Figure 1.3 Age-eligible turnout in New Zealand, 1946–2020

Note: The data are the percentages of valid votes cast on a base of all those qualified to be enrolled, rather than official turnout, which includes disallowed and informal votes on a base of only those enrolled to vote.

Sources: Nagel (1988); Electoral Commission (2020).

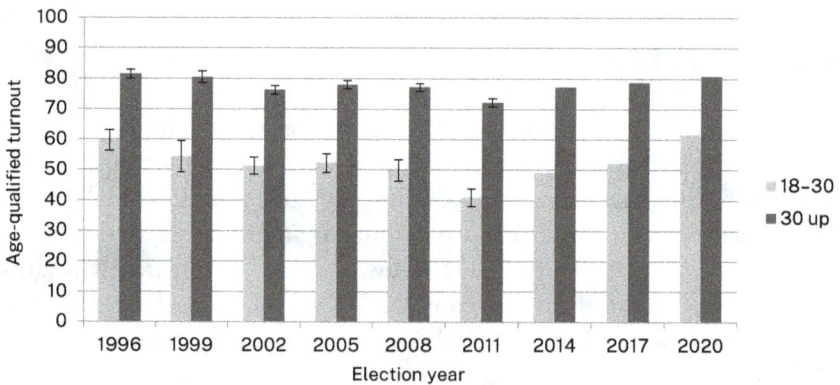

Figure 1.4 Age-eligible turnout by age, 1996–2020

Sources: NZES (1996–2011); New Zealand Electoral Commission (2014–20).

---

4   Calculations based on data from the Electoral Commission (2014, 2017, 2020) and the comparisons of age-eligible populations and enrolment by age available from the commission.

As Figure 1.3 shows, the increase in turnout has been from a low base as, in 2011, electoral turnout reached an all-time low in New Zealand (Vowles 2014). The trend has since been consistently upward. The post-1996 developments are of particular significance given New Zealand's transition to the MMP system. The expectation that turnout could recover was not initially borne out (Vowles 2010). Part of the reason for continued decline was generational replacement. Earlier generations of voters with stronger habits of voting have been replaced with new generations with weaker habits established well before the electoral system change.

Figure 1.4 shows that the post-2011 turnout increase has, since 2014, been predominantly driven by younger adults. On a qualified-to-vote basis, turnout among those aged 18–29 has increased by 50 per cent since its low point in 2011. A pessimistic narrative of global electoral turnout decline that has captured the literature needs revision, particularly as there have been similar recent recoveries in the United Kingdom and the United States. An in-depth analysis of the potential reasons for this increase in turnout is conducted in Chapter 4.[5]

The vote shifts

As noted, the 2020 election produced a net shift of votes between parties that was the greatest in New Zealand's electoral history (Vowles 2020b).[6] However, below the surface there are always much greater movements as individuals go with or against the main currents (also see Vowles 2020c). Appendix Table A1.3 provides an estimate of the total vote flows between the two elections, including flows in and out of nonvoting. It is derived from a weighted cross-tabulation of data from the Vote Compass post-election sample of just over 26,000 people. Of most interest are the flows of votes away from National and New Zealand First, followed by the flows to Labour.

---

5   The referendum concurrent with the election on cannabis law reform could have helped to increase youth turnout, as youth tend to be the predominant consumers of the substance (Oldfield and Greaves 2021). This proposition is tested in Chapter 4 of this volume.

6   A standard vote volatility calculation uses the aggregated election results and summing all the vote share changes between the parties in the two elections in question, dividing them by two, giving an index that would be zero if all parties received the same vote shares as before and 100 if all the parties were replaced with completely different ones. For 2020/2017, this index is just over 24—somewhat higher than the previous New Zealand record of just over 21 at the 1935 election.

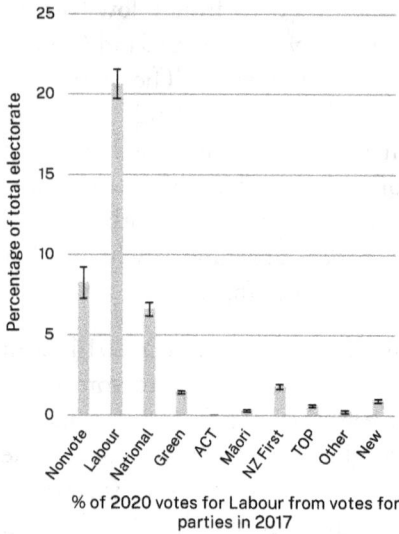

% of 2020 votes for Labour from votes for
parties in 2017

Figure 1.5 Where the 2020 Labour votes came from

Source: Appendix Table A1.3.

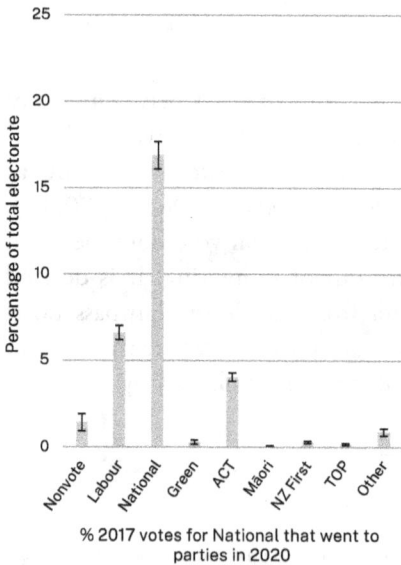

% 2017 votes for National that went to
parties in 2020

Figure 1.6 Where the 2017 National votes went

Source: Appendix Table A1.3.

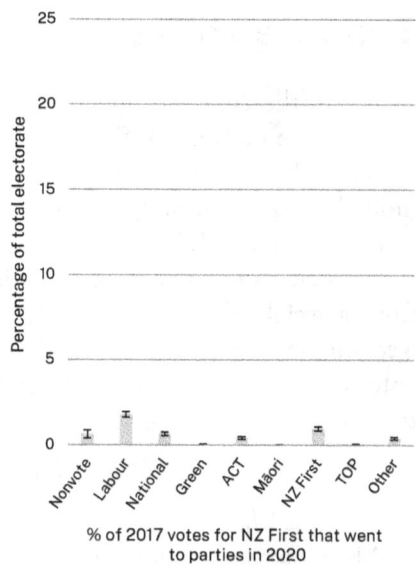

% of 2017 votes for NZ First that went
to parties in 2020

Figure 1.7 Where the 2017 New Zealand First votes went

Source: Appendix Table A1.3.

Drawing on data in the Appendix Table A1.3, Figure 1.5 displays Labour's inflows as percentages of the electorate including nonvoters. Labour won just more than 40 per cent of those enrolled to vote in 2020. Only half of that vote came from those who had voted Labour in 2017. About one-fifth came from previous nonvoters, a little less than one-fifth from previous National voters, a little less than 2 per cent from New Zealand First, and 1 per cent from new voters. Labour also picked up a few former Green voters but, among new voters entering the electorate, the Greens may have done slightly better than Labour.

Figure 1.6 examines National's outflows on the same baseline as percentages of the total electorate. National retained a little more than half its 2017 voters: 55 per cent. While National lost votes to ACT, it lost more to Labour: about 20 per cent of those who had voted National in 2017. Figure 1.7 shows New Zealand First's outflows. New Zealand First retained only one-fifth of its 2017 vote. Those leaving New Zealand First split on a ratio of about 1.7:1 for Labour compared with those who shifted to National or ACT.

A question in Vote Compass asked the left–right position of its participants. Its large sample means that estimates can also be generated for the average left–right positions of the people within each cell of Appendix Table A1.3. Those voting Labour at both elections had a mean of 3.2 ('most left' being zero, 'most right', 10). Those consistently National had a mean of 6.8, while 2017 National voters who moved to Labour in 2020 scored an average of 4.9—almost exactly corresponding to the median voter or centre-ground of politics. Overall, new voters scored an average of 4.2, putting them moderately to the left of centre. New Zealand First to Labour voters scored 4.1, New Zealand First to National voters 6.6, and those who remained with New Zealand First had an average of exactly five. All this is exactly what one would expect if the shifts had a reasonable correlation with self-placed ideology.

As a proportion of all those enrolled to vote in 2020, about 43 per cent voted for the same party as before (not much less than in 2017), which is a surprising finding given the increase in net change (see Appendix 1.1). The big increase in Labour's vote share was due in part to the increase in turnout. But there was more consistent directionality in vote switching than normal. There was less movement against the overall trend, thereby generating higher net effects. Under the surface, the 2020 election may have been less of an earthquake than it appears.

The shift to Labour produced significant gains in provincial electorates, many of which tend to be regarded as relatively safe seats for National because of their concentrations of farmers—normally strong National voters. Not long after the election, Federated Farmers of New Zealand Mid-Canterbury president David Clark speculated that 'plenty of farmers have voted Labour so they can govern alone rather than having a Labour–Greens government'; in other words, they cast a 'strategic' rather than sincere vote (Murphy 2020). However, analysis of the NZES fails to confirm this (Van Veen et al. 2021). Most (57 per cent) of those in farming occupations voted for National and 21 per cent voted for Labour. These numbers contrast with those in 2017 when National received 67 per cent of the farming vote and Labour received just 8 per cent. But if National lost, ACT gained. Its share of the farming vote increased from 2 per cent to 16 per cent. Meanwhile, the New Zealand First farmer vote collapsed from 13 per cent to less than 1 per cent. It is tempting to assume that most farmers who had supported New Zealand First went to Labour, but our data can only suggest rather than confirm this.[7] These observations are based on a very small subsample (N = 102 in the 2020 NZES) and should therefore be interpreted with great caution. But the combined centre-right National–ACT vote among farmers appears to have been relatively unchanged between the two elections, ruling out significant strategic behaviour by those formerly voting for those two parties. The key shift was one of farmers from National to ACT, giving National a warning that it would need to try to reconnect with its hitherto strongest supporters in the election aftermath.

The social foundations of the vote

All this suggests that the 2020 election, despite its drama, did not shatter the foundations of the New Zealand party system; it represented a big swing of the pendulum across the existing dial. Analysis of the correlates of voting choices in social structure and organisation supports this inference. By the 2017 election, the probability of people in households primarily dependent on a person with a manual or service occupation voting for Labour was only very slightly higher than for a person in a non-manual occupation—in other words, traditionally defined occupational-class voting was very low. Only

---

7   One can only speculate about the motives of farmers who voted New Zealand First in 2017 and shifted to Labour in 2020. While they might have wanted Labour to be able to govern alone, there were plenty of other reasons for them to change their behaviour.

farmers—separately identified in these categories—showed a strong class-voting effect (Vowles 2020a, 55–58). The same findings apply in 2020. While this very simple manual–non-manual approach to the measurement of class voting has been rejected in more recent theory, compared with data from previous elections, it does present a well-defined time series.

A huge international literature on class and class voting discusses alternative measurements of class that many claim continue to structure voting choices despite the decline of these manual–non-manual occupational effects (see, for example, Evans 2017; Connolly et al. 2016). Indeed, long ago, some of these were discussed and compared in the New Zealand context in analysis of the 1987 and 1990 elections (Vowles 1992). It is frequently claimed that these more sophisticated sociological analyses of class voting continue to demonstrate strong effects. Most of the schema rely on a larger number of occupational groupings and move beyond occupation to estimate the effects of employment status and workplace authority. One of the more popular recent models is that of Daniel Oesch (2006). But applying it to our NZES data from the 2020 election in an alternative analysis also confirms little or no effect.

Recent work also emphasises the importance of political party mobilisation of class interests, particularly on the left. It is argued that parties traditionally representing working-class interests no longer do so. Compounding the problem, Labour parties elect politicians most of whom are not from working-class backgrounds. If both tendencies apply, a lower level of class voting is to be expected. Meanwhile, class differences persist but are shaped by more factors than in the past. Indeed, we now live in a context of greater social and economic inequality than was the case a half-century ago when most of these class theories were being developed. Our understanding of class must expand beyond occupational groupings to include not only incomes, employment status, and workplace authority, but also the ownership of assets (Vowles et al. 2017, 66–68). Trade union membership is another important indicator of a potential residual working-class–based identity. In the 2020 election data, we have developed a further measure of workplace authority that relies on questions about employment status and supervisory authority.[8]

---

8   Theoretically, intersectional effects could be modelled by various interactions of the variables discussed here, and indeed others including gender and ethnicity. Practically, the small size of most of the subgroups means that few if any of these analytic options would generate findings that would be statistically significant.

Investigating all this, Appendix Table A1.3 displays the results of a multinomial logit model using demographics and social structure to identify the underpinnings of voting choices. In this multivariate model, the estimates for all variables take account of all the others, so they should be understood as 'all else being equal'. In this table, voting for Labour is the reference category against which the values of the coefficients are estimated. The analysis includes nonvoting, vote choices for New Zealand First and the Māori Party, and a residual 'other' category. We mainly focus on the parties most supported, for whom there are enough respondents in the sample to give meaningful results.

Occupational status has no effect on vote choice for manual and non-manual workers, with the exception of farmers. Manual/non-manual or farmer occupational status has an effect on vote choice only for farmers. In terms of workplace authority, one can identify a continuum between having in the household an employer, someone who is self-employed, a person with supervisory responsibilities in their job, or a non-supervisory employee; these differences did matter with respect to both turnout and vote for National. Not voting is more likely among men, the young, non-union members, and employees who have no supervisory responsibilities. National and ACT voters are found less in urban than in rural areas. Higher incomes and wider ownership of assets are associated with National, as is non-membership of a trade union. The Green Party has a higher concentration of young voters than the other parties and appeals most in large cities. ACT does not appeal so much to women voters. Green voters are less likely to be church attendees and are much more likely to have a university degree than those voting for other parties. Māori were less likely than non-Māori to vote for National and ACT and Asian voters were less likely to vote for Green or ACT.[9]

---

9   While many other polls and surveys indicate Chinese voters are more likely to vote for the centre-right parties, they form only about half of the NZES Asian sample. Meanwhile, voters from other Asian backgrounds tended towards Labour. Response rates for ethnic minorities are relatively low in the NZES so their detailed breakdown must be treated with caution. Of 115 respondents declaring Chinese ethnicity, 22 per cent did not vote, 29 per cent voted Labour, and 32 per cent voted National. The next largest Asian group was 58 of Indian ethnicity; of those, 33 per cent did not vote, 45 per cent voted Labour, and only 11 per cent voted National.

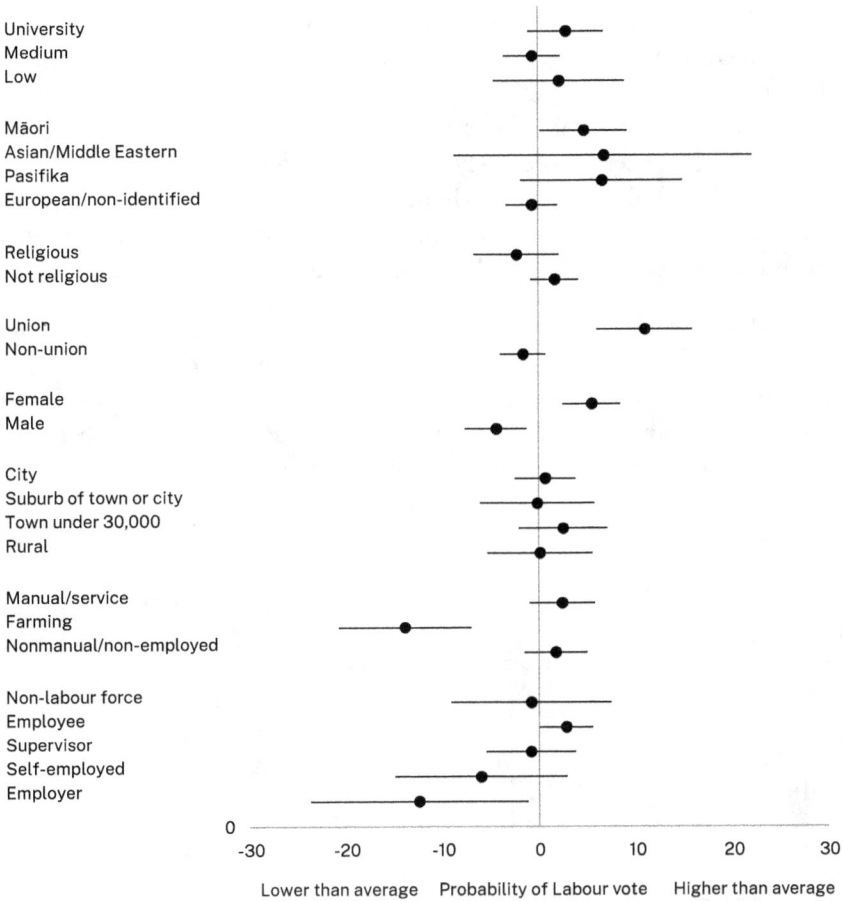

Figure 1.8 The percentage probabilities of voting Labour based on social structure and demographics

Source: Estimates from the model in Appendix Table A1.3.

Voting for Labour is, of course, the other side of the coin and, using estimates derived from the model, Figures 1.8 and 1.9a–c display these findings visually. As in the table, the probabilities are estimated across the whole electorate, including those who did not vote. On this basis, about 40 per cent voted Labour. The probabilities have been adjusted to represent their difference from the 40 per cent Labour vote across the whole sample. The confidence intervals give an estimate of certainty and uncertainty according to the size of the subsample. Most groups represented in the figures have confidence intervals that touch the yardstick at the zero mark, indicating their effect on voting choice was either insignificant or at best marginally significant. People in those groups were as likely as everyone

19

else to vote Labour. We highlight those who are further away. The most striking relationship is, again, that of employment status and workplace authority. Labour's status as the party of the worker is narrowly confirmed, but someone in the household of a non-supervisory employee or employees is only about 3 per cent more likely than average to vote Labour. Employers appear much less likely to vote Labour, but their number in the sample is small, making for wider confidence intervals. The same applies to farmers. Labour's votes were relatively evenly spread across the country.

Labour did much better among women than men and had strong support from people who had a union member in their household—a 10 per cent higher probability of a Labour vote than average. The nonreligious were a little more likely to vote Labour than the religious. All else being equal, Māori and Pasifika were more likely than average to vote Labour.

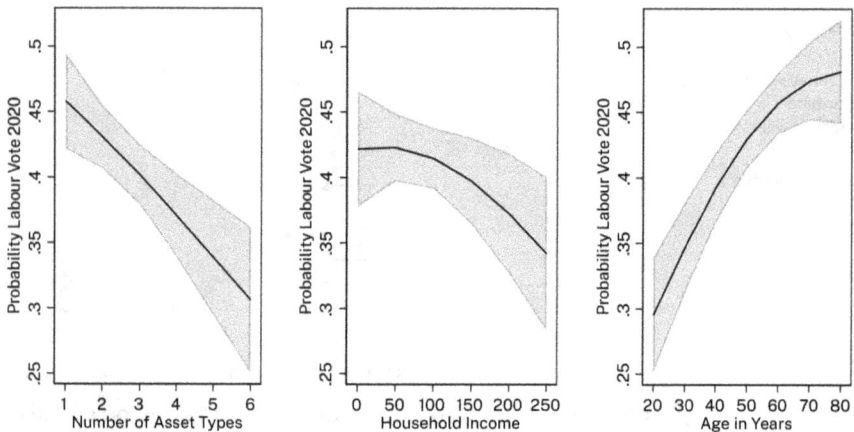

Figures 1.9a–c The probability of a Labour vote by asset types, household income, and age

Source: Estimates from the model in Appendix Table A1.3.

Figures 1.9a–c show some of the strongest correlates of the Labour vote: the number of different types of assets people own, household income, and age. The weaker propensity of the young than the old to vote Labour is largely because the young are more likely to not vote at all. According to our data, 39 per cent of those aged 18–31 voted Labour. National and the Green Party each took 13 per cent, and ACT 5 per cent, while 29 per cent of those on the roll in that age group did not vote. The assets in question are a house, a business, a second house for leisure or investment, stocks and shares, any savings, and membership of KiwiSaver or other retirement savings scheme.

A wide dispersion of assets has a very strong negative association with a Labour vote. The slope for income is not as steep, but it is in the same direction. Class, in terms of income and assets, still counts in New Zealand voting behaviour and party choice and the pattern is much as it was in 2017. Both elections partially but not entirely support claims that class voting in relatively high-income countries has shifted towards differences in income, asset ownership, and education (Gethin et al. 2021). In the case of education, it is significant for the Green vote, but not for Labour's.

The chapters to come

We conclude this chapter with an expanded discussion of our key research questions and a summary of what is to come. We explore the extent to which the Team of Five Million could represent the idea of a new, more united New Zealand or whether it is a discursive reframing of politics as 'business as usual'. New Zealand is a country of increasing cultural diversity, with a gap between rich and poor that has grown in recent decades. In that context, one might be dubious that a call to collective action would unite a public that many believe is increasingly divided.

These questions are unpacked from various directions. In Chapter 2, Jack Vowles starts with the most obvious initial inquiry: how important was the response to Covid-19 in securing Labour's victory? That importance is undeniable, but other, albeit related, factors were evident. Effective leadership and clear communication enhanced the soaring popularity of Prime Minister Jacinda Ardern. Her most significant achievement was to be perceived as trustworthy. A strong stimulus attenuated the economic effects. There was no ideological shift to the left. As discussed earlier, most of those who moved to Labour were centrists—those voters closest to the median left–right position—and it was approval of the Covid-19 response that pulled them to Labour in their voting choices, but that approval did not appear to shift their ideological or policy preferences across other dimensions.

In Chapter 3, Mona Krewel and Matthew Gibbons discuss the increased shift to campaigning on social media and its implications. Campaigning in the shadow of Covid-19 meant that parties and candidates placed a greater emphasis on social media as a possible fallback option should lockdowns resume. The defining debates revolving around the government's Covid-19 response were avidly taken up on social media. While Ardern was answering the Team of Five Million's questions through positive messaging on Facebook Live, the National Party and its leader, Judith Collins, went negative on social media. Alongside this, Advance NZ and the New Zealand Public Party spread conspiracy theories and other disinformation about Covid-19 online, while the Māori Party turned out to be one of the most engaged campaigners on social media. Using text analysis data from the New Zealand Social Media Study (NZSMS), the chapter investigates how, and around what issues, the parties and candidates mobilised on social media. Specifically, it asks what roles were played by fake news, half-truths, negative campaigning, and populist communication strategies, especially around Covid-19. By linking this analysis to data from the 2020 NZES, it estimates how much voters used the internet during the campaign and the extent to which voters were aware of, and able to identify, disinformation on social media.

In Chapter 4, Jennifer Curtin, Celestyna Galicki, and Jack Vowles explore the implications of Covid-19 on electoral turnout and election administration. The original September election date had been set before the virus was recognised as a pandemic and the second outbreak in August posed a serious challenge. Because of the risks associated with in-person voting, and the limits that lockdowns and social distancing placed on campaigning, the election was postponed by one month. The decision was based on advice from the Electoral Commission, which had undertaken considerable research into alternative voting processes. The result saw increased turnout overall, and specifically among young people, stalling a longstanding downward trend. The chapter draws on several datasets, including the NZES, to examine voters' confidence in electoral administration, their take-up of extended advance voting options, and the extent to which voters engaged with two high-profile referendums. Indeed, the referendums—particularly that on cannabis legalisation—could have had significant effects on drawing people to the polls.

One might expect that Māori and other groups marginalised by continuing inequality, poverty, and discrimination, and most vulnerable to Covid-19, might feel less a part of the Team of Five Million. Historically, diseases introduced by early European contact, later colonial settlement, and increasing international travel had devastating consequences for Māori well into the early twentieth century—most notably, the influenza epidemic after World War I. Many Māori and Pasifika people live in large households, work in exposed occupations, find it more difficult than others to self-isolate, and are more vulnerable to hospitalisation and death if they contract the virus (Steyn et al. 2021). Indeed, when community cases emerged, some *iwi* (tribal councils) and *hapū* (kinship group) in provincial New Zealand set up roadblocks to prevent unauthorised travel into their areas, usually in concert with the police.

As a result of such actions, together with the broader policy response and other factors such as a lower likelihood of international travel, cases among Māori initially remained lower than among the rest of the population. Nonetheless, the response from Māori was not uniform. Notably, the Covid-19 denial campaign of Advance NZ and the New Zealand Public Party was led by two Māori: Jami-Lee Ross and Billy Te Kahika, Jr. Both developments raise questions about the extent to which Māori felt they were part of Ardern's Team of Five Million.

With these issues in the background, Lara Greaves, Ella Morgan, and Janine Hayward in Chapter 5 discuss the Māori Party's return to parliament. Its exit in 2017 took many by surprise but it continued a trend of decline in its support over previous elections. The return of the party to parliament in 2020 was not so predictable. This chapter asks where votes and support for the Māori Party came from in 2020 and tests several explanations suggested since the election: an alleged shift to the left, the change of leadership, and the government's handling of Māori issues. The chapter also considers Māori voters within the context of the Team of Five Million.

In Chapter 6, Fiona Barker and Kate McMillan address attitudes and policy towards immigration, asking the question: 'Who belongs on the Team of Five Million?' The 2020 election campaign unfolded in a rare period of almost zero immigration, which dramatically altered and dampened explicit debate about the issue. Yet, the Covid-19 experience raised questions about the future shape and role of immigration in New Zealand's economy. Recent historically high levels of immigration have increased cultural diversity while also putting pressure on public services and infrastructure, particularly the housing market. Temporary immigrants have also helped to sustain a low-wage, service sector–heavy economy. In recent elections, anti-immigration sentiment has been notable for its limited support as a key issue. Against the backdrop of Covid-19, media coverage highlighted labour shortages and the separation of long-term migrants from their families, sparking regular public debate. The chapter finds evidence of some change but mainly continuity in voters' views of immigration.

In Chapter 7, Jennifer Curtin, Victoria Woodman, and Lara Greaves address the gender implications of the election. During the first six months of 2020, international media attention focussed on whether women political leaders—national and subnational—were more effective than their male counterparts at managing the Covid-19 crisis. New Zealand Prime Minister Jacinda Ardern was front and centre in most of these analyses, given her government's decision to lockdown and her effective messaging and inclusive and reassuring style. What much of the international media missed, however, is that the Ardern-led government's economic recovery packages focussed largely on traditional (male) jobs, with little investment in social infrastructure, and marginal support for those on benefits. The chapter explores the extent to which New Zealand voters' views reflected the international awe of Ardern's leadership and whether women's opinions on key policy issues shed a light on whether they felt sufficiently included in the Team of Five Million—a sporting metaphor that might have appealed more to men than women. However, the result was that Ardern appealed to a record high of women voters, widening the gender gap for Labour to an extent not seen before. This was even though gender impact assessments of the pandemic seldom featured in the government's policy responses.

Echoes of scepticism about the scale and seriousness of the crisis, including attempts to portray the response as authoritarian and illiberal, were heard more broadly throughout 2020. With parliament and committees unable to meet in person, an Epidemic Response Committee was established, led by the Leader of the Opposition, to hear evidence on the government's decisions and their ramifications. A group of academics, self-titled Plan B, were vocal opponents of the government's 'hard and early' response, arguing that the economic costs would outweigh the public health benefits of border closures and lockdowns.

The appearance of unity was indeed challenged in the leadup to the 2020 election by the realities and future implications of New Zealand's elimination approach. As a country with 27 per cent of the population not born within its borders, about one million living overseas, and an economy heavily dependent on tourism, migrant labour, and international education, New Zealand's conception as a Team of Five Million presented significant challenges to sectors of the economy. Such observations point to the precarious nature of the extent to which Ardern's Team of Five Million could be considered inclusive.

Taking up some of these themes, Luke Oldfield and Josh Van Veen in Chapter 8 examine the critics and outsiders of the 2020 election campaign. Outside the usually dominant National Party, some 300,000 New Zealanders voted for right-of-centre parties that had expressed scepticism about the government and its Covid-19 response. These parties cut across both the mainstream of New Zealand politics (for example, the libertarian ACT) and the fringe (for example, the traditionalist New Conservatives and conspiracist Advance NZ). While only ACT gained parliamentary representation, the three parties collectively received more than 10 per cent of the party vote. This chapter explores the characteristics of those 300,000 voters who chose not to join the Team of Five Million.

In Chapter 9, Sam Crawley addresses the challenge to governments and their electorates that will not go away, even if temporarily eclipsed by the Covid-19 crisis: climate change. Before the pandemic, a consensus among elites on climate change had been growing in New Zealand. The chapter examines what happened to the issue during the election campaign, given the high-profile focus on both the pandemic and its economic ramifications. It shows that few people saw climate change as an important election issue, despite most people wanting stronger government action on it. Moreover, even if there was a Team of Five Million for New Zealand's Covid-19 response, there does not seem to be one for climate change. There are clear partisan divides among the public when it comes to the issue, with supporters of right-wing parties tending to have lower levels of support for government action than supporters of left-wing parties.

Chapter 10, by Jack Vowles, Jennifer Curtin, and Lara Greaves, concludes by summarising the key findings and exploring their implications. The metaphor of the Team of Five Million has obvious limitations given New Zealand's relatively high levels of social inequality, differences in wealth and power, and in different people's immediate exposure and vulnerability to the crisis across a diverse society. Yet, it seems to have served a rhetorical purpose, encouraging remarkably high levels of compliance in the first year or more of the crisis. With the intrusion of the greatly more infectious Delta variant in 2021, the challenge posed has become more severe, offset by the introduction of vaccination, but with an increasing number of infections, and cracks emerging in the community response. We update the narrative of events into the middle of 2023.

References

Ardern, J. 2020. 'Speech: Labour Campaign Launch 2020.' 8 August, Auckland Town Hall. Available from: www.labour.org.nz/news-speech-campaignlaunch.

Ardern, J. 2022. 'Post-Peak Plan a Safe Return to Greater Normality.' Speech, 23 March, Wellington. Available from: www.beehive.govt.nz/speech/post-peak-plan-safe-return-greater-normality.

Beattie, A., and R. Priestley. 2021. 'Fighting COVID-19 with the Team of 5 Million: Aotearoa New Zealand Government Communication during the 2020 lockdown.' *Social Sciences and Humanities Open* 4(1): 100209. doi.org/10.1016/j.ssaho.2021.100209.

Blavatnik School of Government (BSG). 2020–23. *COVID-19 Government Response Tracker*. Research Project. Oxford: Blavatnik School of Government, University of Oxford. Available from: www.bsg.ox.ac.uk/research/research-projects/covid-19-government-response-tracker.

Church, A. 2019. 'Why Did KiwiBuild Go So Badly Wrong?' *OneRoof*, [Auckland], 25 June. Available from: www.oneroof.co.nz/news/ashley-church-why-did-kiwibuild-go-so-badly-wrong-36406.

Collins, J. 2020. 'Speech: Judith Collins 2020 Campaign Launch.' 20 September, [Online]. Available from: www.national.org.nz/judith-collins-2020-campaign-launch.

Colmar-Brunton Research. 2017–20. 'Political Polls.' Accessed from: www.colmarbrunton.co.nz/1-news-poll/ [page discontinued].

Connolly, R., V. Gayle, and P.S. Lambert. 2016. 'A Review of Occupation-Based Social Classifications for Social Survey Research.' *Methodological Innovations* 9: 1–14. doi.org/10.1177/2059799116638003.

Cooke, H. 2019a. 'How KiwiBuild Fell Down, and Whether Anything Can Be Saved from the Wreckage.' *Stuff*, [Wellington], 21 June. Available from: www.stuff.co.nz/national/politics/113641010/how-kiwibuild-fell-down-and-whether-anything-can-be-saved-from-the-wreckage.

Cooke, H. 2019b. 'Labour Ahead While National Dips Below 40 in New Stuff Poll.' *Stuff*, [Wellington], 25 November. Available from: www.stuff.co.nz/national/politics/117662933/labour-ahead-while-national-dips-below-40-in-new-stuff-poll.

Curtin, J. 2020. *Home for Progressive Politics? An Analysis of Labour's Success in New Zealand.* Analysis, December. Bonn: Friedrich Ebert Stiftung. Available from: library.fes.de/pdf-files/id/ipa/17207.pdf.

Curtin, J., and D. O'Sullivan. 2023. 'Closing the Borders to COVID-19: Democracy, Politics and Resilience in Australia and New Zealand.' In *Democracy, State Capacity and the Governance of COVID-19 in Asia-Oceania*, edited by A. Croissant and O. Hellmann. London: Routledge. doi.org/10.4324/9781003362456-4.

Edwards, B. 2017. 'Political Roundup: Is a "Youthquake" Looming or Not?' *New Zealand Herald*, 19 September. Available from: www.nzherald.co.nz/nz/political-roundup-is-a-youthquake-looming-or-not/3K7M24EFJIUBAIOFN W6YGZLZIU/.

Electoral Commission. 2014. *2014 General Election: Voter Turnout Statistics for the 2014 General Election.* Wellington: Electoral Commission New Zealand. Available from: elections.nz/democracy-in-nz/historical-events/2014-general-election/voter-turnout-statistics-for-the-2014-general-election/.

Electoral Commission. 2017. *2017 General Election: Voter Turnout Statistics for the 2017 General Election.* Wellington: Electoral Commission New Zealand. Available from: elections.nz/democracy-in-nz/historical-events/2017-general-election/voter-turnout-statistics-for-the-2017-general-election/.

Electoral Commission. 2020. *2020 General Election & Referendums: Voter Turnout Statistics for the 2020 General Election.* Wellington: Electoral Commission New Zealand. Available from: elections.nz/democracy-in-nz/historical-events/2020-general-election-and-referendums/voter-turnout-statistics-for-the-2020-general-election/.

Evans, G. 2017. 'Social Class and Voting.' In *The SAGE Handbook of Electoral Behaviour*, edited by K. Arzheimer, J. Evans, and M.S. Lewis-Beck, 177–98. Thousand Oaks, CA: SAGE Publications. doi.org/10.4135/9781473957978.n9.

Gethin, A., C. Martinez-Toledano, and T. Piketty. 2021. *Political Cleavages and Social Inequalities: A Study of Fifty Democracies, 1948–2020.* Cambridge, MA: Harvard University Press. doi.org/10.4159/9780674269910.

Grieve, D. 2020. 'The Epic Story of NZ's Communications-Led Fight against COVID-19.' *The Spinoff*, [Auckland], 11 May. Available from: thespinoff.co.nz/politics/11-05-2020/a-masterclass-in-mass-communication-and-control/.

Hall, E. 2018. 'How to Create a Youth-Quake: Fostering Political Engagement Amongst Young People in Aotearoa New Zealand.' *Policy Commons Blog*, 1 November. Auckland: Public Policy Institute, University of Auckland. Available from: www.policycommons.ac.nz/2018/11/01/how-to-create-a-youth-quake-fostering-political-engagement-amongst-young-people-in-aotearoa-new-zealand/.

Maxwell, J. 2020. 'Election 2020: Māori Party Gains Second Waka in Stunning Return to Parliament.' *Stuff*, [Wellington], 6 November. Available from: www. stuff.co.nz/national/politics/300152085/election-2020-mori-party-gains-second-waka-in-stunning-return-to-parliament.

Mitchell, C. 2021. 'The Scientist and the Rabbit Hole: How Epidemiologist Simon Thornley Became an Outcast of His Profession.' *Stuff*, [Wellington], 21 May. Available from: www.stuff.co.nz/national/health/coronavirus/125035835/the-scientist-and-the-rabbit-hole-how-epidemiologist-simon-thornley-became-an-outcast-of-his-profession.

Murphy, S. 2020. 'Farmers Want Labour to Govern Alone—Fed Farmers.' *Radio New Zealand*, 19 October. Available from: www.rnz.co.nz/news/country/428684/farmers-want-labour-to-govern-alone-fed-farmers.

Nagel, J. 1988. 'Voter Turnout in New Zealand General Elections 1928–1988.' *Political Science* 40(2): 16–38.

New Zealand Election Study (NZES). 1996–2011. NZES Full Samples, 1996–2011. Data file compiled by Jack Vowles, Victoria University of Wellington.

New Zealand Electoral Commission. 2014–20. Final Rolls to Eligible Population (2014, 2017, 2020). Data files compiled by the Electoral Commission, available on request.

Oesch, D. 2006. 'Coming to Grips with a Changing Class Structure: An Analysis of Employment Stratification in Britain, Germany, Sweden and Switzerland.' *International Sociology* 21(2): 263–88. doi.org/10.1177/0268580906061379.

Oldfield, L., and L. Greaves. 2021. 'The Cannabis and Euthanasia Referendums.' In *Politics in a Pandemic: Jacinda Ardern and New Zealand's 2020 Election*, edited by S. Levine, 263–73. Wellington: Te Herenga Waka University Press.

Palmer, R. 2020. 'Election 2020: Special Votes Explained.' *Radio New Zealand*, 18 October. Available from: www.rnz.co.nz/news/political/428614/election-2020-special-votes-explained.

Reid Research. 2022. *TV3 Poll Results*. Auckland: Reid Research Services. Available from: www.reidresearch.co.nz/TV3+POLL+RESULTS.html.

Roy Morgan. 2022. *New Zealand: Party Voting Intention (2017–2022)*. Auckland: Roy Morgan. Available from: www.roymorgan.com/morgan-poll/new-zealand-party-voting-intention.

Small, Z. 2019. 'KiwiBuild Reset: "Overly Ambitious" 100,000 Houses in 10 Years Promise Dropped, Shared Ownership Schemes In.' *Newshub*, [Auckland], 4 September. Available from: www.newshub.co.nz/home/politics/2019/09/kiwi build-reset-overly-ambitious-100-000-houses-in-10-years-promise-dropped-shared-ownership-schemes-in.html.

Small, Z. 2020. 'COVID-19: Simon Bridges Blasts Coronavirus Response Amid Reports People Being Denied Tests.' *Newshub*, [Auckland], 3 March. Available from: www.newshub.co.nz/home/politics/2020/03/covid-19-simon-bridges-blasts-coronavirus-response-amid-reports-people-being-denied-tests.html.

Smith, C. 2017. 'Christian Smith: What Happened to the Youthquake?' *New Zealand Herald*, 24 October. Available from: www.nzherald.co.nz/nz/christian-smith-what-happened-to-the-youthquake/QZ3CBSHCOQC3PW6IXKN5 RC7SA4/.

Steyn, N., R.N. Binny, K. Hannah, S. Hendy, A. James, A. Lustig, K. Ridings, M.J. Plank, and A. Sporle. 2021. 'Māori and Pacific People in New Zealand Have Higher Risk of Hospitalisation for COVID-19.' *New Zealand Medical Journal* 134(1538): 28–43. doi.org/10.1101/2020.12.25.20248427.

Van Veen, J., J. Vowles, J. Curtin, L. Greaves, and S. Crawley. 2021. 'Anniversary of a Landslide: What Swung the 2020 "Covid Election".' *Stuff*, [Wellington], 15 October. Available from: www.stuff.co.nz/national/politics/300431178/anniversary-of-a-landslide-what-swung-the-2020-covid-election.

Vote Compass. 2020. *Post-Election Study, New Zealand 2020 Election*. Toronto: Vox Pop Labs.

Vowles, J. 1992. 'Social Groups and Electoral Behaviour.' In *Electoral Behaviour in New Zealand*, edited by M. Holland, 91–118. Oxford: Oxford University Press.

Vowles, J. 2010. 'Electoral System Change, Generations, Competitiveness and Turnout in New Zealand, 1963–2005.' *British Journal of Political Science* 40(4): 875–95.

Vowles, J. 2014. 'Down, Down, Down: Turnout from 1946 to 2011.' In *The New Electoral Politics in New Zealand: The Significance of the 2011 Election*, edited by J. Vowles, 53–71. Wellington: Institute for Governance and Policy Studies.

Vowles, J. 2020a. 'Populism and the 2017 General Election: The Background.' In *A Populist Exception? The 2017 New Zealand General Election*, edited by J. Vowles and J. Curtin, 35–69. Canberra: ANU Press. doi.org/10.22459/pe.2020.02.

Vowles, J. 2020b. 'The 2020 NZ Election Saw Record Vote Volatility—What Does That Mean for the Next Labour Government?' *The Conversation*, 20 October. Available from: theconversation.com/the-2020-nz-election-saw-record-vote-volatility-what-does-that-mean-for-the-next-labour-government-148330.

Vowles, J. 2020c. 'Where Did National's Votes Go?' Newsroom, [Auckland], 16 November. Available from: www.newsroom.co.nz/ideasroom/where-did-nationals-votes-go.

Vowles, J., F. Barker, M. Krewel, J. Hayward, J. Curtin, L. Greaves, and L. Oldfield. 2022. *2020 New Zealand Election Study*. [Online]. ADA Dataverse, V3. doi.org/10.26193/BPAMYJ.

Vowles, J., H. Coffé, and J. Curtin. 2017. *A Bark But No Bite: Inequality and the 2014 New Zealand General Election*. Canberra: ANU Press. doi.org/10.22459/bbnb.08.2017.

Vowles, J., and J. Curtin (eds). 2020. *A Populist Exception? The 2017 New Zealand General Election*. Canberra: ANU Press. doi.org/10.22459/pe.2020.

Vowles, J., and M. Gibbons. 2023. *A Bigger Data Turnout Dataset, 2014–2020*. Wellington: Victoria University of Wellington.

Appendix 1.1

Table A1.1 Issue salience

Issue	%
Covid-19	26
None named	16
Economy	15
Housing	7
Environment	5
Government	4
Health	4
Cannabis	3
Party bias	3
Welfare, inequality, poverty	6
Tax	2
Immigration	1
Education	1
Euthanasia	1
Other (below 1%)	5

Appendix Table A1.2 provides an estimate of the total vote flows between the two elections, including flows in and out of nonvoting. It is derived from a weighted cross-tabulation of data from the Vote Compass post-election sample of just over 26,000 people. There are similar NZES data but, subject to some limitations, the much larger size of the post-election Vote Compass sample makes it a better source.[10] The table's cells show total percentages of the entire Vote Compass sample. The 2020 votes are read down by column, and the 2017 votes across by row. This vote flow matrix draws on the post-election dataset from Vote Compass and a study of turnout using a 'bigger' sample from the electoral rolls (Vowles and Gibbons 2023). The table is weighted by a process of 'raking' from the results of the election, drawing on the vote shares reported in the official results and data from the electoral rolls to further calibrate the proportions of previously ineligible voters and those who did not vote at both elections. This includes those who joined the roll in 2020, many of whom were eligible to be enrolled in 2017.

---

10   The NZES has similar data based on a panel: people who participated in both the 2020 and the 2017 NZESs. Replicating the same weighting process on the NZES panel subsample produces almost the same cell percentages across the diagonal of consistent behaviour in 2017 and 2020.

Table A1.2 Flow of the votes between 2017 and 2020 (per cent)

Vote 2020 (by col.)	DNV	Labour	National	Green	ACT	Māori	NZ First	TOP	Other	New	All 2020	N
						Vote 2017 (by row)						
DNV	13.72	1.67	1.42	0.19	0.00	0.08	0.65	0.04	0.05	0.70	18.51	217
Labour	8.27	20.63	6.61	1.44	0.03	0.30	1.79	0.61	0.22	0.92	40.82	9,980
National	1.59	0.54	16.88	0.04	0.06	0.07	0.65	0.11	0.10	0.85	20.89	4,269
Green	0.85	1.45	0.29	2.40	0.01	0.05	0.05	0.25	0.05	1.04	6.44	5,789
ACT	0.75	0.23	4.03	0.05	0.24	0.02	0.42	0.10	0.05	0.32	6.21	2,755
Māori	0.36	0.14	0.06	0.03	0.00	0.21	0.01	0.03	0.02	0.03	0.89	182
NZ First	0.39	0.27	0.27	0.02	0.00	0.03	0.96	0.02	0.04	0.09	2.10	590
TOP	0.16	0.15	0.16	0.11	0.01	0.02	0.04	0.45	0.02	0.11	1.23	1,181
Other	0.87	0.28	0.87	0.03	0.01	0.03	0.39	0.07	0.19	0.13	2.92	639
All 2017	26.96	25.38	30.57	4.31	0.38	0.81	4.96	1.68	0.73	4.24	100	
N	538	8,372	7,248	4,413	481	311	1,788	1,134	435	885		26,507

Note: Numbers show unweighted figures. Total percentages estimated by raking: iterated weighting and reweighting the table margins.

Sources: Vote Compass (2020); Vowles and Gibbons (2023).

Table A1.3 Sociodemographic correlates of voting choice in 2020

	Nonvote	National	Green	NZ First	ACT	Māori	Others
[Employer]							
Self-employed	-0.694	-0.768*	0.154	0.953	0.312	-1.208	1.002
	(0.676)	(0.411)	(0.729)	(1.058)	(0.581)	(1.166)	(0.854)
Supervisor	-0.698	-0.556*	-0.081	-0.325	0.101	-2.014**	-0.525
	(0.535)	(0.337)	(0.658)	(1.105)	(0.526)	(0.930)	(0.765)

	Nonvote	National	Green	NZ First	ACT	Māori	Others
Employee	-1.088**	-0.808**	-0.072	-0.143	0.135	-1.886**	-0.104
	(0.518)	(0.326)	(0.640)	(1.041)	(0.505)	(0.928)	(0.710)
Not employed	-0.546	-0.652*	0.256	-1.017	-0.408	-1.909**	-0.672
	(0.587)	(0.391)	(0.716)	(1.109)	(0.654)	(0.945)	(0.825)
[Nonmanual/not employed]							
Farmer	0.494	1.014***	0.445	0.261	0.768**	1.305*	0.713
	(0.428)	(0.211)	(0.394)	(0.829)	(0.305)	(0.679)	(0.544)
Manual/service	-0.104	-0.080	-0.044	0.254	0.027	0.584	0.113
	(0.207)	(0.133)	(0.173)	(0.290)	(0.186)	(0.373)	(0.285)
[Rural]							
Town	0.698*	-0.414**	-0.334	-0.115	-0.761***	-0.565	0.090
	(0.389)	(0.184)	(0.329)	(0.539)	(0.242)	(0.517)	(0.408)
Suburb	0.746*	-0.277	0.695**	0.390	-1.524***	-0.320	0.078
	(0.433)	(0.223)	(0.327)	(0.574)	(0.340)	(0.582)	(0.415)
City	0.504	-0.349**	0.745***	0.318	-0.949***	0.493	0.164
	(0.376)	(0.171)	(0.275)	(0.539)	(0.232)	(0.450)	(0.337)
Age	-0.038***	0.009**	-0.041***	0.024**	-0.002	0.003	-0.022***
	(0.006)	(0.004)	(0.005)	(0.012)	(0.005)	(0.010)	(0.006)
Income	-0.005**	0.006***	0.000	-0.000	0.006***	0.002	-0.001
	(0.002)	(0.001)	(0.001)	(0.002)	(0.001)	(0.003)	(0.003)
Assets	0.072	0.253***	0.160***	-0.074	0.114*	0.114	-0.103
	(0.078)	(0.050)	(0.060)	(0.124)	(0.068)	(0.125)	(0.122)
Female [male]	-0.469**	-0.078	-0.572***	-0.741**	-0.723***	-0.353	-1.019***
	(0.205)	(0.122)	(0.157)	(0.306)	(0.173)	(0.297)	(0.247)

	Nonvote	National	Green	NZ First	ACT	Māori	Others
Union [non-union]	-0.669**	-0.794***	0.114	-0.348	-0.970***	-0.568	0.022
	(0.271)	(0.180)	(0.171)	(0.363)	(0.269)	(0.362)	(0.294)
Religious [not]	0.131	0.261*	-0.511**	0.055	-0.234	0.476	0.895***
	(0.265)	(0.145)	(0.232)	(0.299)	(0.233)	(0.330)	(0.240)
[European/other]							
Asian	-0.004	-0.201	-0.856***	-13.931***	-1.040**	-12.619***	-0.262
	(0.355)	(0.234)	(0.283)	(0.326)	(0.475)	(0.705)	(0.418)
Pasifika	0.700	-1.195**	-2.053*	0.531	-0.652	-12.448***	-3.250***
	(0.479)	(0.584)	(1.050)	(0.998)	(0.751)	(0.655)	(0.808)
Māori	-0.014	-1.155***	-0.358*	1.074***	-0.951***	3.650***	0.136
	(0.225)	(0.163)	(0.184)	(0.313)	(0.260)	(0.689)	(0.315)
[No qualification]							
School/certificate	-0.159	0.217	0.658*	0.125	0.312	0.203	0.220
	(0.300)	(0.187)	(0.396)	(0.384)	(0.269)	(0.456)	(0.481)
University	-0.570	-0.305	1.466***	0.202	-0.303	0.879	0.854*
	(0.360)	(0.217)	(0.405)	(0.502)	(0.314)	(0.588)	(0.501)
Constant	2.028**	-1.201**	-1.317	-4.301***	-1.427**	-5.053***	-0.998
	(0.802)	(0.482)	(0.881)	(1.576)	(0.694)	(1.285)	(1.098)
Observations	3,286	3,286	3,286	3,286	3,286	3,286	3,286
r²_p	0.127						
LL	-4,602						

*** p < 0.01
** p < 0.05
* p < 0.1

Notes: Robust standard errors in parentheses; multinomial logit model; Labour vote is the reference category; explanatory variable reference categories in square brackets.

Sociodemographic variables (Table A1.3, Figure 1.8)

For employment and occupation, participants' position is estimated to represent the nature of the household and its relation to the labour market. To avoid either gender bias (by using male head of household) or individualist bias (disregarding the other person in the household), we assign the participant to a category according to that person or their partner having the most theoretically significant characteristics first.

Employment status

Estimated from responses of respondent and their partner if data for the latter are available. 1) A participant in a household with an employer is classified as such; 2) any household with someone self-employed but not an employer is classified as such; 3) any participant in a household with someone who is a supervisor but not an employer or self-employed or a supervisor is classified as such; leaving 4) a participant in a household containing only non-supervisory employees as the residual category for those with employment status data. Those with no data on employment status form an additional category (5).

Occupation

Any household with a person reporting involvement in farming by industry or occupation is classified as a farmer. Any household with a person in a manual or service occupation (but not a farmer) is classified as such. The rest form a residual non-manual or not-employed category.

Ethnicity

A participant reporting Māori ethnicity is classified as Māori; a participant reporting Pasifika but not Māori ethnicity is Pasifika; a participant reporting Asian or Middle East origin but not Māori or Pasifika is Asian; the rest are a residual category who are mostly European/Pākehā.

Education

Low education is those without any qualifications. The middle category is anyone with a level 1–7 qualification without a university degree.

Income

Income is scored by the midpoints of the ranges measured by six income categories.

Assets

Constructed as the number of asset types: a house, a business, a second house for leisure or investment, stocks and shares, any savings, and membership of KiwiSaver or any retirement savings scheme. By simple addition, this is made into a scale from zero to six.

Union household

Any household that contains a union member, or not.

Religious

Attends religious services more than once a year, or not.

2

Shock, Bounce, and Reward?

Jack Vowles

This chapter analyses how New Zealand's experience of Covid-19 affected electoral change at the 2020 general election. It also provides a schematic comparative overview of the electoral consequences of the pandemic in several other countries. The local focus is on the shift of votes to Labour. The chapter considers four arguments and tests them as much as is possible from the available literature and evidence:

1. Voters can evaluate the success or failure of crisis management and governments will stand or fall based on their judgement.

2. A government cannot simply rely on a 'rally round the flag' impetus; its competence in managing the crisis matters more.

3. Political trust was a primary factor in generating political support for measures to contain the pandemic and the ability of the Labour government to reap an electoral reward.

4. Successful government response to a major crisis may trigger not only short-term but also longer-term political support.

As explained in Chapter 1, the 2020 election rewarded the New Zealand Labour Party with a landslide victory. It generated the biggest net transfer of votes from one election to the next in New Zealand's electoral history and the highest turnout in 20 years. Labour gained a comfortable single-party parliamentary majority unusual in a country with a proportional electoral system. There is wide agreement that the government's Covid-19 response was effective (Jefferies et al. 2020). An elimination strategy kept New Zealand free of the pandemic for long periods when its global severity and contagion were at their peak. The result of the election gave the government a mandate to continue its elimination policy until it was no longer required. A strong stimulus attenuated the economic effects. The success of the government's strategy illustrated the advantages of social cohesion and a sense of responsibility for others.

The next section explains the idea of an unexpected exogenous shock beyond the normal conditions underpinning electoral politics and the party system, the literature underpinning the concept, and its implications for this analysis. Next, attention moves to the broader context of the crisis, examining post-Covid elections around the world. When aligned with case-to-population ratios, the results of 19 post-Covid elections in high-income democracies test whether a country's pandemic response effectiveness enhanced the chances of incumbent government survival. Returning to New Zealand, a summary of the government response leading up to the election is followed by analysis of opinion and behavioural changes between 2017 and 2020, and then of the election itself.

The politics of an exogenous shock and the international context

The Covid-19 pandemic generated an exogenous shock: an event precipitated outside the boundaries of the system that it affects—in this case, the patterns of 'normal' electoral politics in New Zealand. Such shock events can dramatically affect political behaviour. The number of political parties, the votes cast for them, their foundations in society, and the extent and nature of their ideological differences may all be affected.

The theoretical framework of the social psychological Michigan model still defines much current scholarly inquiry of electoral behaviour. Early Michigan theorists argued that party systems in long-established representative democracies tend to mature. Electoral choices should become less volatile and more stable, underpinned by increasing levels of party identification (Converse 1969; Shively 1972). Early political research on Western Europe confirmed a similar consistency in the development of party systems. It emphasised the persistence and apparent consolidation of political cleavage structures, most of them 'frozen' at the point of the achievement of universal male suffrage (Lipset and Rokkan 1967; Bartolini and Mair 1990).

The Michigan model of political behaviour also accommodated the possibility of an exogenous shock that could disrupt behaviour and trigger a 'critical election' (Key 1955). A shock followed by a critical election could potentially lead to a realignment of parties and partisan choices that would, in time, consolidate and restabilise the system (Inglehart and Hochstein 1972). The Great Depression of the 1930s provided the first example. The experience and aftermath of World War II further consolidated party systems. New Zealand provides one of the best examples of a realignment generated by the Depression. The three-party system of the 1920s was transformed into a two-party system at the 1935 and 1938 elections (Leithner 1997, 1119).

But just as the Michigan model was being applied to explain apparent party system stability, in the early 1970s, a sharp increase in the price of oil induced a new economic shock. The tendency towards consolidation began to reverse. Party systems began to de-align, not realign. Electoral volatility tended to increase, and levels of partisan identification to decline, although with much intercountry variation (Särlvik and Crewe 1983; Dalton and Wattenberg 2000; Franklin et al. 2009). New Zealand party politics exhibited many of these developments. Closer to the present, compared with most other high-income representative democracies in the early twenty-first century, New Zealand politics has been both stable and only moderately polarised. Volatility surged after the first election under proportional representation in 1996. By the 2008 election, the two major parties of the centre-right and centre-left, National and Labour, respectively, had recovered dominance (Vowles 2014).

Meanwhile, from the early 1990s, the economies of high-income democracies entered a period of stability described as 'the great moderation' (Bernanke 2012), only marginally disrupted by regional crises in Latin America and Asia. Research in electoral politics had turned to the estimation of the effects of short-term change rather than long-term stability and thus more modest variation in the business cycle (Kramer 1971; Fair 1978; Fiorina 1981). Here, the focus was not on shocks but on the policy performance of incumbent governments. It was assumed that those governments could be assigned most, if not all, responsibility for economic outcomes. Through a sense of general wellbeing, volatility in economic growth and levels of employment could affect the re-election or defeat of incumbent governments. Where growth and employment were strong, voters tended to reward governments. In recessions and with increasing unemployment, voters tended to punish them.[1]

Doubts about the competence of ordinary voters to have coherent and stable political attitudes had been confirmed by survey research in the 1950s and 1960s (Converse 2005). With that scepticism in mind, the theory of retrospective democratic accountability for economic performance could take on considerable normative weight. If voters were not sufficiently informed to vote 'correctly' on issues of the day, at least they might be capable of holding the government to account for their country's economic performance. However, this argument is vulnerable to the observation that, even in the largest and most closed economies, patterns of growth and recession are affected by factors outside one country's borders. Voter incompetence could be even worse than a simple lack of 'real' attitudes. Blind voters are prone to blame governments for outcomes beyond their control. Myopic voters are focussed on short-term rather than long-term performances (Achen and Bartels 2016). This would deny one of the key arguments outlined above: that voters can deliver a meaningful electoral response on the record of a government that has faced a crisis.

An alternative interpretation addresses this challenge: rather than retrospective reward and punishment, there is a process of selection. Collectively, voters are capable of discounting exogenous factors and can extract a 'competency signal' from performance. They apply it to their assessment of a government party into the future (Duch and Stevenson 2008). The test becomes how governments meet an economic challenge or crisis, and their success or failure in so doing. Applying this approach to natural disasters confirms that governments can be rewarded for an effective response, potentially over more than one subsequent election (Bechtel and Hainmueller 2011; Bechtel and Mannino 2022).

The Global Financial Crisis (GFC) of 2008–09 was the biggest shock to hit the global economy since the Great Depression. Identification of short-term effects first followed the logic of retrospective economic voting theory. Initial findings suggested that the great recession that followed the GFC adversely affected the electoral prospects of incumbent governments regardless of

---

1   Gardener (2016) tests the extent of economic voting in New Zealand using NZES data from 1990 to 2014.

their ideological complexion. Election timing also mattered (Bartels 2014). In many cases, voters appeared to be punishing governments for a crisis they did not create, thus casting doubt on selection theory.

More recent research challenges these findings. The depth of the crisis alone did not predict the success or failure of incumbents (Hernández and Kriesi 2016; Talving 2018). If sufficient people are indirectly informed by cues from elite and media sources, they are collectively capable of taking account of both institutional constraints on government and the state of the global economy. They can identify the effects of their own government's performance (Kayser and Peress 2012). The selection model directs the focus not so much to the crisis itself, but to what governments do to meet the challenge. The effects of the economy on voter choice were much stronger after the crisis than either during or before it. The odds of incumbent government survival post-GFC were significantly increased if there was an economic stimulus underpinning a robust recovery. These differences were conditional on the balance between austerity and stimulus in policy responses—parties of the centre-right usually doing best under austerity conditions and those on the centre-left making gains under stimulus (Hellwig et al. 2020, 147–55, 169–79).

As the challenges of the GFC faded into the background, the Covid-19 crisis emerged. The economic effects of Covid-19 have been much more severe than those of the GFC: an estimated 3.3 per cent decline in global gross domestic product (GDP) in 2020 compared with only 0.1 per cent in 2009 during the GFC (IMF 2021). The extent of the GFC and the ability to recover from it were not entirely the responsibility of governments. Some had less of a crisis to manage and more tools and resources available to respond, making the extraction of a competency signal more difficult. Traditional left–right policy differences could also be mobilised. There were competing diagnoses of the causes of the GFC lying in market or government failure.

The pandemic's impact has been felt much more widely, led initially by high-income countries, but rapidly extending everywhere. Its effects were not just economic; they have also been life-threatening, particularly among the elderly, with the potential to unleash 'a primal, deep-seated fear of death' (Baekgaard et al. 2020, 6). The timing of the Covid-19 intrusion varied. There were minor advantages to countries where exposure was delayed and where those countries were better prepared, but because of its high rates of infection, the virus was bound to spread. At first glance, unprepared health systems provided some grounds for punishment of governments, but systems of public health are embedded institutions in which change is slow and difficult (Forest and Denis 2012; Braithwaite et al. 2016). It would therefore be less credible to blame incumbent governments for circumstances equally the responsibility of previous governments. Incumbents' immediate policy responses were the centre of attention and thus shaped perceptions of competence.

With all this in mind, the argument foreshadowed comes to the fore: that an electorate can effectively judge government performance in a crisis. Following the simple logic of reward and punishment, governments that failed to control Covid-19 would be expected to lose votes given basic expectations about a state's duty to protect its citizens. However, one analysis claims that most US voters in 2020 lacked sufficient knowledge about the positions of presidential candidates in dealing with the pandemic to vote effectively on the matter (Guntermann and Lenz 2022). Presenting evidence that challenges this scepticism, county-level analysis of the 2000 US presidential election estimates that the rate of Covid-19 cases negatively affected the vote for Donald Trump and could have helped mobilise voters to turn out to vote for Joe Biden (Baccini et al. 2021).

Another way of denying a competence effect is the idea of a 'rally round the flag'. People support the government out of a sense of national loyalty and social cohesion. In other words, the underlying causes of voter choices are emotional and not based on even minimal evaluation or judgement. Similarly, a simple search for security could lead voters to opt for status-quo candidates (Bisbee and Honig 2021).

Emotions clearly played a role in the New Zealand public's response, but collective public opinion is a complex mixture of reason and emotion. A public 'mood' is based on a combination of the two. The first lockdown experience in New Zealand was successful because it drew on the idea of collective effort, in tune with the appeals of the government (Sibley et al. 2020). The comparative research hitherto finds little evidence that the crisis alone boosted government support. A public mood of approval requires perceptions that a government has acted effectively (Bol et al. 2021). A failure to be seen to act effectively, perhaps compounded by opposition criticism, might see no effect at all. Even an effective policy response might generate only a short-term boost in approval (Kritzinger et al. 2021). Considerable variation in trust and democratic satisfaction has been uncovered in Europe, linked to the immediate aftermath of lockdowns and variation in responses (Bol et al. 2021).

Meanwhile, another line of inquiry has taken a different direction, identifying in government responses to the pandemic a danger of authoritarian governments triggering an authoritarian response in public opinion. For example, research in the United States and Poland has suggested that fear of Covid-19 promoted social conservatism and a greater propensity to vote for the right (Karwowski et al. 2020). But, despite some questioning of the legal basis of some government actions, there is little support for these concerns in the New Zealand context (Vowles 2022).

Comparative data can be brought to bear to test the claim that assessment of performance mattered. Several other countries held elections during the period in question. There was considerable variation in governments' responses, particularly when the threat from the virus first emerged. Before infection and death rates were fully understood, governments and their advisors in many countries with health services with high capacity to deal with respiratory disease hoped that modest restrictions to discourage transmission would be sufficient to manage Covid-19 (Shokoohi et al. 2020, 437). Stronger restrictions would inevitably constrain economic activity. Many feared an economic recession. As it turned out, the experience of the uncontained virus had dire economic effects anyway, much stronger than the effects of restrictions (Hasell 2020). Countries seeking to maintain economic activity with lower levels of restriction were often forced into more severe measures, seesawing back and forth between levels, causing uncertainty and disruption. Where elimination has been feasible it has been the best response for both health and the economy (Oliu-Barton et al. 2021). Only with high levels of vaccination and less fatal variants have lower-level restrictions become effective, albeit at the continuing cost of infections and deaths.

Research on the effects of Covid-19 on electoral behaviour requires selection of cases during the relevant period of crisis. A significant number of studies have already appeared although systematic analysis remains limited (see the summary in Yu et al. 2022). Only eight national elections were held in high-income democracies during 2020; 12 followed in 2021 and into early 2022. The best estimate of the effectiveness of a government's Covid-19 response is the ratio of cases to population. As an estimate of actual cases, differences across countries will contain some errors (Greer et al. 2021, 6–7). For our purposes, one can observe that these are data about which voters in the countries concerned would have been directly or indirectly aware. In the world of electoral politics, perceptions matter more than precise estimates.[2]

Some simple statistical analysis shows a relationship between the survival or defeat of incumbent governments associated with the log of the number of Covid-19 cases per million reported at the time of the election. The log of cases is used because, above a certain level, their effects tend to flatten out. The main incumbent is the party of the prime minister or president. It is necessary to control for the number of months since the advent of Covid as the effects diminish over time. As shown in Figure 2.1, simply dichotomising re-election versus defeat produces a relationship between the number of cases and outcomes.[3] The partisanship of governments, added in another unreported model, has little or no effect. The diminishing effects of the case ratio serve as a warning to post-Covid comparative electoral analysts. The longer the delay between the onset of the pandemic and the election, the harder it could be to identify the effects.

Among the elections featured, two stand out: South Korea and New Zealand. In both, there were low case numbers because of effective government action at a time when many other countries were struggling to contain the pandemic. Landslide victories followed for incumbent centre-left government parties. In South Korea in April 2020, the allied Democratic and Platform parties won the largest parliamentary majority since the restoration of democracy in 1987. The voting turnout was 66 per cent—the highest in 28 years. The government had been under attack for scandals and poor economic growth, but those concerns were overshadowed by the effective pandemic response. Pride in the success of the country's containment drive greatly enhanced the popularity of president Moon Jae-in (Kim 2020). Like other East Asian countries, South Korea was better prepared in its health response because of its recent experience with early pandemic threats, giving its government some advantages. Trust in government was a powerful mediating factor in shaping the public response (Yu et al. 2022). As discussed below, the Korean experience has many parallels with that of New Zealand.

---

2   For this reason, reporting of the number of cases rather than deaths is more appropriate. While the latter are arguably the best data available in 'objective' terms, reports of these data were delayed and less likely to be considered by mainstream media.

3   The analysis incorporates a jack-knife test that corrects the confidence intervals for the possible effects of influential cases. The logged case ratio variable has negative values because some of its values were fractions of one. It is possible more sophisticated statistical modelling could dig more deeply into these data, but the small number of cases and large number of other potential variables would almost certainly confound the analysis.

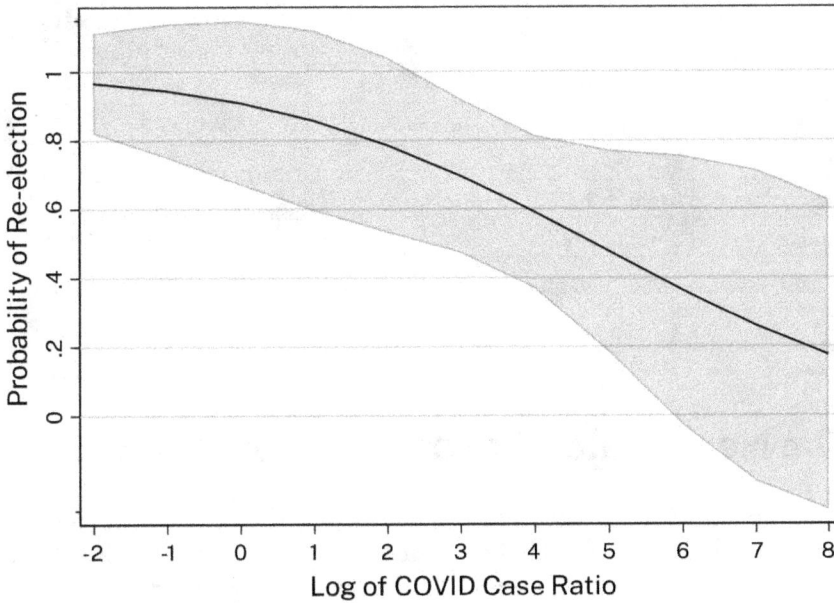

Figure 2.1 The relationship between Covid-19 cases and the survival or defeat of incumbent governments, 2020–2022

Source: Appendix Table A2.1.

Table 2.1 General elections held since Covid-19 (high-income countries only)

Country	Date	Main incumbent	Cases (per million)	Vote change
Israel	2 March 2020	Re-elected	0.10	4.4
Ireland	30–31 March 2020	Defeated	51.64	−4.7
South Korea	15 April 2020	Re-elected	0.58	12.9
Singapore	10 July 2020	Re-elected	27.71	−8.6
Lithuania	11 October 2020	Defeated	48.96	−4.4
New Zealand	16 October 2020	Re-elected	0.39	13.1
United States	6 November 2020	Defeated	331.89	0.8
Israel	23 March 2021	Defeated	107.42	−5.3
Netherlands	17 March 2021	Re-elected	350.88	0.6
Norway	13 September 2021	Defeated	217.15	−4.7
Canada	20 September 2021	Re-elected	114.17	−0.5
Iceland	25 September 2021	Re-elected	88.32	−1.0
Germany	26 September 2021	Defeated	92.39	−8.8
Czechia	8–9 October 2021	Defeated	77.79	−2.5

Country	Date	Main incumbent	Cases (per million)	Vote change
Japan	31 October 2021	Re-elected	2.09	1.4
Chile	21 November 2021	Re-elected	123.92	0.3
Portugal	30 January 2022	Re-elected	5,480.27	5.1
South Korea	9 March 2022	Defeated	5,191.07	3.5
Hungary	3 April 2022	Re-elected	142.6	4.9

Notes: Cases per million and official election results by country. See Appendix 2.1 for the regression model.
Source: Global Change Data Lab (2022).

The New Zealand experience of Covid-19

Less emphasised in the international literature is the quality of leadership. Assessment of the New Zealand case, backed up by other research, highlights the effectiveness of the authorities in ensuring strong communication to elicit community support (Grieve 2020; McGuire et al. 2020; Beattie and Priestly 2021a, 2021b). Labour framed the battle as one to be fought by citizens together with their government, to protect the health of all citizens but particularly the most vulnerable, in line with the social democratic principles of the party.[4] As a high-profile woman leader, Jacinda Ardern may also have had an advantage in being able to project herself as honest, trustworthy, and competent at dealing with health issues (Piazza and Diaz 2020). Chapter 7 of this volume expands on this theme.

In sharp contrast to the South Korean example, the reasons for New Zealand's strong response can be found not in preparedness but in its absence. There was a pandemic response plan in place, but it was geared to a new strain of influenza. Because of its high infection rate, Covid-19 posed a much more serious threat (Kvalsvig and Baker 2021). After years of constrained health expenditure under New Zealand governments of both the centre-right and the centre-left, the number of intensive care unit beds

---

4   Announcing the first Covid-19 response package in the House of Representatives, Finance Minister Grant Robertson explicitly framed his government's response as being in line with the Labour principles behind the creation of New Zealand's welfare state in the 1930s, saying: '[I]n New Zealand, we have been here before, with major economic and social crises. In my lifetime, we have seen Governments respond with austerity—an ideology that has done enormous damage to the fabric of our society. We have also seen other examples, such as the first Labour Government, who responded with investment, pragmatism, optimism, and kindness. It is from them that I take my lesson on how we recover and rebuild in a just, fair, and far-sighted manner' (Robertson 2020).

was the second lowest across 22 countries of the Organisation for Economic Co-operation and Development (OECD). New Zealand's ratio of hospital beds to population was sixth lowest in the OECD, but slightly higher than in Sweden, Denmark, the United Kingdom, and Canada (World Bank 2022).[5]

New Zealand's first case of Covid-19 was reported on 28 February 2020. On 11 March, the World Health Organization declared an official pandemic. Beginning on 14 March, all those entering New Zealand were required to self-isolate. Public events were cancelled and public places began to close. Community transmission was anticipated. On 19 March, the border was closed to almost all but returning New Zealand citizens and residents. It remained closed on that basis until early 2022.[6] On 25 March, on the advice of medical and epidemiological experts, the entire country moved into a comprehensive 'Level 4' lockdown—one of the most stringent enacted anywhere. The objective of the lockdown was 'elimination'—defined as

> reduction of the incidence of a disease to zero in a defined geographical area. While absence of disease is the ultimate goal, elimination criteria … allow for occasional outbreaks or imported cases, provided they are stamped out within a defined time period. (Baker et al. 2020: 198; Cameron 2020)[7]

Travel and tourism together constituted 15 per cent of New Zealand GDP in 2019. Tourism generated about 8 per cent of employment (OECD 2021a, 2021b). The border closure also revealed the dependence of the tourist industry on the employment of low-budget backpackers and other temporary migrant workers. Agriculture and horticulture suffered from a lack of seasonal labour, much of it also supplied by migrant workers from offshore.

On 28 April, the lockdown was eased to Level 3, and cases began to peter out. On 14 May, restrictions were eased to Level 2 and, on 9 June, to Level 1, restoring much of everyday life to how it was before the pandemic. Days began to pass with no new cases other than at the border. All those entering the country were in managed isolation in hotels in the three major cities for

---

5   New Zealand was somewhat better placed in its availability of doctors and nursing staff, sitting at close to the OECD mean, with slightly more nurses than average but somewhat fewer doctors (OECD 2020, 7–13). The ratio of beds to population dropped by more than half between 2002 and 2009. Most of that period was under a Labour-led government.

6   With limited exceptions for those deemed to be making an economic contribution, such as people with highly valuable skills, entertainers, and actors for television and film production.

7   Description of the conditions specified for the various alert levels and a timeline of the Covid-19 response measures can be found in New Zealand Government (2021b).

a 14-day quarantine period. One hundred and two days followed without community transmission. On 11 August, four community cases emerged in Auckland—their source never identified—with others following. Auckland went into Level 3 lockdown, the rest of the country into Level 2. Capacity testing and contact tracing had been very poor at the outset; by then they had been improved (Roche et al. 2020). Almost all cases were detected and moved into isolation. The coming general election, scheduled for 19 September, was postponed until 17 October.

On 21 September, all areas outside Auckland moved to Level 1, with Auckland itself following on 7 October. Cases once again petered out except at the border. Consequently, the 2020 general election could be held without the need for social distancing. However, provisions for advance voting had been extended. Many more people than at previous elections cast early votes, reducing congestion at voting places (see Chapter 4, this volume).

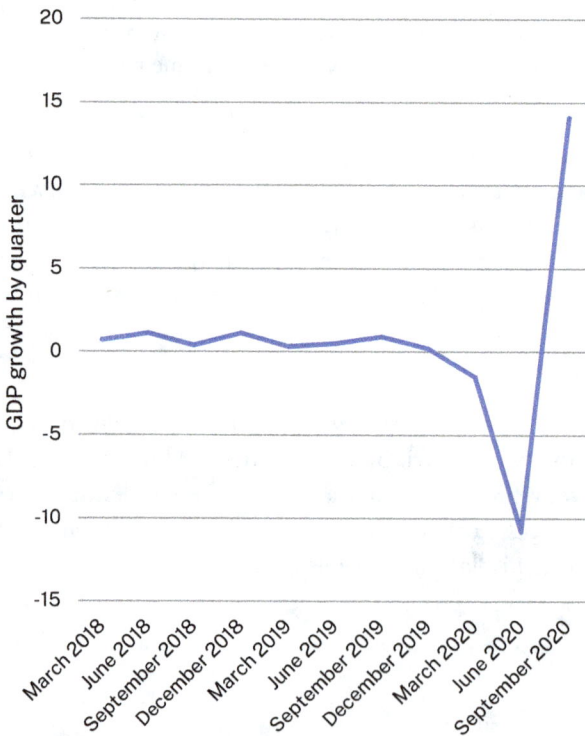

Figure 2.2 Quarterly GDP growth
Source: StatsNZ (2021).

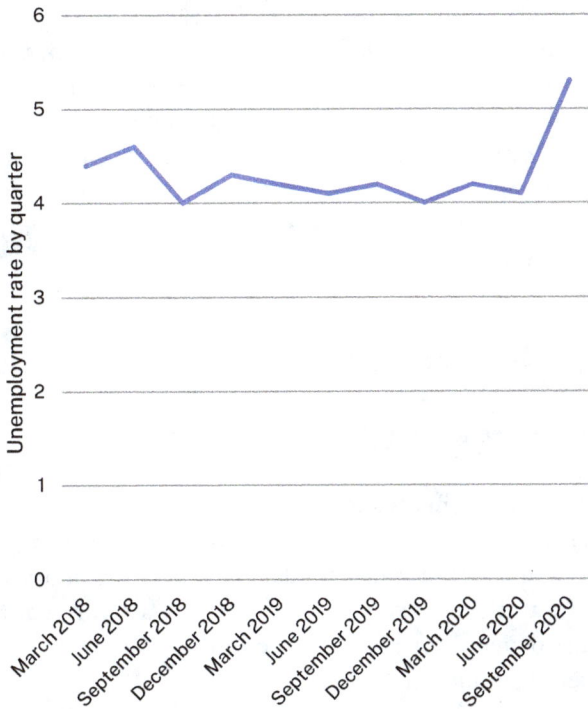

Figure 2.3 Unemployment rate
Source: StatsNZ (2021).

Even before the first lockdown, the economy had been weakening. On 17 March 2020, the government announced a stimulus package of NZ$12.5 billion—equivalent to 4 per cent of New Zealand's GDP. It increased health expenditure and boosted benefits for those on low incomes. About three-quarters of the package supported business and employment with a wage subsidy to businesses. In the budget delivered on 14 May, a further NZ$50 billion package was announced. The International Monetary Fund (IMF) has estimated that New Zealand's stimulus in 2020 was equivalent to 19.3 per cent of that year's GDP—in global comparison, second only to that of the United States (IMF Fiscal Affairs Department 2021). New Zealand's net core government debt grew from 19 per cent of GDP in 2019 to 27 per cent at the end of 2020—expected to peak at 48 per cent in 2023, which is still relatively low by comparative standards (New Zealand Government 2021b). Much of this debt was funded internally by bond purchases through the New Zealand Reserve Bank's program of quantitative easing.

As Figure 2.2 shows, the economy contracted by just less than 11 per cent in the year to the June quarter of 2020. As shown in Figure 2.3, the wage subsidy held off the effects on unemployment. Stimulus pushed the economy to bounce back by 14 per cent in the September quarter, despite the Auckland lockdown at the end of that period. Unemployment increased, but only marginally above 5 per cent. By the election on 17 October, community transmission had been stopped and the economy was on a relatively stable footing.

Explaining the shift to Labour in 2020

With the background to the election established, the next step is to test the arguments under examination with the evidence from the 2017 and 2020 NZESs. The possibility of long-term effects is considered first. The extent of the landslide and the increase in turnout could have been the early stages of a realignment. A renewed sense of social solidarity could shift political priorities towards the left, as did the experience of World War II in many countries, driving a 'huge demand for social protection that needed to be addressed by policymakers' (Obinger et al. 2018, 426).

The 2020 New Zealand general election sparked both an electoral landslide and a sharp increase in turnout, particularly among the young. The latter is potentially important, as realignments can take place in at least two ways: conversion, whereby voters shift from previous loyalties to new ones, or the mobilisation of new voters either hitherto not regularly voting or becoming eligible to vote for the first time. For example, a realignment of parties in the United States that consolidated in the 1940s was primarily by way of generational recruitment. The shift to the Democratic Party during the 1930s was a short-lived conversion effect (Norpoth et al. 2013).

The 2020 general election in New Zealand therefore had the potential to become a realigning or critical election. Early evidence suggested a shift to the left in public opinion, yet caution is in order. Strong as it was, the impact of Covid-19 is unlikely to have such far-reaching effects on political values as the experiences of those coming to maturity in the 1930s and 1940s during and after an economic depression that was followed by a global war.

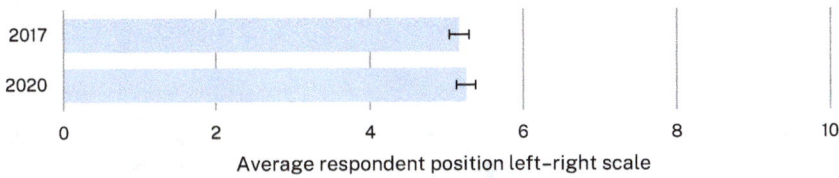

Figure 2.4 Average right–left scale positions, 2017 and 2020
Source: Vowles et al. (2022).

The 1,259 people who responded to the 2020 NZES represent 62 per cent of those who participated in the 2017 NZES.[8] Descriptive statistics from this panel data indicate that there was no ideological shift to the left. If anything, as Figure 2.4 shows, average self-placement on the right–left scale shifted marginally further to the right of the centre although well within confidence intervals. Because they tend to converge around the midpoint and tend to have a larger number of missing values than other instruments, left–right scales can be criticised as imprecise instruments, but they are widely used and defended in the literature (Kroh 2007).

A more substantive estimate should correlate with the left to right positions: opinions about inequality. Increasing social and economic inequality has been a theme of recent social commentary. NZES analysis of the 2014 election indicated strong majority support for government action to reduce inequality, but this was not followed with sufficient votes to elect a centre-left government (Vowles et al. 2017). Only in 2017 did the centre-left come to power—although through a coalition rather than winning a vote plurality (Vowles and Curtin 2020). Post-pandemic, inequality has worsened. Monetary stimulus boosted the property market and pumped asset values (see, for example, Hickey 2021). As a partial offset, welfare benefits were increased. While progress towards the government's target of reduced child poverty has been called into question, as of mid-2021, the key estimates of deprivation had trended somewhat downwards since 2018 (StatsNZ 2022). Figure 2.5, however, shows that, while the belief that the government should act to reduce income differences still had strong majority support, it fell back in 2020.

---

8   Comparison of the full data from both the 2017 and the 2020 NZESs finds the same changes—or the same absence of changes—as those reported below, although the gaps are slightly smaller.

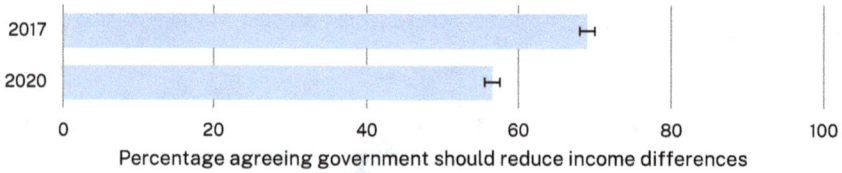

Percentage agreeing government should reduce income differences

Figure 2.5 Opinion on government action to reduce inequality

Note: The question was agreement or disagreement across a five-point scale with the statement: 'The government should take measures to reduce differences in income levels.'

Source: Vowles et al. (2022).

Preferences for government expenditure show little evidence of big attitudinal shifts in the four most salient policy areas. Figure 2.6 shows that preferences for higher health and housing expenditure have good majority support but dropped marginally from 2017 to 2020, while minority preferences for higher expenditure on welfare and unemployment benefits marginally increased. Longitudinal analysis of the NZES shows strong majority support for health expenditure that benefits almost everyone and declining minority support for benefits that are targeted at those in need (Humpage 2014). Meanwhile, New Zealand faces a crisis of housing underprovision and inflated values (Mitchell 2021). These inter-election expenditure preference shifts are hard to explain. The data clearly refute any concerted shift to the left. Marginal increases in favour of greater support for the unemployed and those on other benefits hint at some movement in favour of greater support for those worst affected.

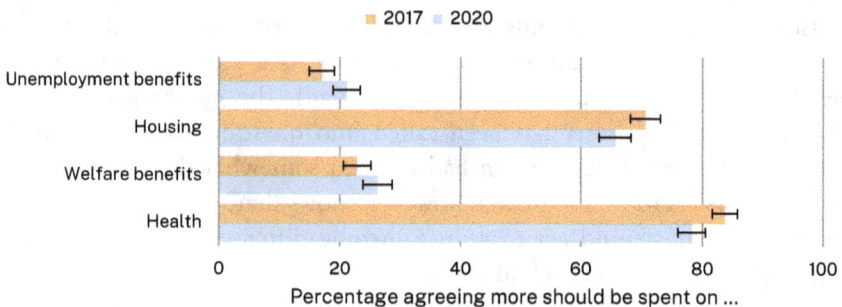

Percentage agreeing more should be spent on ...

Figure 2.6 Government expenditure preferences, 2017 and 2020

Note: The question was: 'Should there be more or less public expenditure in ... Remember if you say "more" or "much more" it could require a tax increase, and if you say "less" or "much less" it could require a reduction in those services.'

Source: Vowles et al. (2022).

Prior Bias   Covid-19 Effects   OUTCOME

Labour Vote 2017

Trust in Arden

Labour Vote 2020

Response Approval

Right-Left Position

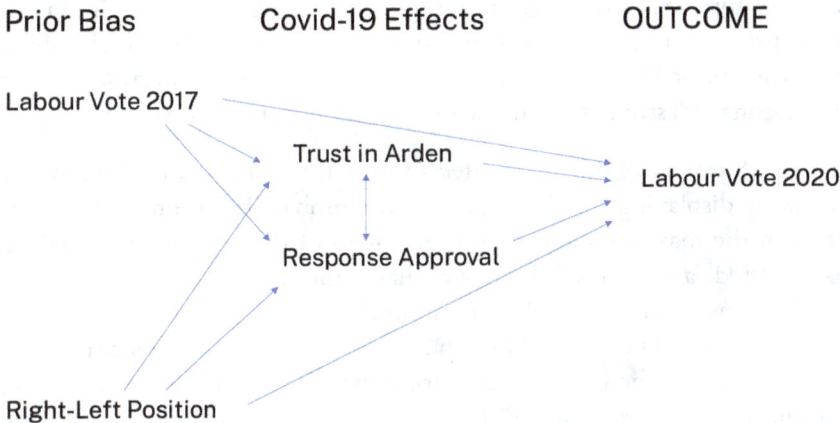

Figure 2.7 A model of the shift to Labour in 2020

To move on to the direct examination of the 2020 shift to Labour, the model displayed in Figure 2.7 is informed by a combination of theory and exploratory analysis. It is based on change. Most people who voted in 2020 had voted at previous elections and brought to their 2020 behaviour their habits and memories of previous behaviour. As a result, most had 'prior bias'. We know from a wealth of research in cognitive psychology that people resist new information that is inconsistent with their existing assumptions and past behaviour (see Kahneman 2012).[9]

The change model is given effect by using an individual's 2017 vote and right–left ideological position as baseline variables. While the panel data show there was some shifting in ideological positions from 2017 to 2020 (r = 0.62), Figure 2.4 shows there was virtually no net movement. This change approach facilitates reduction of the variables to a relatively small number that accounts for the shifts. Our data also include the crucial question: approval or disapproval of the Covid-19 response.[10] The model posits both trust in Prime Minister Ardern and response approval as variables mediating between previous behaviour and right–left ideological position on the road to a Labour vote. We assume both direct and indirect influences of the prior variables and reciprocal effects between trust in Ardern and

9   An alternative estimate of prior bias would be partisan identification, but in New Zealand this is relatively fluid and the previous vote is a better estimate. In 2020, those replying to the question on party identification saying they were 'generally speaking, close to Labour' increased from 19 to 28 per cent in the inter-election panel.
10   'Do you approve or disapprove of the way the government has responded to the coronavirus (Covid-19) outbreak?' A five-point scale.

response approval. Indeed, given the endogeneity inevitably built into most relationships between variables in public opinion and political behaviour, except for prior Labour vote, causality could go in both directions.[11] One can reasonably assume that the main direction was towards vote choice.

Figure 2.8 estimates the direct effects for each variable net of those of the others by displaying the differences in the probability of one's 2020 vote between the maximum and minimum values of the explanatory variables. As expected, a previous Labour vote has a big influence; a Labour voter in 2017 was about 30 per cent more likely to vote Labour in 2020 than someone who did not vote Labour in 2017 (a probability difference of about 0.3, as shown in the figure). Comparing the highest and lowest degrees of trust in Ardern (a probability difference of about 0.5) and response approval (about 0.3), one can see that these perceptions strongly shifted votes to Labour. Those on the right were more likely to resist the pull to Labour, but approval of the Covid-19 response nonetheless pulled many in the centre and centre-right to Labour, as Figure 2.9 shows.

Figure 2.9 shows how right–left positions condition the effect of response approval on the change to Labour. Left is estimated at point two on the 10-point scale. Leftists were almost entirely unaffected by their approval or disapproval of the pandemic response, although the majority approved. Those on the right, at eight on the scale, became almost as likely as people on the left to vote Labour if they strongly approved of the pandemic response. Perhaps the most telling slope is that for the median voter: the more the government response met approval, the higher was the probability of a shift to Labour. Appendix 2.1 provides further detail, including an expanded model with more control variables that tells the same story.[12]

The last addition to the picture is a model showing what factors lay behind approval or disapproval of the Covid-19 response. Approval was very high at 83 per cent. Figure 2.10 displays the differences and confidence intervals between the maximum and minimum probability values of the variables of theoretical and/or substantive significance.

---

11   Realistically, one should also accept a small degree of endogeneity even here because of recall error.
12   Many of the normal sociodemographic factors associated with a Labour vote do not register as significant, simply because they are absorbed by the prior bias of a 2017 Labour vote.

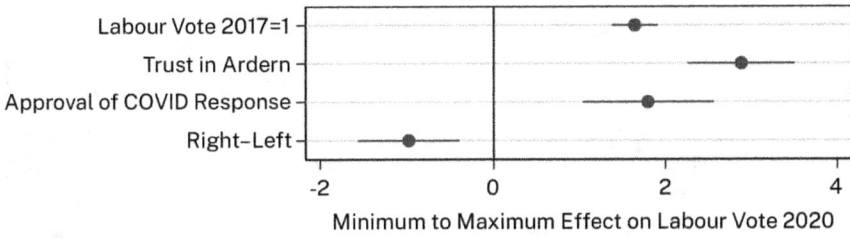

Figure 2.8 Labour vote in 2020: Effects of trust in Jacinda Ardern, approval of Covid-19 response, and previous vote

Source: Model II presented in Appendix Table A2.2.

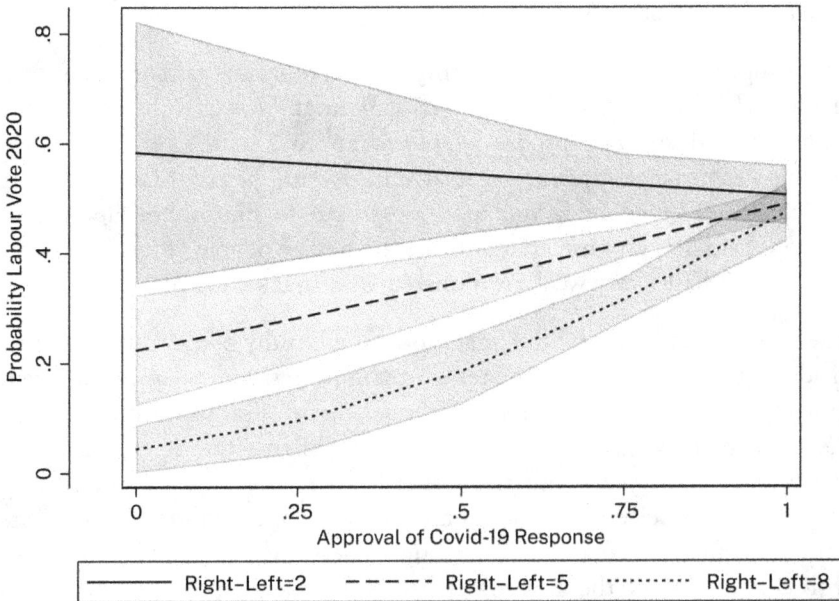

Figure 2.9 How left–right position conditioned the effect of response approval on the shift to Labour

Source: Model III presented in Appendix Table A2.4.

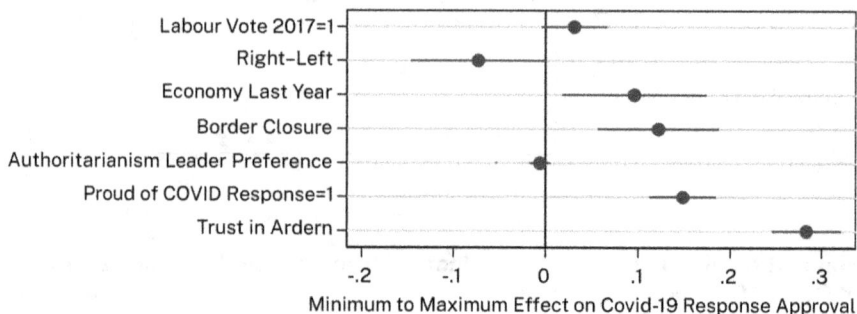

Figure 2.10 Approval of the Covid-19 response
Source: Appendix Table A2.3.

Following the same logic as the voting model, one expects the background factors that measure prior bias towards Labour and towards the left to have underlying effects that dispose people to approve of the response. They do, but the variance explained is relatively low at 7 per cent (see Appendix Table A2.4).[13] Once the factors more proximate to approval or disapproval of the Covid-19 response are controlled, whether people voted Labour or not in 2017 had a very weak relationship with that sentiment.

The variance explained by the final model is a healthy 34 per cent. In terms of ideology, those on the right remained more resistant to approval, even though, as the earlier analysis has shown, many did approve and made the move to Labour. A positive appreciation of the state of the economy over the previous year—much boosted by the government's stimulus by the time of the election—had significant effects, as did approval of the border closure.[14] Preferences for strong leadership were weakly associated with disapproval of the government response, not approval, but had no significant effect—indicated by the confidence internal touching the 'zero' or no-effect line.[15] The feeling of pride in the country's response also had a high correlation with approval of the Covid-19 response: 38 per cent of

---

13 A model without these baseline controls can be found in Chapter 8 of this volume, giving a different picture of the sociodemographic and other ideological elements behind approval or disapproval.
14 'When should New Zealand open its borders to tourists, students, and temporary workers from countries where there is community transmission of Covid-19? Immediately, only when community outbreaks can be safely contained, only after they go through 14 days' quarantine and two negative tests, only when there is a vaccine available?' Operationalised as a four-point scale, with 'Don't know' set to missing.
15 An alternative childhood socialisation values index was used in another model; its effects were insignificant.

the sample expressed that emotion.[16] Overall, the biggest effect was, again, that of trust in Ardern. This picture presents an image of an electorate making a sound collective judgement based on two of the most important elements of the policy response. Emotion certainly played a role, but it was a supplementary one underpinned by knowledge and experience.

Discussion and conclusions

This chapter presents evidence that governments can benefit electorally from successful crisis management after a strong unexpected 'shock', and that success can be both deserved and understood by the electorate. Despite scepticism (Achen and Bartels 2016; Guntermann and Lenz 2022), voters are collectively capable of assessing government performance and assigning credit or blame in conditions of crisis. Moreover, this was more than a simple 'rally round the flag'. Success and competence mattered. That said, more is needed than simple competence. The perception of competence must be supported by good leadership and clear communication and underpinned by trust. The New Zealand case clearly bears out these claims. International evidence suggests that electorates responded similarly, but the further the election was from the emergence of the crisis, the smaller was the effect.

There is little preliminary evidence to confirm or even suggest that a successful government response to the crisis triggered not only short-term but also longer-term political support. Other than the size of the shift, and the increase in turnout, one finds little evidence of a critical and realigning election. As Chapter 1 reports, turnout did increase, particularly among the young, but there is no evidence Labour benefited more than other parties from the youth vote. The turnout increase could have more to do with something else, as Chapter 4 will suggest. Nor does one find evidence of an ideological shift that would provide the foundations for significant changes in public policy settings on social and economic issues.

Despite the increase in welfare benefits and a slight reduction in child poverty, the social and economic outcomes of the government response were not redistributive and have exacerbated wealth inequality. While understandable in a post-Covid world facing an intensifying climate crisis,

---

16 'Which, if any, of the following describe your feelings about the government's response to Covid-19: angry, happy, disgusted, hopeful, uneasy, confident, afraid, proud, none of these?' A variable of zero or one on 'proud'.

the government's post-pandemic fiscal caution will mean only marginal changes in a redistributive direction are likely in the short to medium terms. The final chapter in this book discusses Labour's retreat from its ambitious policy agenda as the 2023 election was approaching.

Differences between those who situate themselves on the political right and the political left continued to underpin voting choice between Labour and its opponents on the right and centre-right. But the correlation between left–right position and voting choice weakened in 2020. Significant numbers situating themselves in the centre or on the right moved to Labour because they approved of the government's policy response. The explanation of this movement lies in selection theory, based on expectations of future competence and underpinned by enhanced trust in leadership and the successful elimination strategy. When Jacinda Ardern stepped down as prime minister in January 2023, New Zealand remained one of the very few countries in the world with no estimated excess deaths as the result of the Covid-19 pandemic.

References

Achen, C.H., and L.M. Bartels. 2016. *Democracy for Realists: Why Elections Do Not Produce Responsive Government*. Princeton, NJ: Princeton University Press. doi.org/10.1515/9781400882731.

Australian and New Zealand Intensive Care Society (ANZICS). 2019. *ANZICS Centre for Outcome and Resource Evaluation: 2018 Report*. Melbourne: ANZICS. Available from: www.anzics.com.au/wp-content/uploads/2019/10/2018-ANZICS-CORE-Report.pdf.

Baccini, L., A. Bordeur, and S. Weymouth. 2021. 'The COVID-19 Pandemic and the 2020 US Presidential Election.' *Journal of Population Economics* 34: 739–67. doi.org/10.1007/s00148-020-00820-3.

Baekgaard, M., J. Christensen, J.K. Madsen, and K.S. Mikkelsen. 2020. 'Rallying around the Flag in Times of Covid-19: Societal Lockdown and Trust in Democratic Institutions.' *Journal of Behavioral Public Administration* 3(2): 1–12. doi.org/10.30636/jbpa.32.172.

Baker, M.G., A. Kvalsvig, and A.J. Verrall. 2020. 'New Zealand's COVID-19 Elimination Strategy.' *Medical Journal of Australia* 213(5): 198–200. doi.org/10.5694/mja2.50735.

Bartels, L.M. 2014. 'Ideology and Retrospection in Electoral Responses to the Great Recession.' In *Mass Politics in Tough Times: Opinions, Votes and Protest in the Great Recession*, edited by N. Bermeo and L.M. Bartels, 185–223. Oxford: Oxford University Press. doi.org/10.1093/acprof:oso/9780199357505.003.0007.

Bartolini, S., and P. Mair. 1990. *Identity, Competition, and Electoral Availability: The Stabilisation of European Electorates 1885–1985*. Cambridge: Cambridge University Press.

Beattie, A., and R. Priestley. 2021a. 'Fighting COVID-19 with the Team of 5 Million: Aotearoa New Zealand Government Communication During the 2020 Lockdown.' *Social Sciences & Humanities Open* 4(1): 100209. doi.org/10.1016/j.ssaho.2021.100209.

Beattie, A., and R. Priestley. 2021b. 'We Rewatched Last Year's 1pm Briefings. Today, the Team of Five Million Needs a Pep Talk.' *The Spinoff*, [Auckland], 23 March. Available from: thespinoff.co.nz/politics/23-03-2021/we-rewatched-last-years-1pm-briefings-today-the-team-of-five-million-needs-a-pep-talk/.

Bechtel, M.M., and J. Hainmueller. 2011. 'How Lasting Is Voter Gratitude? An Analysis of the Short- and Long-Term Electoral Returns to Beneficial Policy.' *American Journal of Political Science* 55(4): 851–67. doi.org/10.1111/j.1540-5907.2011.00533.x.

Bechtel, M.M., and M. Mannino. 2022. 'Retrospection, Fairness, and Economic Shocks: How Do Voters Judge Policy Responses to Natural Disasters?' *Political Science Research and Methods* 10(2): 260–78. doi.org/10.1017/psrm.2020.39.

Bernanke, B. 2012. 'The Great Moderation.' In *The Taylor Rule and the Transformation of Monetary Policy*, edited by R. Leeson, E.F. Koenig, and G.A. Kahn, 145–62. Stanford, CA: Hoover Institution.

Bisbee, J., and D. Honig. 2021. 'Flight to Safety: COVID-Induced Changes in the Intensity of Status Quo Preference and Voting Behavior.' *American Political Science Review* 116(1): 70–86. doi.org/10.1017/S0003055421000691.

Bol, D., M. Giani, A. Blais, and P.J. Loewen. 2021. 'The Effect of COVID-19 Lockdowns on Political Support: Some Good News for Democracy?' *European Journal of Political Research* 60(2): 497–505. doi.org/10.1111/1475-6765.12401.

Braithwaite, J., Y. Matsuyama, R. Mannion, J. Johnson, D.W. Bates, and C. Hughes. 2016. 'How to Do Better Health Reform: A Snapshot of Change and Improvement Initiatives in the Health Systems of 30 Countries.' *International Journal for Quality in Health Care* 28(6): 843–46. doi.org/10.1093/intqhc/mzw113.

Cameron, B. 2020. 'Captaining a Team of 5 Million: New Zealand Beats Back Covid-19, March–June 2020.' In *Global Challenges Covid-19: Innovations for Successful Societies Case Study*. Princeton, NJ: Princeton School of Public and International Affairs. Available from: successfulsocieties.princeton.edu/sites/g/files/toruqf5601/files/NewZealand_COVID_FInal.pdf.

Converse, P.E. 2005 [1964]. 'The Nature of Belief Systems in Mass Publics.' *Critical Review* 18(1–3): 1–74. doi.org/10.1080/08913810608443650.

Converse, P.E. 1969. 'Of Time and Partisan Stability.' *Comparative Political Studies* 2(2): 139–71. doi.org/10.1177/001041406900200201.

Dalton, R., and M. Wattenberg (eds). 2000. *Parties without Partisans: Political Change in Advanced Industrial Democracies*. Oxford: Oxford University Press.

Duch, R., and R. Stevenson. 2008. *The Economic Vote: How Political and Economic Institutions Condition Election Results*. Cambridge: Cambridge University Press. doi.org/10.1017/cbo9780511755934.

Fair, R.C. 1978. 'The Effect of Economic Events on Votes for President.' Review of Economics and Statistics 60(2): 159–73. doi.org/10.2307/1924969.

Fiorina, M. 1981. Retrospective Voting in American National Elections. New Haven, CT: Yale University Press.

Forest, P.G., and J.L. Denis. 2012. 'Real Reform in Health Systems: An Introduction.' *Journal of Health Politics, Policy and Law* 37(4): 575–86. doi.org/10.1215/03616878-1597430.

Franklin, M.N., T. Mackie, and H. Valen (eds). 2009. *Electoral Change: Responses to Evolving Social and Attitudinal Structures in Western Countries*. 2nd edn. Colchester: ECPR Press.

Gardener, L. 2016. 'The Economic Vote in New Zealand: An Analysis of How Macroeconomic Conditions and Perceptions of the Economy Affect Voter Behaviour.' MA thesis, University of Otago, Dunedin, New Zealand.

Global Change Data Lab. 2022. 'Coronavirus (COVID-19) Cases: Daily New Confirmed COVID-19 Cases Per Million People.' *Our World in Data*. London: Global Change Data Lab. Available from: ourworldindata.org/covid-cases.

Greer, S.L., E.J. King, and E.M. da Fonseca. 2021. 'Introduction: Explaining Pandemic Response.' In *Coronavirus Politics: The Comparative Politics and Policy of COVID-19*, edited by S.L. Greer, E.J. King, E.M. da Fonseca, and A. Peralta-Santos, 3–33. Ann Arbor, MI: University of Michigan Press. doi.org/10.3998/mpub.11927713.

Grieve, D. 2020. 'The Epic Story of NZ's Communications-Led Fight against Covid-19.' *The Spinoff*, [Auckland], 11 May. Available from: thespinoff.co.nz/politics/11-05-2020/a-masterclass-in-mass-communication-and-control/.

Guntermann, E., and G. Lenz. 2022. 'Still Not Important Enough? COVID-19 Policy Views and Vote Choice.' *Perspectives on Politics* 20(2): 547–61. doi.org/10.1017/S1537592721001997.

Hasell, J. 2020. 'Which Countries Have Protected Both Health and the Economy in the Pandemic?' *Our World in Data*, 1 September. London: Global Change Data Lab. Available from: ourworldindata.org/covid-health-economy.

Hellwig, T., Y. Kwan, and J. Vowles. 2020. *Democracy Under Siege? Parties, Voters and Elections After the Great Recession*. Oxford: Oxford University Press.

Hernández, E., and H. Kriesi. 2016. 'The Electoral Consequences of the Financial and Economic Crisis in Europe.' *European Journal of Political Research* 55(2): 203–24. doi.org/10.1111/1475-6765.12122.

Hickey, B. 2021. 'The Real Impact of New Zealand's Economic Response to Covid-19.' *The Spinoff*, [Auckland], 6 December. Available from: thespinoff.co.nz/money/06-12-2021/the-real-impact-of-new-zealands-economic-response-to-covid-19.

Humpage, L. 2014. *Policy Change, Public Attitudes and Social Citizenship: Does Neoliberalism Matter?* Bristol: The Policy Press. doi.org/10.1332/policypress/9781847429650.001.0001.

IMF Fiscal Affairs Department. 2021. *Fiscal Monitor Database of Country Fiscal Measures in Response to the COVID-19 Pandemic*. Washington, DC: International Monetary Fund. Available from: www.imf.org/en/Topics/imf-and-covid19/Fiscal-Policies-Database-in-Response-to-COVID-19.

Inglehart, R., and A. Hochstein. 1972. 'Alignment and Dealignment of the Electorate in France and the United States.' *Comparative Political Studies* 5(3): 343–72. doi.org/10.1177/001041407200500304.

International Monetary Fund (IMF). 2021. 'Real GDP Growth: Annual Percent Change.' In *World Economic Outlook*. Washington, DC: International Monetary Fund. Available from: www.imf.org/external/datamapper/NGDP_RPCH@WEO/WEOWORLD.

Jefferies, S., N. French, C. Gilkison, G. Graham, V. Hope, J Marshall, C. McElnay, A. McNeill, P. Muellner, S. Paine, N. Prasad, J. Scott, J. Sherwood, L. Yang, and P. Priest. 2020. 'COVID-19 in New Zealand and the Impact of the National Response: A Descriptive Epidemiological Study.' *Lancet Public Health* 5(11): e612–e623. doi.org/10.1016/S2468-2667(20)30225-5.

Kahneman, D. 2012. *Thinking, Fast and Slow*. London: Penguin.

Karwowski, M., M. Kowal, A. Groyecka, M. Białek, I. Lebuda, A. Sorokowska, and P. Sorokowski. 2020. 'When in Danger, Turn Right: Does Covid-19 Threat Promote Social Conservatism and Right-Wing Presidential Candidates?' *Human Ethology* 35: 37–48. doi.org/10.22330/he/35/037-048.

Kayser, M.A., and M. Peress. 2012. 'Benchmarking across Borders: Electoral Accountability and the Necessity of Comparison.' *American Political Science Review* 106(3): 661–84. doi.org/10.1017/s0003055412000275.

Key, V.O., jr. 1955. 'A Theory of Critical Elections.' *Journal of Politics* 17: 3–18. doi.org/10.2307/2126401.

Kim, S.C. 2020. 'South Korea's Election Amid COVID-19.' *East Asian Policy* 12(3): 49–62. doi.org/10.1142/S1793930520000227.

Kramer, G.H. 1971. 'Short-Term Fluctuations in U.S. Voting Behavior, 1896–1964.' American Political Science Review 65(1): 131–43. doi.org/10.2307/1955049.

Kritzinger, S., M. Foucault, R. Lachat, J. Partheymüller, C. Plescia, and S. Brouard. 2021. '"Rally Round the Flag": The COVID-19 Crisis and Trust in the National Government.' *West European Politics* 44(5–6): 1205–31. doi.org/10.1080/01402382.2021.1925017.

Kroh, M. 2007. 'Measuring Left–Right Political Orientation: The Choice of Response Format.' *The Public Opinion Quarterly* 71(2): 204–20. doi.org/10.1093/poq/nfm009.

Kvalsvig, A., and M.G. Baker. 2021. 'How Aotearoa New Zealand Rapidly Revised Its Covid-19 Response Strategy: Lessons for the Next Pandemic Plan.' Journal of the Royal Society of New Zealand 51(S1): S143–66. doi.org/10.1080/03036758.2021.1891943.

Leithner, C. 1997. 'Of Time and Partisan Stability Revisited: Australia and New Zealand 1905–1990.' *American Journal of Political Science* 41(4): 1104–27. doi.org/10.2307/2960483.

Lipset, S.M., and S. Rokkan. 1967. *Party Systems and Voter Alignments*. New York: Free Press.

McGuire, D., J. Cunningham, K. Reynolds, and G. Matthews-Smith. 2020. 'Beating the Virus: An Examination of the Crisis Communication Approach Taken by New Zealand Prime Minister Jacinda Ardern during the Covid-19 Pandemic.' Human Resource Development International 23(4): 361–79. doi.org/10.1080/13678868.2020.1779543.

Mitchell, C. 2021. 'The Housing Affordability Crisis Is Likely Worse Than You Think.' *Stuff*, [Wellington], 4 July. Available from: www.stuff.co.nz/life-style/home-property/300339165/the-housing-affordability-crisis-is-likely-worse-than-you-think.

New Zealand Government. 2021a. *History of the COVID-19 Alert System.* Wellington: New Zealand Government. Available from: covid19.govt.nz/alert-levels-and-updates/history-of-the-covid-19-alert-system/ [page discontinued].

New Zealand Government. 2021b. *Wellbeing Budget 2021: Securing Our Recovery.* Wellington: New Zealand Government. Available from: www.treasury.govt.nz/publications/wellbeing-budget/wellbeing-budget-2021-securing-our-recovery#from-the-prime-minister.

Norpoth, H., A.H. Sidman, and C.H. Suong. 2013. 'Polls and Elections: The New Deal Realignment in Real Time.' *Presidential Studies Quarterly* 43(1): 146–66. doi.org/10.1111/psq.12007.

Obinger, H., K. Petersen, and P. Starke. 2018. *Warfare and Welfare: Military Conflict and Welfare State Development in Western Countries.* Oxford: Oxford University Press. doi.org/10.1093/oso/9780198779599.001.0001.

Oliu-Barton, M., B.S.R. Pradelski, P. Aghio, P. Artus, I. Kickbusch, J.V. Lazarus, D. Sridhar, and S. Vanderslott. 2021. 'SARS-CoV-2 Elimination, Not Mitigation, Creates Best Outcomes for Health, the Economy, and Civil Liberties.' *The Lancet* 397(10291): 2234–36. doi.org/10.1016/S0140-6736(21)00978-8.

Organisation for Economic Co-operation and Development (OECD). 2020. *Beyond Containment: Health Systems Responses to COVID-19 in the OECD.* Paris: OECD Publishing. Available from: read.oecd-ilibrary.org/view/?ref=119_119689-ud5comtf84&title=Beyond_Containment:Health_systems_responses_to_COVID-19_in_the_OECD.

Organisation for Economic Co-operation and Development (OECD). 2021a. *Strengthening the Recovery: The Need for Speed—OECD Economic Outlook, Interim Report March 2021.* Paris: OECD Publishing. Available from: www.oecd.org/economic-outlook/march-2021/.

Organisation for Economic Co-operation and Development (OECD). 2021b. *OECD Policy Responses to Coronavirus (COVID-19):* Tourism Policy Responses to the Coronavirus (COVID-19). [Updated 2 June.] Paris: OECD Publishing. Available from: www.oecd.org/coronavirus/policy-responses/tourism-policy-responses-to-the-coronaviruscovid-19-6466aa20/#figure-d1e253.

Piazza, K.S., and G. Diaz. 2020. 'Light in the Midst of Chaos: COVID-19 and Female Political Representation.' *World Development* 136: 105125. doi.org/10.1016/j.worlddev.2020.105125.

Robertson, G. 2020. 'COVID-19—Emergency Economic Package.' *Hansard (Debates)*, Vol. 745, Tuesday, 17 March. Wellington: New Zealand Parliament. Available from: www.parliament.nz/en/pb/hansard-debates/rhr/combined/HansD_20200317_20200317.

Roche, B., W. Moetara, M. Poore, L. Read, and P. Hill. 2020. *Final Report on the Contact Tracing System*. Contract Tracing Assurance Committee Report, 16 July. Wellington: Ministry of Health. Available from: www.health.govt.nz/system/files/documents/pages/final-contact-tracing-assurance-committee-report-2020.pdf.

Särlvik, B., and I. Crewe. 1983. *Decade of Dealignment: The Conservative Victory of 1979 and Electoral Trends in the 1970s*. Cambridge: Cambridge University Press.

Shively, W.P. 1972. 'Party Identification, Party Choice, and Voting Stability: The Weimar Case.' *American Political Science Review* 66(4): 1203–27. doi.org/10.2307/1957174.

Shokoohi, M., M. Osooli, and S. Stranges. 2020. 'COVID-19 Pandemic: What Can the West Learn from the East?' *International Journal of Health Policy and Management* 9(10): 436–38. doi.org/10.34172/ijhpm.2020.85.

Sibley, C., L. Greaves, N. Satherly, M. Wilson, N.C. Overall, C.H.J. Lee, P. Milojev, J. Bulbulia, D. Osborne, T.L. Milfont, C.A. Houkamau, I.M. Duvk, R. Vickers-Jones, and F.K. Barlow. 2020. 'Effects of the COVID-19 Pandemic and Nationwide Lockdown on Trust, Attitudes Toward Government, and Well-Being.' *American Psychologist* 75(5): 618–30. doi.org/10.1037/amp0000662.

StatsNZ. 2021. *Gross Domestic Product: March 2021 Quarter*. Wellington: New Zealand Government. Available from: www.stats.govt.nz/information-releases/gross-domestic-product-march-2021-quarter.

StatsNZ. 2022. 'Child Poverty Statistics Show All Measures Trending Downwards Over the Last Three Years.' News release, 24 February. Wellington: New Zealand Government. Available from: www.stats.govt.nz/news/child-poverty-statistics-show-all-measures-trending-downwards-over-the-last-three-years.

Talving, L. 2018. 'Economic Voting in Europe: Did the Crisis Matter?' *Comparative European Politics* 16: 695–723. doi.org/10.1057/s41295-017-0092-z.

Vowles, J. 2014. 'Putting the 2011 Election in its Place.' In The New Electoral Politics in New *Zealand*, edited by J. Vowles, 27–52. Wellington: Institute for Governance and Policy Studies.

Vowles J. 2022. 'Authoritarianism and Mass Political Preferences in Times of COVID-19: The 2020 New Zealand General Election.' *Frontiers in Political Science* 4. doi.org/10.3389/fpos.2022.885299.

Vowles, J., F. Barker, M. Krewel, J. Hayward, J. Curtin, L. Greaves, and L. Oldfield. 2022. *2020 New Zealand Election Study*. [Online]. ADA Dataverse, V3. doi.org/ 10.26193/BPAMYJ.

Vowles, J., H. Coffé, and J. Curtin (eds). 2017. *A Bark But No Bite: Inequality and the 2014 New Zealand General Election*. Canberra: ANU Press. doi.org/ 10.22459/bbnb.08.2017.

Vowles, J., and J. Curtin (eds). 2020. *A Populist Exception? The 2017 New Zealand General Election*. Canberra: ANU Press. doi.org/10.22459/pe.2020.

World Bank. 2022. 'Hospital Beds (Per 1,000 People): OECD Members.' *Data*. Washington, DC: The World Bank. Available from: data.worldbank.org/ indicator/SH.MED.BEDS.ZS?locations=OE.

Yu, S., E.J. Yoo, and S. Kim. 2022. 'The Effect of Trust in Government on Elections during the COVID-19 Pandemic in South Korea.' *Asian Politics and Policy* 14: 175–198. doi.org/10.1111/aspp.12631.

Appendix 2.1

Covid-19 and global elections

Table A2.1 reports the statistical details of the model used to construct Figure 2.1.

Table A2.1 Covid-19 and the re-election or defeat of main incumbent parties, high-income democracies, 2020–2022

Outcome: Defeat or re-election of main incumbent	
Log of Covid-19 cases per million at election	–0.561*
	(0.443)
Time by month since January 2020	0.115
	(0.091)
Constant	0.807
	(1.163)
R^2	0.185
Log-likelihood	–10.5407
Obs	19

*** $p < 0.01$

** $p < 0.05$

* $p < 0.1$

Note: OLS coefficients, jack-knife standard errors in parentheses.

Table A2.2 Labour vote change models

Labour vote in 2020	I	II	III	IV	V
Voted Labour in 2017	1.976***	1.646***	1.627***	1.557***	1.567***
	(0.119)	(0.135)	(0.135)	(0.139)	(0.143)
Right–left	–1.842***	–0.980***	–6.915***	–0.106***	–0.096***
	(0.264)	(0.299)	(1.615)	(0.034)	(0.034)
Approve of Covid-19 response		1.800***	6.711***		1.298***
		(0.390)	(1.832)		(0.413)
Right–left* response approval			–1.798*		
			(1.066)		
Trust in Ardern		2.879***	2.876***	2.499***	2.181***
		(0.318)	(0.323)	(0.376)	(0.365)
Age				0.006*	0.005*
				(0.003)	(0.003)
Female				0.228*	0.207*
				(0.120)	(0.121)
Māori				0.054	0.069
				(0.147)	(0.149)
Economy				–0.037	–0.068
				(0.079)	(0.080)
Income				–0.126	–0.154
				(0.251)	(0.253)
Assets				–0.050	–0.046
				(0.048)	(0.049)
Satisfaction				0.417	0.235
				(0.274)	(0.273)
Strong leader				–0.037	–0.047
				(0.054)	(0.054)
Reduce inequality				0.029	0.002
				(0.064)	(0.065)
Ardern's competence				2.147***	1.883***
				(0.387)	(0.401)
Constant	0.054	–4.105***	–0.887	–4.538***	–4.896***
	(0.155)	(0.462)	(1.002)	(0.560)	(0.611)
Observations	3,730	3,613	3,613	3,434	3,406
r²_p	0.173	0.2663	0.272	0.278	0.281
ll	–2,096	–1,799	–1,786	–1,675	–1,652

*** p < 0.01

** p < 0.05

* p < 0.1

Note: Logit coefficients, robust standard errors in parentheses.

Source: 2020 NZES (Vowles et al. 2022).

Table A2.3 Approval or disapproval of the Covid-19 response

Covid response approval	I	II
Voted Labour in 2017	1.022***	0.352*
	(0.209)	(0.208)
Right–left	−2.244***	−0.803*
	(0.316)	(0.415)
Economy good		1.054**
		(0.451)
Border closure		1.340***
		(0.362)
Strong leadership		−0.065
		(0.064)
Proud of response		2.083***
		(0.441)
Ardern trustworthy		3.113***
		(0.245)
Constant	2.705***	−1.330***
	(0.215)	(0.448)
Observations	3,730	3,650
r²_p	0.0655	0.323
ll	−1,526	−1,084

*** p < 0.01

** p < 0.05

* p < 0.1

Note: Robust standard errors in parentheses.

Source: 2020 NZES (Vowles et al. 2022).

Table A2.2 contains the first three models discussed in the chapter text: baseline (I), augmented (II), and interactive (III). The final two models test for the possible confounding effects of other variables. However, the pseudo r-squared statistic reporting the fit of the various models hardly improves between model III and models IV and V, indicating that model III captures most of the story. Most of the other variables do not register as statistically significant. It is worth noting the tendency of older people and women to be more likely to shift to Labour, even given these other controls.

Running alternative versions of these models and possible interactions between variables of interest (too many to report) indicates that some expectations were not borne out. There is no evidence that the movement to Labour represented a generational shift; age barely registered as a covariate in most models. Economic voting based on household circumstances did not stand out significantly when tested across various social groups. So far, other than the elderly and women there is no evidence that demographic or social categories of voters were affected in their voting choices by different levels of exposure or vulnerability to the crisis.

One can also note that while competence features in perceptions that led people to Labour, and remained highly significant in the final model, the stronger perception was trust, giving both empirical and theoretical reasons for its emphasis. The two perceptions were highly correlated.

3

Between Selfies and Conspiracy Theories: Social media campaigning in 2020

Mona Krewel and Matthew Gibbons

Introduction

Social media has become increasingly important to political parties and voters in recent years. Using content analysis results from Facebook posts by New Zealand political parties and their leaders, this chapter describes how the parties and leaders campaigned on social media. It also uses NZES survey data (Vowles et al. 2022a) to document how most New Zealanders used the internet. And just over one-third used social media to inform themselves during the 2020 election campaign.

This chapter first briefly considers the growing importance of the internet and social media in political campaigning in New Zealand. This reflects the decline of traditional media, the desire by politicians to publish unfiltered messages, and the social distancing rules in effect in 2020. The focus then switches to the New Zealand Social Media Study (NZSMS) analysis of the Facebook communications of all significant political parties and their leaders in the last four weeks of the campaign.[1] The high use of Facebook by

---

1   The NZSMS analysed all Facebook posts made by the Labour Party, National Party, Green Party, ACT, The Opportunities Party (TOP), New Zealand First, Māori Party, New Conservative Party, Advance NZ/The New Zealand Public Party; and the party leaders Jacinda Ardern, Judith Collins, Marama Davidson, James Shaw, David Seymour, Geoff Simmons, Winston Peters, John Tamihere, Debbie Ngarewa-Packer, Leighton Baker, and Billy Te Kahika between 16 September and 16 October 2020.

parties and leaders to publicise policies and mobilise potential supporters is discussed. The much more positive campaigning of Labour and its leader, Jacinda Ardern, is contrasted with the negative campaigning of the National Party and its leader, Judith Collins. This chapter shows that fake news and half-truths in Facebook posts were relatively rare, and most were made by fringe anti-establishment parties and their leaders.

Data from the 2020 NZES are then used to quantify voters' high use of the internet and the growing use of social media for accessing political information during the campaign. About one-third of voters reported coming across online misinformation or disinformation during the election campaign. Māori and supporters of fringe anti-establishment parties were most likely to state they had come across misinformation and disinformation. More than half of all voters were at least somewhat confident in their ability to identify made-up online content, with those who were most interested in politics, the young, and men most confident about their abilities.

In the final section of this chapter, NZES data are used to assess the effects of social media campaigns on voters' evaluations of the leaders of the two major parties. The results indicate that using Facebook and Instagram to access political news was associated with high ratings for Labour's Jacinda Ardern on a 0-10 'liking' scale. Ardern was extremely popular with voters. In contrast, using Instagram to access political news was associated with disliking National's unpopular leader, Judith Collins.

The internet and social media in campaigning

The internet and social media have made it easier, cheaper, and often more necessary for politicians to bypass traditional media sources such as newspapers, radio, and broadcast news (Enli and Rosenberg 2018, 50). People are also increasingly using social media platforms, which did not exist until the early 2000s, as a source of news. Parties and their leaders are now active on social media platforms such as Facebook, Instagram, and Twitter, and use these to communicate unfiltered messages quickly and directly to potential supporters (Allcott and Gentzkow 2017, 211; Hendricks and Schill 2017; Semetko and Tworzecki 2017, 331). As one New Zealand journalist commented, by the time of the 2020 election, the internet had 'allowed politicians to go around us' (Cooke 2021, 142).

In addition, many traditional news sources now have fewer staff to cover political events than in the past. A slow decline of newspapers in many developed countries became much more rapid from the early 2000s as advertising migrated to the internet. This reduced the resources available for news reporting and resulted in newspapers charging higher cover prices, which further reduced readership (Chyi and Tenenboim 2019). In New Zealand, newspaper readership has sharply fallen, print newspapers are now stocked by few retailers, and the number of New Zealand journalists halved between 2001 and 2018 (Loan et al. 2021, iv; Williams 2018). By the time of the 2020 election, New Zealand Media and Entertainment was increasingly putting its content behind paywalls for its flagship *New Zealand Herald* and its regional papers and focussing on stories that appealed to its relatively old and well-off readers. Although the rival *Stuff* newspaper group kept its content free, its news coverage was much more limited than in the past. New providers of news stories, such as *Newsroom* and *The Spinoff*, along with the long-established *National Business Review*, were only available through the internet, and were often paywalled.

Covid-19 regulations also resulted in the suspension of the printing of community newspapers and magazines. Overseas owners and investors had already been despairing about the prospects for the New Zealand newspaper and magazine industry, and the closure of many long-established titles seemed imminent (Greive 2020). Television news was also struggling for advertising and resources. In addition, the 2014 election was the last at which parties were provided with time on television to broadcast the opening and closing of the campaign; at the 2017 and 2020 elections, these broadcasts were only available on the internet. As a result of the decline of traditional media, and changes in campaigning methods, it is important to study social media use by political actors and by voters.

Because of its widespread use and the ease with which information can be posted, Facebook is in most countries regarded as the most valuable social media platform by political parties. In contrast, Instagram use is strongly skewed towards young people and is primarily a visual medium used for sharing highly filtered photos and videos with friends and family, and for following celebrities and social media influencers. Because the young are less likely to vote, and because of the difficulty of posting links, Instagram tends to be a relatively low priority for political parties. Twitter is predominantly used by professionals to share relatively serious written messages (Kreiss et al. 2018, 16, 18; Walker and Matsa 2021). There are also other less politically important social media platforms, such as LinkedIn and TikTok. LinkedIn is used by some candidates to connect with people. TikTok is very youth-focussed and does not allow political parties to advertise. In New Zealand, as in other countries, politicians usually use social media as a way of broadcasting information, rather than for discussions (Muchison 2016; Ross et al. 2015).

#NZvotes: Social media in the 2020 election campaigns of parties and candidates

This section describes the high level of social media posts by parties and their leaders, and the political issues they covered. It then discusses use of positive and negative messages by the main parties. Whereas Labour and its leader conducted a positive campaign, the results show that National and its leader became more negative over time. The low prevalence of fake news and half-truths in social media posts by most political actors is then quantified.

Because Facebook is the most widely used social media platform, the total number of posts by parties and their leaders made on Facebook during the four weeks before election day is an important indicator of the importance they placed on social media. The nine parties and their leaders in our dataset collectively made 3,037 posts on Facebook during this 'hot campaign phase'. During the final two weeks of this period, early voting was both permitted and encouraged and, in 2020, most New Zealanders voted before election day. The main parties posted several times each day, with posts increasing as the electioneering ended (Krewel and Vowles 2020d).

Facebook posts were downloaded by the newly created New Zealand Social Media Study (NZSMS) at Victoria University of Wellington using Facebook's CrowdTangle tool for academic researchers (Meta 2022; Smalley 2022). They were then analysed using the Campaigning for Strasbourg (CamforS) methods that were applied to European elections in 2019 (Fenoll et al. 2021).

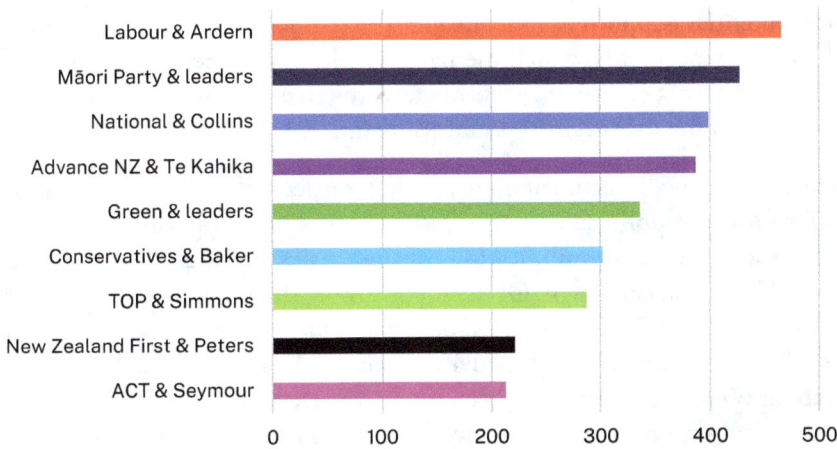

Figure 3.1 Total number of Facebook posts by parties and their leaders
Source: NZSMS (2020).

Figure 3.1 shows that Labour and its leader, Jacinda Ardern, made the most posts in the 30 days before the election, with 465 Facebook posts. This is consistent with expectations: Ardern was known to be highly visible on the internet. Second were the Māori Party and its leaders. Indeed, Māori Party co-leader John Tamihere posted the most of all the leaders, and co-leader Debbie Ngarewa-Packer also frequently posted. Third were National and its leader, Judith Collins, which was expected given National's status as the main opposition party. Fourth was Advance NZ and its co-leader Billy Te Kahika; their other co-leader, Jamie-Lee Ross, did not use Facebook during the campaign. The Green Party and its two co-leaders came next, followed by the New Conservative Party and The Opportunities Party (TOP). The two least active parties on Facebook were New Zealand First and ACT.

The relatively high number of Facebook posts by the Māori Party shows that social media, where it is easy to self-publish information and messages, can be used effectively by a minor party with limited resources. Before the 2020 election, the Māori Party had no parliamentary representation, a small campaign budget, and its prospects of returning to parliament seemed poor. Apart from Māori television, coverage of this party by media outlets was often low. However, the Māori Party had as its leaders two skilled social media practitioners (Krewel and Vowles 2020d), who circumvented traditional media gatekeepers and communicated directly with potential supporters (Shoemaker 1991; Shoemaker and Vos 2009). Policy announcements, which the party would have once hoped would be published by a newspaper, were made through social media, along with mobilisation messages (Greaves and Morgan 2021, 322).

While social media campaigning is often suspected of being a relatively shallow form of political communication, this is not supported by analysis of the social media communications of the parties and their leaders during the 2020 election campaign. Of the slightly more than 3,000 Facebook posts coded, more than 2,500 contained policy or issue content. Figure 3.2 shows that the proportion of social media posts about an issue gradually declined to about 60 per cent in the five days before the election as the proportion of posts mobilising people to vote increased.[2] About 4.9 per cent of the posts in our study referred to a political actor's private life, such as candidates talking about hardships their family had experienced or alluding to their children (McGregor 2018; McGregor et al. 2017; Ross et al. 2023, 7).

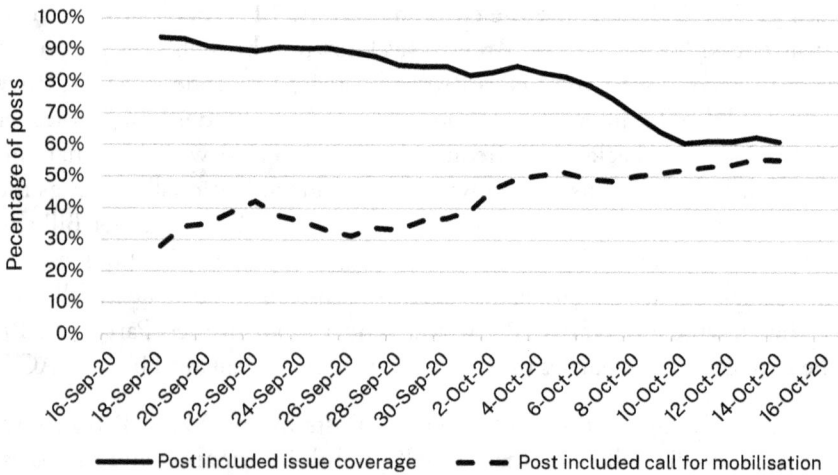

Figure 3.2 Percentage of posts by all actors that included issue coverage or a call for mobilisation (five-day moving average)

Source: NZSMS (2020).

---

2   However, these two categories were not mutually exclusive.

The economy was consistently the dominant issue—included in almost 31 per cent of posts that covered a specific issue. Social issues (18.4 per cent of posts about a specific issue) and the environment (13.5 per cent) were also important. The next most important were domestic issues in general (7.5 per cent), health (6.7 per cent), and transport (6.5 per cent). The relatively low importance of health may seem surprising; however, New Zealand had few Covid-19 cases and it escaped the overloaded hospitals that occurred in some countries. Indeed, the country's death rate during lockdown was slightly lower than usual, probably because infectious diseases such as influenza were unable to spread (Kung et al. 2021).

It is not surprising that most parties focussed their campaigning on the economy, as Figure 1.2 (Chapter 1, this volume) revealed that voters identified the economy as the second most important election topic after Covid-19. However, the Green Party mentioned the environment the most in its posts. The Māori Party campaigned more on social issues to achieve better outcomes for Māori than on the economy and maintained the strongest focus on the Treaty of Waitangi (Krewel and Vowles 2020c, 2020d). In addition, Advance NZ and the New Conservatives focussed more on domestic policies in general than on the economy.

Figure 3.2 shows that by the time early voting began in New Zealand, two weeks before election day, more than half of Facebook posts by parties and their leaders included a mobilisation message. However, despite initially matching and then surpassing other actors in the percentage of mobilisation messages it made, New Zealand First issued relatively few mobilisation messages in the final week of the election campaign (Krewel and Vowles 2020d). This could have been to its electoral cost.

Election campaigns have often been criticised, particularly in the United States, for involving insults, mudslinging, and distortion. Negative campaigning can be effective as negative information is more psychologically 'sticky' in people's memories than positive information (Boydstun et al. 2019). However, the effects of negative advertising seem to vary between countries, work best in two-party systems, and are affected by the prior beliefs of voters (Flanaghan 2014, 145–160).

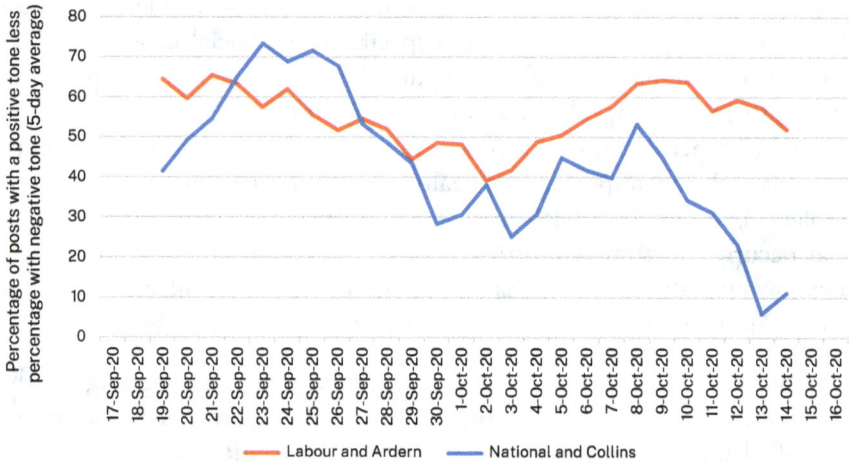

Figure 3.3 Positive minus negative references in Facebook posts by Labour and Jacinda Ardern and by National and Judith Collins (five-day moving average)
Source: NZSMS (2020).

Figure 3.3 shows that the net tone of posts by Labour and Ardern remained strongly positive during the campaign. Ardern's personal posts remained 'relentlessly positive', as she had promised when she became Labour's leader in 2017 and pledged again in 2020 (Edwards 2017; Sachdeva 2020). Indeed, Ardern did not personally express any negative statements or emotions in her posts. In contrast, National's and Collins's posts began positive but became more negative as the campaign progressed, almost falling into negative territory by the last few days. With opinion polls showing it was making no ground, the National Party appears to have become increasingly desperate. For instance, Collins stated that Labour would introduce a disastrous wealth tax[3] and argued that it had not met its 2017 campaign commitments. Incumbents usually run more positive campaigns than challengers (Benoit 1999; Druckman et al. 2009; Haynes and Rhine 1998) because they must work harder for the media attention that negativity produces (Hopmann et al. 2012; Schoenbach et al. 2001; Shoemaker 2006). Indeed, Ardern had appeared daily on television during lockdowns and was well known to voters. In contrast, Collins was National's third leader in 2020.

---

3   The Green Party leaders believe this worked in their favour as their supporters favoured a wealth tax (Davidson and Shaw 2021, 85).

Of Labour's two partners in government, the Green Party and its leaders also maintained a positive tone in their posts. New Zealand First and its leader adopted a more negative tone towards the end of the campaign, but still made more positive than negative posts. All the minor parties retained a positive tone at the end of the campaign, although there were periods when Advance NZ's posts were negative. Posts by its leader, Billy Te Kahika, and by the New Conservative Party's Leighton Baker were sometimes negative in tone (Krewel and Vowles 2020c).

An important indicator of the quality of a campaign is the spread of misinformation and disinformation. In measuring misinformation and disinformation in New Zealand social media campaigns, the NZSMS distinguished between fake news and half-truths. Fake news was 'content of a post which is completely or for the most part made up and intentionally and verifiably false to mislead voters' (Krewel and Vowles 2020a).[4] In contrast, half-truths were content that 'is not entirely' or for the most part made up, however, it still contains 'some half-truths or is questionable regarding its factual accuracy' (Krewel and Vowles 2020a). The half-truths variable was introduced because fake news, in its pure form, was rare. Instead, posts more frequently contained information that was not entirely accurate. Examples included assertions by the New Conservative's Baker about poll results and rising crime, and claims by Te Kahika about mandatory vaccinations. While not fake news, these posts were a distortion.

Advance NZ and Te Kahika made the most half-true statements, followed by the New Conservative Party and Baker, the National Party and Collins, New Zealand First and its leader, Winston Peters, and ACT and David Seymour. The number of half-truths by parties in Facebook posts remained relatively constant during the campaign, while for leaders the number fell over time (Krewel and Vowles 2020c, 2020d).

---

4   The usual disagreements between and accusations made by political actors were not coded as fake news. If a coder assumed that a post included fake news but they were not fully sure, they fact-checked the post, including whether a reliable news site had already identified a statement as false. If they were still unsure, coders were told to not code the story as fake news. This conservative definition of fake news ensured that normal political disagreements between parties and candidates, which are an integral part of the democratic discourse, were not counted as fake news. Furthermore, on a scale from one (very confident) to four (not at all confident), the coders gave a self-assessment of how sure they were they had identified fake news (Krewel and Vowles 2020a). All posts for which coders had not indicated that they were very confident were double-checked by a NZSMS principal investigator. Apart from one post, which was removed from the sample, the principal investigators agreed with the coders' initial assessments.

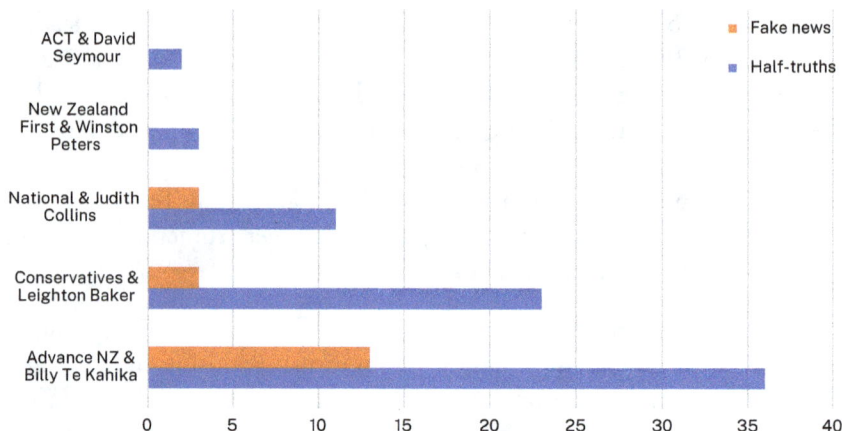

Figure 3.4 Total number of Facebook posts by each party and their leader containing fake news and half-truths
Source: NZSMS (2020).

During the 2020 election campaign, parties and their leaders together posted only 75 half-truths. This reflects the high quality of democratic political discourse in New Zealand (Krewel and Vowles 2020d). However, continuation of the NZSMS in 2022 shows that as polarisation has increased around Covid-19 vaccination mandates, misinformation and disinformation have increased (Krewel 2022).

Figure 3.4 shows that Advance NZ and Te Kahika made the most fake news posts during the 2020 campaign, followed by the New Conservatives and Baker, and then National and Collins (Krewel and Vowles 2020c, 2020d). Most of the fake news posts by Advance NZ and the New Conservatives and their leaders were about Covid-19; however, Advance NZ also attacked the media, including social media providers. Some New Conservatives' fake news and half-truths posts also attacked the media, including the exclusion of the party from the leaders' television debates (Krewel and Vowles 2020c, 2020d). In the posts containing half-truths or fake news neither Advance NZ nor the New Conservatives and their leaders had a very strong or explicit focus on Labour or on Jacinda Ardern, or even on the government in general.

Collins and the National Party both posted a selectively edited clip from the leaders' debate that made it appear that Ardern had described a defence of dairy farming as 'the view of a world that has passed'. Ardern's comment was specifically about the unsustainability of 'dirty dairying'—the practice and defence of which she ascribed to a minority of dairy farmers. Ardern also applauded farmers meeting sustainability challenges as 'climate change warriors'. This incident met the NZSMS definition of fake news (Krewel and Vowles 2020b) and was also identified as a distortion by newspaper fact-checkers (Cooke 2020). With only 19 fake news posts among more than 3,000 posts in four weeks, however, for the most part, New Zealand's parties and their leaders campaigned fairly in 2020 (Krewel and Vowles 2020d).

Only 0.4 per cent of posts featured a meme, where text was added to a picture. ACT and Seymour had the most meme posts, with their memes acting like the billboards used in earlier elections (Robinson 2019, 193). Perhaps the efforts parties put into crafting their posts will increase in the future, especially if they start publishing posts they hope will be noticed by other media and the public. Currently, most Facebook posts are targeted at those sympathetic to a party.

Voters 2.0? Usage and perception of social media campaigning in the 2020 election

This section first considers voters' high use of the internet and social media, and in particular Facebook, for political information. The ways in which voters were contacted by political parties in 2020, including the continued dominance of direct mail, are then considered. About one-third of voters reported coming across some online misinformation or disinformation, with Māori and supporters of anti-establishment parties the most likely to do so. The results also show that those who are more interested in politics, younger people, and men are the most confident in their ability to identify fake news.

Election study data show that during the 2020 election campaign, 80 per cent of New Zealand voters used the internet to access news or information about the election. However, these results must be interpreted cautiously because 85.8 per cent of New Zealanders reported having internet access at home, newspapers (including paywalled content) and broadcast news are increasingly accessed through the internet, and only 6.7 per cent of New Zealanders reported having no access to the internet. People could have interpreted this question in varying ways.

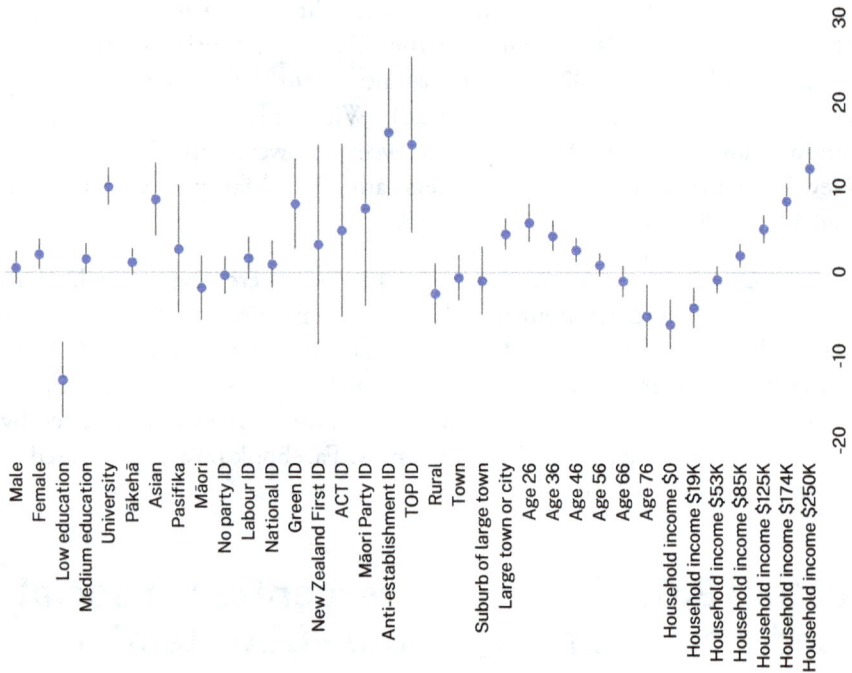

Figure 3.5 Percentage by which internet use for political information differed from mean use

Source: 2020 NZES (Vowles et al. 2022a).

Nevertheless, Figure 3.5 shows—as expected—that the use of the internet for political information was greatest among the youngest age groups, and steadily decreased with age. While the proportions of men and women using the internet for political information were similar, internet use for political information increased with household income and education and was higher for those living in a big city. For ethnicity, Asians were most likely to use the internet for political information, whereas Māori were least likely to do so.

For party identification the differences were usually not significant; however, those who identified with the Green Party were a little more likely to use the internet than those who did not identify with any party. A group of small parties can be classified as 'anti-establishment': the New Conservatives, Advance NZ, the NZ Outdoors & Freedom Party, as well as traditionalist religious parties. Those who identified with these parties were also highly likely to use the internet for political information, but the confidence intervals were wide because of the small number in this group. It is not surprising that the supporters of the anti-establishment parties more strongly used the internet to inform themselves about politics, as they prefer alternative information channels to the 'mainstream media' (Holt 2018; Moffitt 2016).

Narrowing the focus to the use of social media, Facebook, as in other countries, was the dominant platform. Indeed, 34.1 per cent of respondents used Facebook for political information, whereas 8.3 per cent used Instagram, and 4.3 per cent used Twitter. This supports the New Zealand Social Media Study's decision to concentrate on analysing parties' Facebook messages. Facebook was even used by parties to broadcast their campaign opening speeches and, because of Covid restrictions, National's campaign launch was a virtual experience for all except a small number of guests (Walls 2020). The total combined use of these three platforms was 36.8 per cent.

Figure 3.6 shows that in a multivariate model the use of Facebook for political information purposes in New Zealand was higher among younger voters. Instagram use was even more heavily concentrated among the youngest voters (Figure 3.7), with the small group of those born after 2000 the heaviest users of Instagram for political information. Because the relationship between Instagram use and age is nonlinear, Figure 3.7 uses age cohorts. In contrast, Twitter use, which is shown in Figure 3.8, was only slightly higher among the youngest age groups, probably because Twitter attracts older people who use it for professional purposes.

Figures 3.6 to 3.8 show that before the 2020 election women made greater use of Facebook and Instagram for political information purposes than men, whereas the percentage of men using Twitter was greater, but statistically not significant. Except for Facebook, where the effects were weak, household income was poorly correlated with the use of social media for political information. Facebook use was similar across education levels. In contrast, those with a university education were more likely to use Instagram and Twitter for political information than those with only a basic education.

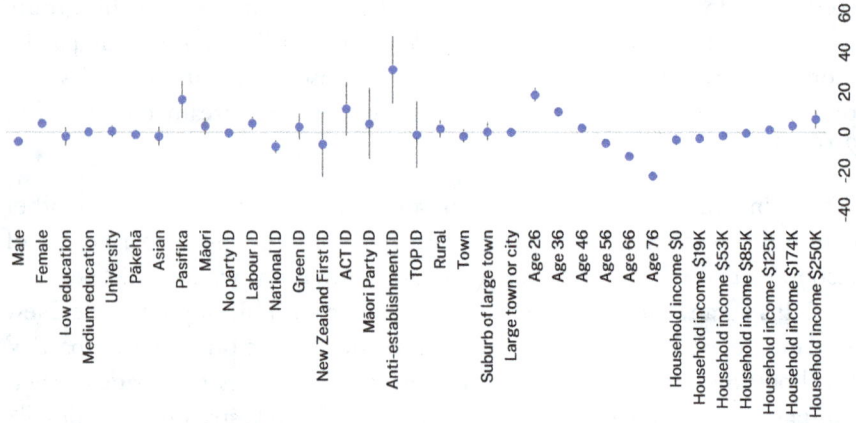

Figure 3.6 Percentage by which Facebook use for political information differed from mean use

Source: 2020 NZES (Vowles et al. 2022a).

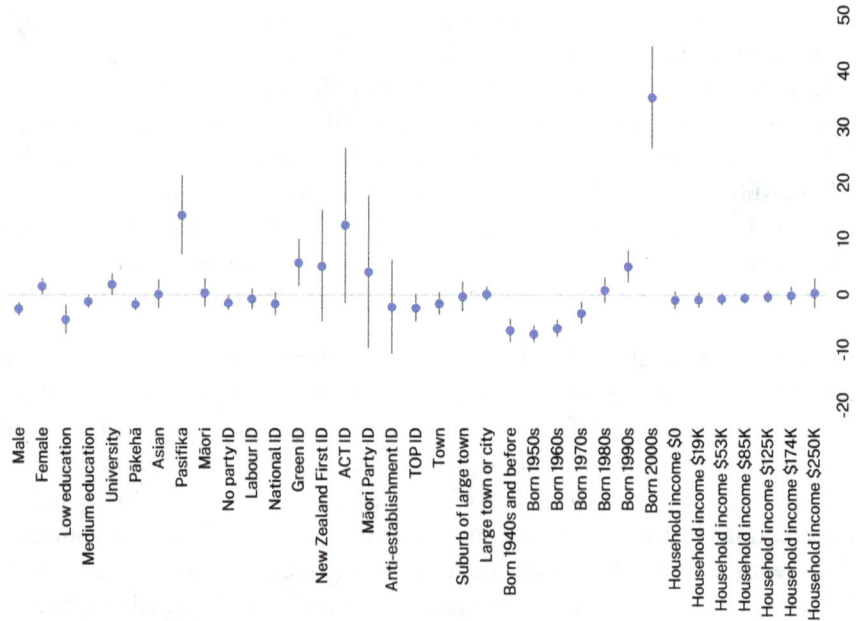

Figure 3.7 Percentage by which Instagram use for political information differed from mean use

Source: 2020 NZES (Vowles et al. 2022a).

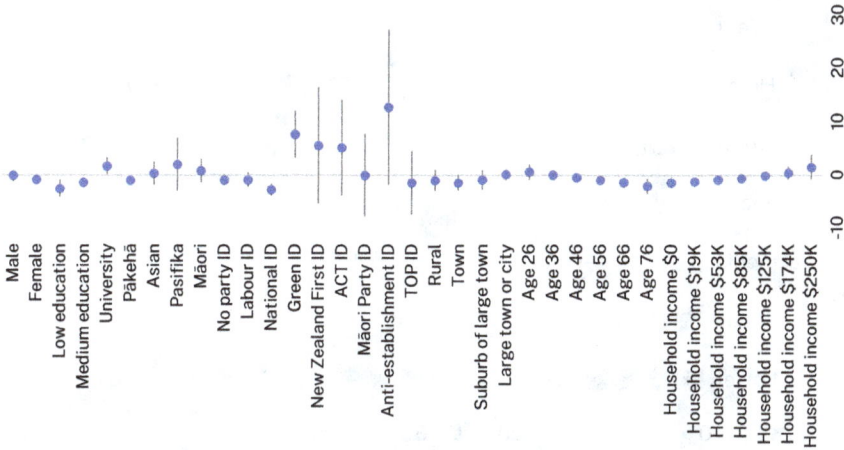

Figure 3.8 Percentage by which Twitter use for political information differed from mean use

Source: 2020 NZES (Vowles et al. 2022a).

Those who identified with anti-establishment parties were more likely to use Facebook for political information than those with no identification, or those who identified with Labour, National, Green, or New Zealand First. For Twitter, the point estimates for the anti-establishment parties and for the Greens, New Zealand First, and ACT New Zealand were all high. However, wide confidence intervals meant that only for the Greens were these point estimates statistically different from those with no identification or those who identified with the established parties. The results indicate Pasifika people were high users of Facebook and Instagram for political information.

As well as actively seeking political information, voters were directly contacted by political parties. Parties targeted messages at core and potential supporters as they outlined policies, introduced candidates, asked people to donate their time and money, and reminded them to vote. Whereas voters are increasingly using social media to learn about political topics, in developed countries, the main ways parties contact voters are usually by direct mail or phone. Between 2011 and 2016, New Zealand parties used direct mail, including leaflets, more than parties in any other country except the United Kingdom and Canada. For face-to-face contact, New Zealand was in the middle of the range, and it ranked slightly higher than average in the use of email and social media. Social media was the method by which the young were most likely to be contacted by parties (Magalhães et al. 2020, 608, 611).

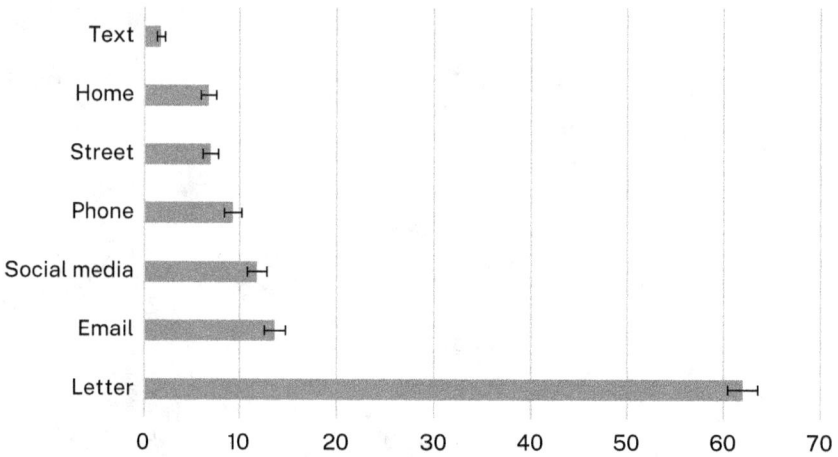

Figure 3.9 Percentage of voters contacted by political parties via different campaign channels
Source: 2020 NZES (Vowles et al. 2022a).

Figure 3.9 (and Figure 4.4 in the next chapter) shows that direct mail still dominated New Zealand canvassing methods in the 2020 election. In 2020, 62 per cent of New Zealand voters received a letter from a political party before the election. In contrast, just 13.6 per cent of New Zealand voters received an email from a party, and only 11.8 per cent were contacted through social media. Even fewer New Zealand voters (9.2 per cent) received a phone call and only 1.7 per cent received a text message from a party. Despite the pandemic, 6.8 per cent of New Zealand voters had a home visit and 7.0 per cent were contacted in the street. Traditional campaign channels are still important, and sometimes dominant, despite the rise of social media campaigning (Semetko and Tworzecki 2017, 332).

Because of the absence of national email or mobile phone contact lists, it is difficult for parties to contact voters by these methods in the way they can using postal addresses for mailing. However, parties have sought to collect people's email addresses and leaders regularly send emails to those who subscribe to these lists. New Zealand continues to lag behind democracies like the United States, Taiwan, and Iceland in terms of online electoral contacts, but is similar to Australia (Gibson 2020, 46–48).

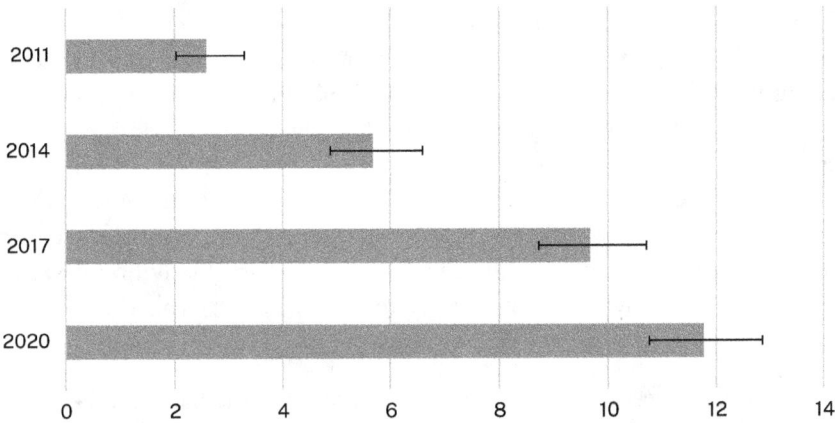

Figure 3.10 Percentage of voters contacted by political parties via social media since 2011
Sources: Vowles et al. (2022a, 2022b, 2022c, 2022d).

Nevertheless, contact by social media has been steadily increasing since the 2011 election, when a question about party contact via social media was included in the NZES for the first time. As Figure 3.10 shows, in 2011, just 2.6 per cent of voters were contacted by a party on social media. Contact with parties on social media over three elections increased a little more than fourfold. However, most use of social media for political purposes is still initiated by users, rather than by political parties and their leaders.

Whereas Ardern had 1.7 million Facebook followers at the time of the 2020 election, just 68,000 people followed Collins. This difference probably occurs because Ardern, who had been prime minister for three years, had a high profile in New Zealand and overseas, whereas Collins only became National's leader in July 2020 after Todd Muller's surprise resignation after 53 days in the job. Ardern received 1,382,238 responses to her Facebook posts over the last four weeks of the campaign, compared with only 255,528 for Judith Collins.[5] Because of differences in the number of followers, however, on average, Collins's followers were more active in responding to her posts than Ardern's followers.

People who follow and engage with the content of parties and candidates are usually supportive of or sympathetic towards a political actor. This is reflected in the way they invariably leave a positive rather than a negative reaction to content. Responses to Ardern were overwhelmingly 'like'

---

5   These were downloaded from Facebook's CrowdTangle platform for academic researchers.

85

(71 per cent) and 'love' (24 per cent), with few 'sad' (2 per cent), 'care' (2 per cent), or 'ha ha' (1 per cent) responses, and even fewer 'wow' (0.2 per cent) or 'angry' (0.2 per cent) responses.[6] For Collins, an even higher proportion of reactions were 'like' (88 per cent), but fewer were 'love' reactions (9 per cent), while the proportions of 'ha ha' (2 per cent), 'angry' (1.5 per cent), 'care' (0.4 per cent), 'sad' (0.2 per cent), and 'wow' (0.2 per cent) were all low. However, posts by Collins towards the end of the campaign stating Labour would introduce a wealth tax that would strip elderly homeowners of their assets resulted in higher angry reactions, which peaked at 4.4 per cent of reactions to Collins on 11 October.

Because there is less gatekeeping than in traditional media, there has been concern that social media is less accurate than traditional media (Semetko and Tworzecki 2017, 332). Almost 33.9 per cent of respondents in the NZES believed they had come across some kind of online political misinformation or disinformation at least sometimes, while 8.7 per cent thought they often encountered misinformation or disinformation during the campaign; 13.9 per cent said they never did and 19.6 per cent did not know.

The level of disinformation in the 2020 social media campaigns of the parties and party leaders was low and, as Figure 3.4 shows, came from two sources: Advance NZ and the New Conservatives. Only those who followed those two parties would have frequently encountered fake news and half-truths. Given this, most voters presumably overstated how often they encountered online misinformation or disinformation during the 2020 campaign. It is likely that many people considered unwanted political information that challenged their own political views as false. Deeply ingrained cognitive biases influence the perceived strength of political arguments (Arceneaux 2012, 273).

Asking people about the level of false online information they encountered could reveal more of a media hostility effect than an accurate assessment of the level of online misinformation and disinformation. This effect highlights the tendency of people with strong attitudes about political candidates or issue-based media coverage to perceive that coverage is biased when it goes against their political position and in favour of their political opponents (Vallone et al. 1985). While this effect has been found

---

6   The 'sad' responses to Ardern's posts related to the death of US Supreme Court justice Ruth Bader Ginsburg and of a New Zealand police officer working in the United Kingdom. The 'ha ha' responses related to humorous images and captions Ardern posted to humanise herself. Collins also made humorous posts and posted about Police Remembrance Day.

in response to traditional media for decades, it is also important for social media and extends to 'motivated fake news perception' (Tsang 2022, 824). The percentage of those who reported coming across misinformation or disinformation often or sometimes increased with political interest, further supporting this interpretation, as people with high political interest usually also have stronger political attitudes.

Those who identified with the Māori Party or the anti-establishment parties were most likely to perceive online misinformation or disinformation. For anti-establishment party supporters, this is not surprising, as it is an integral part of their identity to deny widely accepted political and scientific facts (Holt 2018). For Māori Party supporters, the high level of perceived misinformation and disinformation could reflect disapproval of a Western, Pākehā-shaped online political discourse in which they do not feel adequately represented (Iseke-Barnes and Danard 2007; Kamira 2003).

When it comes to people's self-assessment of their own ability to identify fake news during the campaign, about half of all New Zealanders (54.6 per cent) were at least somewhat confident that they could recognise made-up online content. Only 16.7 per cent were very confident, while almost 16 per cent were not confident, and 4.9 per cent were not at all confident. Figure 3.11 indicates that as interest in politics increased, so did people's confidence in their ability to spot fake news. Younger people also felt more confident about their ability, perhaps because they have grown up in 'post-truth' societies and are used to online misinformation and disinformation. Men felt more confident than women in their ability to perceive misinformation, and the difference was statistically significant. Men tend to feel more confident in their own abilities in a wide range of areas, which reflects gendered socialisation (Beyer and Bowden 1997; Niederle and Vesterlund 2011). Asian people were less confident in their ability to recognise misinformation, although the results varied for different Asian population groups and the confidence interval overlapped with that for Pasifika. Those with a university education were more confident in their ability to spot misinformation than those with low education. Differences were usually not statistically significant for party identification; however, Green Party identifiers were more confident than those with no identification.

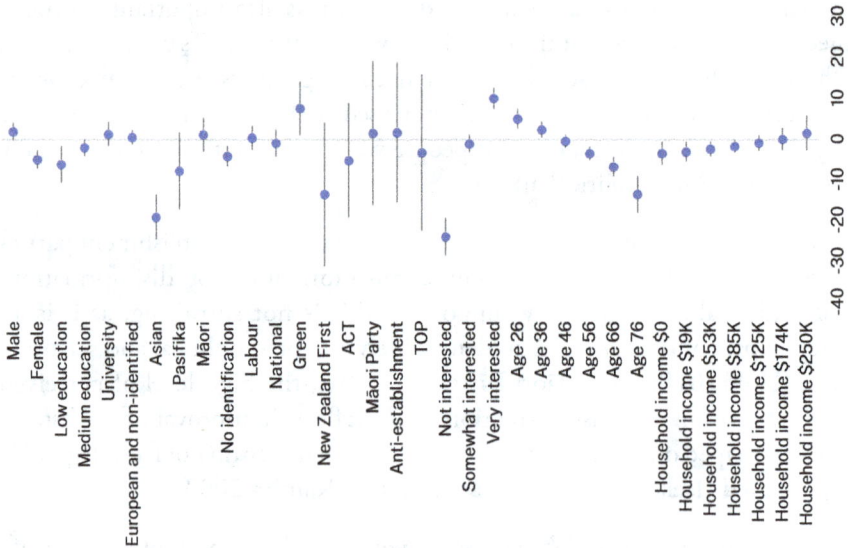

Figure 3.11 Voters' self-assessment of their ability to identify misinformation and disinformation (deviations from the mean)
Source: 2020 NZES (Vowles et al. 2022a).

Effects of social media campaigning on party leader evaluations

Candidate evaluations can be reinforced, and sometimes even changed, by social media as its content is usually highly personalised. Candidate and leadership evaluations, then, can influence voting decisions (King 2002). Fewer people these days identify with political parties and, even when they express an identification, it is now weaker and less consistent over time than in the past (Dalton 2021).[7] Candidate and leader evaluations have therefore become more electorally important (Bean 1992) and also more affected by campaign influences including social media use (Hendricks and Schill 2017). This section considers the significantly different effects of social media use on approval by New Zealanders of the leaders of the two main parties.

---

7   A little less than 60 per cent were 'usually close to' a political party in 2020, but NZES panel data suggest that about one-third of those were either not close to a party or were close to a different party in 2017. For trends in party identification in New Zealand over time, see Karp (2010) and Vowles (2014). For instability in party identification in New Zealand as far back as the 1980s, see Aimer (1989).

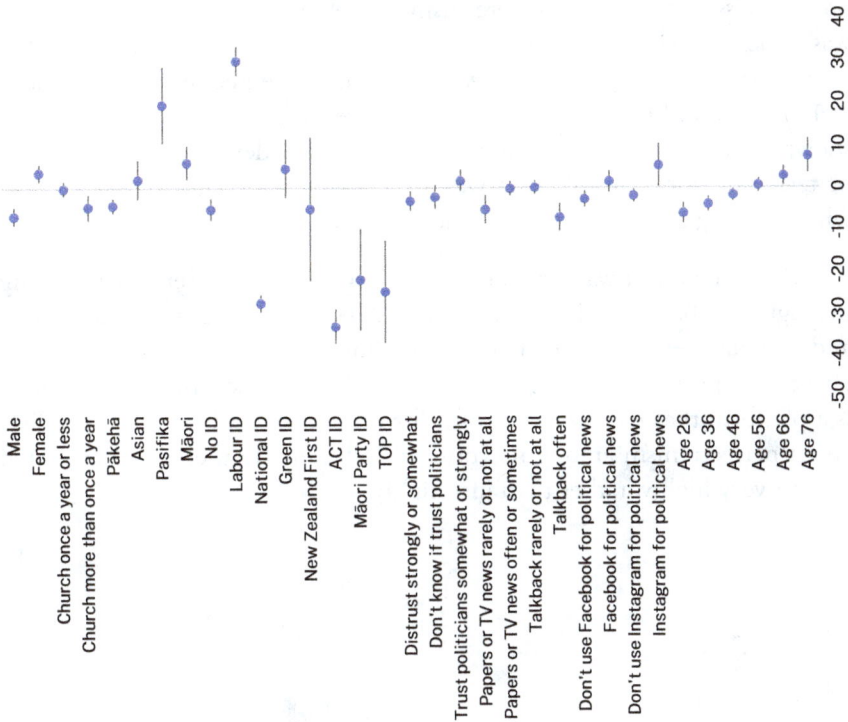

Figure 3.12 Multivariate analysis results for rating Jacinda Ardern as 10 for likeability (deviations from mean)
Source: 2020 NZES (Vowles et al. 2022a).

Labour's Jacinda Ardern was a very popular incumbent leader in the 2020 election, with 34.5 per cent of voters rating her with a 10 on a scale from zero (strongly dislike) to 10 (strongly like), and only 5.4 per cent rating her as zero. Almost half the voters rated her likeability as an eight or higher. In contrast, National's Judith Collins was not popular, with almost 25 per cent of the electorate rating her with a zero, and only 3.1 per cent rating her with a ten. Almost half of voters scored Collins as zero to three. In the following analyses, those who scored the party leaders as eight, nine, or 10 are considered voters who liked them. Since the distribution for Collins is so skewed towards dislikes, those who disliked her are those who scored her as zero to three.

Using multivariate analysis, Figure 3.12 shows that identifying with Labour and being Pasifika were mostly strongly associated with rating Ardern as a ten. Green Party identifiers, women, and Māori were also more likely to rate Ardern as a 10, as were older voters and those who only went to church

89

once or less a year. Furthermore, using Facebook to access political news was associated with rating Ardern as a ten. Similarly, Figure 3.12 shows that using Instagram for political news resulted in more people scoring Ardern at 10 for likeability, rather than a lower score. In contrast, Twitter use (not shown) did not seem to be important for liking Ardern. Using newspapers or television for political news was associated with people liking Ardern, whereas using talkback radio had the opposite association.

The Facebook effect was evident when liking Ardern was defined as scoring her eight to 10, rather than just as a ten. The television or newspaper news and talkback effects remained strong; however, the positive Instagram effect disappeared. This suggests that people who used Instagram, which is a platform that has been criticised for promoting and reinforcing beliefs about perfectionism among its youthful followers (Lup et al. 2015), rated Ardern very highly, rather than just highly.

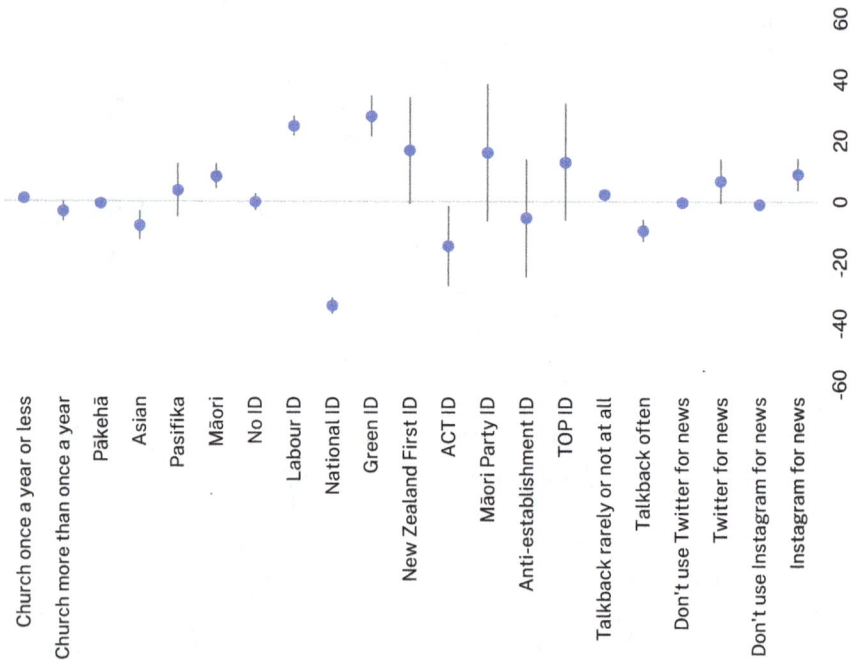

Figure 3.13 Multivariate analysis results for rating Judith Collins as a zero to three (deviations from mean)
Source: 2020 NZES (Vowles et al. 2022a).

For Collins, identifying as a National Party supporter was, not surprisingly, strongly associated with liking her, as was being religious and listening to talkback radio. With the controls shown in Figure 3.13, using Instagram was associated with people being more likely to dislike her. Using Twitter for news also was associated with people disliking Collins, but there was a significance level of only 0.081 for this effect. As Figure 3.13 indicates, the Twitter result might therefore change in a larger sample. Not surprisingly, the party identification controls have a strong effect. Similar results for Instagram occurred when the full range of likeability scores was used for Collins. The Twitter result became much weaker, and the variable for Twitter was dropped. However, there was weak evidence Facebook use was associated with people disliking Collins.

These results suggest that Jacinda Ardern's reputation as a social media 'powerhouse', which is also discussed in Chapter 7 of this volume, was well deserved (Krewel and Vowles 2020b; Wilson 2020). Ardern's Facebook and Instagram performances had a particularly positive effect on people's evaluations of her. She used both these channels frequently and attracted large audiences. In contrast, Judith Collins did not benefit from her social media presence, with those using Instagram for political news tending to dislike her.

Conclusion

This chapter described how parties and their leaders campaigned on Facebook during the 2020 general election campaign, how New Zealanders used the internet to inform themselves about politics, and what effects parties' and leaders' social media campaigns had on voters' evaluations of the likeability of party leaders. NZSMS data showed that the governing Labour Party and its leader, Jacinda Ardern, made the most Facebook posts during the final four weeks of the election campaign. However, some parties with no parliamentary representation also used Facebook heavily as a convenient and low-cost way of communicating with voters and bypassing media gatekeepers. Most Facebook posts contained policy or issue content, although less so as the campaign progressed. Labour and its leader were polling well and maintained a strongly positive focus. The opposition parties and their leaders increasingly attacked Labour. Fake news and half-truths mostly came from the anti-establishment parties and their leaders. In contrast, the quality of political discourse by the established parties was usually high.

Election study survey data showed that more than 80 per cent of New Zealand voters now use the internet to access political information. Use tended to be higher among the young, the educated, and high-income earners and, although the confidence intervals are very large, those who identified with fringe parties are distrustful of the established media. About 34.1 per cent of New Zealanders used Facebook for political information, about 8.3 per cent used Instagram, and 4.3 per cent used Twitter. Instagram use was strongest among the youngest voters. In contrast, age effects were smaller for Facebook and very weak for Twitter. Women made greater use than men of Instagram and Facebook. Pasifika and, with less confidence, Māori made high use of Facebook for political information, as did those who identified with anti-establishment parties. However, traditional campaign channels such as direct mail and person-to-person meetings still dominate political campaigning in New Zealand and were used most by the largest parties.

About one-third of people reported coming across online misinformation or disinformation. Those who identified with an anti-establishment party were most likely to do so, followed by those who identified with the Māori Party. Almost 55 per cent of New Zealanders were confident in their ability to recognise 'made-up' online content.

The popularity of Jacinda Ardern was high at the start of the campaign after a tight lockdown that had effectively eliminated Covid-19 from New Zealand. In contrast, Judith Collins, who became leader of the internally divided National Party only shortly before the start of the election campaign, struggled for popularity. Whereas post-election survey data show that almost half of the voters evaluated Ardern as eight or higher on an 11-point scale for likeability, almost half of the voters evaluated Collins as zero to three. Multivariate analysis shows that those who used Facebook and Instagram for news were more likely than non-users to evaluate Ardern as 10 for likeability. Instagram use, in particular, was associated with users giving Ardern a perfect score for likeability, rather than just a very high score. Twitter use, on the other hand, did not seem to be important. In a multivariate model for Collins, using Instagram for political news was associated with people being more likely to dislike her. These results confirm Jacinda Ardern's reputation as a social media 'powerhouse'.

Ardern retired from politics in early 2023, partly because of the threats and misogynist personal attacks she and her family increasingly faced (Bradley 2023). It seemed unlikely that Labour and its new leader, Chris Hipkins, could dominate the social media campaign in 2023 in the same way as Labour did under Ardern in 2020. Admittedly, Hipkins was seen by voters as more relatable than National's new leader, Christopher Luxon (Newshub 2023). Hipkins adeptly used social media to promote Labour's policies and policy delivery, including a much stronger focus on cost-of-living issues; to record his attendance at official events; to be seen promoting the interests of business; and to remind voters that he is an ordinary, strongly nationalist New Zealander with a love of sausage rolls. However, Hipkins made it clear that he would be keeping his children entirely out of politics (Daalder 2023). In his first four months as leader, Hipkins ignored opposition parties in his Facebook posts, although Labour also ran some 'You can't trust National' posts on Facebook. National and Luxon ran a relatively critical social media campaign in the first half of 2023, strongly focussed on a promise to 'Get New Zealand back on track'. National's use of artificial intelligence to create images for Facebook attack advertisements was controversial (New Zealand Herald 2023). With National and ACT far ahead in fundraising (Malpass 2023) and all the major newspaper companies paywalling some content, there were strong incentives for Labour and the minor parties to rely heavily on social media for campaigning during the 2023 election.

References

Aimer, P. 1989. 'Travelling Together: Party Identification and Voting in the New Zealand General Election of 1987.' Electoral Studies 8(2): 131–42. doi.org/10.1016/0261-3794(89)90030-9.

Allcott, H., and M. Gentzkow. 2017. 'Social Media and Fake News in the 2016 Election.' The Journal of Economic Perspectives 31(2): 211–35. doi.org/10.1257/jep.31.2.211.

Arceneaux, K. 2012. 'Cognitive Biases and the Strength of Political Arguments.' American Journal of Political Science 56(2): 271–85. doi.org/10.1111/j.1540-5907.2011.00573.x.

Bean, C. 1992. 'Party Leaders and Local Candidates.' In Electoral Behaviour in New Zealand, edited by M. Holland, 141–68. Oxford: Oxford University Press.

Benoit, W.L. 1999. Seeing Spots: A Functional Analysis of Presidential Television Advertisements, 1952–1996. Westport, CT: Praeger.

Beyer, S., and E.M. Bowden. 1997. 'Gender Differences in Self-Perceptions: Convergent Evidence from Three Measures of Accuracy and Bias.' *Personality and Social Psychology Bulletin* 23(2): 157–72. doi.org/10.1177/0146167297232005.

Boydstun, A.E., A. Ledgerwood, and J. Sparks. 2019. 'A Negativity Bias in Reframing Shapes Political Preferences Even in Partisan Contexts.' *Social Psychological and Personality Science* 10(1): 53–61. doi.org/10.1177/1948550617733520.

Bradley, A. 2023. 'The Hatred and Vitriol Jacinda Ardern Endured "Would Affect Anybody".' *Radio New Zealand*, 20 January. Available from: www.rnz.co.nz/news/political/482761/the-hatred-and-vitriol-jacinda-ardern-endured-would-affect-anybody.

Chyi, H.I., and O. Tenenboim. 2019. 'Charging More and Wondering Why Readership Declined? A Longitudinal Study of U.S. Newspapers' Price Hikes, 2008–2016.' *Journalism Studies* 20(14): 2113–29. doi.org/10.1080/146167 0x.2019.1568903.

Cooke, H. 2020. 'National MPs are Twisting Jacinda Ardern's Words on Social Media.' *Stuff*, [Wellington], 24 September. Available from: interactives.stuff.co.nz/2020/08/election-2020-the-whole-truth/#/1193324691/national-mps-are-twisting-jacinda-ardern-s-words-on-social-media.

Cooke, H. 2021. 'Covering the 2020 Election: Platforms and the Plague.' In *Politics in a Pandemic: Jacinda Ardern and the 2020 Election*, edited by S. Levine, 141–48. Wellington: Te Herenga Waka University Press.

Daalder, M. 2023. 'Chris Hipkins Wants to Make Politics Boring Again.' *Newsroom*, [Auckland], 23 January, [Updated 28 January]. Available from: www.newsroom.co.nz/chris-hipkins-want-to-make-politics-boring-again.

Dalton, R.J. 2021. 'Party Identification and Its Implications.' In *Oxford Research Encyclopedia of Politics*. Oxford: Oxford University Press. doi.org/10.1093/acrefore/9780190228637.013.72.

Davidson, M., and J. Shaw. 2021. 'Growing Green Support from a Position of Government.' In *Politics in a Pandemic: Jacinda Ardern and Labour's 2020 Election*, edited by S. Levine, 81–87. Wellington: Te Herenga Waka University Press.

Druckman, J.N., M.J. Kifer, and M. Parkin. 2009. 'Campaign Communications in U.S. Congressional Elections.' *American Political Science Review* 103(3): 343–66. doi.org/10.1017/S0003055409990037.

Edwards, B. 2017. 'Political Roundup: The Jacinda Ardern Effect Characterised By "Relentless Positivity".' *New Zealand Herald*, 2 August. Available from: www.nzherald.co.nz/nz/political-roundup-the-jacinda-ardern-effect-characterised-by-relentless-positivity/24WPOZIV4GGC5KYMGNPKYSR6IU/.

Enli, G., and L.T. Rosenberg. 2018. 'Trust in the Age of Social Media: Populist Politicians Seem More Authentic.' *Social Media + Society* 4(1). doi.org/10.1177/2056305118764430.

Fenoll, V., J. Haßler, M. Magin, and U. Russmann. 2021. 'Campaigning for Strasbourg on Facebook: Introduction to a 12-Country Comparison on Parties' Facebook Campaigns in the 2019 European Parliament Election.' In *Campaigning on Facebook in the 2019 European Parliament Election: Informing, Interacting With, and Mobilising Voters*, edited by J. Haßler, M. Magin, U. Russmann, and V. Fenoll, 3–21. Cham: Palgrave Macmillan. doi.org/10.1007/978-3-030-73851-8_1.

Flanagan, T. 2014. *Winning Power: Canadian Campaigning in the Twenty-First Century*. Montreal, QC: McGill-Queen's University Press. doi.org/10.1515/9780773590366.

Gibson, R.K. 2020. *When the Nerds Go Marching In: How Digital Technology Moved from the Margins to the Mainstream of Political Campaigns*. Oxford: Oxford University Press. doi.org/10.1093/oso/9780195397789.001.0001.

Greaves, L., and E. Morgan. 2021. 'Maori and the 2020 Election. In *Politics in a Pandemic: Jacinda Ardern and New Zealand's 2020 Election*, edited by S. Levine, 316–27. Wellington: Te Herenga Waka University Press.

Greive, D. 2020. 'Bauer's Shocking Fall Reveals the Government's Poisonous Media Dilemma.' *The Spinoff*, [Auckland], 3 April. Available from: thespinoff.co.nz/business/03-04-2020/bauers-shocking-fall-reveals-the-governments-poisonous-media-dilemma.

Haynes, A.A., and S.L. Rhine. 1998. 'Attack Politics in Presidential Nomination Campaigns: An Examination of the Frequency and Determinants of Intermediated Negative Messages against Opponents.' *Political Research Quarterly* 51(3): 691–721. doi.org/10.1177/106591299805100307.

Hendricks, J.A., and D. Schill. 2017. 'The Social Media Election of 2016.' In *The 2016 US Presidential Campaign: Political Communication and Practice*, edited by R.E. Denton, jr, 121–50. Cham: Palgrave Macmillan. doi.org/10.1007/978-3-319-52599-0_5.

Holt, K. 2018. 'Alternative Media and the Notion of Anti-Systemness: Towards an Analytical Framework.' *Media and Communication* 6(4): 49–57. doi.org/10.17645/mac.v6i4.1467.

Hopmann, D.N., P. Van Aelst, and G. Legnante. 2012. 'Political Balance in the News: A Review of Concepts, Operationalizations and Key Findings.' *Journalism* 13(2): 240–57. doi.org/10.1177/1464884911427804.

Iseke-Barnes, J.M., and D. Danard. 2007. 'Indigenous Knowledges and Worldview: Representations and the Internet.' In *Information Technology and Indigenous People*, edited by L.E. Dyson, M. Hendriks, and S. Grant, 27–37. Hershey, PA: IGI Global. doi.org/10.4018/978-1-59904-298-5.ch003.

Kamira, R. 2003. 'Te Mata o te Tai—The Edge of the Tide: Rising Capacity in Information Technology of Maori in Aotearoa-New Zealand.' *The Electronic Library* 21(5): 465–75. doi.org/10.1108/02640470310499858.

Karp, J.A. 2010. 'How Voters Decide.' In New Zealand Government and Politics, edited by R. Miller, 287–301. 5th edn. Melbourne: Oxford University Press.

King, A. 2002. *Leaders' Personalities and the Outcomes of Democratic Elections.* Oxford: Oxford University Press. doi.org/10.1093/0199253137.001.0001.

Kreiss, D., R.G. Lawrence, and S.C. McGregor. 2018. 'In Their Own Words: Political Practitioner Accounts of Candidates, Audiences, Affordances, Genres, and Timing in Strategic Social Media Use.' *Political Communication* 35(1): 8–31. doi.org/10.1080/10584609.2017.1334727.

Krewel, M. 2022. *The New Zealand Social Media Study, Wave 1–3.* [Computer file].

Krewel, M., and J. Vowles. 2020a. Codebook: New Zealand Social Media Study (NZSMS).' Unpublished document.

Krewel, M., and J. Vowles. 2020b. 'From Dirty Dairying to Dirty Campaigning? The Duel between Jacinda Ardern and Judith Collins on Facebook.' *Election 2020: Key Social Media Trends*, [Blog], 2 October. Wellington: Victoria University of Wellington. Available from: www.wgtn.ac.nz/research/strengths/election/The-Facebook-duel-between-Ardern-and-Collins.

Krewel, M., and J. Vowles. 2020c. 'Negative Campaigning, Fake News, and Half-Truths among the Minor Parties. And the Question: Is Advance New Zealand Really "Populist"?' *Election 2020: Key Social Media Trends*, [Blog], 16 October. Wellington: Victoria University of Wellington. Available from: www.wgtn. ac.nz/research/strengths/election/is-advance-new-zealand-populist.

Krewel, M., and J. Vowles. 2020d. '#nzvotes: The Dynamics of Campaign Communication on Facebook.' *Election 2020: Key Social Media Trends*, [Blog], 27 October. Wellington: Victoria University of Wellington. Available from: www. wgtn.ac.nz/research/strengths/election/facebook-campaign-communication? fbclid=IwAR2otnQiaqBg7Ylw0BtC_FrXKhC6j6h4bOyOr9iDM07TQazp KCXR3TCq3A4.

Kung, S., M. Doppen, M. Black, T. Hills, and N. Kearns. 2021. 'Reduced Mortality in New Zealand during the COVID-19 Pandemic.' *The Lancet* 397(10268): 25. doi.org/10.1016/S0140-6736(20)32647-7.

Loan, J., K. Murray, R. Pauls, and K. Woock. 2021. *The Implications of Competition and Market Trends for Media Plurality in New Zealand*. A report for the Ministry for Culture and Heritage, November. Wellington: Sapere Research Group. Available from: www.mch.govt.nz/sites/default/files/2023-10/sapere-report-media-plurality-nz-feb22.pdf

Lup, K., L. Trub, and L. Rosenthal. 2015. 'Instagram #Instasad?: Exploring Associations Among Instagram Use, Depressive Symptoms, Negative Social Comparison, and Strangers Followed.' *Cyberpsychology, Behavior, and Social Networking* 18(5): 246–52. doi.org/10.1089/cyber.2014.0560.

Magalhães, P.C., J.H. Aldrich, and R.K. Gibson. 2020. 'New Forms of Mobilization, New People Mobilized? Evidence from the Comparative Study of Electoral Systems.' *Party Politics* 26(5): 605–18. doi.org/10.1177/1354068818797367.

Malpass, L. 2023. 'ACT Declares Almost $1 Million In One Day from Big Money Donors.' *Stuff*, [Wellington], 25 March. Available from: www.stuff.co.nz/national/politics/131600565/act-declares-almost-1-million-in-one-day-from-big-money-donors.

McGregor, S.C. 2018. 'Personalization, Social Media, and Voting: Effects of Candidate Self-Personalization on Vote Intention.' *New Media & Society* 20(3): 1139–60. doi.org/10.1177/1461444816686103.

McGregor, S.C., R.G. Lawrence, and A. Cardona. 2017. 'Personalization, Gender, and Social Media: Gubernatorial Candidates' Social Media Strategies.' *Information, Communication & Society* 20(2): 264–83. doi.org/10.1080/1369118X.2016.1167228.

Meta. 2022. 'CrowdTangle: About us.' [Online]. Menlo Park, CA: Meta. Available from: help.crowdtangle.com/en/articles/4201940-about-us.

Moffitt, B. 2016. *The Global Rise of Populism: Performance, Political Style and Representation*. Stanford, CA: Stanford University Press. doi.org/10.1515/9780804799331.

Muchison, A. 2016. 'Online Media in New Zealand.' In *Politics and the Media*, edited by J. Kemp, B. Bahador, K. McMillan, and C. Rudd, 214–25. Auckland: Auckland University Press.

Newshub. 2023. 'Newshub-Reid Research Poll Results: Nearly Half of New Zealanders Believe Christopher Luxon is Out of Touch.' *Newshub*, [Auckland], 14 May. Available from: www.newshub.co.nz/home/politics/2023/05/newshub-reid-research-poll-results-nearly-half-of-new-zealanders-believe-christopher-luxon-is-out-of-touch.html.

New Zealand Herald. 2023. 'National Party Uses AI in Attack Ads: Christopher Luxon "Not Aware".' *New Zealand Herald*, 23 May. Available from: www.nz herald.co.nz/nz/national-party-uses-ai-in-attack-ads-luxon-not-aware/EA32SU 4L35D7LFCHTJ5PGCFRCA/.

New Zealand Social Media Study (NZSMS). 2020. Victoria University of Wellington. Available from: www.wgtn.ac.nz/hppi/centres/isprl/new-zealand-social-media-study.

Niederle, M., and L. Vesterlund. 2011. 'Gender and Competition.' *Annual Review of Economics* 3(1): 601–30. doi.org/10.1146/annurev-economics-111809-125122.

Robinson, C. 2019. *Promises, Promises: 80 Years of Wooing New Zealand Voters*. Auckland: Massey University Press.

Ross, K., S. Fountaine, and M. Comrie. 2015. 'Facing Up to Facebook: Politicians, Publics and the Social Media(ted) Turn in New Zealand.' *Media, Culture & Society* 37(2): 251–69. doi.org/10.1177/0163443714557983.

Ross, K., S. Fountaine, and M. Comrie. 2023. 'Gender, Party and Performance in the 2020 New Zealand General Election: Politicking on Facebook with Jacinda and Judith.' *Media, Culture & Society* 45(2): 388–405. doi.org/10.1177/01634437221127366.

Sachdeva, S. 2020. 'Labour Put Its Chips On "Positive Politics" In Election Year.' *Newsroom*, [Auckland], 24 January. Available from: www.newsroom.co.nz/labour-puts-its-chips-on-positive-politics-in-election-year.

Schoenbach, K., J. De Ridder, and E. Lauf. 2001. 'Politicians on TV News: Getting Attention in Dutch and German Election Campaigns.' *European Journal of Political Research* 39(4): 519–31. doi.org/10.1111/1475-6765.00586.

Semetko, H.A., and H. Tworzecki. 2017. 'Campaign Strategies, Media, and Voters: The Fourth Era of Political Communication.' In *The Routledge Handbook of Elections, Voting Behavior and Public Opinion*, edited by J. Fisher, E. Fieldhouse, M.N. Franklin, R. Gibson, M. Cantijoch, and C. Wlezien, 331–43. London: Routledge. doi.org/10.4324/9781315712390-25.

Shoemaker, P. 1991. *Gatekeeping: Communication Concepts 3*. Thousand Oaks, CA: SAGE. doi.org/10.4324/9780203931653.

Shoemaker, P. 2006. 'News and Newsworthiness: A Commentary.' *Communications* 31(1): 105–11. doi.org/10.1515/COMMUN.2006.007.

Shoemaker, P., and T. Vos. 2009. *Gatekeeping Theory*. London: Routledge.

Smalley, S. 2022. 'Meta Won't Comment on its Plans to Abandon CrowdTangle.' *Factually*, 18 August. St Petersburg, FL: Poynter Institute for Media Studies. Available from: www.poynter.org/reporting-editing/2022/meta-wont-comment-on-its-plans-to-abandon-crowdtangle/.

Tsang, S.J. 2022. 'Issue Stance and Perceived Journalistic Motives Explain Divergent Audience Perceptions of Fake News.' *Journalism* 23(4): 823–40. doi.org/10.1177/1464884920926002.

Vallone, R.P., L. Ross, and M.R. Lepper. 1985. 'The Hostile Media Phenomenon: Biased Perception and Perceptions of Media Bias in Coverage of the Beirut Massacre.' *Journal of Personality and Social Psychology* 49(3): 577–85. doi.org/10.1037//0022-3514.49.3.577.

Vowles, J. 2014. 'Putting the 2011 Election in Its Place.' In *The New Electoral Politics in New Zealand*, edited by J. Vowles, 27–52. Wellington: Institute for Governance and Policy Studies.

Vowles, J., F. Barker, J. Hayward, J. Curtin, and L. Greaves. 2022a. *2020 New Zealand Election Study*. [Online]. ADA Dataverse, V3. doi.org/10.26193/BPAMYJ.

Vowles, J., H. Coffé, J. Curtin, and G. Cotterell. 2022b. *2014 New Zealand Election Study*. [Online]. ADA Dataverse, V3. doi.org/10.26193/MF9DNL.

Vowles, J., G. Cotterell, R. Miller, and J. Curtin. 2022c. *2011 New Zealand Election Study*. [Online]. ADA Dataverse, V3. doi.org/10.26193/YZDMF3.

Vowles, J., K. McMillan, F. Barker, J. Curtin, J. Hayward, L. Greaves, and C. Crothers. 2022d. *2017 New Zealand Election Study*. [Online]. ADA Dataverse, V3. doi.org/10.26193/28JJFB.

Walker, M., and K.E. Matsa. 2021. 'News Consumption Across Social Media in 2021.' News, 20 September. Washington, DC: Pew Research Center. Available from: www.pewresearch.org/journalism/2021/09/20/news-consumption-across-social-media-in-2021/.

Walls, J. 2020. 'Election 2020: Judith Collins in "Bittersweet" Campaign Launch, Attacks Labour as "Erratic" and "Lazy".' *New Zealand Herald*, 20 September. Available from: www.nzherald.co.nz/nz/election-2020-judith-collins-in-bittersweet-campaign-launch-attacks-labour-as-erratic-and-lazy/AC3W2IHWY37ZDNB5DJZTVZR47E/.

Williams, D. 2018. 'The Future of Newspapers.' *Newsroom*, [Auckland], 8 January. Available from: www.newsroom.co.nz/summer-newsroom/the-future-of-newspapers.

Wilson, S. 2020. 'Three Reasons Why Jacinda Ardern's Coronavirus Response Has Been a Masterclass in Crisis Leadership.' *The Conversation*, 6 April. Available from: theconversation.com/three-reasons-why-jacinda-arderns-coronavirus-response-has-been-a-masterclass-in-crisis-leadership-135541.

Appendix 3.1

Table A3.1 Model of party leader approval for Jacinda Ardern

Variables	(1) Ardern as 10	(2) Strongly like (8–10)
Female	0.637***	0.454***
	(0.092)	(0.088)
Age	0.014***	0.010***
	(0.003)	(0.003)
Attends church more than once a year	–0.286**	–0.406***
	(0.114)	(0.108)
Asian	0.382**	0.426***
	(0.153)	(0.149)
Pasifika	1.396***	0.661**
	(0.268)	(0.295)
Māori	0.618***	0.441***
	(0.129)	(0.137)
Labour identifier	1.598***	1.860***
	(0.104)	(0.142)
National identifier	–1.773***	–1.476***
	(0.169)	(0.112)
Green identifier	0.469***	0.762***
	(0.172)	(0.191)
New Zealand First identifier	0.006	0.085
	(0.452)	(0.400)
ACT identifier	–3.296***	–2.120***
	(1.243)	(0.442)
Māori Party identifier	–1.112*	–0.628
	(0.579)	(0.471)
TOP identifier	–1.408*	–0.789*
	(0.721)	(0.434)
Anti-establishment identifier		–3.975***
		(1.269)

Variables	(1) Ardern as 10	(2) Strongly like (8–10)
Politicians trustworthy, neither, don't know, or missing	−0.243**	−0.276**
	(0.119)	(0.119)
Politicians trustworthy, distrust strongly/somewhat	−0.302***	−0.733***
	(0.108)	(0.106)
Follow TV or papers = 2, rarely, or not at all	−0.318***	−0.888***
	(0.123)	(0.115)
Follow talkback = 3, rarely, or not at all	0.462***	0.715***
	(0.125)	(0.113)
Visited Facebook for information	0.264**	0.259**
	(0.103)	(0.101)
Visited Instagram for information	0.439***	0.019
	(0.161)	(0.167)
Constant	−2.319***	−0.493**
	(0.245)	(0.225)
Observations	3,029	3,063

*** $p < 0.01$

** $p < 0.05$

* $p < 0.1$

Note: Standard errors in parentheses.

Table A3.2 Model of party leader approval for Judith Collins

Variables	(1) Strongly dislike (0–3)	(2) Like (0–10)
Age		−0.004
		(0.003)
Female		0.127
		(0.106)
Attends church more than once a year	−0.226**	0.612***
	(0.101)	(0.128)
Asian	−0.379***	0.531***
	(0.138)	(0.182)
Pasifika	0.227	−0.299
	(0.239)	(0.317)
Māori	0.471***	−0.603***
	(0.123)	(0.159)
Labour identifier	1.097***	−1.680***
	(0.100)	(0.135)

Variables	(1) Strongly dislike (0–3)	(2) Like (0–10)
National identifier	−1.832***	2.365***
	(0.131)	(0.141)
Green identifier	1.268***	−1.641***
	(0.195)	(0.234)
New Zealand First identifier	0.715*	−0.486
	(0.405)	(0.554)
ACT identifier	−0.632**	0.835**
	(0.321)	(0.418)
Māori Party identifier	0.681	−1.387**
	(0.513)	(0.644)
Anti-establishment identifier	−0.226	−0.057
	(0.426)	(0.598)
TOP identifier	0.545	−1.279**
	(0.426)	(0.591)
Another party identifier	0.289	−1.876
	(1.477)	(2.135)
Follow TV or papers, sometimes, rarely, or not at all		0.190*
		(0.110)
Follow talkback rarely or not at all	0.622***	−0.746***
	(0.107)	(0.133)
Visited Facebook for information		−0.209*
		(0.120)
Visited Twitter for information	0.372*	−0.355
	(0.205)	(0.256)
Visited Instagram for information	0.521***	−0.513**
	(0.153)	(0.201)
Constant	−0.657***	4.716***
	(0.113)	(0.261)
Observations	3,055	3,127
R-squared		0.251

*** $p < 0.01$

** $p < 0.05$

* $p < 0.1$

Note: Standard errors in parentheses.

4

Mobilising Voters from the 'Team of Five Million': Electoral administration and turnout in the 2020 election

Jennifer Curtin, Celestyna Galicki, and Jack Vowles

Introduction

Two features of the 2020 election in New Zealand stand out above all others: the landslide victory of the Labour Party and a significant increase in electoral turnout, particularly among the young. This chapter analyses the latter. From the international literature and theories of turnout, one would not have expected a turnout increase as the result of an election held in 2020, given the onset of the Covid-19 pandemic. Most research began from the inference that the fear of catching Covid-19 would discourage people from going out to vote (Picchio and Santolini 2021; Santana et al. 2020). Where risk is high, turnout should be down; where risk is lower, turnout should be less affected.

The case of New Zealand is distinctive because, by the time of the election, there were no Covid-19 cases in the community. That said, life in New Zealand had not returned to pre-pandemic 'normal'. Mask-wearing was still expected and Covid-19 vaccinations were not available in the country until four months after the 2020 election. Moreover, the election was postponed briefly because some cases emerged just before the date on which parliament was to be dissolved. These were contained within a few weeks, but some restrictions remained in place, and no one could be sure that new cases would not emerge during the campaign. Yet, the final vote count revealed that the 2020 election had the highest official turnout since 1999, at 82.2 per cent, and the highest voter enrolment since 2008.

After reviewing changes in turnout over time, this chapter proceeds by exploring three possible reasons for its increase and why fears about a potential decline proved to be ill-founded in the New Zealand case. The first relates to electoral integrity and trust in the democratic system. Internationally, commentators expressed fears that the effect of such restrictions could be to reduce trust and create fears of an authoritarian government. Election postponements along with the emergency powers required to implement lockdowns could erode democracy and turnout and exacerbate declining trust in public institutions (James and Alihodzic 2020; Landman and Splendore 2020). In preparation for such a possibility, the New Zealand Electoral Commission made significant efforts to protect the integrity of the election and to encourage turnout. Drawing on qualitative data and secondary survey analysis from the Electoral Commission, we assess whether a high level of electoral integrity and trust in New Zealand's democratic process contributed to increased turnout.

Second, we examine whether voters saw this election as mattering more than normal given the context of Covid-19. In other words, did the pandemic have a mobilising effect, reinforcing the feeling that elections are important, thus leading to increased engagement between voters and political parties, their messages, and their candidates (Franklin 2004; see also Santana et al. 2020; Constantino et al. 2021)? And, we ask to what extent was political engagement hampered by Covid-19 and the restricted ability of parties to campaign at in-person events in 2020, compared with the 2017 election? Drawing on earlier arguments in Chapter 2, we also explore whether trust in the democratic process was important to increased turnout.

In the final section of this chapter, we examine a third potential explanation. Research in the United States reports that high-profile referendums held concurrently with legislative elections can have the effect of increasing turnout for the latter (for example, Childers and Binder 2016; Smith and Tolbert 2004). The 2020 election was held concurrently with two referendums: one on euthanasia or the end of life, and the other on legalisation of cannabis. Some have argued that the strong increase in youth turnout in 2020 was encouraged by the cannabis referendum, which was only narrowly lost. Drawing on NZES data, we test whether the increased turnout was indeed a referendum effect and therefore perhaps had little to do with Covid-19.

The context of New Zealand's high voter turnout

On 28 January 2020, Prime Minister Jacinda Ardern announced that the next New Zealand general election would be held on Saturday, 19 September. This announcement came just two days before the World Health Organization declared Covid-19 a Public Health Emergency of International Concern. Six weeks later, on 11 March, when Covid-19 was relabelled a pandemic, New Zealand had five confirmed cases of the virus (New Zealand Doctor 2022). Case numbers began to increase substantially, leading the government to close the border, introduce a four-tier alert system, and implement a two-month nationwide lockdown (see Chapter 2 for further details). What became known as the 'elimination' approach was initially successful. Community case numbers ebbed.

By the time Ardern launched her party's re-election campaign on 7 August 2020, New Zealand had experienced 99 days without community transmission. However, Covid-19 returned on 13 August, eight days before parliament was due to be dissolved. The government put Auckland into a Level 3 lockdown, restricting travel and social gatherings, initially for three days. Political parties had to postpone or cancel campaign events. The prime minister initially advised the governor-general to delay for several days both the dissolution of parliament and the issue of the electoral writ (Knight 2021). Less than a week later, after consultations with political parties and electoral officials, the prime minister announced that the election would be delayed until 17 October 2020. This represented the first electoral postponement since World War II and the first for a public health emergency. But New Zealand was not alone in its decision to postpone its general election. In 2020, the International Institute for Democracy and Electoral Assistance (IDEA 2021) calculated that at least 70 countries and territories globally had experienced a delay in their elections.

As Chapter 1 has shown, turnout in New Zealand elections hit a low point in 2011 and has since been in recovery: incremental increases in turnout across the past three elections, with the greatest upsurge evident among younger voters, whose rates have always been significantly lower than turnout overall. They remain lower than among the elderly, but the gap has narrowed. Table 4.1 provides additional detail by age bands from 2014.

Estimating how Covid-19 and the associated changes to the election date, campaigning, and voting methods influenced turnout is beyond the reach of our NZES data, but we can provide a qualitative context.

Before the pandemic, there was limited theoretical literature on the effects of such a crisis (Scheller 2021). Cross-national analysis of participation in both national and local elections held between January and July 2020 suggested that turnout decline was most common. While in some cases falls in turnout were a result of electoral integrity concerns, in established democracies, public abstention was attributed to the health risks associated with Covid-19 (Garnett et al. 2022). Several other studies found that higher levels of deaths and infections in a polity were correlated with lower voter turnout, especially among older voters (Santana et al. 2020; Constantino et al. 2021; Picchio and Santolini 2021).

Table 4.1 Voter turnout by age, 2014–2020 (per cent)

Age band	Turnout as percentage of eligible population				Turnout as percentage of those enrolled			
	2014	2017	2020	Change	2014	2017	2020	Change
18–24	48.0	50.1	60.9	10.8	62.7	69.3	78.0	8.7
25–29	50.8	54.1	62.6	8.5	62.1	67.6	74.4	6.8
30–34	59.3	63.8	67.9	4.1	67.4	70.9	74.5	3.6
35–39	70.4	72.2	73.0	0.8	72.8	74.3	76.0	1.7
40–44	74.7	75.4	77.1	1.7	76.2	77.8	78.7	0.9
45–49	77.0	78.3	79.4	1.1	78.6	80.0	81.5	1.5
50–54	79.3	80.3	83.1	2.8	80.8	81.9	83.2	1.3
55–59	82.1	83.7	85.1	1.4	83.3	84.1	85.2	1.1
60–64	84.8	85.1	87.4	2.3	86.0	86.2	87.3	1.1
65–69	86.9	86.9	88.5	1.6	88.1	88.2	89.1	0.9
70+	81.7	84.8	85.3	0.5	85.8	86.3	86.8	0.5

Source: Electoral Commission (n.d.).

However, given few countries undertook an elimination approach, one would not expect such concerns to apply. In addition to alternative procedures put in place by the Electoral Commission detailed in the next section, there was no community transmission of Covid-19 in the three weeks leading up to the election. The risks associated with voting were thus comparatively low.

That said, the continued presence of alert levels, the closed border, managed isolation for arrivals, and social distancing, in addition to economic uncertainty, meant a sense of crisis remained. The literature on crises and voter turnout is useful here; building on Downs's (1957) rational choice framework, it proposes that external shocks could have a mobilising effect because they reinforce the feeling that elections are important and could provide an opportunity for more engagement between voters and politicians (Santana et al. 2020; Constantino et al. 2021). Assuming voters conduct a cost–benefit analysis of turning out to vote, the argument would follow that, if costs related to time, access, and knowledge are reduced, the benefits of a vote making a difference could increase (Riker and Ordeshook 1968). Or, to put it another way, the costs of not voting may be perceived as too high (Niemi 1976).

Maintaining electoral integrity during a time of crisis

Easing the pathway to casting a vote was already a priority in the minds of New Zealand's election administrators. New Zealand rates high on most indicators of the quality of democracy. As observed by one authoritative source, the country has 'a rich history of free and fair elections and the electoral process is characterised by a very high level of integrity' (Bertelsmann Stiftung 2022). New Zealand has an independent Electoral Commission. Over the past decade, it has pursued an apparently successful voter participation strategy, removing as many barriers as possible to the act of casting a ballot. This includes allowing electoral registration up to and including election day and extensive provision of advance voting facilities that were already in place before the pandemic. New Zealand's election administrators were able to face the challenge with a considerable stock of resources and experience and a relatively high level of public trust in politicians (Vowles 2022, 5).

There has been considerable discussion and dissection of electoral integrity in recent decades and the ways in which it should be defined and measured (Garnett et al. 2022; James 2020; Norris 2014). For the most part, such research has focussed on elections that have occurred, rather than those that have not. This is despite natural disasters and humanitarian crises causing election delays in the past (Hyde and Marinov 2012; James and Alihodzic 2020). The advent of Covid-19 has reignited scholarly interest in the impacts of natural disasters and humanitarian crises on the democratic process. Holding elections at a time when human life is at risk may necessitate a time-limited postponement, but the decision is not risk-free (James and Alihodzic 2020). Labelled the 'postponement paradox', such a delay could result in innovative alternatives but could also compromise electoral management quality, deliberation, contestation, and participation. There could be increasing distrust in electoral processes and democratic institutions exacerbated by the increase in executive powers to instigate emergency measures and the reduction in parliamentary oversight (see Rapeli and Saikkonen 2020; Landman and Splendore 2020; Gaskell and Stoker 2020; Flinders 2020).[1]

Prime Minister Jacinda Ardern justified her decision to delay New Zealand's 2020 general election by the need to ensure voter and candidate safety and to make it possible for parties to campaign fairly. The Electoral Commission was also keenly cognisant of the complexities and challenges that the initial Covid-19 state of emergency announcement and Alert Level 4 conditions presented to the conduct of the 2020 election.[2] If in-person voting was perceived as unsafe, and if alternative voting measures proved inadequate, this could have led to reduced turnout, a decline in confidence in the quality of election management, and potentially a questioning of the legitimacy of the election (Electoral Commission 2021; James and Alihodzic 2020).

To avoid these potentially harmful outcomes, the Electoral Commission immediately began reviewing the election planning process that was already under way. Advance voting in supermarket foyers had been introduced in 2017 and was to be expanded into other high-traffic locations. But this was potentially less viable if voters were required to socially distance or remain in their homes. While postal voting is used for local elections, introducing this option for national elections would have required a legislative change with a 75 per cent majority in parliament. Even if passed, it would have involved significant logistical investment. Nor was it deemed feasible to extend the system used by overseas voters who log in online and print out voting papers and a declaration, the completion of which requires an in-person witness. In addition, the commission had already identified the need for increased

---

1   We do not include a question on mistrust in the NZES, so have not canvassed the mistrust literature here.
2   Under Level 1 there were no domestic restrictions; Level 2 included some limits on gatherings and involved social distancing; Level 3 increased restrictions on gatherings and travel; while Level 4 allowed only essential travel and all gatherings were banned. Levels 3 and 4 are viewed as equivalent to a form of lockdown.

levels of security to prevent cyber and physical threats and disinformation campaigns, precluding consideration of electronic voting options, even had those been possible to implement in the time available.

In response to this multitude of challenges, the Electoral Commission made several changes that would enable in-person voting under Alert Level 2 conditions of group gathering limits and social distancing, while scaling up remote voting services for those most at risk of illness. Larger numbers of and more spacious voting places were provided. Education campaigns suggested that voters bring their own pen and vote close to home to avoid the need to cast a more time-consuming special vote outside their electorate. Single-use pens were also provided and the advance voting period was increased to include an additional weekend. In consultation with the Ministry of Health, a range of safety protocols were put in place, many of which were already familiar to New Zealanders. In addition, procedures were put in place to facilitate 340,000 remote voters, which involved temporary amendments to electoral regulations to allow voters to apply for remote voting by phone, and discretion for the commission to waive the need for a witness if home visits became high risk. An additional NZ$28 million was requested by the Minister of Justice to support these provisions, which supplemented a previously allocated $8 million.

These initiatives complemented two legal changes that were in train before Covid-19 but which also had the potential to expand enrolment and increase turnout. In June 2020, an amendment to the *Electoral (Registration of Sentenced Prisoners) Act* came into force and allowed for the re-enfranchisement of prisoners serving sentences of less than three years. Three months earlier, an amendment had been passed that enabled election day enrolment for voters in New Zealand. In 2017, the Electoral Commission processed more than 200,000 enrolment transactions during the advance voting period of which more than 94,000 were made in the last three days of the advance voting period.

Previous research has found that requiring enrolment well in advance of voting can pose a barrier for some groups, including young people who frequently move between addresses (Galicki 2018a, 2018b). In the case of New Zealand, previous enrolment settings had effectively made voting a two-step task that required planning, rather than a single task that could be done spontaneously. Alongside the law change, the commission increased its use of text messaging to reach people who had moved homes and made improvements to its digital enrolment processes. Digital enrolment transactions increased from 8 per cent in 2017 to 56 per cent in 2020, while 80,000 people used the single-step enrolment-voting option. This could have included about 5,000 newly eligible voters who turned 18 because of the delay.

One challenge remained unsolved, with some New Zealanders living overseas raising concerns about their ability to cast a vote in 2020. Citizens are eligible to vote if they have been in New Zealand within the three years before the election; for permanent residents, the requirement is within 12 months. The rationale behind these criteria is that returning to New Zealand within the time frame demonstrates a physical connection to the country. However, border closures in March 2020 meant the three-year eligibility period was reduced by seven months, and some overseas New Zealanders reported they could not enter the country due to travel restrictions, managed isolation availability, and costs, leading to them being ineligible to vote (Every Kiwi Vote Counts 2021). The need for a printer with scanning capacity was an additional barrier for overseas voters during the pandemic since those who did not have this equipment at home were unable to access it at another location due to restrictions. Disabled overseas voters faced additional barriers (Kelly-Costello 2021). Indeed, now travel restrictions have been removed there are concerns some citizens and permanent residents overseas who face financial, health, and logistical barriers to travelling home will be disenfranchised from voting in the 2023 general election. To address this, the Treasury has made a case for a temporary change to eligibility criteria for overseas voters in 2023.[3]

While the change of election date created some logistical challenges for the implementation of the election, the Electoral Commission has maintained it had a positive effect on the campaign to increase enrolments. The commission used the extra time to reconnect with community partners, undertake additional digital and in-person events, and design a digital strategy to communicate the location of new and existing voting places. The commission 'used data driven advertising displayed on 290 outdoor digital screens across the country and, on mobile phones, showing people how far they were from the nearest voting place on a map' (Electoral Commission 2021, 25). The aim of this campaign was to reach unenrolled voters and reduce the costs of searching for local voting places.

---

3   A number of the issues raised here are also being considered by an Independent Electoral Review Panel set up (in 2022) to review a large range of electoral law provisions.

In this way, the Electoral Commission intentionally sought to undertake critical initiatives to limit the risks to electoral integrity associated with postponement recommended by analysts (James and Alihodzic 2020). These initiatives included transparency and inclusiveness in the decision to postpone and in the procedures to be followed. The analysts recommended low-tech solutions like advance voting, along with maintaining access to quality information and ensuring opportunities for a diversity of viewpoints from trusted media sources. Not all initiatives were within the Electoral Commission's remit, but their proposed plans were deemed acceptable by the government and the parliamentary parties consulted in the process of implementation.

Election results, data from the Electoral Commission's post-election survey, and the NZES indicate that the quality and integrity of the 2020 election were maintained despite the pandemic, and the services delivered by the commission were well received by voters. The number of disallowed votes fell from 6 per cent in 2017 to 2 per cent in 2020 (11,000 votes, down from 27,000). Confidence in the Electoral Commission's fairness and impartiality increased to 87 per cent and 85 per cent, respectively—up from 78 per cent and 79 per cent in 2017 (Electoral Commission 2021). Alongside this, satisfaction with the privacy of the voting screen increased from 69 per cent rating it as excellent in 2017 to 74 per cent in 2020. Voting screens were placed further apart to comply with social distancing and this could have allayed some migrant communities' fears regarding secrecy and voting (Galicki 2018b). In 2020, Asian voters' satisfaction with the voting screens increased to 75 per cent—up from 59 per cent in 2017.

Extending the advance voting period resulted in a historically high 68 per cent of voters (almost two million) choosing this option. Figure 4.1 compares the accumulation of advance votes over the equivalent days of the three campaigns, pegged to the 2020 dates. This great increase in advance voting mitigated the public health risks by spreading out the numbers at voting places and had the added benefit of reducing the incidence of people having to queue: 31 per cent in 2017 to 22 per cent in 2020 (Kantar 2020). Uncertainty about possible changes to Covid-19 alert levels that could result in further restrictions and the perceived risk of getting sick influenced the significant increase in advance voting. Those aged over 60 were more likely to cast an early vote than younger age groups, but there was a pronounced increase in advance voting across all age groups.

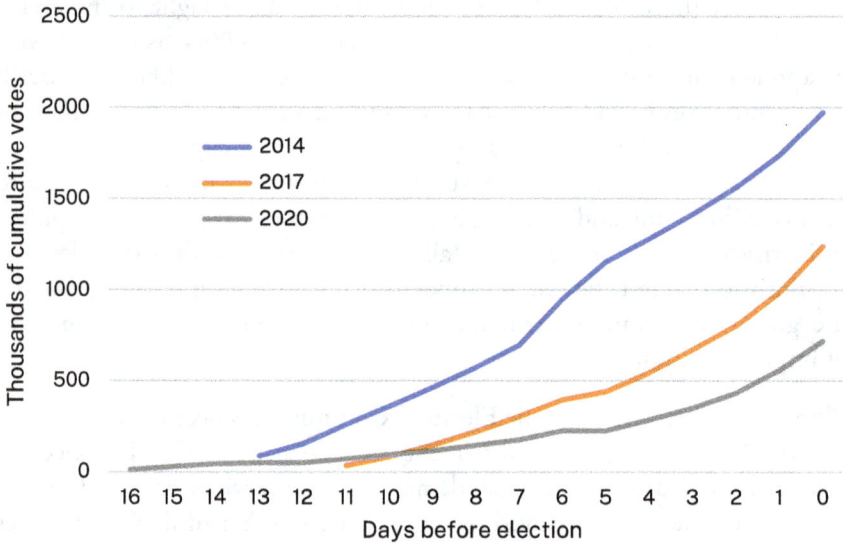

Figure 4.1 Cumulative advance votes in 2014, 2017, and 2020
Source: Electoral Commission (2022).

In its review of the 2020 election, the Electoral Commission recommended that there be legal recognition for advance voting with a minimum prescribed period, and that applying for a special vote by phone be an ongoing option. Digitising the processes associated with casting postal, dictation, and takeaway votes was also resolved to be a valuable next step to allow for scalability and greater efficiencies in future crises (Electoral Commission 2021, 2).

In 2021, New Zealand was held up as an example of how elections can be credibly managed under the restrictions imposed by Covid-19 in the International IDEA's Asia-Pacific report (International IDEA 2021). Many other countries in the region experienced democratic backsliding.

Indeed, satisfaction with democracy in New Zealand greatly increased between the two elections: from 64 per cent to 77 per cent among those in the 2017 to 2020 NZES panels, respectively. Satisfaction with democracy tends to be associated with those happy with the result of an election (Blais and Gélineau 2007). The big vote for Labour would therefore increase the number of those satisfied for that reason. More generally, satisfaction with democracy reflects how well people feel a democratic regime works in practice (Linde and Ekman 2003). Satisfaction with democracy also correlates with approval of the Covid-19 response, but causality probably runs in both directions. Cross-nationally, it is found most in countries where political institutions are transparent, responsive, and free of corruption (Foa et al. 2020). The increase in satisfaction with democracy in New Zealand in 2020 puts it at one of the highest levels in the world.

However, this increase in confidence was not reflected across a range of attitudes related to external political efficacy: the idea that politicians are responsive to popular opinion. Most of these showed little or no movement from their 2017 settings.[4] Figure 4.3 shows the comparison of agreement or disagreement with a very optimistic statement expressing maximum political trust, 'Most politicians can be trusted', comparing the mean scores of a five-point scale, adjusted to run between zero and one hundred. The small difference is entirely within confidence intervals. New Zealanders are relatively evenly split between trust and distrust of politicians—a more positive balance than in many other countries (Vowles 2022, 5).

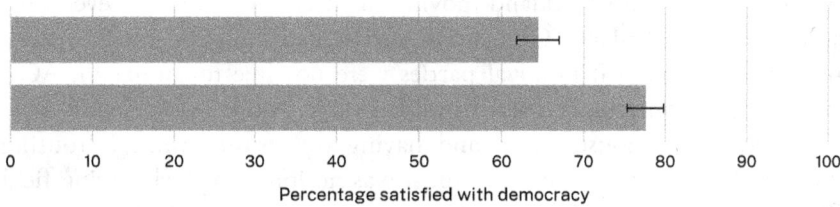

Figure 4.2 Change in satisfaction with democracy, 2017 and 2020
Note: The question was: 'How satisfied are you with the way democracy works in New Zealand?'
Source: Vowles et al. (2022a).

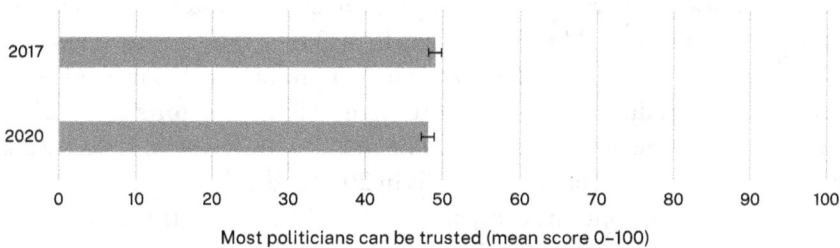

Figure 4.3 'Most politicians can be trusted', 2017 and 2020
Sources: Vowles et al. (2022a, 2022b).

---

4   These statements include 'Most MPs are out of touch with the rest of the country', on which agreement increased between 2017 and 2020; 'People like me don't have any say about what the government does', little or no difference; 'Voting makes a big difference/not any difference to what happens', no change; and 'I don't think politicians and public servants care what people like me think', no change.

While support for the Labour government's handling of the pandemic and trust in Ardern are likely to have enhanced turnout and satisfaction with democracy, this brief overview suggests adjustments to the electoral administration process did nothing to reduce and probably facilitated continued relative trust and confidence in, and satisfaction with, New Zealand's democratic process during Covid-19. But the underlying pattern of attitudes about politicians in general remained remarkably unaffected.

Campaigning and canvassing during Covid-19

Before the prime minister's announcement to delay the election, most political parties had begun to campaign around the country. However, the re-emergence of community transmission threw the election campaign into a kind of limbo, with Auckland moving to Alert Level 3, with Level 2 for the rest of New Zealand. Opposition parties had indicated their concern about a fair election if political parties were not free to campaign. ACT leader David Seymour claimed candidates and voters in Auckland were 'effectively under house arrest' and having the prime minister fronting daily Covid-19 press briefings meant it was no longer a level playing field (Curtin and Greaves 2020).

However, our analysis of NZES responses indicates that despite political parties being unable to hold political events such as campaign launches, meet-and-greets in malls or on the street, and door-to-door canvassing, they did not appear to improve their direct contact with voters electronically during the campaign. The data go back to 2011, the election at which turnout hit its lowest level in New Zealand's electoral history since universal suffrage was introduced. We see increasing mobilisation efforts up to 2017 and, apart from the new media, a decline in 2020. In Figure 4.3, we see big drops in contact via telephone and visits in 2020 and only marginal increases in the use of online options compared with 2017. From this evidence, it is hard to infer that the turnout increase had anything to do with parties' efforts to make campaign contacts; overall, they were lower than in 2017 and probably lower than in 2014 as well.

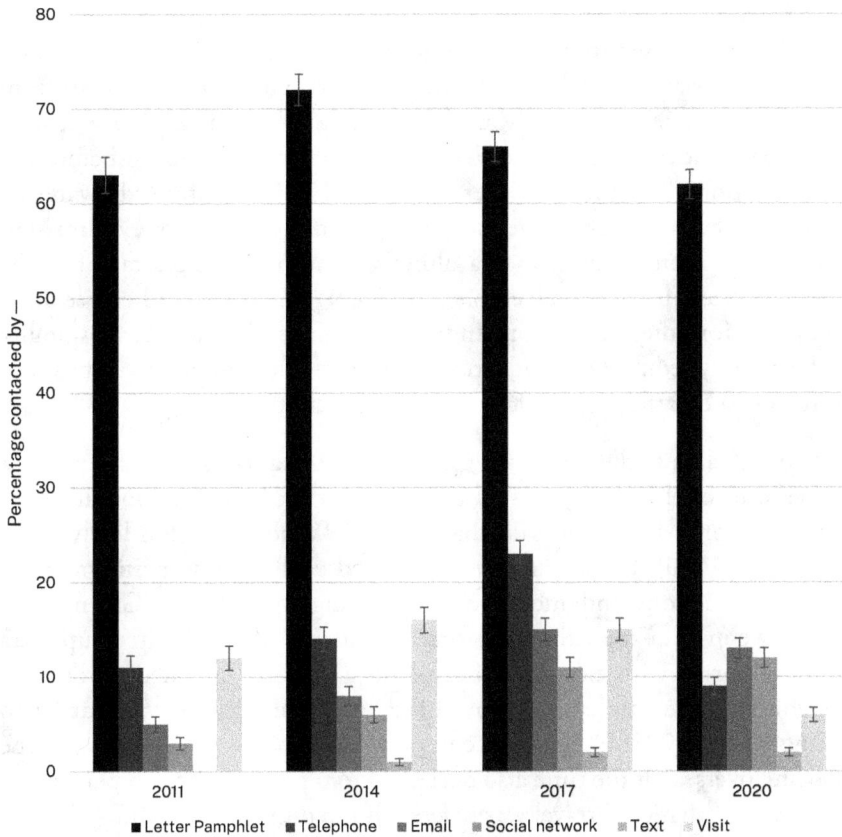

Figure 4.4 Campaign contacts by political parties, 2011–2020
Sources: Vowles et al. (2022a, 2022b).

The decline in phone contact could have been a result of Covid restrictions on volunteers working from call centres; letter or pamphlet contact also declined a little in 2020 (from 66 per cent to 62 per cent), perhaps because of reduced postal services (implemented before Covid-19). However, this form of contact remained the primary source for most respondents. Some pamphlets could have been dropped by party workers rather than through the mail. Nevertheless, despite the advent of lockdowns, there was no dramatic explosion in outreach by political parties to voters directly via non-traditional sources.[5]

---

5   We do not know whether parties were actively pursuing alternative online contact options that were not canvassed via the NZES.

The Electoral Commission's research indicates that awareness of electoral advertising increased from 52 per cent in 2017 to 72 per cent in 2020 and this increase was even more pronounced among younger voters—up from 43 per cent to 80 per cent (Kantar 2020). In addition, 27.5 per cent of NZES respondents visited the Electoral Commission's website before the 2020 election—up from 16.5 per cent in 2017. This improved awareness could have been a result of the increased presence of Electoral Commission advertising through social media although another possible factor is the sharp decrease in other advertising in 2020 that would otherwise have competed for voters' attention. Industries such as tourism and hospitality had markedly reduced their advertising given restrictions on travel, business activities, and gatherings (Nothling-Demmer 2020).

In New Zealand, the Electoral Commission's Kantar survey found that 15 per cent of eligible voters said that Covid-19 made them more likely to vote while only 1 per cent said that Covid-19 made them less likely to do so (Kantar 2020). Given there was a marked decline in domestic mobility due to restrictions and more people working from home (Green et al. 2020), we might expect that this forced reduction of activity freed up extra time to engage with election information and vote. In other words, it is possible that the pandemic removed the 'life getting in the way' barrier to voting (Galicki 2018b). The percentage of nonvoters who did not vote due to being overseas at the time also decreased to 0 per cent, from 5 per cent in 2017, as international travel was severely limited (Kantar 2020).

NZES data can help us here: according to these conjectures, interest in politics and attention to the media for political news should have increased. But interest in politics was, if anything, slightly down overall. A small 6–7-point shift from 'somewhat interested' to 'very interested' is slightly concealed in the summary data. As for attention to politics in the media, overall, it was slightly up in 2020. But these are small differences: given the rise in turnout, one would have expected more.

Finally, the high level of compliance with lockdown measures and high support for how the government handled the outbreak could have had a spill-over effect into a greater propensity towards following the law in general. While in 2017 only 17 per cent said that the reason for initially enrolling was 'you have to, it's the law', in 2020, 33 per cent gave this as the reason for enrolling (Kantar 2020). As Figure 4.5 reports, when asked, somewhat more than half of our participants said that for them voting was a duty, not just a choice. However, there is no comparable question from the 2017 study.

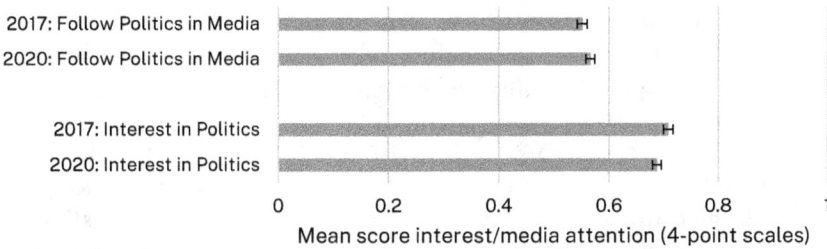

Figure 4.5 Interest in politics and attention to the media, 2017 and 2020
Sources: Vowles et al. (2022a, 2022b).

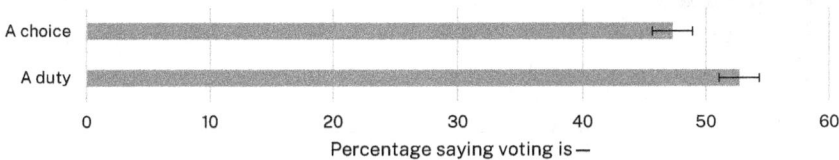

Figure 4.6 Voting as a choice or a duty
Source: Vowles et al. (2022a).

The mobilising effect of the referendums

In 2020, New Zealand's general election was accompanied by two high-profile referendum questions. One asked voters whether they endorsed the passage of the *End of Life Choice Act 2019*, which gave people with a terminal illness the option of requesting an assisted death. The second asked voters whether they supported the proposed Cannabis Legalisation and Control Bill, which if passed would legalise the recreational use of cannabis. While the end-of-life referendum passed easily with 65.1 per cent in favour of the Act coming into force, the cannabis referendum received only 48.4 per cent support (Oldfield and Greaves 2021).

As noted earlier, there is evidence that high-profile referendums concurrent with general representative elections can increase voter turnout. The Kantar post-election survey indicated some support for this argument, with 8 per cent of young people who voted in the general election saying they voted only because of the referendums, but the question did not specify which referendum (Kantar 2020). As it is unlikely that young people were highly motivated by a question that was of much more interest to the elderly, one can infer they were more interested in the choice proposed on cannabis.

Indeed, young people are more likely than older people to be cannabis users (Ministry of Health 2015). Most polling taken on the issue found they were more likely to support cannabis legalisation (for example, Vowles 2020).

The cannabis referendum was also highly significant to Māori due to the disproportionate harm existing cannabis laws have on them. Experts argued that legalising cannabis would result in fewer Māori arrests but legalisation would have to be balanced with support measures and regulation (NZ Drug Foundation 2020). Immediately before the referendum, support for cannabis law reform was significantly higher among Māori than among the general population. Opinion polls conducted in 2019 and 2020 indicated about 75 per cent of Māori supported cannabis legalisation (Dempster and Norris 2022).

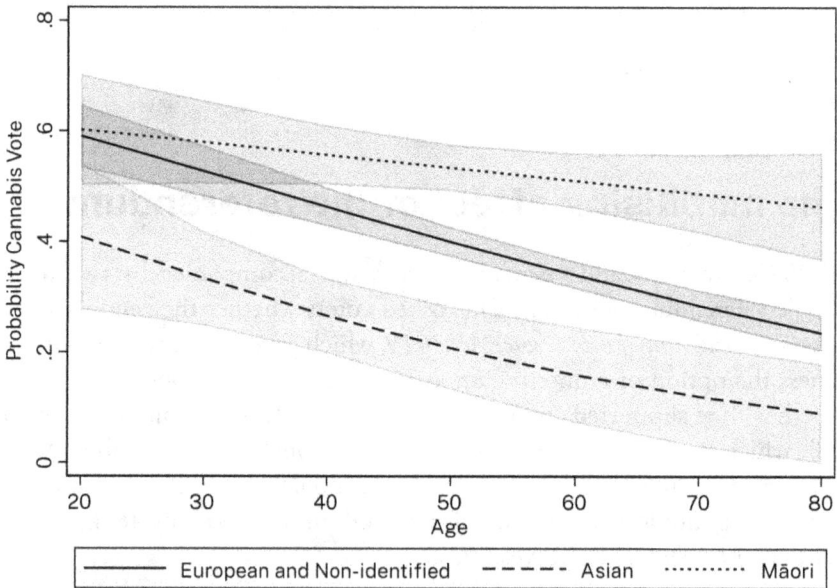

Figure 4.7 The probability of voting in favour of the legalisation of cannabis by age and ethnicity
Source: Appendix Table A4.1: Model 2.

Appendix Table A4.1 reports analysis of the two referendum votes by age and main ethnic group. Figure 4.7 displays the estimates derived from the cannabis model. The end-of-life referendum vote was only weakly affected by age and ethnicity; indeed, age had no significant effect on the vote. Asian and Pasifika people were somewhat more likely to oppose the introduction of assisted death for people who qualified by way of a terminal illness.

Age and ethnicity were much more associated with the cannabis vote. Ethnicity is here defined by priority, removing multiple identifications to simplify the analysis. All Māori identifiers are coded as Māori, and Pasifika who do not identify with Māori are coded as Pasifika, disregarding any other non-Māori identifications. Those who identify with an Asian ethnicity are coded similarly, leaving a residual group most of whom are of European ethnicity. While policy-relevant research in New Zealand is moving away from this approach, if used with caution, it is recognised as being useful for understanding the relationship between ethnicity and outcomes (Boven et al. 2020).

The number of Pasifika in our sample is too small for statistical significance although their opinions seem to have been closer to those of Māori than to the European/other population. Young Māori and young people in the European/residual group are equally likely to have favoured legalisation—at about 60 per cent. Asian identifiers are much less likely to have supported legalisation, although their young were more prone to do so, with about 40 per cent voting in favour. Following the age gradient, age had little effect on Māori, who remained in favour of legalisation into older age groups. But older people in the Asian and European/residual groups were much less likely to support legalisation, with the oldest being particularly opposed. Here is some further prima facie evidence that youth turnout could have been affected by the cannabis referendum.

However, inferring whether the cannabis referendum enhanced turnout or not is more difficult than it might at first seem. We can gauge interest in the referendums from those who visited a website established by the Electoral Commission to provide basic information. But this means we cannot distinguish between the effects of the two referendums. However, no one has suggested a turnout effect for the end-of-life referendum. There is no obvious reason why there should have been one. It was much less sharply contested and the practical benefits of change were relevant to only a small minority—although for those affected it was very important.

Of more concern, a simple correlation between those reporting visiting the referendum's website and electoral turnout proves little or nothing; many who visited were intending to vote anyway. We must apply multivariate regression analysis, allowing us to control for other factors that could dispose people towards voting: age, income, ethnic identity, previous vote, closeness to a political party, and whether people feel there is a duty to vote or not (for more details, see Appendix Table A4.2).

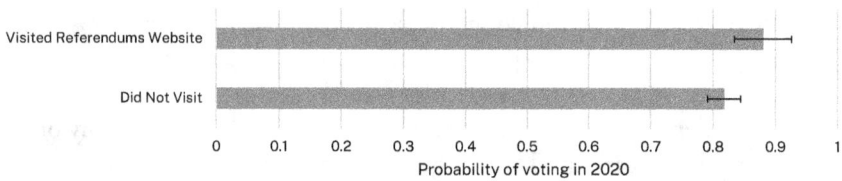

Figure 4.8 The effect of interest in the referendums on turnout in 2020
Source: Estimates derived from Appendix Table A4.2, net of the effects of all other variables in the model.

As displayed in Figure 4.8, estimates derived from this model tell us that people who visited the referendum's website were 6 per cent more likely to vote than those who did not, taking all these other matters into account. This is just significant at the 95 per cent level—in 19 of 20 possible samples we could hypothetically have taken—and the confidence intervals only very marginally overlap.

One further problem remains. Methodologically, whether people visited the site is a 'treatment effect'. Statistically speaking, such effects should be random, not intentional, as such a visit clearly was. A possible problem of self-selection bias towards confirmation of the effect on voting or not voting remains, even despite the controls in the regression. Fortunately, a statistical test is available to check whether such a bias remains: a recursive bivariate probit model, which tests two models—one with the visit as outcome variable and the other on voting or not (Marra and Radice 2011). Residuals from these models did not significantly correlate, indicating no significant selection bias. The estimate from our model can stand.

Our data indicate that nearly half of those aged between 18 and 24 visited the referendum's website, compared with 15 per cent or fewer of those aged 70 and over. However, there was no apparent difference in people's propensity to vote by age associated with visiting the website. However, visiting the site did enhance turnout, and it was visited much more by the young than the elderly. About 26 per cent of the NZES participants visited the referendum's site, but across the whole electorate, this means that the overall turnout effect could have been at best a modest 1.5 per cent. If there was a strong youth mobilisation in tandem with the cannabis referendum, this seems small. However, the cannabis referendum could have motivated young people to vote regardless of whether they visited the referendum's website.

Conclusion

This chapter proposed three possible explanations for the turnout increase at the 2020 general election. The first rested on the high level of electoral integrity and the resources of trust and confidence in New Zealand's democratic process, and in its Electoral Commission. This made it possible for politicians and administrators to rise to the challenge of the Covid-19 crisis, taking the postponed election in their stride. We provide a wealth of qualitative data and secondary survey analysis from the Electoral Commission to underpin this claim. Voters had no reason to fear catching Covid-19 when they went to vote. The government's elimination strategy had reduced the risk to a microscopic level and the provision of extensive advance voting and the relative absence of crowding in voting places reduced it even further. But if this claim is convincing as an explanation of an absence of turnout decline, it does not work so well for its increase. Levels of trust in politicians remained much as they were in 2017: relatively high by international standards, although far from perfect.

The second potential explanation posits that the election 'mattered', reinforcing perceptions that elections are important, and encouraging greater engagement between voters and politicians. However, such engagement did not happen directly between parties and voters; campaign contacts were lower than at previous elections and small increases in electronic engagement do not appear to have filled the gap. High levels of compliance with government restrictions could have encouraged a greater sense of collective solidarity. Restrictions could have given people more time to think about politics and the democratic process and engage with the process themselves through the mainstream and social media. Some evidence from Electoral Commission data suggests that a significant number of people thought their Covid-19 experience had made them more likely to vote. However, small shifts in attention to the media and interest in politics do not support the idea that engagement and interest increased significantly.

The NZES dataset is better able to test the third potential explanation: that of a referendum effect. Visiting the referendum's website did show a significant effect, even after controls were applied and with a more robust statistical test for a possible selection effect. Political efficacy and agreement with a civic norm underpinning the vote also play a large part. However, political efficacy, as measured by perceptions of the effectiveness of the vote, did not shift between 2017 and 2020. Neither interest in politics nor attention to the media has significant effects on the model when added to alternative versions. On balance, the best evidence is for our third explanation, although a broader engagement is not entirely ruled out in our findings.

As it grew near, what this would mean for the election in 2023 was a matter for speculation. If a sense of crisis prompted engagement in 2020, this was lacking in 2023. Moreover, there was no high-profile referendum to attract young and new voters. Polling in late 2022 hinted at a competitive election in 2023, which could have boosted turnout at the margins. Research indicates that competitiveness at the previous election has a lagged effect on turnout (Vowles 2014). The 2020 election was spectacularly uncompetitive. After three elections at which turnout has increased, the 2023 election was most likely to see a regression towards the mean. There remained a hope—strong among youthful social movement activists—that the young are the vanguard of progressive change, that they will continue to vote in larger numbers, and that a new generation will enrich the political process and underpin significant advances in social justice and the fight against climate change. No one can deny the importance of such aspirations.

References

Bertelsmann Stiftung. 2022. 'New Zealand.' *Sustainable Governance Indicators*. Gütersloh: Bertelsmann Stiftung. Available from: www.sgi-network.org/2020/New_Zealand/Quality_of_Democracy.

Blais, A., and F. Gélineau. 2007. 'Winning, Losing and Satisfaction with Democracy.' *Political Studies* 55: 425–41. doi.org/10.1111/j.1467-9248.2007.00659.x.

Boven, N., D. Exeter, A. Sporle, and N. Shackleton. 2020. 'The Implications of Different Ethnicity Categorisation Methods for Understanding Outcomes and Developing Policy in New Zealand.' *Kōtuitui: New Zealand Journal of Social Sciences Online* 15(1): 123–39. doi.org/10.1080/1177083X.2019.1657912.

Childers, M., and M. Binder. 2016. 'The Differential Effects of Initiatives and Referenda in the United States, 1890–2008.' *Chapman Law Review* 19(1): 35–59. Available from: www.chapman.edu/law/_files/publications/Volume%2019/clr-19-childers-binder.pdf.

Citizens Advice Bureau (CAB). 2020. *Face to Face with Digital Exclusion: A CAB Spotlight Report into the Impacts of Digital Public Services on Inclusion and Wellbeing*. February. Wellington: Citizens Advice Bureaux New Zealand. Available from: www.cab.org.nz/assets/Documents/Face-to-Face-with-Digital-Exclusion-/FINAL_CABNZ-report_Face-to-face-with-Digital-Exclusion.pdf.

Constantino, S.M., A.D. Cooperman, and T.M.Q. Moreira. 2021. 'Voting in a Global Pandemic: Assessing Dueling Influences of Covid-19 on Turnout.' *Social Science Quarterly* 102(5): 2210–35. doi.org/10.1111/ssqu.13038.

Curtin, J., and L. Greaves. 2020. 'Jacinda Ardern Delays New Zealand's Election to Allow Conventional Campaigning—But Where Are Voters Really Getting Information?' *The Conversation*, 17 August. Available from: theconversation.com/jacinda-ardern-delays-new-zealands-election-to-allow-conventional-campaigning-but-where-are-voters-really-getting-information-144560.

Dempster, C., and A.N. Norris. 2022. 'The 2020 Cannabis Referendum: Māori Voter Support, Racialized Policing, and the Criminal Justice System.' *Decolonization of Criminology and Justice* 4(1): 57–80. doi.org/10.24135/dcj.v4i1.40.

Downs, A. 1957. 'An Economic Theory of Political Action in a Democracy.' *Journal of Political Economy* 65(2): 135–50. www.jstor.org/stable/1827369.

Electoral Commission. n.d. *New Zealand Election Results*. Wellington: Electoral Commission New Zealand. Available from: elections.nz/stats-and-research/participation-in-voting/.

Electoral Commission. 2021. *Report of the Electoral Commission on the 2020 General Election and Referendums*. May. Wellington: Electoral Commission New Zealand. Available from: elections.nz/assets/2020-general-election/Report-of-the-Electoral-Commission-on-the-2020-General-Election-and-referendums.pdf.

Electoral Commission. 2022. 'Advance Voting Statistics for the 2020 General Election.' In *2020 General Election and Referendums*. Wellington: Electoral Commission New Zealand. Available from: elections.nz/democracy-in-nz/historical-events/2020-general-election-and-referendums/advance-voting-statistics-for-the-2020-general-election/.

Every Kiwi Vote Counts. 2021. 'Submission to the Inquiry into the 2020 General Election and Referendums.' 5 July. Wellington: New Zealand Parliament. Available from: www.parliament.nz/resource/en-NZ/53SCJU_EVI_104172_JU1876/dabc0c8309f1d3e78bb37c63989d75547859fee2.

Flinders, M. 2020. 'Gotcha! Coronavirus, Crises and the Politics of Blame Games.' *Political Insight* 11(2): 22–25. doi.org/10.1177/2041905820933371.

Foa, R.S., A. Klassen, M. Slade, A. Rand, and R. Collins. 2020. *The Global Satisfaction with Democracy Report 2020*. January. Cambridge: Centre for the Future of Democracy. Available from: www.cam.ac.uk/system/files/report2020_003.pdf.

Franklin, M. 2004. *Voter Turnout and the Dynamics of Electoral Competition in Established Democracies Since 1945.* Cambridge: Cambridge University Press. doi.org/10.1017/CBO9780511616884.

Galicki, C. 2018a. 'Barriers to Voting and the Cost of Voting among Low Socioeconomic, Young and Migrant Voters in New Zealand.' *Political Science* 70(1): 41–57. doi.org/10.1080/00323187.2018.1473014.

Galicki, C. 2018b. 'The Costs of Voting: Barriers to Voting among Young, Low-Socioeconomic and Migrant Voters in New Zealand and Sweden.' PhD thesis, University of Auckland. researchspace.auckland.ac.nz/handle/2292/45168.

Garnett, H.A., T.S. James, and M. MacGregor. 2022. *Electoral Integrity Global Report 2019–2021.* The Electoral Integrity Project, Royal Military College of Canada/Queen's University and the University of East Anglia. Available from: www.electoralintegrityproject.com/globalreport2019-2021.

Gaskell, J., and G. Stoker. 2020. 'Centralized or Decentralized: Which Governance Systems are Having a "Good" Pandemic?' *Democratic Theory* 7(2): 33–40. doi.org/10.3167/dt.2020.070205.

Green, N., D. Tappin, and T. Bentley. 2020. 'Working from Home Before, During and After the Covid-19 Pandemic: Implications for Workers and Organisations.' *New Zealand Journal of Employment Relations* 45(2): 5–16. doi.org/10.24135/nzjer.v45i2.19.

Hyde, S.D., and N. Marinov. 2012. 'Which Elections Can Be Lost?' *Political Analysis* 20(2): 191–210. doi.org/10.1093/pan/mpr040.

International Institute for Democracy and Electoral Assistance (International IDEA). 2021. *The State of Democracy in Asia and the Pacific 2021: Old Resilience, New Challenges.* Stockholm: International IDEA. Available from: www.idea.int/publications/catalogue/state-democracy-asia-and-pacific-2021.

James, T.S. 2020. *Comparative Electoral Management: Performance, Networks, and Instruments.* New York, NY: Routledge.

James, T.S., and S. Alihodzic. 2020. 'When Is It Democratic to Postpone an Election? Elections During Natural Disasters, COVID-19, and Emergency Situations.' *Election Law Journal: Rules, Politics, and Policy* 19(3): 344–62. doi.org/10.1089/elj.2020.0642.

Kantar. 2020. *Report into the 2020 General Election: Prepared by Kantar New Zealand for the Electoral Commission.* December. Auckland: Kantar New Zealand. Available from: elections.nz/assets/2020-general-election/Voter-and-non-voter-satisfaction-survey-2020.pdf.

Kelly-Costello, A. 2021. 'Submission to the Inquiry into the 2020 General Election and Referendums.' 6 May. Wellington: New Zealand Parliament. Available from: www.parliament.nz/resource/en-NZ/53SCJU_EVI_104172_JU1231/d3b3353 f90a7e3a068d07c6caeb750731634436c.

Knight, D. 2021. 'New Zealand: 2020 General Election—Not An Ordinary Election, Not An Ordinary Time.' *Public Law: The Constitutional and Administrative Law of the Commonwealth*: 439–42. doi.org/10.25455/wgtn.21753323.

Landman, T., and L. Splendore. 2020. 'Pandemic Democracy: Elections and COVID-19.' *Journal of Risk Research* 23(7–8): 1060–66. doi.org/10.1080/13669877.2020.1765003.

Linde, J., and J. Ekman. 2003. 'Satisfaction with Democracy: A Note on a Frequently Used Indicator in Comparative Politics.' *European Journal of Political Research* 42: 391–408. doi.org/10.1111/1475-6765.00089.

Marra, G., and R. Radice. 2011. 'Estimation of a Semiparametric Recursive Bivariate Probit Model in the Presence of Endogeneity.' *The Canadian Journal of Statistics* 39(2): 259–79. doi.org/10.1002/cjs.10100.

Ministry of Health. 2015. *Cannabis Use 2012/13: New Zealand Health Survey*. Wellington: New Zealand Government.

Ministry of Health. 2023. *Covid-19 Data and Statistics*. Wellington: New Zealand Government. Available from: covid19.govt.nz/news-and-data/covid-19-data-and-statistics/#covid-19-cases.

Ministry of Justice. 2022. *Regulatory Impact Statement: Temporary Change to Eligibility Criteria for Overseas Voters for the 2023 General Election*. 5 April. Wellington: New Zealand Government. Available from: www.treasury.govt.nz/sites/default/files/2022-07/ria-justice-tcec-apr22.pdf.

New Zealand Doctor. 2022. *Timeline: Coronavirus*. Auckland: The Health Media Ltd. Available from: www.nzdoctor.co.nz/timeline-coronavirus.

New Zealand Parliament. 2021. *Inquiry into the 2020 General Election and Referendums: Interim Report of the Justice Committee*. Wellington: New Zealand Parliament. Available from: www.parliament.nz/en/pb/sc/business-before-committees/document/INQ_104172/inquiry-into-the-2020-general-election-and-referendums.

Niemi, R.G. 1976. 'Costs of Voting and Nonvoting.' *Public Choice* 27(Fall): 115–19.

Norris, P. 2014. *Why Electoral Integrity Matters*. Cambridge: Cambridge University Press. doi.org/10.1017/CBO9781107280861.

Nothling-Demmer, D. 2020. 'Beyond 2020: Media and Advertising Spend Outlook.' *New Zealand Marketing Magazine*, 4 December. Available from: nzmarketingmag.co.nz/beyond-2020-media-and-advertising-spend-outlook/.

NZ Drug Foundation. 2020. 'A Māori Perspective on the Cannabis Referendum.' News, 13 August. Wellington: NZ Drug Foundation. Available from: www.drug foundation.org.nz/news-media-and-events/a-maori-perspective-on-the-cannabis-referendum/.

Oldfield, L., and L. Greaves. 2021. 'The 2020 Cannabis and Euthanasia Referendums.' In *Politics in a Pandemic: Jacinda Ardern and New Zealand's 2020 Election*, edited by S. Levine, 263–67. Wellington: Te Herenga Waka University Press.

Picchio, M., and R. Santolini. 2021. 'The Covid-19 Pandemic's Effects on Voter Turnout.' *European Journal of Political Economy* 73(June): 102161. doi.org/10.1016/j.ejpoleco.2021.102161.

Rapeli, L., and I. Saikkonen. 2020. 'How Will the COVID-19 Pandemic Affect Democracy?' *Democratic Theory* 7(2): 25–32. doi.org/10.3167/dt.2020.070204.

Santana, A., J. Rama, and F.C. Bértoa. 2020. 'The Coronavirus Pandemic and Voter Turnout: Addressing the Impact of COVID-19 on Electoral Participation.' *SocArXiv*, 18 November. doi.org/10.31235/osf.io/3d4ny.

Scheller, D.S. 2021. 'Pandemic Primary: The Interactive Effects of COVID-19 Prevalence and Age on Voter Turnout.' *Journal of Elections, Public Opinion and Parties* 31(S1): 180–90. doi.org/10.1080/17457289.2021.1924728.

Smith, D.A., and C.J. Tolbert. 2004. *Educated by Initiative: The Effects of Direct Democracy on Citizens and Political Organizations in the American States*. Ann Arbor, MI: University of Michigan Press. doi.org/10.3998/mpub.11467.

StatsNZ. 2019. *2018 Census Totals by Topic—National Highlights*. Wellington: New Zealand Government. Available from: www.stats.govt.nz/information-releases/2018-census-totals-by-topic-national-highlights-updated/.

Vowles, J. 2014. 'Down, Down, Down: Turnout from 1946 to 2011.' In *The New Electoral Politics in New Zealand: The Significance of the 2011 Election*, edited by J. Vowles, 53–74. Wellington: Institute for Governance and Policy Studies.

Vowles, J. 2020. 'The Numbers Suggest the Campaign for Cannabis Reform in NZ Will Outlive the Generations That Voted Against It.' *The Conversation*, 16 November. Available from: theconversation.com/the-numbers-suggest-the-campaign-for-cannabis-reform-in-nz-will-outlive-the-generations-that-voted-against-it-150073.

Vowles, J. 2022. 'Authoritarianism and Mass Political Preferences in Times of COVID-19: The 2020 New Zealand General Election.' *Frontiers in Political Science* 4: 885299. doi.org/10.3389/fpos.2022.885299.

Vowles, J., F. Barker, M. Krewel, J. Hayward, J. Curtin, L. Greaves, and L. Oldfield. 2022a. *2020 New Zealand Election Study*. [Online]. ADA Dataverse, V3. doi.org/10.26193/BPAMYJ.

Vowles, J., K. McMillan, F. Barker, J. Curtin, J. Hayward, L. Greaves, and C. Crothers. 2022b. *2017 New Zealand Election Study*. [Online]. ADA Dataverse, V3. doi.org/10.26193/28JJFB.

Appendix 4.1

Table A4.1 Age and ethnicity and the two referendum votes

Logistic regression	(1) Cannabis	(2) Cannabis	(3) End of life	(4) End of life
Age	−0.023***	−0.026***	−0.003	−0.004
	(0.003)	(0.003)	(0.003)	(0.003)
Asian	−0.805***	−0.604	−0.685***	−1.025**
	(0.186)	(0.531)	(0.181)	(0.480)
Pasifika	0.153	−0.852	−1.113***	−0.772
	(0.349)	(0.843)	(0.349)	(0.873)
Māori	0.440***	−0.281	−0.250**	−0.463
	(0.123)	(0.376)	(0.120)	(0.368)
Asian*Age		−0.007		0.008
		(0.013)		(0.010)
Pasifika*Age		0.025		−0.009
		(0.018)		(0.018)
Māori*Age		0.016**		0.005
		(0.007)		(0.007)
Constant	0.748***	0.883***	0.623***	0.675***
	(0.156)	(0.176)	(0.164)	(0.188)
Observations	3,618	3,618	3,618	3,618
Pseudo r²	0.0424	0.0449	0.0124	0.0128
ll	−2,333	−2,327	−2,410	−2,409

*** p < 0.01

** p < 0.05

* p < 0.1

Note: Robust standard errors in parentheses.

Table A4.2 Identifying the effects of interest in the referendums on turnout

Logistic regression	Voted	Logistic regression	Voted
Voted in 2017	0.859***	University degree (no degree)	0.084
	(0.234)		(0.246)
Age	0.026***	Voting is a choice, not a duty	−0.940***
	(0.006)		(0.222)
Closeness to party	0.174	Visited referendums site	0.648**
	(0.109)		(0.320)
Household income	0.005**	No internet access	−0.632*
	(0.002)		(0.379)
Assets	−0.085	Visited no site for information	−0.134
	(0.080)		(0.256)
Female (male)	0.114	Voting makes a difference	0.383***
	(0.216)		(0.078)
(European/other)		Visited party or candidate site	0.935***
Asian	−0.335		(0.314)
	(0.340)	Constant	−1.817***
Pasifika	−1.508**		(0.516)
	(0.587)	Observations	3,301
Māori	−0.385	Pseudo r²	0.248
	(0.237)	ll	−1,105

*** p < 0.01

** p < 0.05

* p < 0.1

Notes: Robust standard errors in parentheses. The challenge in the analysis reported here is to test the possible effect in robust fashion without overloading the model. Several other control variables were added and discarded because they were not statistically significant, did not add appreciably to the fit of the model, and had no effect on the 'treatment'. These included interest in politics, the extent of following politics in the media, satisfaction with democracy, trust in politicians, trust in Jacinda Ardern, approval or disapproval of the Covid-19 response, and emotions about the Covid-19 response. While several of these are positively correlated with the choice to vote or not, their effects are absorbed by a combination of habitual voting (voted in 2017), civic norms (voting is a choice or a duty), and political efficacy (voting makes a difference).

5

Resisting the Red Wave? The Māori Party's return to parliament

Lara Greaves, Ella Morgan, and Janine Hayward

On election night 2020, voters watched as a so-called red wave of support for Labour swept across many safe National seats (RNZ 2020). The final election result led to the first single-party majority government since the introduction of the mixed-member proportional (MMP) electoral system in 1996—a feat very few predicted in the leadup to the election (1News 2020). While the election night coverage focussed on the historic Labour victory, Māori Party candidate for Waiariki, Rawiri Waititi, celebrated his fortieth birthday, joining in a televised rendition of 'Happy Birthday to You' with musician Rob Ruha. It was a birthday Waititi will never forget; as the evening progressed, his whānau (family) and supporters watched the gap between him and Labour Party incumbent Tāmati Coffey narrow, and then build in Waititi's favour. A tense wait for the special votes over the following weeks confirmed that Waititi had won the electorate and the Māori Party had maintained its 2017 share of the overall party vote at 1.2 per cent. As a result, wahine (woman) Māori Party co-leader Debbie Ngarewa-Packer joined Waititi in the fifty-third parliament. Waiariki was the only electorate lost by a Labour incumbent in 2020.

The victory by the Māori Party (Te Pāti Māori) in Waiariki was significant not only in the context of Labour's historic win, but also because it returned the party to parliament. Te Pāti Māori had first entered parliament in 2004 when former Labour MP Tariana Turia won the Te Tai Hauāuru by-election after walking away from the Labour Party over the *Foreshore and Seabed Act 2004*. Turia and others subsequently established the Māori Party (Godfery 2015). In 2005, the Māori Party won four of the seven Māori electorates, with just over 2 per cent of the party vote. In 2008, the party had its best result, winning five of the Māori electorates, with its highest percentage of the party vote, at almost 2.5 per cent. The party supported the National-led coalition from 2008 to 2017, during which time its popularity declined, from winning three electorates in 2011 to just one in 2014. In 2017, the Māori Party found itself out of parliament entirely (Greaves and Hayward 2020). The win in Waiariki in 2020 was unexpected; even Māori Party co-leader John Tamihere had lamented that 2020 was not going to be their year and that he had set his hopes on 2023 for a Māori Party return (Manch 2020).

How did the Māori Party get back into parliament in 2020, particularly when the Labour Party was so dominant? In this chapter, we use data from the NZES to test four possible explanations. We base these on speculation in the media at the time of the election in conjunction with existing scholarship from previous elections. First, had Labour lost Māori support over its handling of issues such as the situation at Ihumātao and Covid-19? Second, did Māori voters perceive Te Pāti Māori's 'unapologetically Māori' campaign as a shift to the left, thereby competing more with Labour ideologically? Third, did the new Māori Party leaders win the party greater support, despite the popularity of Labour leader Jacinda Ardern? Fourth, did the Māori Party's campaign for the electorate vote and efforts to contact Māori roll voters boost its election result? Our analysis of these questions reveals, overall, that Te Pāti Māori is building its relationship with Māori on the Māori roll. Even in the face of Labour's historic victory, Te Pāti Māori held or increased its voter support. Before turning to these questions, we describe the election study, explain how we define Māori voters, and provide an overview of the election results in the Māori electorates.

Rangahau Tōrangapū o Aotearoa/ the New Zealand Election Study

Like other chapters in this book, we draw on data from the NZES. For the 2020 election, we trialled new design elements that were more inclusive of Māori. The survey was available in te reo Māori (the Māori language) online, the survey logo was updated to include the te reo Māori name 'Rangahau Tōrangapū o Aotearoa', and a te reo Māori coversheet was added. All translations were provided by Hēmi Kelly, an expert translator and creator of the 'Everyday Māori' initiatives. As the NZES had done in 2005, the survey included additional questions specifically for Māori participants relating to, for example, identity, cultural connection, Treaty settlements, and voting in *rūnanga* (*iwi*/tribal council) elections.[1] In addition, following past NZES waves, we 'oversampled' Māori voters by sending more surveys to that group than their representation in the population to ensure sufficient numbers to make robust conclusions.[2] The final response rate for voters of Māori descent was 19.9 per cent, which compares favourably with similar studies (for a discussion, see Greaves et al. 2020).

Voters of Māori descent have a choice to enrol to vote on either the Māori roll or the general roll. Those who choose the Māori roll (currently 52 per cent of the Māori descent population; Electoral Commission 2018) vote in the Māori electorates. Recognising this, we took several steps to identify Māori voters and construct categories for data analysis. We have discussed elsewhere the complexity of Māori identity and the minimum level of acknowledgement required to register on the Māori roll (Greaves and Hayward 2020). The *Electoral Act 1993* defines a Māori elector as 'a person of the Māori race of New Zealand; and includes any descendant of such a person'. We drew descent from the roll: 33.4 per cent of the total NZES sample said they were of Māori ancestry on the roll; 66.6 per cent did not.[3] Identifying as Māori is a fluid process, so we took the broadest possible definition of Māori for our analyses: if someone recognised their *whakapapa* (Māori descent) on *either* the roll *or* the survey, we counted them as a Māori voter. Overall, we considered 35.1 per cent of the sample to be Māori voters (*n* = 1,310—that is, of Māori descent and thus able to register on the Māori roll).

---

1   In 1999, the NZES commissioned a Māori Election Study using face-to-face interviews.

2   Oversamples date from 1996 and, until 2020, were of those on the Māori roll only. The 1999 main dataset had no oversample, but Māori respondents were added from the Māori Election Study.

3   We also asked all NZES participants the same ancestry question in the survey: 33.4 per cent of participants said 'yes' to being of Māori descent, 64.1 per cent said 'no', and 2.4 per cent 'don't know'. However, these survey responses did not perfectly align with the electoral roll. For example, we found that 1.9 per cent of participants had said they were Māori on the roll but did not say they were Māori in the descent question in the survey (2.5 per cent went the other way). Of those who said they 'don't know' about descent in the survey, 77.5 per cent were on the general roll and 22.5 per cent were on the Māori roll.

As with our analysis of the 2017 general election (Greaves and Hayward 2020), we split voters into three categories for comparison:

1. Māori on the Māori roll (n = 603)
2. Māori on the general roll (n = 707)
3. all non-Māori (n = 2,420).[4]

We now provide an overview of the key election events and results in the Māori electorates, before moving on to explore the NZES data.

The Māori electorate results in 2020

The Māori Party won only the Waiariki electorate in 2020 but, before the election, it appeared that three of the seven Māori electorates were potentially winnable by Māori Party candidates: Waiariki, Te Tai Hauāuru, and Tāmaki Makaurau (Te Ao 2020a, 2020c, 2020d; Neilson 2020a). We discuss the results of these three electorates to set the scene for our subsequent analysis of the broader dynamics between the Māori and Labour parties.

The Waiariki electorate encompassing Tauranga, Whakatāne, Rotorua, and Taupō was previously held by former Māori Party leader Te Ururoa Flavell (2005–17). As the 2020 campaign unfolded, it proved to be a close race between incumbent Labour MP Tāmati Coffey and Rawiri Waititi of the Māori Party. Waititi had experience campaigning in Waiariki, having contested the seat for Labour in 2014 before announcing his support for the Māori Party in 2016. Several electorate-specific issues were highlighted during the campaign that could have impacted on the choices of Waiariki voters, although it is difficult to test whether this is the case due to small sample sizes (90 NZES participants were enrolled in Waiariki). At debates and *hui* (gatherings), the issue of overlapping Treaty claims between the Tauranga Moana Iwi Collective and Pare Hauraki Collective was often a central topic of discussion. Tauranga Moana have criticised the settlement practices of the Crown and claimed that redress has been allocated incorrectly to Pare Hauraki (Macfarlane 2020). Waititi repeatedly expressed support for the Tauranga Moana viewpoint at electorate debates and highlighted a need for Treaty settlement reform (Te Ao 2020b). Other key issues in

---

4   These numbers slightly over-represent Māori on the general roll: 54 per cent of our sample were on the general roll compared with 48 per cent on the Māori roll after the 2018 Māori electoral option (Electoral Commission 2018).

Waiariki included concerns from Whareroa Marae about the effects of air pollution from industrial areas in Tauranga and court challenges to the bottling of water from Otakiri Springs (Jones 2019; Tebbutt 2020). Some speculated that Hannah Tamaki, Waiariki candidate for Vision NZ, split the vote (Te Ao 2020b). Māori Television polling showed Coffey ahead of Waititi by only 12 per cent in the leadup to the election (Te Ao 2020c). When Rawiri Waititi won the Waiariki electorate in 2020 by 836 votes, he credited the victory to a 'comprehensive ground game and social media campaign' (Neilson 2020a).

Waiariki was not the only Māori electorate to watch, as Te Tai Hauāuru and Tāmaki Makaurau looked to be close races. In Te Tai Hauāuru, Labour Party incumbent Adrian Rurawhe was challenged by Māori Party candidate Debbie Ngarewa-Packer, a former local councillor and environmental campaigner. An extra boost to Ngarewa-Packer's profile came when she was named co-leader of the Māori Party in April 2020. Rurawhe is descended from several Western Māori MPs and Rātana movement founder, Tahupōtiki Wiremu Rātana, an important figure in Māori politics and religion who led the Rātana movement into a political alliance with Labour in the 1930s. Rurawhe had held the seat since 2014 and, in 2017, he retained it by a margin of only 1,039 votes against the Māori Party candidate. This result, combined with Ngarewa-Packer's profile and history in the *rohe* (region), led many to speculate that the Te Tai Hauāuru electorate would be the closest race across the Māori electorates (TVNZ 2020). However, Rurawhe ultimately won the electorate, holding his 2017 margin with 1,053 votes. Additionally, due to Waititi's win in Waiariki, Ngarewa-Packer was able to enter parliament from the party vote (1.2 per cent overall).

The third electorate in play, Tāmaki Makaurau, covers a large part of Auckland. Here, Labour incumbent Peeni Henare was challenged by several high-profile Māori politicians. These included controversial figure John Tamihere of the Māori Party, as well as Marama Davidson, the Green Party co-leader. Just 10 days before the election, Māori Television polling showed Tamihere trailing only 6 per cent behind Henare (Te Ao 2020d). Henare was ultimately successful in retaining his seat; however, the results demonstrated a move towards the Māori Party in the electorate.

Table 5.1 shows the final election results across the Māori electorates. From 2017 to 2020, Labour increased its share of the party vote in every Māori electorate, although in two cases—Waiariki and Tāmaki Makaurau— the electorate vote for Labour candidates declined. Across all the Māori electorates, the Māori Party vote was up marginally, by 0.6 per cent to 12.8 per cent. The Māori Party electorate vote increased significantly more, up by 5.4 per cent to 34 per cent. Labour's electorate votes dropped by 1.6 per cent to 51.8 per cent, but its party vote increased by 2.1 per cent to 62.2 per cent. By exploring NZES data, we can observe possible patterns of discontent among Māori voters with Labour or moves towards the Māori Party. We begin by exploring whether there was any signal of growing dissatisfaction with Labour across the data, particularly in relation to how it handled the major issues relating to Māori in its first term of government.

Table 5.1 Election results in the Māori electorates for the 2017 and 2020 general elections

Electorate	2017 party vote	2020 party vote	2017 candidate vote winner (vote majority)	2020 candidate vote winner (vote majority)
Te Tai Tokerau	57.9% Labour 11.1% NZ First	60.1% Labour 10.2% Māori Party	Kelvin Davis, Labour (4,807)	Kelvin Davis, Labour (8,164)
Tāmaki Makaurau	59.3% Labour 11.0% Māori Party	60.0% Labour 12.7% Māori Party	Peeni Henare, Labour (3,809)	Peeni Henare, Labour (927)
Hauraki-Waikato	61.5% Labour 11.3 % Māori Party	63.4% Labour 12.0% Māori Party	Nanaia Mahuta, Labour (9,223)	Nanaia Mahuta, Labour (9,660)
Waiariki	58.1% Labour 19.4% Māori Party	59.8% Labour 17.5% Māori Party	Tāmati Coffey, Labour (1,719)	Rawiri Waititi, Māori Party (836)
Ikaroa-Rāwhiti	64.7% Labour 13.0% Māori Party	66.1% Labour 11.9% Māori Party	Meka Whaitiri, Labour (4,210)	Meka Whaitiri, Labour (6,045)
Te Tai Hauāuru	58.5% Labour 15.0% Māori Party	61.0% Labour 15.4% Māori Party	Adrian Rurawhe, Labour (1,039)	Adrian Rurawhe, Labour (1,053)
Te Tai Tonga	55.8% Labour 12.5% National	58.7% Labour 11.5% Green Party	Rino Tirikatene, Labour (4,676)	Rino Tirikatene, Labour (6,855)

Note: For a full overview of Māori electorate results from 2002, see Greaves and Hayward (2020, 219–20).

Source: Electoral Commission (2020).

Did Labour generally lose Māori voter support?

Our first possible explanation for the Māori Party's return to parliament via Waiariki is that the Labour Party had generally lost Māori voter support in 2020. In the leadup to the 2020 election, the Labour Party (and particularly Prime Minister Jacinda Ardern) was enjoying very high levels of popularity due to the successful Covid-19 response. The Labour-led government elected in 2017 also had a sizeable Māori caucus after winning all the Māori electorates. But despite this general support, there were areas of vulnerability in Labour's response to Māori policy issues. Where did Māori voters see themselves in relation to the 'Team of Five Million'? Since the 2017 election, Labour had grappled with a situation at Ihumātao, in Auckland, involving Māori land, and Oranga Tamariki (the Ministry for Children) had been strongly criticised for the uplifting of *tamariki* Māori (Māori children) (Greaves and Morgan 2021). The emergence of Covid-19, which began in late 2019, added further tension to Labour's relationship with Māori voters. Health experts—aware of the impacts of the Spanish flu on Māori communities in the early twentieth century, the H1N1 pandemic, and general health inequities—advocated strongly for a targeted policy response for Māori, which was something the government was reluctant to do (Te Rōpū Whakakaupapa Urutā n.d.). As a result, *iwi* leaders and community organisations mobilised to address the specific needs of Māori (Parahi 2020). Community-based action included *hapū*-led roadblocks to educate the public about the lockdowns and the formation of Te Rōpū Whakakaupapa Urutā, a national Māori pandemic group (Bargh and Fitzmaurice 2021). Perhaps it was not entirely surprising that the Māori Party withstood the red wave in one electorate. And perhaps the policy solutions for the Team of Five Million did not work for Māori. To test this possibility, we consider Māori responses to the government's actions on Ihumātao and Covid-19.

The government's handling of Ihumātao

In 2016, the site of a proposed housing development in South Auckland was contested by activist group Save Our Unique Landscape (SOUL). Described as 'protectors', the group lived on the *whenua* (land) at Ihumātao with the goal of preventing construction and spurring the government to return the land to *mana whenua* (those with original territorial rights to the land). How the land was originally taken from Māori and the possible solutions to redress the historical grievance were complex matters that attracted widespread media attention (Godfery and Hayward 2021). The Māori Party was among those who called for the government to purchase the land and return it to *mana whenua* (McCarron et al. 2019). Labour's coalition partner, New Zealand First, was vocal in its opposition to government intervention at Ihumātao. In 2019, the government paused construction at Ihumātao but it had not resolved the issue by the 2020 election.

Given the prominence of the Ihumātao situation, the NZES included two questions on the topic to gauge voters' opinions on the government's handling of the situation: one for a general audience and one just for Māori voters. We asked all NZES survey participants, 'Do you approve or disapprove of the government's handling of the dispute over land ownership at Ihumātao?', on a five-point scale (from strongly disagree to strongly agree). The first finding was the degree to which the issue was too complex for a proportion of the population to form an opinion on. In survey development, a high percentage of the sample saying they 'don't know' normally indicates that the topic (or question wording) is beyond the participants' knowledge (De Vaus 2013). A large minority of non-Māori (38.4 per cent) and Māori on the general roll (32.6 per cent) selected 'don't know' in response to the Ihumātao question, compared with 20.1 per cent of Māori on the Māori roll. These findings suggest that Ihumātao is a complex issue that a significant proportion of the electorate could not understand or on which they did not form an opinion. The issue was best understood by Māori on the Māori roll.

Māori on the Māori roll also rated the government's response to Ihumātao more favourably than other groups. Of those who did rank the government's handling of the situation, there was a small but statistically significant difference: Māori on the Māori roll and Māori on the general roll both had a higher average approval rating of the government's response compared with non-Māori.[5] However, when we controlled for the extent to which each group 'likes' Labour, the effect was no longer statistically significant. This indicates that there is no real difference between Māori on the Māori

---

5   Māori on the Māori roll (M = 2.69) and Māori on the general roll (M = 2.61; p = 0.861) both had a higher average approval rating of the government's response than non-Māori (M = 2.51; ps < 0.05; $F(2, 2,409)$ = 5.16, p = 0.006).

roll and Māori on the general roll in support of the government's handling of the Ihumātao issue. Any small difference is likely due to participants on the Māori roll holding higher support for the Labour government generally.

Ihumātao also raised the question of the extent to which government action (or inaction) can precipitate a collective Māori political response. To test this with a Māori audience in 2020, we returned to the 2005 NZES, which asked participants how much they agreed with the statement: 'The foreshore and seabed legislation unfairly discriminated against Māori.' As mentioned earlier, when the Labour government legislated to ensure Māori could not test their claim to the foreshore and seabed in the courts, it evoked substantial protests from Māori and led to the creation of the Māori Party (Godfery 2015).

In the 2005 NZES, there was a high level of negative sentiment among Māori towards Labour over its handling of the foreshore and seabed issue. The striped bar in Figure 5.1[6] shows the results for Māori-descent voters for four parties in 2005. The results from 2005 showed that Māori Party voters agreed the most that the Act unfairly discriminated against Māori, with an average score of 4.4 out of five. But Māori Labour (M = 3.8) and Green (M = 3.9) voters also tended to agree. To test whether there was residual feeling about the foreshore and seabed issue in 2020, we asked participants to rank the statement again. The solid dark-grey bar represents sentiment about the foreshore and seabed issue and shows that, 15 years on, there is a strong sentiment that the fifth Labour government's response was unfairly discriminatory towards Māori. Indeed, our results suggest that this view could have grown among Green and National party Māori voters.

Inspired by the wording of the 2005 study, in 2020, we swapped out the name of the issue ('Ihumātao' for 'foreshore and seabed') and asked Māori participants to rate their level of agreement. Māori Party (M = 3.8) and Green Party voters (M = 3.6) agreed more than Labour voters (M = 3.1) that Labour's Ihumātao solution discriminated against Māori, while National Party voters disagreed the most (M = 2.4). Therefore, Māori Party and Green voters carry the most negative sentiment towards Labour over its handling of Ihumātao, but more voters have retained negative opinions over time for the foreshore and seabed response.

---

6   In some parts of this chapter, we present results according to whether someone voted for a certain party using both party *and* electorate vote. That is, someone is counted as a voter for X party if they gave *either* the electorate *or* the party vote to that party. We do this to boost sample size, given that the Māori Party had an electorate vote–only strategy (discussed later); in 2020 only 84 of our participants gave their party vote to the Māori Party, but 205 gave it their electorate vote.

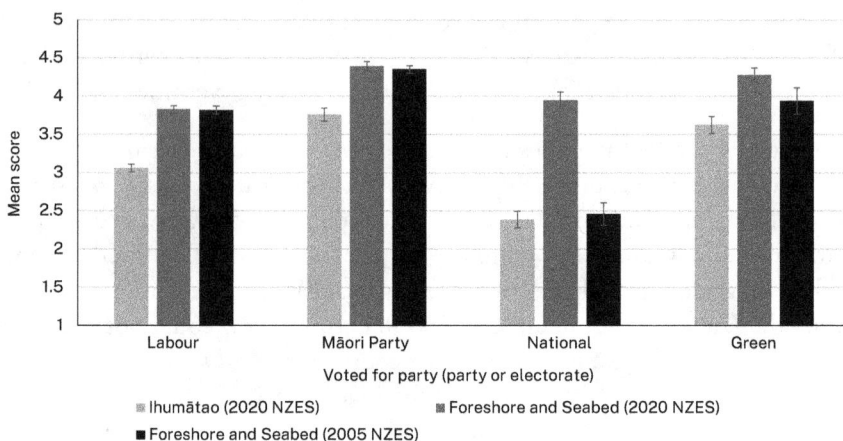

Figure 5.1 The average level of agreement among participants of Māori descent with statements about events unfairly discriminating against Māori, broken down by vote (party and electorate vote combined)
Source: 2020 NZES (Vowles et al. 2022).

Ultimately, NZES data suggest that for Māori voters Ihumātao was an issue that created some negative sentiment. However, there was not the same degree of negative sentiment towards Labour as there was (and still is) over the foreshore and seabed legislation, which led to the formation of the Māori Party in 2004. It may be that the regional nature of Ihumātao meant that it was not seen as an injustice towards Māori as a collective, or that Labour had learnt from past mistakes and improved its response generally. In addition, the issue was ambiguous and complex, with different opinions among *mana whenua*. Thus, although Ihumātao sheds light on some important issues for Māori, the NZES data suggest it has had a limited impact on voting.

Covid-19 and other 'big' issues

The second topic we consider in terms of Labour's handling of issues of policy significance to Māori is the Covid-19 response. As soon as the Covid-19 threat emerged, concerns were raised that the virus would disproportionately affect Māori when it arrived in Aotearoa New Zealand (Steyn et al. 2020). So, how did Māori rank the government's response to Covid-19 by the time of the election in 2020? We asked respondents to rank their approval of the government's response to Covid-19 on a scale of one (strongly disapprove) to five (strongly approve). Māori on the Māori roll had an average score of 4.5—significantly higher than both Māori on the general roll (*M* = 4.3) and non-Māori (M = 4.3).[7] The NZES results show that, if anything, Māori on the Māori roll had a *more* positive view of the government's Covid-19 performance than did others. To that extent at least, the idea of the Team of Five Million might have resonated with Māori voters.

Given the strength of support, we explored the importance of the Covid-19 response for Māori relative to other major policy issues. The NZES asked participants to identify the single most important issue for them in the 2020 election. Participants wrote their issue into an open-ended survey question, and we coded the data and further grouped them into categories based on similar issues (for example, we combined the economy, tax, and business). We then tested where there were statistically significant differences across groups. The biggest issues for Māori on the Māori roll related to poverty, housing, and inequality (19.6 per cent), followed by Covid-19 (17.9 per cent), then the economy, tax, or business (8.8 per cent). In contrast, the biggest issues for Māori on the general roll were related to Covid-19 (19.8 per cent), followed by inequality (16.1 per cent), and the economy (11.9 per cent). More non-Māori named Covid-19 as the biggest issue (23.5 per cent), with the economy second (18.1 per cent), and inequality third (13.3 per cent). Therefore, while Māori on the Māori roll gave the government its highest Covid-19 approval ranking, this group considered issues of inequality to be more important than the pandemic.

For the three groups of issues—the economy, inequality, and Covid-19— there was a statistically significant difference between Māori on the Māori roll, Māori on the general roll, and non-Māori ($p < 0.05$). We also explored which party the survey respondents thought dealt best with the issue. These responses came only from those participants who named each issue as the most important for them. Those participants who named Covid-19 as the most important issue overwhelmingly thought that Labour was the best party to respond to the pandemic (Māori on the Māori roll at 95.3 per cent and non-Māori at 88.9 per cent). Māori on the Māori roll, who were most concerned about issues relating to inequality, were also significantly more likely to think that the Labour Party was best placed to respond to the issue (57.0 per cent) than Māori on the general roll (45.9 per cent) and non-Māori (42.8 per cent). In relation to the economy, only Māori on the Māori roll were more likely to rank Labour higher than National, and here the contrast was very clear: 55.8 per cent of Māori on the Māori roll

---

7    $p < 0.001$; $F(2, 3,660) = 11.94$, $p < 0.001$.

chose Labour, while 51.8 per cent of Māori on the general roll and 62.3 per cent of non-Māori chose National as best suited to deal with the economy. Only 25 per cent of those on the Māori roll who rated the economy, tax, or business as their top issue thought National was best placed to deal with it. This illustrates that the National Party must continue to work to build a relationship with Māori on the Māori roll even for those who prioritise similar issues to that party. At the time of the 2020 election, National had not stood candidates in the Māori electorates since 2005.

In summary, 2020 was the Covid-19 election and Labour enjoyed substantial support for its pandemic response—most of all from Māori on the Māori roll. But those voters were also still more concerned about issues of poverty and inequality than Covid-19, and they will be looking to the government's response to these issues as they head into the 2023 election. Moving beyond the specific issues of the 2020 election, how much do Māori voters 'like' Labour overall? We turn to this question next.

How much did Māori voters generally 'like' Labour?

Stepping back from specific policy issues such as Ihumātao and Covid-19, we sought to understand the extent to which the fortunes of the Labour and Māori parties were entwined in 2020. Previous research has shown a more complicated relationship between the two parties than the simple assumption that the Māori Party will do well when the Labour Party declines in popularity among Māori (Sullivan et al. 2014; Greaves and Hayward 2020). In 2020, did the Māori Party's gain mean Labour's loss, or vice versa?

To answer this question, we explored the degree to which our voter groups 'liked' Labour and Te Pāti Māori. The results in Figure 5.2 show that all three groups followed the same general trend of liking Labour less in 2014, with increases in 2017 and 2020. Māori on the Māori roll, however, consistently liked Labour more than Māori on the general roll and non-Māori. More specifically, in 2017, the mean likeability of Labour among voters on the Māori roll was 7.4, increasing to 8.1 in 2020. Trends for liking the Māori Party over time show a different pattern. Figure 5.3 shows that voters on the Māori roll had an increase in support for Te Pāti Māori, from 6.1 in 2017 to 6.5 in 2020. But for Māori on the general roll the mean likeability of the Māori Party decreased between 2014 and 2020, from 5.0 to 4.4, and for non-Māori, likeability slightly increased in 2014, then stayed steady across 2017 and 2020. These results suggest that the Māori Party appealed least to Māori roll voters in 2014, while simultaneously appealing more to Māori on the general roll, potentially due to the party's support for successive National governments. The average likeability of Labour for Māori on the Māori roll increased by 0.7 of a point between 2017 and 2020, but only increased by 0.4 for the Māori Party. However, overall, there is no evidence that Labour Party likeability faltered for Māori voters in 2020 or that the Māori Party experienced a substantial increase in likeability among Māori roll voters. This trend suggests that the Māori Party could be appealing more to voters on the Māori roll over time.

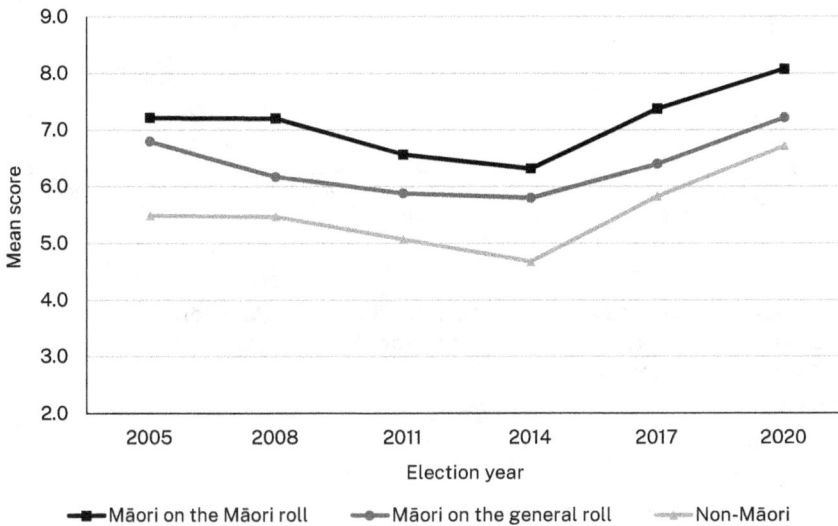

Figure 5.2 How much participants liked the Labour Party on a scale of 0 (dislike) to 10 (like) across elections for Māori on the Māori and general rolls, alongside non-Māori
Source: 2020 NZES (Vowles et al. 2022).

In addition, Figure 5.4 shows the percentages of Māori on the Māori roll, Māori on the general roll, and non-Māori who said they trusted the Labour Party across elections. Unfortunately, data were not collected in 2017 and the NZES did not ask a question about trust in the Māori Party. Overall, however, there was a trend of decreasing trust in the Labour Party over time, with a large increase in trust around 2020. This result adds to the picture that there seems to be no great break with Labour for Māori voters: Māori on the Māori roll liked and trusted Labour *more* in 2020, while simultaneously liking the Māori Party a little more. Thus, there is no evidence that Māori moved away from Labour and none to suggest that it is a zero-sum game between Labour and the Māori Party for support; a decline in likeability of one party does not mean an increase for the other.

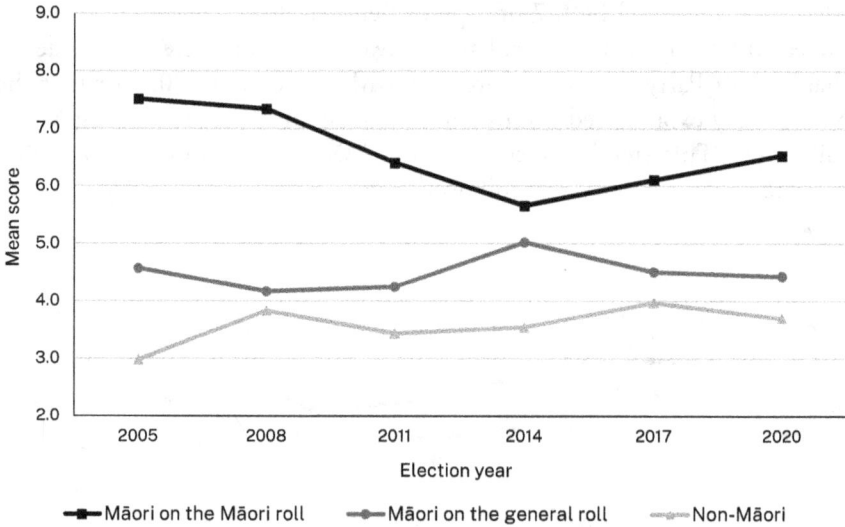

Figure 5.3 How much participants liked the Māori Party on a scale of 0 (dislike) to 10 (like) across elections for Māori on the Māori and general rolls, alongside non-Māori

Source: 2020 NZES (Vowles et al. 2022).

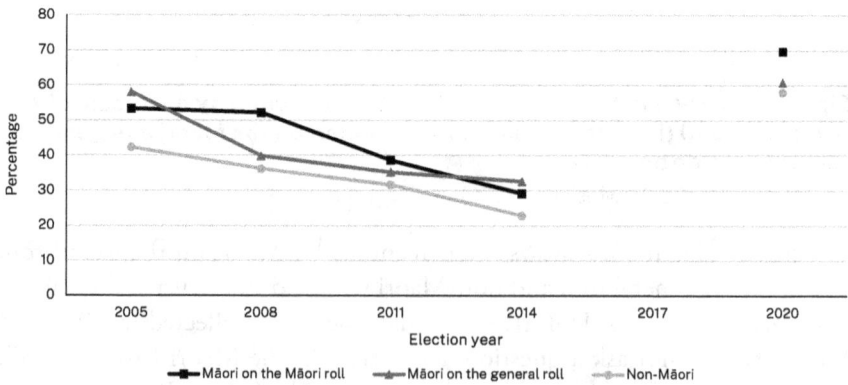

Figure 5.4 The percentage of participants who said they trusted Labour split by Māori on the Māori roll, Māori on the general roll, and non-Māori

Source: 2020 NZES (Vowles et al. 2022).

Did the Māori Party shift to the left?

The second possible explanation we explore is the suggestion that voters saw the Māori Party as ideologically repositioning itself in 2017. Since it was first established, the Māori Party has promised to be 'neither left nor right, but Māori' (Godfery 2017). But when the Māori Party failed to have any candidates elected to parliament in 2017, analysis of NZES data from that election showed that this was the result of a continued decline in support for the party during its years supporting National-led coalition governments (Greaves and Hayward 2020). Māori on the Māori roll are consistently shown to be more left-wing than Māori on the general roll (Greaves and Hayward 2020) and more concerned about issues aligned with a left-wing platform such as poverty (Te Ao 2020a, 2020b, 2020d). The renewal of the Māori Party for the 2020 campaign involved policies that voters could have viewed as taking a more left-wing position, such as lifting the minimum wage, doubling welfare benefits, and making them easier to access (Te Pāti Māori 2021). But did voters perceive this shift to the left and did this bring the party more in line with Māori roll voters?

The NZES asked voters to place all the main parties on a scale of zero (left-wing) to 10 (right-wing). Figure 5.5 presents the results for voters' perceptions of the ideological position of the Māori Party going back to 2005. As an overall trend, Māori on the Māori roll view the Māori Party as further to the right (that is, with a higher score in Figure 5.5) than do Māori on the general roll and non-Māori. In 2020, Māori on the Māori roll gave the Māori Party a score of 4.1, not far below (or to the left of) the scale midpoint of five, yet it was rated as 3.6 by Māori on the general roll and 3.2 by non-Māori. Although these are small differences, they show that Māori on the Māori roll view the Māori Party as closer to the centre than do other voters. All voters viewed the party as more right-wing in 2014 (Māori on the Māori roll rated it 5.3), although this perception shifted to the left in 2017 (4.7), and then further left again in 2020 (4.1). Generally, although voters overall consider the Māori Party to be shifting left, does the rating further right by Māori on the Māori roll simply reflect their own position as more left-wing than other Māori voters?

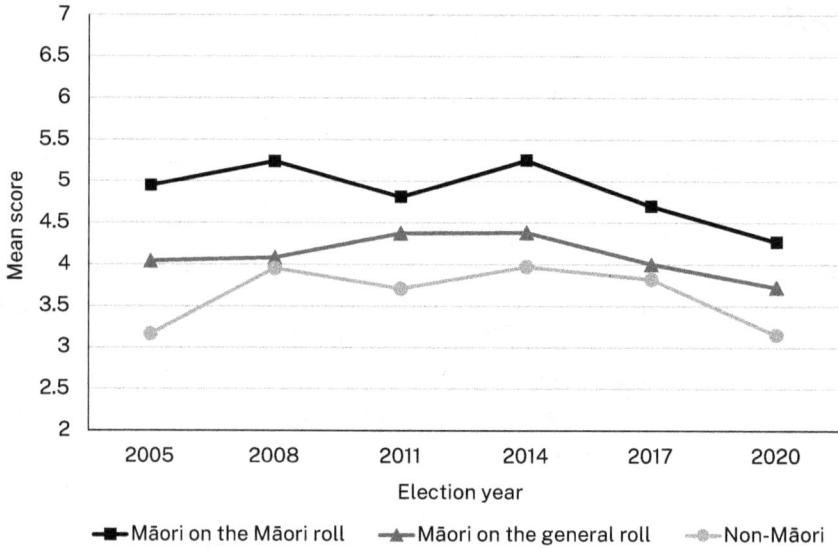

Figure 5.5 Differences across Māori on the Māori roll, Māori on the general roll, and non-Māori for 0 (left) to 10 (right) ratings of the ideological position of the Māori Party

Source: 2020 NZES (Vowles et al. 2022).

Table 5.2 The position in which participants placed the Māori Party on a scale of 0 (left) to 10 (right) minus where they placed themselves on that same scale

Election	Māori on the Māori roll	Māori on the general roll	Non-Māori
2005	0.33	–0.79	–2.31
2008	0.10	–1.31	–1.63
2011	–0.05	–0.83	–1.92
2014	0.28	–0.86	–1.89
2017	0.26	–0.88	–1.58
2020	–0.64	–1.36	–2.14

Source: 2020 NZES (Vowles et al. 2022).

Table 5.2 shows where each voter group placed the Māori Party on the scale from zero (left) to 10 (right), minus the average of where the group placed themselves on that same scale. A negative score indicates that the group viewed themselves as more left-wing than the Māori Party, a positive score as more right-wing. Te Pāti Māori has been consistently within one point of Māori on the Māori roll over time, suggesting it has been well aligned ideologically with its potential voter base. Māori on the Māori roll (on average) now view the party as slightly more left-wing than themselves, but note that this is less than one point on an 11-point scale. Therefore, there is no evidence in the NZES data to suggest that the Māori Party shifted closer to the average Māori roll voter on perceived ideology at the 2020 election. When we explore where voters generally place themselves on a left to right scale, we see that Labour voters rated themselves as a 4.6 (4.6 for non-Māori and 4.8 for voters of Māori descent), whereas Māori Party voters gave a rating of 4.7 for themselves. This shows that both Labour and the Māori Party were well aligned ideologically with the average Māori roll voter in 2020 and that both parties were viewed as slightly left of centre.

We also considered the suggestion that the Māori Party is 'neither left nor right but Māori' to understand voters' perceptions of the party's positioning. In 2020, Te Pāti Māori ran an 'unapologetically Māori' campaign to advocate for Māori interests (Neilson 2020a). The 2020 survey asked participants of Māori descent: 'Thinking about your life as a whole, how important is it for you to be involved in things to do with Māori culture?' Answers were given on a five-point scale from 'not important at all' to 'very important' (drawn from the Māori social survey Te Kupenga; StatsNZ 2018). As established elsewhere (Fitzgerald et al. 2007; Greaves et al. 2017), Māori on the Māori roll view their culture as more important to them than do other Māori voters, with 73.0 per cent rating it as quite or very important, compared with 29.6 per cent of Māori on the general roll. Only 3.4 per cent of Māori on the Māori roll rated it as 'not important at all' versus 20.2 per cent of Māori on the general roll. Figure 5.6 displays the importance of Māori culture to Māori voters, grouped according to the party for which they vote. It shows that Māori who find their Māori culture most important tend to vote for the Māori Party.

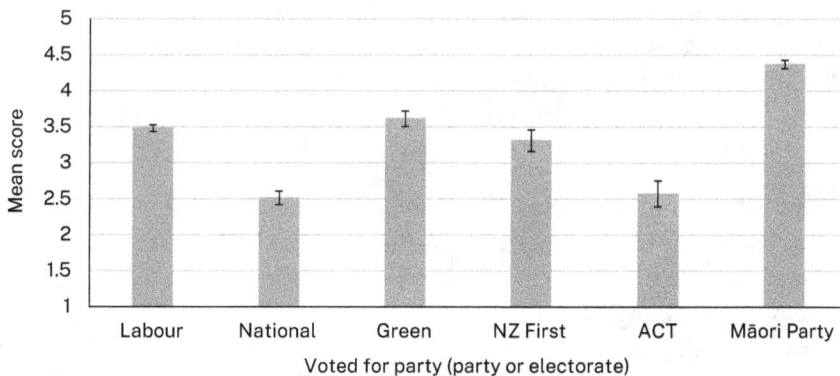

Figure 5.6 Differences in self-ratings of how important being involved in Māori culture is for voters of Māori descent

Source: 2020 NZES (Vowles et al. 2022).

Overall, voters *do* see the Māori Party as shifting to the left after its time supporting the National-led governments. More importantly for the party, our data show that Māori who have close associations with Māori politics and culture are much more likely to support the Māori Party. The original party mantra, 'neither left nor right but Māori', is still relevant for Māori on the Māori roll, but perhaps not for other voters, who view the party as more left-wing.

What did Māori voters think of the parties' leaders?

A third possible explanation for the Māori Party's success is that its change of leadership for the 2020 election impacted on the result. After the 2017 election result, both Māori Party co-leaders, Te Ururoa Flavell and Marama Fox, resigned. The Māori Party renewed its party leadership and a new, younger executive leadership was announced: Che Wilson became president and Kaapua Smith deputy president of the party (aged 42 and 35, respectively). In 2018, Debbie Ngarewa-Packer and John Tamihere were selected as wahine and tāne (man) party co-leaders. Ngarewa-Packer has a track record in local government politics, having served as the Deputy-Mayor of South Taranaki District Council. She was also a campaigner against seabed mining and a long-term advocate for Māori health and environmental issues. Tamihere has held several political roles over the past two decades and is CEO of the Whānau Ora Commissioning Agency. His appointment as co-leader attracted some controversy due to his statements suggesting that women in the Labour Party received preferential treatment due to their gender and making victim-blaming comments regarding a high-profile sexual assault case (Palmer 2019). In this section, we consider Māori roll voters' views of different political leaders, including the new Māori Party co-leaders and Labour leader Jacinda Ardern.

Figure 5.7 shows the average likeability score of each leader for Māori on the Māori roll, Māori on the general roll, and non-Māori. Jacinda Ardern was significantly more popular than any other leader among all voters, and more popular among Māori on the Māori roll than with other voters. It also shows that both Māori Party co-leaders were liked by Māori on the Māori roll considerably more than by other Māori and non-Māori voters. This indicates that they were a popular choice for the party to attract support from those voters. Other leaders who were more popular with Māori roll voters than other voters were the Green Party co-leaders and Winston Peters from New Zealand First (the party that won all the Māori electorates from Labour in 1996). Only two leaders were significantly less popular among voters on the Māori roll, Judith Collins (National) and David Seymour (ACT).

Next, we tested whether there was a significant gender difference in support for the party leaders. Gender and leadership are explored in more detail in Chapter 7 of this volume. Here we test the idea that John Tamihere, in particular, was unpopular among Māori women due to his past controversial comments. We test for differences in mean likeability between *wāhine* and *tāne* Māori for each leader. *Wāhine* Māori liked Tamihere more ($M = 4.1$) than did Māori men ($M = 3.6$), which is surprising and contradicts our expectations. However, *wāhine* Māori consistently rated leaders higher than did *tāne* Māori, except for David Seymour and Winston Peters (the differences were not significant), and Judith Collins, whom *wāhine* Māori ($M = 2.6$) liked significantly less than did *tāne* Māori ($M = 3.1$). Overall, this shows that although the new Māori Party leadership was relatively liked by Māori roll voters, Ardern's popularity was high in 2020 and, despite various controversies about Māori issues, she was even more popular among Māori on the Māori roll than among other voters.

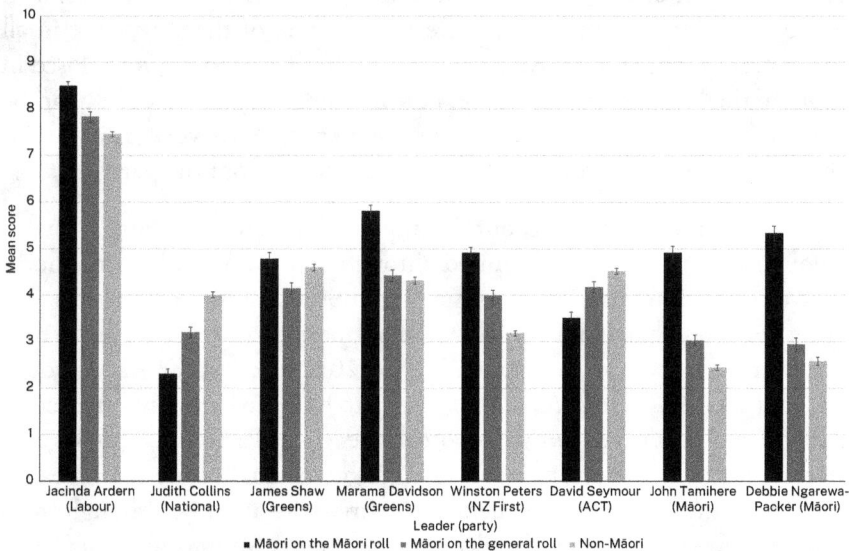

Figure 5.7 How voters across Māori on the Māori roll, Māori on the general roll, and non-Māori rated the likeability of each leader on a scale from 0 (strongly dislike) to 10 (strongly like)

Source: 2020 NZES (Vowles et al. 2022).

Did the Māori Party's campaign strategy change?

The fourth and final possible explanation for the Māori Party's relative success in 2020 that we test is that the party's campaign strategy had a positive impact on the result. We analyse results with a particular focus on how changes between the 2017 and 2020 campaigns may have helped the Māori Party. In 2020, Te Pāti Māori actively promoted a 'two ticks for Māori' strategy, which the media described as the 'Māori two-fer' (Maxwell 2020b). More than ever before, Māori Party candidates encouraged Māori electorate voters to give their electorate vote to the Māori Party and their party vote to Labour. The 'two for one' message was delivered by all Māori Party candidates at every opportunity (Maxwell 2020a). The purpose of this strategy was to maximise the impact of the Māori vote by electing Māori Party MPs in the Māori electorates, while at the same time returning Labour's Māori candidates to parliament through the Labour Party list ('two-fer' the price of one; Neilson 2020b). It was precisely this strategy that returned Labour candidate Tāmati Coffey to parliament via the Labour Party list despite his loss in Waiariki to Māori Party candidate Rawiri Waititi. But was this two-fer strategy a success beyond Waiariki? At a glance (as shown in Table 5.1), the Labour Party increased its share of the party vote in all the Māori electorates, even where the margin in the electorate vote closed in favour of the Māori Party candidate. Furthermore, despite not calling for the party vote, the Māori Party won 1.2 per cent of the party vote (as in 2017), which got Debbie Ngarewa-Packer into parliament from the party list.

What do NZES data reveal about the impact of this strategy? First, a caveat: although this is a sample recruited through statistically robust methods, some of these results are based on small numbers. Acknowledging this, our results are nonetheless revealing. We asked participants which party they most wanted to be in government after the 2020 election. Of the 81 voters who said they *most wanted* the Māori Party to be in government on election day, 65.7 per cent gave their party vote to the Māori Party and 82.6 per cent gave the party their electorate vote. This suggests that among their greatest supporters, the majority gave them their party vote anyway, although there is some difference between the electorate and party votes, suggesting some supporters followed the strategy. It is interesting to note also that not all of those who preferred the Māori Party voted for them; it could be that some voters were concerned the Māori Party would not win a seat and voted for

Labour instead. Indeed, 11.6 per cent of those who most wanted the Māori Party to be in government gave their electorate vote to Labour, and 22.9 per cent gave Labour their party vote.

More broadly and recognising that under MMP many parties may form a government, the NZES also asked which parties participants wanted in government. Some 57.7 per cent of Māori on the Māori roll, 21.5 per cent of Māori on the general roll, and 11.2 per cent of non-Māori wanted to see the Māori Party in government, suggesting that the majority of those on the Māori roll wanted to see the Māori Party have influence in government. We next explored the reported party and electorate votes for those who said they wanted the Māori Party to be in government. Most of those on the Māori roll who wanted the Māori Party in government gave their electorate vote to the Māori Party candidate (54.1 per cent), whereas many still gave their electorate vote to Labour (38.9 per cent). This reinforces the inference that many of those on the Māori roll simultaneously support the Māori and the Labour parties. Turning to the electorate vote, of those who wanted the Māori Party to be in government and were voting on the Māori roll, 22.1 per cent gave their party vote to the Māori Party, versus 59.3 per cent to the Labour Party. The difference in numbers between the electorate (54.1 per cent) and party (22.1 per cent) votes for those who wanted the Māori Party in government, and between electorate (82.6 per cent) and party (65.7 per cent) votes for those who *most wanted* the Māori Party in government suggests that to some extent the voters who support the Māori Party followed the party's 'two-fer' strategy. In summary, while many voters followed the party's wishes, many others still wanted to give their party vote to the Māori Party, especially those who liked them the best. This indicates that, although many voters on the Māori roll vote strategically for what is likely to be a range of reasons, many will still vote for their favourite party.

Another significant aspect of the Māori Party campaign was the extent to which it directly contacted potential voters in the Māori electorates. The NZES provides data relating to the extent to which participants were contacted by political parties across a range of mediums, from pamphlets and door-knocking to social media. Table 5.3 presents the results of all these added together to answer the question: what percentage of Māori on the Māori roll were contacted by the Māori Party?

Table 5.3 The percentage of Māori on the Māori roll, Māori on the general roll, and non-Māori contacted by each party in the leadup to the 2020 general election

	Māori on the Māori roll	Māori on the general roll	Non-Māori
Labour	65.2	61.8	61.4
National	**43.4**	**57.4**	**64.1*****
Green	28.9	26.4	28.7
New Zealand First	18.6	18.5	15.6
ACT	**13.6**	**18.7**	**18.3***
Māori Party	**39.6**	**11.3**	**5.0*****
TOP	9.6	11.9	9.4
New Conservatives	**8.8**	**14.9**	**14.3*****
Advance NZ	10.8	10.3	9.0

* $p < 0.05$

** $p < 0.01$

*** $p < 0.001$

Note: Statistically significant differences are presented in bold; n Māori roll = 603; n Māori on the general roll = 707; n non-Māori = 2,420.

Source: 2020 NZES (Vowles et al. 2022).

These results show that the Māori Party placed its efforts in contacting Māori roll voters, contacting 39.6 per cent of Māori roll voters versus 11.3 per cent of Māori on the general roll and only 5.0 per cent of non-Māori. This was a slight increase from 2017 when the party had contacted 38.0 per cent of Māori on the Māori roll, 8.9 per cent of Māori on the general roll, and 4.3 per cent of non-Māori. In contrast, Labour had contacted 61.4 per cent to 65.2 per cent of all voters. These results show that the Māori Party in 2020 managed to contact a large minority of those on the Māori roll, although by no means as many voters as Labour, which had more funding and a larger campaign team. However, 2017 and 2020 make an interesting comparison: in 2017, Labour contacted 70.3 per cent of Māori on the Māori roll—a greater proportion than Māori on the general roll (63.7 per cent) and non-Māori (59.9 per cent). Indeed, this difference was statistically significant in 2017, but not in 2020, perhaps speaking to Labour's aggressive commitment to win the Māori electorates in 2017. During that campaign, Labour candidates in the Māori electorates took an all-or-nothing approach; they did not stand on the Labour Party list but rather ran electorate-only campaigns to show their commitment to winning all seven electorates back from the Māori Party (Greaves and Hayward 2020).

Based on the observation that the Māori Party was particularly active on social media (Greaves and Morgan 2021) and that Māori politics is increasingly taking place online (Waitoa et al. 2015), we tested whether there was a significant difference in social media contact by each party across the rolls. There were differences for both the Labour and the Māori parties, indicating that the parties were more likely to contact Māori on the Māori roll (compared with Māori on the general roll or non-Māori) on 'Facebook or other social media'. The Labour Party contacted 11.9 per cent of Māori on the Māori roll, 10.0 per cent of Māori on the general roll, and 7.5 per cent of non-Māori. In comparison, the Māori Party contacted 8.6 per cent of the Māori on the Māori roll, 2.8 per cent of Māori on the general roll, and 1.5 per cent of non-Māori. This gap (of 11.9 per cent for Labour versus 8.7 per cent for the Māori Party) is much smaller than the overall contact gap between parties (of 65.2 per cent versus 39.6 per cent of Māori roll voters). NZES data show that, taken together, the Māori Party contacted a similar proportion of its potential Māori roll voters in 2020 as it did in 2017, with Labour contacting relatively fewer when compared across both elections. However, the Māori Party (39.6 per cent) was able to contact fewer Māori roll voters than Labour (65.2 per cent). Minor parties such as the Māori Party have fewer resources for campaigning than Labour, which is important to note given the huge geographical size of some Māori electorates. However, using social media could help to even this out in future, as there is greater capacity to target potential voters, even with limited budgets.

Overall, in terms of the impact of the new strategy, we conclude that Te Pāti Māori campaigns did not deter some voters from supporting the party despite the campaign encouraging voters to be strategic with their party vote.

Conclusion

This chapter has drawn on data from a sample of Māori voters in the NZES to understand the dynamics that led to the Māori Party's unexpected victory in Waiariki. We tested several possible explanations. First, only Māori on the Māori roll felt that Labour discriminated against Māori in the handling of Ihumātao, and that group gave the government its highest rating in terms of the Covid-19 response by the time of the 2020 election. It seems difficult to argue therefore that Labour lost support generally among Māori voters through these policies. We followed up this line of inquiry by asking which party voters like most. This showed that despite some specific Māori policy challenges for Labour, Māori on the Māori roll had a positive evaluation of Labour in 2020 with no associated uptick in support for the Māori Party.

Second, in relation to whether the Māori Party shifted to the left in 2020, our findings indicate that both Labour and the Māori Party were ideologically aligned with the average Māori roll voter in 2020 and both were viewed as left of centre. Our findings suggest that the idea of the Māori Party as 'neither left nor right but Māori' is fertile ground for future campaigns. Voters who identify more with Māori culture are more likely to vote for the Māori Party and this is a better predictor than left–right ideology. Third, regarding the impact of leadership, although the new Māori Party leadership was reasonably popular with Māori roll voters, they were much less liked than Labour leader Jacinda Ardern. Fourth, perhaps the best example of the two-fer strategy in action was the win in Waiariki. The 'unapologetically Māori' campaign seems to be an effective one, given that Te Pāti Māori appeals most to Māori voters who connect strongly with Māori politics and are motivated by issues of relevance to Māori.

Overall, these results suggest that the Māori Party is building relationships with Māori on the Māori roll and could be appealing more to them over time. Even in the exceptional circumstance of the 2020 red wave, Te Pāti Māori held or increased support among its core voter base. Consequently, the two Māori Party MPs effectively served as opposition from a pro-*hāpori* (community) Māori perspective in the fifty-third parliament and held the Labour government (and opposition parties) to account at every turn.

References

1News. 2020. '"Really Hard Ask" for Māori Party to Return to Parliament, Political Scientist Says.' *1News*, [Auckland], 3 August. Available from: www.1news.co.nz/2020/08/02/really-hard-ask-for-maori-party-to-return-to-parliament-political-scientist-says/.

Bargh, M., and L. Fitzmaurice. 2021. *Stepping Up: COVID-19 Checkpoints and Rangatiratanga*. Wellington: Huia.

De Vaus, D. 2013. *Surveys in Social Research*. 6th edn. Oxford: Routledge. doi.org/10.4324/9780203519196.

Electoral Commission. 2018. *Māori Electoral Option*. Wellington: Electoral Commission New Zealand. Available from: www.elections.nz/democracy-in-nz/what-is-an-electoral-roll/what-is-the-maori-electoral-option/.

Electoral Commission. 2020. *New Zealand Election Results*. Wellington: Electoral Commission New Zealand. Available from: www.electionresults.govt.nz.

Fitzgerald, E., B. Stevenson, and J. Tapiata. 2007. *Māori Electoral Participation: A Report Produced for the Electoral Commission*. May. Palmerston North: School of Māori Studies, Massey University. Available from: www.academia.edu/1559 198/Māori_Electoral_Participation.

Godfery, M. 2015. 'The Māori Party.' In *New Zealand Government and Politics*, edited by J. Hayward, 240–50. Melbourne: Oxford University Press.

Godfery, M. 2017. 'The End of "Neither Left nor Right, But Māori".' *The Spinoff*, [Auckland], 30 September. Available from: thespinoff.co.nz/politics/30-09-2017/the-end-of-neither-left-nor-right-but-maori.

Godfery, M., and J. Hayward. 2021. 'Te Tiriti o Waitangi.' In *Government and Politics in Aotearoa New Zealand*, edited by J. Hayward, L. Greaves, and C. Timperley, 116–25. Melbourne: Oxford University Press.

Greaves, L., and J. Hayward. 2020. 'Māori and the 2017 General Election: Party, Participation and Populism.' In *A Populist Exception? The 2017 New Zealand General Election*, edited by J. Vowles and J. Curtin, 213–45. Canberra: ANU Press. doi.org/10.22459/pe.2020.07.

Greaves, L.M., and E. Morgan. 2021. 'Māori and the 2020 Election.' In *Politics in a Pandemic: Jacinda Ardern and New Zealand's 2020 Election*, edited by S. Levine, 316–27. Wellington: Te Herenga Waka University Press.

Greaves, L.M., L.D. Oldfield, M. Von Randow, C.G. Sibley, and B.J. Milne. 2020. 'How Low Can We Go? Declining Survey Response Rates to New Zealand Electoral Roll Mail Surveys Over Three Decades.' *Political Science* 72(3): 228–44. doi.org/10.1080/00323187.2021.1898995.

Greaves, L.M., D. Osborne, C.A. Houkamau, and C.G. Sibley. 2017. 'Identity and Demographics Predict Voter Enrolment on the Maori Electoral Roll.' *MAI Journal* 6(1): 3–16. doi.org/10.20507/MAIJournal.2017.6.1.1.

Jones, C. 2019. 'Community Takes Fight Against Water Bottling Plant to High Court.' *Radio New Zealand*, 27 December. Available from: www.rnz.co.nz/news/national/406291/community-takes-fight-against-water-bottling-plant-to-high-court.

Macfarlane, K. 2020. 'Covid 19 Halts Tauranga Moana, Hauraki Kaumātua Hui Sparked by Treaty Claim.' *Bay of Plenty Times*, [Tauranga, NZ], 18 August. Available from: www.nzherald.co.nz/bay-of-plenty-times/news/covid-19-halts-tauranga-moana-hauraki-kaumatua-hui-sparked-by-treaty-claim/HMUKJL6Q XLXLSLNFBM52DPLGOQ/.

Manch, T. 2020. 'Election 2020: John Tamihere on Why 2020 Isn't the Māori Party's Year.' *Stuff*, [Wellington], 24 August. Available from: www.stuff.co.nz/national/politics/122524904/election-2020-john-tamihere-on-why-2020-isnt-the-mori-partys-year.

Maxwell, J. 2020a. 'Election 2020: How Did Labour Lose a Seat in the Midst of a Red Tidal Wave?' *Stuff*, [Wellington], 18 October. Available from: www.stuff.co.nz/national/politics/123125478/election-2020-how-did-labour-lose-a-seat-in-the-midst-of-a-red-tidal-wave.

Maxwell, J. 2020b. 'Election 2020: Māori Party Pushes One Waka Towards Shore in "Red Tsunami".' *Stuff*, [Wellington], 18 October. Available from: www.stuff.co.nz/national/politics/300131378/election-2020-mori-party-pushes-one-waka-towards-shore-in-red-tsunami.

McCarron, H., D. Satherley, and L. Reymer. 2019. '"Racism" Behind Why Govt Won't Buy Ihumātao Land: Māori Party.' *Newshub*, [Auckland], 29 July. Available from: www.newshub.co.nz/home/politics/2019/07/racism-behind-why-govt-won-t-buy-ihumatao-land-maori-party.html.

McClure, T. 2022. 'Jacinda Ardern Acknowledges "Difficult Period" As Labour Party Slumps Again in Polls.' *The Guardian*, 4 May. Available from: www.theguardian.com/world/2022/may/04/jacinda-ardern-acknowledges-difficult-period-as-labour-party-slums-again-in-polls.

Neilson, M. 2020a. 'Election 2020: Māori Party's Rawiri Waititi Says Priority is to Tackle Systemic Racism.' *New Zealand Herald*, 18 October. Available from: www.nzherald.co.nz/nz/election-2020-maori-partys-rawiri-waititi-says-priority-is-to-tackle-systemic-racism/4BHRKDTYEH3CZ2C6QR6UEXMIDI/.

Neilson, M. 2020b. 'Election Results 2020: Māori Party Back in Parliament as Rawiri Waititi Wins Waiariki.' *New Zealand Herald*, 18 October. Available from: www.nzherald.co.nz/nz/election-results-2020-maori-party-back-in-parliament-as-rawiri-waititi-wins-waiariki/U2KUOHTTTYXCW3WMSN4U7IH25E/.

Palmer, S. 2019. 'John Tamihere's Most Controversial Moments.' *Newshub*, [Auckland], 26 January. Available from: www.newshub.co.nz/home/politics/2019/01/john-tamihere-s-most-controversial-moments.html.

Parahi, C. 2020. 'Labour's Māori MPs Need to Push Their Party to Do More for Māori.' *Stuff*, [Wellington], 18 October. Available from: www.stuff.co.nz/national/politics/opinion/300135285/labours-mori-mps-need-to-push-their-party-to-do-more-for-mori.

Radio New Zealand (RNZ). 2020. 'Red Wave Sweeps Country.' *Radio New Zealand*, 18 October. Available from: www.rnz.co.nz/national/programmes/morning report/audio/2018768876/red-wave-sweeps-country.

StatsNZ. 2018. *Differences between Te Kupenga 2013 and 2018 Surveys*. 23 March. Wellington: New Zealand Government. Available from: www.stats.govt.nz/methods/differences-between-te-kupenga-2013-and-2018-surveys.

Steyn, N., R.N. Binny, K. Hannah, S.C. Hendy, A. James, T. Kukutai, A. Lustig, M. McLeod, M.J. Plank, K. Ridings, and A. Sporle. 2020. 'Estimated Inequities in COVID-19 Infection Fatality Rates by Ethnicity for Aotearoa New Zealand.' *medRxiv*. Available from: www.medrxiv.org/content/10.1101/2020.04.20.2007 3437v1. doi.org/10.1101/2020.04.20.20073437.

Sullivan, A., M. von Randow, and A. Matiu. 2014. 'Māori Voters, Public Policy and Privatisation.' In *The New Electoral Politics in New Zealand: The Significance of the 2011 Election*, edited by J. Vowles, 141–60. Wellington: Institute for Governance and Policy Studies.

Te Ao. 2020a. 'Voters Undecided Over Te Tai Hauāuru Candidates—Poll Result.' *Te Ao Māori News*, [Auckland], 28 September. Available from: www.teaonews. co.nz/2020/09/28/voters-undecided-over-te-tai-hauauru-candidates-poll-result/.

Te Ao. 2020b. 'Māori Electoral Debate—Waiariki.' *Te Ao Māori News*, [Auckland], 4 October. Available from: www.facebook.com/watch/live/?ref=watch_permalink &v=255435312470672.

Te Ao. 2020c. 'Māori Party's Waititi Hard on the Heels of Labour's Coffey.' *Te Ao Māori News*, [Auckland], 4 October. Available from: www.teaonews.co.nz/2020/10/04/maori-partys-waititi-hard-on-the-heels-of-labours-coffey/.

Te Ao. 2020d. 'Tāmaki Makaurau Seat Up for Grabs? Poll Results.' *Te Ao Māori News*, [Auckland], 11 October. Available from: www.teaonews.co.nz/2020/10/11/tamaki-makaurau-seat-up-for-grabs-poll-results/.

Tebbutt, L. 2020. 'Whareroa Marae Sets Govt 10-Year Deadline for Mount Maunganui Heavy Industry Retreat.' *Bay of Plenty Times*, [Tauranga, NZ], 8 July. Available from: www.nzherald.co.nz/bay-of-plenty-times/news/whareroa-marae-sets-govt-10-year-deadline-for-mount-maunganui-heavy-industry-retreat/KSQ G6BJXEHA4IU4AJEYXFTRH3Q/.

Te Pāti Māori. 2021. *Incomes Policy: Executive Summary.* 6 August. [Online]. Available from: www.maoriparty.org.nz/income.

Te Rōpū Whakakaupapa Urutā [National Māori Pandemic Group]. n.d. *COVID-19 Advice for Māori.* [Online]. Available from: www.nzhealthgroup.com/covid-19-advice-for-maori/.

TVNZ. 2020. 'Māori Party Fights to Re-Enter Parliament.' *TVNZ.* Available from: www.youtube.com/watch?v=fTYjLE-qIT0.

Vowles, J., F. Barker, M. Krewel, J. Hayward, J. Curtin, L. Greaves, and L. Oldfield. 2022. *2020 New Zealand Election Study.* [Online]. ADA Dataverse, V3. doi.org/10.26193/BPAMYJ.

Waitoa, J., R. Scheyvens, and T.R. Warren. 2015. 'E-Whanaungatanga: The Role of Social Media in Māori Political Empowerment.' *AlterNative: An International Journal of Indigenous Peoples* 11(1): 45–58. doi.org/10.1177/117718011501100104.

6

Who Belongs in the 'Team of Five Million'? Immigration and the 2020 election

Fiona Barker and Kate McMillan

Introduction

The 2020 New Zealand general election took place during a period of closed borders, near-zero immigration, and an all-consuming focus on the domestic and international impacts of the Covid-19 pandemic. Things were very different three years earlier: migration into New Zealand had reached record highs and, in the broader context of concerns about the country's infrastructural capacity, immigration was an issue of growing importance to voters at that year's election (McMillan and Gibbons 2020).

In this chapter, we ask whether Covid-19 and the associated disruptions impacted New Zealanders' views about immigration. First, we compare public opinion about immigration in 2020 with that in previous elections and, second, we examine what voters thought future immigration into New Zealand should look like, including which kinds of immigrants they wanted to see enter the country once the border reopened. We also examine whether the factors found to be important determinants of opinions about immigration in previous elections remained important in 2020.

We find a clear reduction in the salience of immigration between 2017 and 2020, which we attribute not just to the relatively greater importance voters placed on pandemic-related issues (such as health) but also to the dramatic drop in inward migration in the months leading up to the election. In other respects, public opinion about immigration remained relatively stable. This general stability of opinion sits alongside both a perceptible decrease in the proportion of voters who worried about the cultural and economic consequences of immigration and some hardening of opinion among those wanting immigration reduced. Looking to future immigration policy, we find public opinion to be broadly supportive of most types of immigration, with the notable exception of the investor category, which a large majority of participants oppose. Beyond views about which immigrants should be granted access to the labour market, there is some reluctance to allow non-resident foreign buyers into the housing market and to provide immigrants with access to welfare.

The chapter first details immigration policy and patterns ahead of the 2020 election. It then examines pre-pandemic and emerging literature on how public opinion about immigration is affected by events such as pandemics. A third section presents our findings and, in the final section, we consider implications for future immigration policy.

Immigration policy and politics in 2020: Setting the context

On 19 March 2020, the New Zealand Government shut the country's border to almost all non-citizen and non–permanent residents (Knight 2021). The Team of Five Million was now sealed off from the rest of the world and, by November 2020, a drop of 98 per cent in overall arrivals to New Zealand was reported (Ministry of Business, Innovation and Employment 2020). Annual net migration was less than 10,000 by early 2021, contrasting dramatically with net migration of almost 92,000 in the year to March 2020 (Infometrics 2021).[1] There was a similar dramatic decline in migration globally after the initial flurry of people trying to travel before borders shut. Permanent migration to OECD countries, for example, fell by more than 30 per cent in 2020, to the lowest levels seen in almost two decades, with particular impacts on family migration (OECD 2021). New Zealand was, nonetheless, unusual in that its border closure halted whole classes of migration—notably, of international student, working holidaymaker, and other temporary work visa categories.

---

1   Citizens returning to New Zealand after the pandemic broke out dominated incoming long-term flows.

Even before the pandemic, some changes in immigration patterns and policy had been emerging. The previous National-led government had, in its last year of office (2017), already placed restrictions on some work visas and begun removing the 'residents-in-waiting' logic of temporary migration categories (Woodhouse 2017). The briefing to the incoming Minister of Immigration after the 2017 election emphasised that significant growth in temporary migration flows over the previous two decades had placed pressure on the residence program and could 'work against the Government's wider objectives for the integrity of the immigration system and the labour market' (Ministry of Business, Innovation and Employment 2017, 4–5). Indeed, temporary work visa holders had come to make up almost 5 per cent of the country's labour force—the highest in the OECD by some distance (Office of the Minister of Immigration 2021).

In line with officials' advice, in 2017, Jacinda Ardern's Labour–New Zealand First government signalled it would address the emerging bottleneck on the permanent migration pathway, as well as reduce immigration levels overall. It had taken only limited steps in this direction—including adjustment to post-study visas, family migration, and work on migrant exploitation—before Covid-19 and the related border closure upended its plans. Policy work had also been underway in housing—an area associated with immigration pressure. Labour had made numerous campaign pledges in this area, given the prolonged crisis of housing availability and affordability and the importance voters placed on it in 2017 (Vowles and Curtin 2020, 43). As well as promising to build 100,000 affordable homes, reduce homelessness, and shrink social housing waiting lists, Labour signalled it would ban 'foreign buyers' from purchasing existing housing (Davison 2017) to try to reduce competition for residential properties and, in turn, slow price increases. As the 2020 election neared, however, the government had reportedly built few of the promised 'KiwiBuild' homes and house prices had risen steeply (Taylor 2020).[2] Legislation had, however, been introduced to stop most 'non-residents' from purchasing residential properties.[3] Across immigration and related policy areas, then, the Labour–New Zealand First government had begun making changes in response to challenges associated with rapid

2   Median house prices rose 11 per cent in the year to September 2020 (Taylor 2020).
3   After this law was passed, non-residents were required to apply to the Overseas Investment Commission for permission to purchase residential property. Australian and Singaporean citizens were exempt from these rules due to bilateral economic and trade agreements. 'Non-resident' in this case meant not just people on a resident visa living overseas, but also those living in New Zealand on a non–residence class visa. Students and other temporary visa holders were not generally eligible to apply for permission (New Zealand Treasury 2018).

and sustained growth in temporary migration over decades. Nonetheless, apparent indecision about specific changes and further increases in the backlog of residency applications attracted criticism (RNZ 2019b); by late 2019, tens of thousands of migrants lived with uncertainty as they waited on residency decisions (Bonnett 2019).

The pandemic context of almost zero immigration gave the government an opportunity to more radically reshape immigration policy. In the short term, it adopted reactive emergency measures to address issues arising from the closed border, including periodic extensions to visas close to expiry, variation of conditions on some visas (for example, allowing working holidaymakers to move to a special seasonal work visa; Faafoi 2020), and some minimal welfare provisions for migrants stranded in New Zealand.[4] While providing short-term relief for visa holders in New Zealand, and for employers struggling to find workers, these measures were criticised as piecemeal and unpredictable, ignoring the plight of visa holders stranded offshore when the border closed, and still not addressing the many thousands in the residency application queue when the pandemic broke out (Bonnett 2020a).

With the government slow to commit to reform of the troubled immigration system, or to offer residence certainty to whole categories of migrants, the perception of an immigration 'policy hole' arose (Fonseka 2020b). Yet, a broader step-change was in the works. Cabinet papers and policy documents from mid-2020 show policymakers' thoughts turning to 'post-pandemic' immigration and foreshadowing the immigration 'reset' eventually announced in May 2021.[5] Stating that 'when our borders fully open again, we can't afford to simply turn on the tap to the previous immigration settings' (Nash and Faafoi 2021), the government signalled substantial reform of skilled migration and, especially, temporary migration—the category whose numbers had doubled in the previous decade. Immigration minister Kris Faafoi told employers they would need to rethink their reliance on foreign workers and that the government had to prioritise New Zealanders for work and training instead (Bonnett 2020b). In immigration, as in post-Covid

---

4   *The Immigration (COVID-19 Response) Amendment Act 2020* introduced extensive time-limited powers to grant visas and to amend visa conditions and duration for whole classes of visa holders (Lees-Galloway 2020).
5   The 2020 post-election briefing restated the 'one-off opportunity to reset' labour market and immigration settings that Covid-19 border closures provided, mentioning specifically the need for a 'reset of skilled residence settings' (Ministry of Business, Innovation and Employment 2020, 5).

tourism and international education, future policy was expected to focus on 'higher value and lower volume strategies' (Ministry of Business, Innovation and Employment 2020, 5).

Commitment to an immigration 'rethink' also appeared in Labour's 2020 election manifesto, which stated a desire to 'make the most of the opportunity provided' by Covid-related disruptions to 'update' immigration settings (Labour Party 2020). Short on details, the manifesto promised to 'review immigration criteria to enable a broader range of workers to enter New Zealand', to continue work on family migration and migrant exploitation, and to establish a new 'Investment Attraction Strategy to encourage targeted and high-value international investment into New Zealand' (Labour Party 2020). Labour increasingly faced a dilemma familiar to centre-left parties internationally: how to respond both to their traditional working-class base, some of whom see immigrants as undermining their working conditions and access to resources, and to those among their supporters who emphasise immigration as a human right and a matter of global solidarity. Labour had been largely shielded from this dilemma by the long period of bipartisan support for immigration as a key plank of economic management and stimulation, extant since the late 1980s. With the breakdown of this consensus, it was more difficult for Labour to either downplay immigration or avoid adopting a clear stance on the issue, both of which are strategies employed by left-wing parties elsewhere (Odmalm and Bale 2015; Carvalho and Ruedin 2020).

Apart from the Green Party, the other main political parties were also short on immigration policy details ahead of the election beyond statements of broad values. Most indicated continuity with previous policy positions. National, Labour, and ACT all expressed continued support for the investor category targeted at high-wealth migrants with capital to invest, whereas the Green Party sought to clamp down on this category (Bonnett 2020b). New Zealand First called most explicitly for a 'fundamental rethink' of policy, arguing that the pre-pandemic scale of immigration 'belongs to another era' (New Zealand First 2020). It advocated for regionalised immigration, caps on some categories, policy oriented more tightly around skill shortage lists, and a population plan. While ACT declared itself 'pro-immigration', it nonetheless aligned with New Zealand First in areas such as 'trimming back overly generous' pension entitlements for immigrants and seeking to require new migrants to sign up to 'New Zealand's values' (ACT 2020). The Green Party's detailed policy platform was notable for its rights focus. It sought further increases in the refugee quota, liberalised residency rules for family members of immigrants, and removal of the ties binding temporary workers to employers, which it argued led to migrant exploitation (Green Party of Aotearoa New Zealand 2020). Across the parties, however, discussion of immigration during the election campaign focussed little on future policy settings. Instead, parties debated border-related issues, such as how best to allocate places in the country's managed isolation and quarantine system and which migrants should receive exemptions to cross a border otherwise firmly shut to those who were neither citizens nor permanent residents (Bonnett 2020b).

Given the many interruptions to business-as-usual immigration caused by the pandemic, we cannot take for granted that the factors usually found to shape voters' attitudes to immigration would exert the same influence in 2020. In the next section, we discuss these factors and identify some expectations about how Covid-19 could affect voters' opinions on immigration.

The effect of major events on immigration attitudes

What effects might we expect the Covid-19 pandemic—with its cascading health, economic, demographic, social, and political consequences—to have on how New Zealanders feel about immigration? In this section, we examine historical literature on the relationship between health and other crises and immigration attitudes, as well as the emerging literature on the Covid-19 pandemic's effects on public opinion about immigration. We explore this literature for its insights into three possible effects of the pandemic on attitudes about immigration: first, that Covid-19 would make people more hostile to immigrants and less open to immigration; second, that it would make people more accepting of immigrants and immigration; and third, that Covid-19 would have little lasting effect on people's opinions about immigrants and immigration.

Historical support for the claim that a pandemic will harden public opinion towards immigration and immigrants can be found in the experience of the 1918 flu epidemic, which is credited with increasing anti-immigrant attitudes in the United States (Eun Kim et al. 2022; Lee et al. 2022; Markel and Stern 2002). Anthropological and psychological theories claim that the spread of disease can lead to the rise of anti-immigrant, xenophobic sentiment, with scholars in the 1960s arguing that societies tend to blame 'outsiders' when faced with a biological threat such as a highly infectious disease (Douglas 1966). More recently, scholars have theorised that xenophobia is an 'evolutionary adaptation to disease' (Daniels et al. 2021), drawing on the behavioural immune system hypothesis to argue that exposure to the Covid-19 threat was associated with negative orientations towards immigrants (Freitag and Hofstetter 2022). Similarly, several nationalism scholars suggested the Covid-19 pandemic would inflame existing nationalist sentiment, possibly at the expense of ethnic minorities and other commonly 'othered' communities (Woods et al. 2020). Initial anecdotal evidence in New Zealand and elsewhere lends support to some of these claims: Chinese New Zealanders and other New Zealanders of Asian descent, for instance, reported being subjected to Covid-related racist abuse and attacks when the pandemic began (Leahy 2020; Tan 2021), and similar experiences were reported by Chinese people in many other countries (Jakovljevic et al. 2020).

Such xenophobia might be expected to translate into opposition to immigration flows. There is some support for this position in the emerging international literature. She et al. (2022) found increased xenophobia towards people from Wuhan among other Chinese nationals in China during the pandemic, while Daniels et al. (2021), in their study of Californians' attitudes towards immigration, diversity, and Asian-Americans during the early period of Covid-19, found 'selective support' for this hypothesis, mainly manifesting in an increase in crimes against Asian-Americans, although they considered this was more likely to be the product of 'politicians' authorisation of scapegoating' than wider racial hostility.

An alternative hypothesis is that Covid-19 would make public opinion more positive towards immigration and immigrants, especially given labour shortages and personal hardships arising from closed borders. There is not a lot of support for this hypothesis in the historical literature; existing studies that point to increasingly favourable attitudes instead identify a broader temporal effect by which attitudes liberalise over time, rather than as a reaction to a specific event. Thus, Boelhouwer et al.'s (2016) study found attitudes in European countries towards immigration and asylum became more generally favourable between 2002 and 2015. Other scholars observed attitudinal shifts in favour of immigration that could reflect a process of habituation to the presence of new immigrants despite initial backlash (Claassen and McLaren 2021) and that tracks generational change more broadly (McLaren and Paterson 2020). Lee et al.'s (2022) study, however, found Covid-19 vulnerability (measured as fear of or anxiety about the pandemic) in five Asian countries to be positively associated with support for immigration post-pandemic. They attribute this surprising result to policy feedback: '[I]nstead of scapegoating out-groups and seeing immigration restrictions as costless protective measures, people concerned about COVID-19 are reminded of (1) the importance of cross-border collaboration in combating the disease, and (2) the economic cost of stringent border controls' (Lee et al. 2022).

The most persuasively articulated position in the literature, though, is the stability-of-opinion hypothesis. Lapinski et al. (1997), for example, argue that while opinions about immigration and immigrants vary significantly across *populations*,[6] variation over *time* within populations tends to occur slowly, as Pryce (2018) also shows in the US context. Of particular interest are studies that have found this continuity of opinion even in the face of external shocks. Stockemer et al. (2020), for instance, found the movement of asylum-seekers into Europe between 2015 and 2017—commonly referred to as a 'crisis'—did not increase anti-immigrant sentiment, concluding that 'even under a strong external shock, fundamental political attitudes remain constant'. Hatton (2016) tested the effects of a different external shock, economic recession, on public attitudes to immigration in 20 European countries, finding that 'shifts in opinion have been remarkably mild'. Kustov et al. (2021, 1,479), confirming these findings of attitudinal stability even in the face of economic and political shocks, note that changes that do occur in response to external shocks tend to be small and of short duration as voters move back to their 'long-term equilibrium'.[7]

Taken together, these kinds of studies tend to support political socialisation theories of voter attitudes and behaviour, and suggest we should expect to see little, if any, change in immigration attitudes because of the pandemic. Indeed, some studies of the effect of the pandemic on public opinion about immigration during its first year provide initial support to the continuity hypothesis. Pickup et al. (2021) found that British attitudes towards immigration during the pandemic were strongly influenced by pre-pandemic views but noted that some existing views could be heightened.

---

6   A voluminous and theory-rich scholarship explains cross-national variation via individual and societal variables. For overviews of this literature, see Victor (2019); Freeman et al. (2013).

7   Conversely, Laaker (2023) argues that the experience of economic shock, in the form of a recession, during voters' formative years can have a long-lasting negative effect on attitudes to immigration. However, such long-term effects cannot be examined with the current data measuring opinions so soon after the onset of the Covid-19 pandemic.

Notably, anti-immigrant attitudes strengthened during the pandemic among Brexit voters (who already had more negative attitudes towards immigrants than did 'Remainers'), while Remainers' immigration attitudes remained relatively unchanged. In the US context, Daniels et al. (2021) similarly found only selective support for the contention that pandemics 'engender xenophobia' or reduce support for diversity.

A more general feature of recent pre-pandemic literature examining public views about immigration is the testing of complex relationships between individual variables and sociopolitical contexts. This literature points to the influence of a variety of mediating factors on immigration attitudes, including the presence or absence of state immigrant integration policies (Artiles and Meardi 2014; Neureiter 2021) and of right-wing parties, media framing (Boomgaarden and Vliegenthart 2009; Freeman et al. 2013; Haynes et al. 2016; McLaren et al. 2018), and elite framing (Bishin et al. 2021). Indeed, Lancaster (2022) shows that, while immigration attitudes are largely stable in the face of economic and political shocks, the change that does occur is primarily due to the *salience* of the immigration issue. This finding underlines the importance of how political elites frame issues, which is also apparent from Lee et al.'s (2022) study. Given the range of contextual variables at work in influencing public opinion, we could expect that the relatively low attention political parties gave to immigration (as opposed to border rules) in 2020 would similarly translate into lower salience of immigration in voters' minds and, thus, less opposition to immigration.

A further element of New Zealand's social and political context, and its possible effects on public opinion about immigration, is also important. Although the leadup to the 2020 election was dominated by the pandemic, New Zealand had experienced a different shock just a year earlier: the 15 March 2019 terror attack by a far-right gunman on the Al Noor Mosque and Linwood Islamic Centre in Christchurch, which killed 51 and injured 49 people. This attack produced an immediate government response that was praised for its compassion towards the targeted Muslim community, as well as law reforms to regulate firearms more tightly (RNZ 2019a; Roy 2019). Could the shock of this attack have contributed to voter attitudes to immigration in 2020? Consistent with the aftermath of a similar attack in Norway, studies so far have found higher levels of satisfaction with government (Satherley et al. 2021), and more positive attitudes towards Muslims (Shanaah et al. 2021), after these attacks. However, Shanaah et al. (2021) caution that the positive effects on attitudes towards Muslims did not extend to other out-group minorities or to immigrants more generally. Second, the positive effects, which were also more pronounced among left-liberal voters, appeared to be of short duration overall. After an immediate boost in positive attitudes towards Muslim communities, and in support for the government, a return to baseline views was observed in the following two to three months (Shanaah et al. 2021).

Thus, like the findings outlined earlier in relation to the impact of exogenous crises like the pandemic, continuity (via a return to baseline attitudes) seems stronger than disruption. The Christchurch attack constituted a profound shock to New Zealand society and to the Muslim community, and elite discourse changed to a more inclusionary stance—notably, in the immediate aftermath. However, given the degree to which the pandemic subsequently crowded out other issues, the longer-term impact of the attack on attitudes to immigration is less certain and we would not expect attitudes to immigration to be substantially changed in the medium term.

Immigration attitudes in pandemic times: Findings

How much, then, did the pandemic affect attitudes to immigration by late 2020? Drawing on data from the NZES 2020 (and earlier NZESs), we turn now to examine public opinion towards immigration and the factors associated with opposition to, or support for, it, in the initial phase of the pandemic. We examine the extent to which people supported levels of immigration as they were before the pandemic and explore some of the factors associated with a desire to see immigration reduced, increased, or kept constant. In so doing, we seek to assess whether voters' attitudes towards immigration became more negative, more positive, or remained largely unchanged.

Our first query relates to a fundamental aspect of immigration: the ability of people to move across borders. We asked participants when they thought New Zealand's border should be reopened to students, tourists, and temporary workers from countries where there was community transmission of the Covid-19 virus. As Figure 6.1 shows, when questioned at the end of 2020, almost 90 per cent of New Zealanders did not want the border reopened unless certain conditions were met: those entering the country had gone through a 14-day quarantine and produced two negative test results

(51 per cent); a vaccine was available to protect New Zealanders against infection (30 per cent); or New Zealand could safely contain outbreaks (13 per cent). Only 3 per cent of people thought the border should be opened immediately. This high level of concern about the risks associated with reopening the border aligned with government practice at the time and is consistent with the very high levels of support for the government's overall pandemic response and acceptance of restrictions that at any other time might have been considered draconian (Beattie and Priestley 2021). Indeed, only 6.5 per cent of NZES participants disapproved of the government's Covid-19 response, which had successfully reduced the spread of the virus. These views form the backdrop to New Zealanders' other views about immigration at the time of the 2020 election.

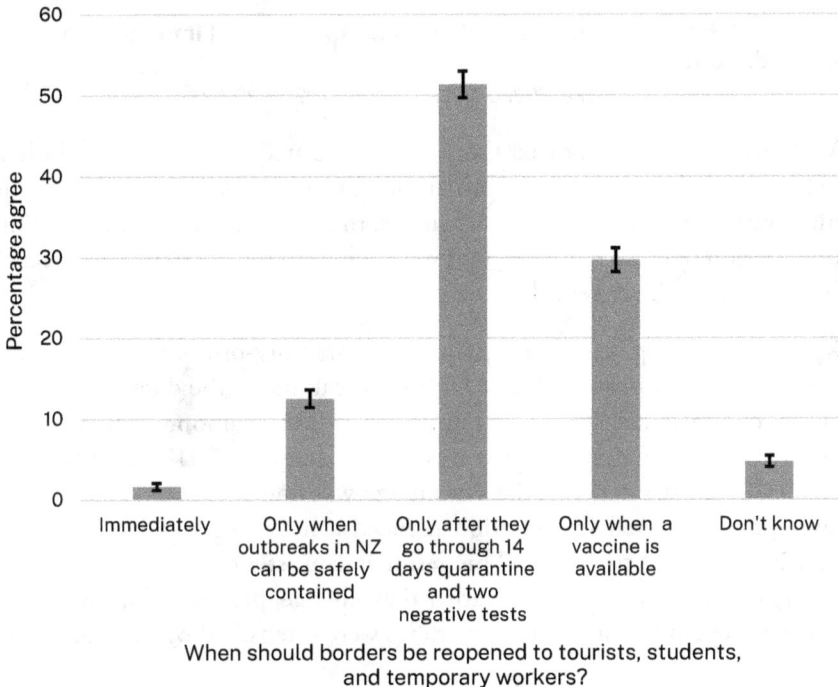

Figure 6.1 Reopening borders to those from countries with Covid-19

Note: The question was: 'When should New Zealand reopen its borders to tourists, students, and temporary workers from countries where there is community transmission of Covid-19?'

Source: Vowles et al. (2022a).

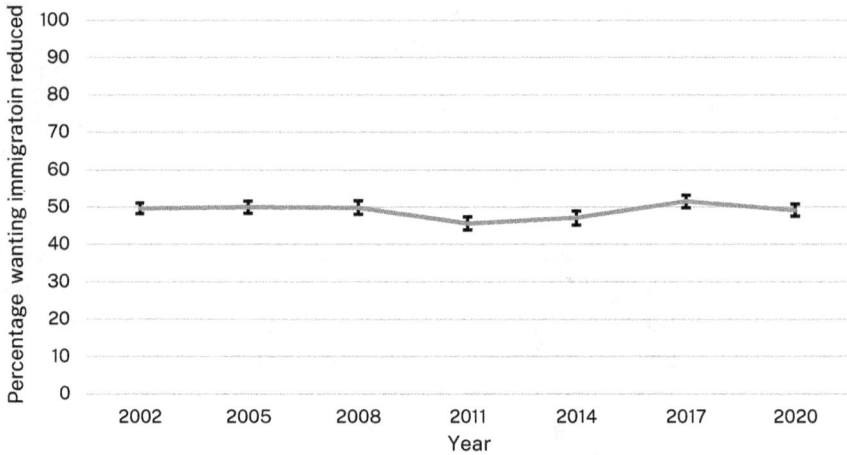

Figure 6.2 Percentage of respondents wanting levels of immigration reduced, 2002–2020
Sources: Vowles et al. (2022a, 2022b, 2022c, 2022d, 2022e, 2022f).

While participants supported the pandemic-related border closures in late 2020, this did not translate into noticeably more negative views about immigration. Indeed, as Figure 6.2 shows, the share of participants wanting immigration reduced a little or a lot was slightly lower in 2020 (49 per cent) than in 2017 (51 per cent).[8]

While Figure 6.2 gives some support to the stability-of-opinion hypothesis (Hatton 2016; Kustov et al. 2021), if we break down the data, they reveal a more complicated picture. As Figure 6.3 indicates, among those wanting a decrease in immigration there was growth between 2017 (22 per cent) and 2020 (28 per cent) in the percentage wanting it reduced a lot, while fewer people wanted immigration reduced a little in 2020 (21 per cent) than in 2017 (30 per cent). This result is consistent with Pickup et al.'s (2021) finding that continuity, rather than change, prevailed, but that some existing (negative) immigration attitudes were intensified by the pandemic.

---

8   As the border was essentially closed at the time of the 2020 survey, the question asked participants to think ahead to when it would be open again. In all other respects, the question was the same as in 2017, asking if the number of immigrants allowed into New Zealand should be: increased a lot, increased a little, about the same as now, reduced a little, reduced a lot, or don't know.

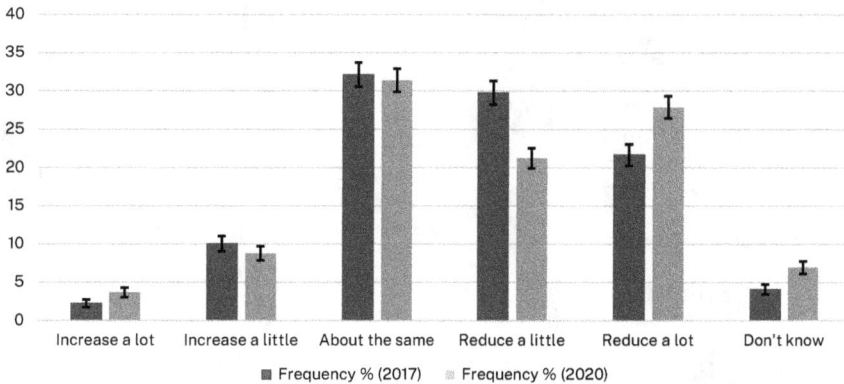

Figure 6.3 What should happen to immigration levels, 2017 and 2020 compared

Sources: Vowles et al. (2022a, 2022f).

Despite some hardening of opinion around the edges, immigration was clearly not at the forefront of New Zealanders' minds at the 2020 election. When participants were asked to identify the single most important issue to them, we found a notable drop between 2017 (5.2 per cent) and 2020 (1.2 per cent) in the share identifying immigration as their most important issue. This decrease appears to be the result of fewer people in 2020 worrying that immigration had damaging effects.[9] With most of the population nervous about the border reopening, and with fully one-quarter of participants identifying Covid-related issues as their biggest concern in 2020, it is unsurprising that attention was drawn away from other issues, such as immigration. Other pressing pandemic-related issues and the great reduction in flows across the border rendered immigration simply less important to many people. In turn, while issues such as the effects of Covid-19 on health and the economy dominated voters' minds, underlying views about immigration were not greatly affected and the picture is one of continuity in immigration attitudes.

Which factors influenced participants' attitudes towards immigration in the pandemic context? Continuity is the story here, too, as the factors explaining immigration opinion in pre-pandemic times, both in New Zealand and internationally, continued to be important in 2020. Being more open to immigration is significantly related to being highly educated, being born in North-East Asia, being of Chinese ethnicity, and voting Green (Figure 6.4).

---

9   The 5 per cent of participants who identified immigration as their most important issue in 2017 were significantly more likely to have negative attitudes towards it than those who did not, and were also more likely to think immigration was bad for New Zealand's culture and level of crime.

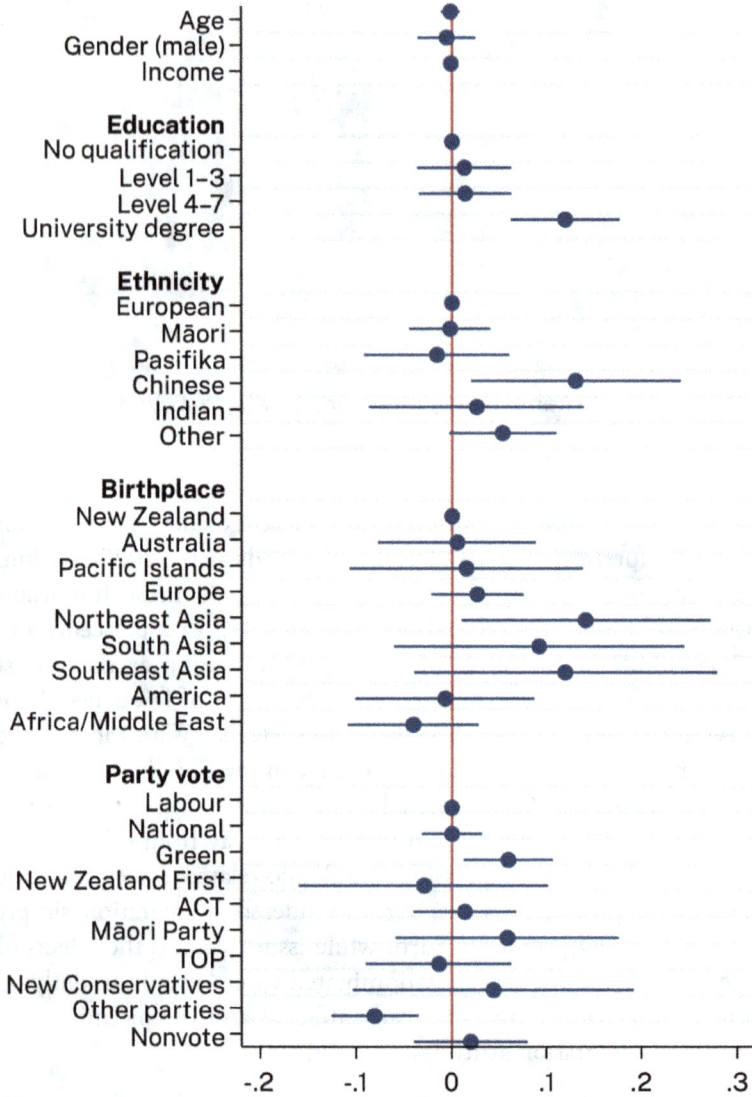

Figure 6.4 Attitudes to levels of immigration by socioeconomic status, ethnicity, country of origin, and party vote

Note: The effects of socioeconomic status, ethnicity, country of birth, and party vote were calculated from four different logistic models, with the last three including socioeconomic controls.

Source: Vowles et al. (2022a).

Conversely, those wanting to see immigration reduced a little or a lot were significantly more likely to be Māori or Pasifika than European or Chinese (Appendix Table 6.1), and New Zealand First voters were significantly more likely than Labour or National voters to want immigration levels reduced. Age and gender were not significantly related to views on levels of immigration (Figure 6.4).

As Figure 6.2 shows, since 2005, about half of New Zealanders have wanted to see immigration reduced. Nonetheless, they have also tended to view immigration as good for the economy; indeed, New Zealanders were even more likely to think immigration was good for the economy nine months into the pandemic (73 per cent) than they were in 2017 (69 per cent) (Figure 6.5). Even among those who wanted immigration reduced a lot, more than 45 per cent considered immigration to be good for the economy. Nor was there much concern that temporary immigrants take jobs from New Zealanders: only 25 per cent considered this to be the case, while 58 per cent disagreed. Even though unemployment was beginning to increase a little as the election approached, tipping over 5 per cent for the first time since 2016 (StatsNZ 2022), the government's success in controlling the pandemic meant that its economic effects were, at that time, less severe than originally feared. The Treasury even noted that the economy had 'bounced back to, or near, pre-COVID-19 levels by July 2020' (New Zealand Treasury 2020). Wage subsidies, income relief packages, and winter energy payment increases (Ministry of Social Development 2020) had all helped to soften the economic impacts of Covid-19, and possibly also to take the sting out of economic dissatisfaction that could otherwise have bolstered demand for populist, anti-immigration policies and parties.

To assess whether the pandemic led to heightened xenophobia and fear of the cultural effects of immigration, as suggested by some of the scholars discussed earlier, we examined whether the share of people thinking that 'New Zealand culture is generally harmed by immigrants' (not asked in the 2008 and 2014 NZESs) had increased. Again, we did not find a statistically significant change between 2017 (22 per cent) and 2020 (19 per cent). The overall trend has, in fact, been in the opposite direction: since 2011, there has been a substantial decrease in the proportion of New Zealanders who believe immigration harms culture (see Figure 6.6). In 2020, 61 per cent of New Zealanders disagreed with the statement that immigrants harm culture.

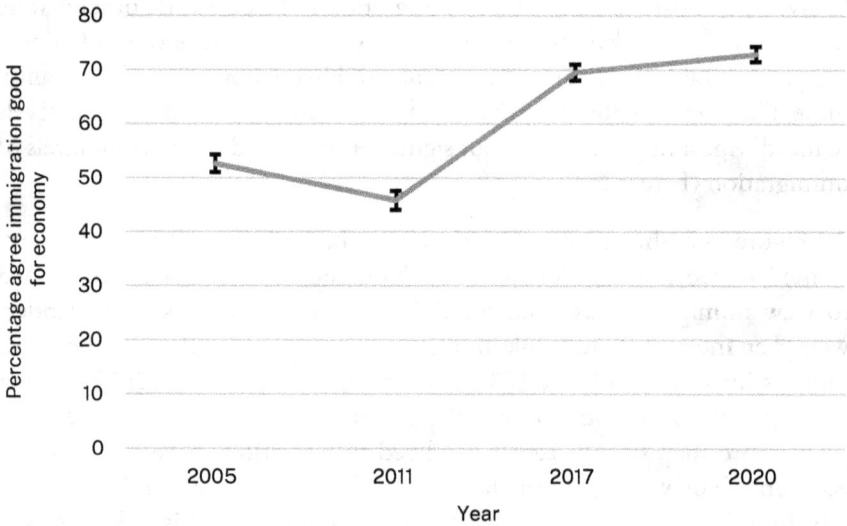

Figure 6.5 Percentage of respondents agreeing that immigrants are good for the economy, 2002–2020

Sources: Vowles et al. (2022a, 2022c, 2022e, 2022f).

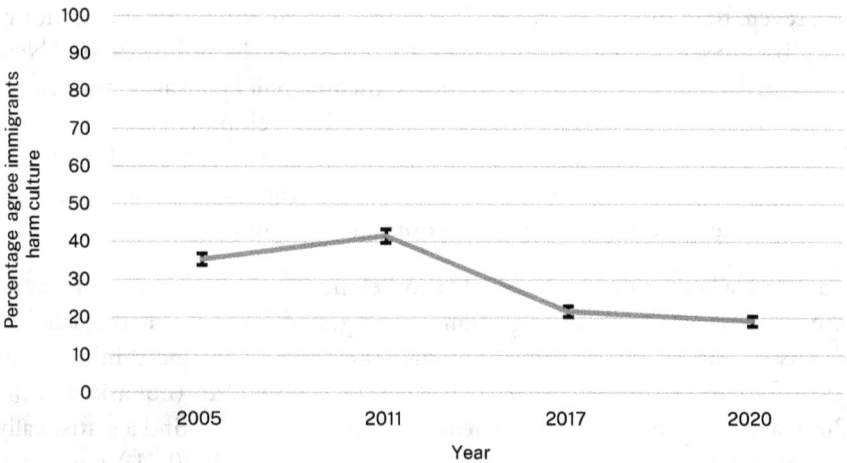

Figure 6.6 Percentage of respondents thinking immigrants harm New Zealand culture, 2002–2020

Sources: Vowles et al. (2022a, 2022c, 2022e, 2022f).

This decline in the proportion of people who believe immigrants harm New Zealand's culture can be viewed alongside a similar decrease in the proportion of participants agreeing with the statement 'Minorities should adapt to the customs and traditions of the majority'. In 2017, 37 per cent of participants agreed, compared with 33 per cent in 2020. This result should be treated with caution, however, because, as Greaves and Vowles (2020) point out, in the New Zealand context, some participants might understand 'minorities' to mean Māori, not immigrant minorities. Nonetheless, an increase in the proportion of New Zealanders who reject the idea that minorities should fully assimilate into the majority group's customs and traditions is consistent with growing support for cultural pluralism in New Zealand between 2017 and 2020.

'Post-pandemic' immigration policy

The shock of the pandemic and sudden border closure did not appear to greatly shift participants' attitudes to immigration or alter the factors shaping these attitudes. However, with the government having stated its intention to rethink immigration policy settings after the pandemic, we asked participants to think about their preferences for future immigration once the border reopened. We were interested, first, in whether New Zealanders supported continued emphasis on temporary rather than permanent migration, as had been characteristic of flows in the previous decade. Views on this were mixed, with many participants expressing uncertainty.[10] Of those who had a view, however, there was a strong preference for permanent (37 per cent) over temporary (23 per cent) migration.

As the government's promise of a 'reset' implied some change to the balance of skills and characteristics it would seek in future immigrants, we next asked participants which kinds of people should be encouraged to come to live in New Zealand when the border reopened (Figure 6.7). Very strong support (89 per cent) was expressed for two categories in particular: 'high-skilled professionals' and 'skilled tradespeople'. There was also strong support (74.5 per cent) for Pasifika seasonal workers. Consistent with the mostly positive attitudes to immigration overall, almost all other migration categories (low-skilled workers, international students, and working holiday visa holders) were also supported by more than 50 per cent of participants.

---

10   The most common answer to this question was 'not sure' (41 per cent), which suggests many New Zealanders are unaware of the differences between permanent and temporary migration policies or of their consequences for immigrants, their families, and the wider community.

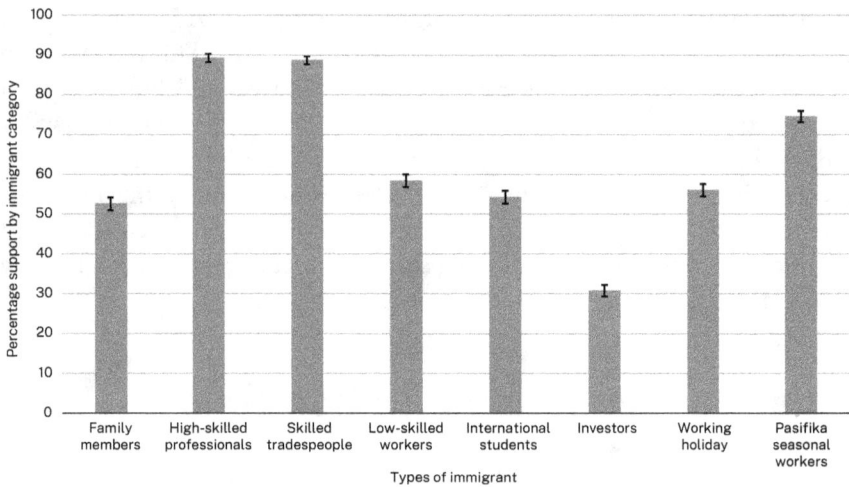

Figure 6.7 Percentage of respondents agreeing that New Zealand should encourage certain kinds of immigrants when the border reopens
Source: Vowles et al. (2022a).

The one immigration category opposed by a clear majority of participants was that of investor immigrants. The comparatively low support (31 per cent) for these migrants is particularly striking given that participants were not asked to make any trade-offs between categories: they could have supported all categories had they wished. It was also the one category for which the Labour Party, alongside National and ACT, had most clearly reaffirmed its support at election time and in subsequent policy initiatives. This clear contradiction between many political parties' support for high-wealth 'investor immigrants' and voters' opposition to such migrants deserves further exploration, and strongly suggests some elements of the entrenched economic logic of New Zealand's immigration policy are not supported by voters.

To further explore these findings on future immigration, we investigated how socioeconomic variables and partisanship affected participants' views.[11] The biggest effects here related to partisanship and country of birth. Voting for New Zealand First was significantly related to lower levels of support for all kinds of immigration when compared with those who voted Labour, except for support for investors, where the difference was not statistically significant. National, ACT, and Te Pāti Māori voters were also less likely

---

11   Detailed models for results in this section are available from the authors on request.

to support family migrants than were Labour voters, and Te Pāti Māori voters were also significantly less likely to support professional and skilled tradespeople. Green voters, by contrast, were significantly more likely to support family migrants, international students, and Pasifika seasonal workers than were Labour voters.

Country of birth emerged as another strong predictor of opinion about different categories of migration. People born in North and East Asia (China, Hong Kong, Taiwan, Japan) were significantly more likely to support the immigration of family members, skilled professionals, international students, and investors than participants born in New Zealand, and significantly less likely to support the immigration of low-skilled workers and Pasifika seasonal workers than the New Zealand–born. Interestingly, those born in the Pacific Islands were no more likely to be supportive of Pasifika seasonal migration than the New Zealand–born, and those born in South or South-East Asia were less likely than the New Zealand–born to be supportive of this migration. While studies reporting attitudes to immigration sometimes elide this dimension of diversity within the sample of participants, these findings show individuals' own immigration background and national origin may affect, in different ways, their attitudes to subsequent immigration to the country.

Social membership and the rights of non-residents

Our final queries concerned New Zealanders' attitudes towards immigrants' access to the property market and welfare benefits. We first asked whether New Zealand should open its housing market to foreign buyers living overseas. An overwhelming majority (87 per cent) of participants opposed this, with only 6.3 per cent in favour.[12] To explore this strong opposition to foreign buyers, we examined a range of factors for their effects on views about who should be able to access homeownership (Figure 6.8). Again, both partisanship and country of origin were significant. Although on average supporters of no party fell to the positive end of the spectrum, National voters were significantly less opposed than Labour voters to opening the housing market to non-residents. Place of birth and ethnicity

---

12   As explained earlier, the ban on property purchases also applied to immigrants living in New Zealand on a non-permanent resident visa, but the question, as asked, does not refer to such immigrants.

were also strong predictors of the degree of feeling on this issue, with those born in North-East Asia and those of Chinese ethnicity significantly less opposed (although still, on average, opposed) to allowing foreign buyers to buy houses than the New Zealand–born.

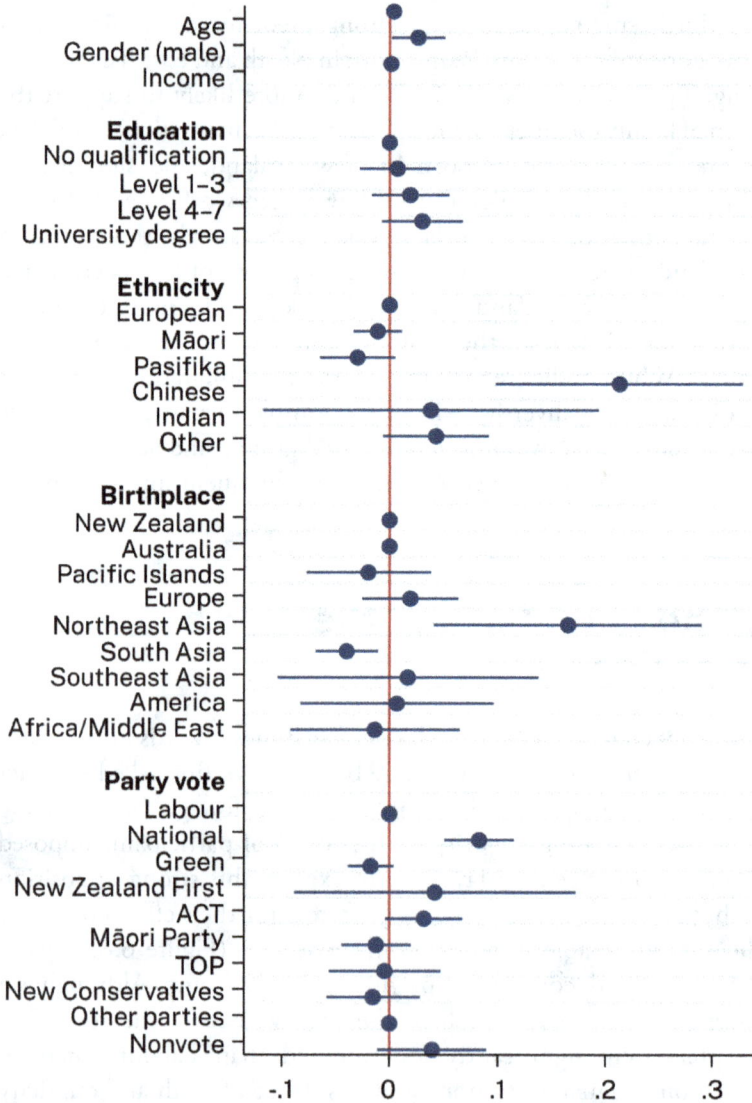

Figure 6.8 Should the housing market be open to foreign buyers living overseas?

Source: Vowles et al. (2022a).

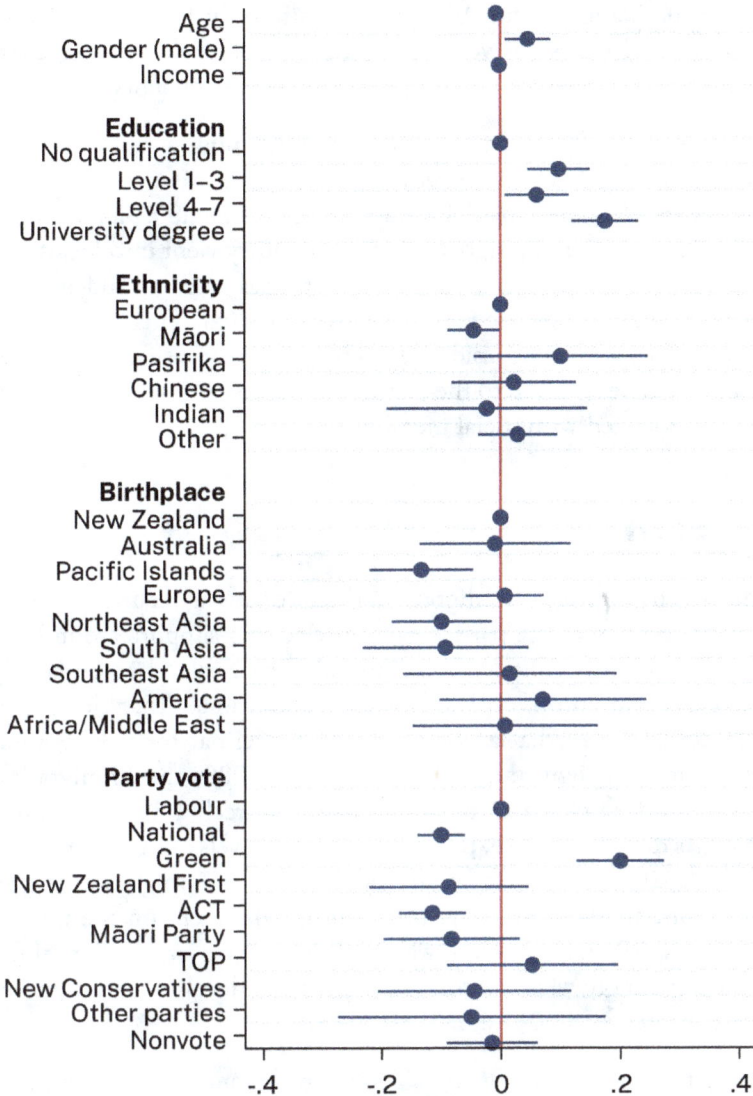

Figure 6.9 Should immigrants have access to welfare?
Source: Vowles et al. (2022a).

We then asked whether immigrants on work visas of two years or more should be eligible to receive welfare benefits (Figure 6.9). More than half of participants replied either 'Definitely no' (32 per cent) or 'Probably no' (26 per cent), while 17 per cent were unsure and less than one-quarter were in favour (23 per cent). A majority opposed extending welfare support to this group of immigrants, but partisanship also played a significant role:

177

those voting for National and ACT were significantly less supportive of giving immigrants access to welfare, whereas almost half (49 per cent) of Green voters supported immigrants' access to welfare benefits.[13]

With the exception of Green voters, then, public opinion in this respect was largely in line with existing government policy. For example, while the government extended the Covid-19 wage subsidy scheme to all workers, regardless of residency or visa status, when the country went into lockdown in March 2020, migrants on non-permanent visas were excluded from other key aspects of the welfare regime (Fonseka 2020a). This exclusion of migrants without permanent residence from emergency welfare reinforced the distinction between access to the New Zealand labour market and access to the rights associated with social membership.

Conclusion

Before the pandemic, anti-immigration rhetoric was a recurrent theme among xenophobic populist parties gaining electoral support around the world. McMillan and Gibbons (2020) found New Zealand to be largely a 'populist exception' in this regard in 2017 but cautioned that changes in the immigration and media landscape created potential for immigration to become a more salient and divisive issue. By 2020, the immigration landscape had indeed changed, but in a manner scarcely imaginable three years earlier. As discussed above, the unprecedented levels of immigration of 2017 had by 2020 given way to border closures. With immigration largely stalled, and with an all-consuming media and public focus on the myriad effects of Covid-19, immigration was of low salience at election time. Perhaps unsurprisingly, views about the appropriate levels of immigration remained stable between 2017 and 2020.

Indeed, voters were more positive about the economic and cultural consequences of immigration in 2020 than they had been previously. This could be due in part to media and elite messaging. News coverage during the pandemic highlighted the absence of immigrant labour in a range of sectors and was largely sympathetic to stories of immigrants' experiences.

---

13   This could indicate acceptance of the current immigration system within which access to permanent status and associated social rights varies substantially based on visa type. Just as likely, however, is that NZES participants, like New Zealanders generally, lack understanding of the complexity in the immigration system and of discrepancies in status and rights available to different groups of immigrants regardless of their contribution to the labour market.

Such stories highlighted the dislocating effect of border closures on the lives of many immigrants, especially long-term workers settled in New Zealand with family who were stranded offshore at the time the border shut but who did not have the permanent resident status required to re-enter the country. In many cases, however, those people most affected by this border exclusion could not vote, and their cause did not mobilise sufficient support for immigration to become a major election issue. Nonetheless, media coverage of migrants' difficulties, combined with extensive coverage of the economic impact of border closures on businesses, potentially reduced the space for anti-immigrant discourse to develop. Also limiting that space was inclusionary elite messaging about immigrants and immigration; this likely played a role in decreasing both the salience of immigration and concerns about its effects. As with the political response to the Christchurch terror attack the year before, the prime minister's language of unity and kindness in the first phase of the pandemic explicitly rejected exclusionary rhetoric. Immigrants on temporary visas were rhetorically included in the Team of Five Million, even if some later came to complain that the policy was exclusionary in practice and the Team of Five Million rhetoric was misleading (Bonnett 2021; The Indian News 2021).

The immigration and broader political contexts of the 2020 election were undoubtedly extraordinary and, as the severity of the pandemic began to wane in 2022 and the border reopened, New Zealand again began to experience high inward migration, as well as high levels of emigration (StatsNZ 2023). Indeed, net migration for the year to March 2023 had risen to 65,400—above the net average for the years 2002–19 (StatsNZ 2023). Breaking with the pre-pandemic trend, though, there also appeared to be a change in emphasis from temporary to permanent migration. In May 2022, the government announced its long-signalled 'rebalancing' of immigration policy (Cooke 2022), which created a streamlined path to residency for migrants whose occupations were on a 'green list', and more than 200,000 people who had been stuck in the country during the pandemic were granted a one-off resident visa.

In late August 2022, however, then new Minister of Immigration, Michael Wood, announced a series of measures to facilitate the entry of temporary migrants to fill labour shortages across a wide range of industries (Wood 2022). This policy was reminiscent of the pre-pandemic reliance on temporary migration to fill labour market gaps and, by June 2023, the media was reporting a return to pre-pandemic migration trends driven by those on student, non-resident work, and tourist visas (MacLeod 2023).

Questions seem likely to continue about where the appropriate balance between permanent and temporary migration lies and the extent to which New Zealand should return to a high-volume economically driven immigration system. Such contestation of immigration settings may grow, especially if associated with ongoing labour market shortages and other negative economic indicators. It could also drive broader public debate about the impacts of immigration on New Zealand society.

References

ACT. 2020. *Immigration*. Auckland: ACT. Available from: www.act.org.nz/immigration.

Artiles, A.M., and G. Meardi. 2014. 'Public Opinion, Immigration and Welfare in the Context of Uncertainty.' *Transfer: European Review of Labour and Research* 20(1): 53–68. doi.org/10.1177/1024258913515368.

Beattie, A., and R. Priestley. 2021. 'Fighting COVID with the Team of 5 Million: Aotearoa New Zealand Government Communication during the 2020 Lockdown.' *Social Sciences & Humanities Open* 4(1): 100209. doi.org/10.1016/j.ssaho.2021.100209.

Bishin, B.G., T.J. Hayes, M.B. Incantalupo, and C.A. Smith. 2021. 'Immigration and Public Opinion: Will Backlash Impede Immigrants' Policy Progress?' *Social Science Quarterly* 102(6): 3036–49. doi.org/10.1111/ssqu.13077.

Boelhouwer, J., G. Kraaycamp, and I. Stoop (eds). 2016. *Trust, Life Satisfaction and Opinions on Immigration in 15 European Countries*. New York, NY: Netherlands Institute for Social Research. doi.org/10.4324/9781003077558-1.

Bonnett, G. 2019. 'Immigration Quota Talks Begin As 35,000 Wait on Residency Decision.' *Radio New Zealand*, 5 December. Available from: www.rnz.co.nz/news/national/404866/immigration-quota-talks-begin-as-35-000-wait-on-residency-decision.

Bonnett, G. 2020a. 'Visa Delays Leave Immigrant Families in "Tricky" Situations.' *Radio New Zealand*, 25 June. Available from: www.nzherald.co.nz/nz/visa-delays-leave-immigrant-families-in-tricky-situations/2CJFZ2GBECQKKYRPR2QRWNVRL4/.

Bonnett, G. 2020b. 'Election 2020: Immigration Reset or a New Normal?' *Radio New Zealand*, 26 September. Available from: www.rnz.co.nz/news/national/426983/election-2020-immigration-reset-or-a-new-normal.

Bonnett, G. 2021. 'Benefits for Migrants to End Today: "What Happened to Our Fabled Kindness?"' *Radio New Zealand*, 31 August. Available from: www. rnz.co.nz/news/covid-19/450385/benefits-for-migrants-to-end-today-what-happened-to-our-fabled-kindness.

Boomgaarden, H.G., and R. Vliegenthart. 2009. 'How News Content Influences Anti-Immigrant Attitudes: Germany, 1993–2005.' *European Journal of Political Research* 48(4): 516–42. doi.org/10.1111/j.1475-6765.2009.01831.x.

Carvalho, J., and D. Ruedin. 2020. 'The Positions Mainstream Left Parties Adopt on Immigration: A Cross-Cutting Cleavage?' *Party Politics* 26(4): 379–89.

Claassen, C., and L. McLaren. 2021. 'Does Immigration Produce a Public Backlash or Public Acceptance? Time-Series, Cross-Sectional Evidence from Thirty European Democracies.' *British Journal of Political Science* 52(3): 1–19. doi.org/ 10.1017/S0007123421000260.

Cooke, H. 2022. 'Immigration Overhaul: Government Introduces "Fast-Track" to Residency for Some Migrants—But with Hefty Pay Requirement.' *Stuff*, [Wellington], 11 May. Available from: www.stuff.co.nz/national/politics/30058 5646/immigration-overhaul-government-introduces-fasttrack-to-residency-for-some-migrants--but-with-hefty-pay-requirement.

Daniels, C., P. DiMaggio, G.C. Mora, and H. Shepherd. 2021. 'Has Pandemic Threat Stoked Xenophobia? How COVID-19 Influences California Voters' Attitudes toward Diversity and Immigration.' *Sociological Forum* 36(4): 889–915. doi.org/10.1111/socf.12750.

Davison, I. 2017. 'Election 2017: Labour and National Appeal to First Home Buyers.' *New Zealand Herald*, 21 August. Available from: www.nzherald.co.nz/ kahu/election-2017-labour-and-national-appeal-to-first-home-buyers/2SA2 U3TYCT5ITQZEOXU527WMDI/.

Douglas, M. 1966. *Purity and Danger: An Analysis of the Concepts of Pollution and Taboo*. London: Routledge & Kegan Paul.

Eun Kim, S., A.J. Shin, and Y. Yang. 2022. 'The Usual Suspects?: Attitudes Towards Immigration during the COVID-19 Pandemic.' *Journal of Asian Public Policy*. doi.org/10.1080/17516234.2022.2046686.

Faafoi, K. 2020. 'Seasonal Work Visa Available to More People.' Media release, 22 September. Wellington: New Zealand Government. Available from: www. beehive.govt.nz/release/seasonal-work-visa-available-more-people.

Fonseka, D. 2020a. 'Three-Tier Welfare System "Lacks Dignity".' *Newsroom*, [Auckland], 24 June. Available from: www.newsroom.co.nz/the-three-tier-welfare-state.

Fonseka, D. 2020b. 'The Immigration "Policy Hole".' *Newsroom*, [Auckland], 24 September, [Updated 25 January 2021]. Available from: www.newsroom. co.nz/the-immigration-policy-hole.

Freeman, G.P., R. Hansen, and D.L. Leal. 2013. *Immigration and Public Opinion in Liberal Democracies*. New York, NY: Routledge. doi.org/10.4324/9780203 095133.

Freitag, M., and N. Hofstetter. 2022. 'Pandemic Threat and Intergroup Relations: How Negative Emotions Associated with the Threat of Covid-19 Shape Attitudes Towards Immigrants.' *Journal of Ethnic and Migration Studies* 48(13): 2985–3004. doi.org/10.1080/1369183x.2022.2031925.

Greaves, L., and J. Vowles. 2020. 'Measuring Populism in New Zealand.' In *A Populist Exception? The 2017 New Zealand General Election*, edited by J. Vowles and J. Curtin, 71–106. Canberra: ANU Press. doi.org/10.22459/PE.2020.03.

Green Party of Aotearoa New Zealand. 2020. *Immigration Policy*. Wellington: Green Party of Aotearoa New Zealand. Available from: www.greens.org.nz/immigration _policy.

Hatton, T. 2016. 'Immigration, Public Opinion and the Recession in Europe.' *Economic Policy* 31(86): 205–46. doi.org/10.1093/epolic/eiw004.

Haynes, C., J.L. Merolla, and S.K. Ramakrishnan. 2016. *Framing Immigrants: News Coverage, Public Opinion, and Policy*. New York, NY: Russell Sage Foundation.

The Indian News. 2021. 'The March of Migrants II—Team of Five Million?' *The Indian News*, [Wellington], 10 July.

Infometrics. 2021. *Coming Home, or Not Leaving? Changing Migration Patterns in New Zealand*. Report prepared for WSP and the Helen Clark Foundation. July. Wellington: Infometrics.

Jakovljevic, M., S. Bjedov, N. Kaksic, and I. Jakocljevic. 2020. 'Covid-19 Pandemia and Public and Global Health from the Perspective of Global Health Security.' *Psychiatria Danubina* 32(1): 6–14. doi.org/10.24869/psyd.2020.6.

Knight, D. 2021. 'New Zealand: Legal Response to Covid-19.' In *The Oxford Compendium of National Legal Responses to Covid-19*, edited by J. King and O.L.M. Ferraz. Oxford, UK: Oxford University Press. doi.org/10.1093/law-occ19/e4.013.4.

Kustov, A., D. Laaker, and C. Reller. 2021. 'The Stability of Immigration Attitudes: Evidence and Implications.' *Journal of Politics* 83(4): 1478–94. doi.org/10.1086/ 715061.

Laaker, D. 2023. 'Economic Shocks and the Development of Immigration Attitudes.' *British Journal of Political Science*: 1–21. doi.org/10.1017/S0007123 42300011X.

Lancaster, C. 2022. 'Value Shift: Immigration Attitudes and the Sociocultural Divide.' *British Journal of Political Science* 52(1): 1–20. doi.org/10.1017/S0007 123420000526.

Lapinski, J.S., P. Peltola, G. Shaw, and A. Yang. 1997. 'Trends: Immigrants and Immigration.' *Public Opinion Quarterly* 61(2): 356–83. doi.org/10.1086/ 297799.

Leahy, B. 2020. 'Coronavirus Outbreak: Calm Urged as Anti-Chinese Sentiment Felt in New Zealand.' *New Zealand Herald*, 31 January. Available from: www.nz herald.co.nz/nz/coronavirus-outbreak-calm-urged-as-anti-chinese-sentiment-felt-in-new-zealand/D4JRRSEFYA2VMQUF7FSMXJYAKM.

Lee, S.-y., S. Yuen, N.H.K. Or, E.W. Cheng, and R.P.H. Yue. 2022. 'Pandemic Vulnerability, Policy Feedback and Support for Immigration: Evidence from Asia.' *British Journal of Social Psychology* 61: 1124–43. doi.org/10.1111/bjso.12529.

Lees-Galloway, I. 2020. 'Pragmatic Changes to Immigration Act to Respond to COVID-19 Passed.' Media release, 13 May. Wellington: New Zealand Government. Available from: www.beehive.govt.nz/release/pragmatic-changes-immigration-act-respond-covid-19-passed.

MacLeod, I. 2023. 'Most Migrants Here for A Good Time, Not A Long Time.' *Business Desk*, [Auckland], 6 June. Available from: businessdesk.co.nz/article/ immigration/most-migrants-here-for-a-good-time-not-a-long-time.

Markel, H., and A.M. Stern. 2002. 'The Foreignness of Germs: The Persistent Association of Immigrants and Disease in American Society.' *The Milbank Quarterly* 80(4): 757–88. doi.org/10.1111/1468-0009.00030.

McLaren, L., H. Boomgaarden, and R. Vliegenthart. 2018. 'News Coverage and Public Concern About Immigration in Britain.' *International Journal of Public Opinion Research* 30(2): 173–93. doi.org/10.1093/ijpor/edw033.

McLaren, L., and I. Paterson. 2020. 'Generational Change and Attitudes to Immigration.' *Journal of Ethnic and Migration Studies* 46(3): 665–82. doi.org/ 10.1080/1369183X.2018.1550170.

McMillan, K., and M. Gibbons. 2020. 'Immigration and Populism in the 2017 New Zealand Election.' In *A Populist Exception? The 2017 New Zealand General Election*, edited by J. Vowles and J. Curtin, 137–78. Canberra: ANU Press. doi.org/10.22459/PE.2020.05.

Ministry of Business, Innovation and Employment. 2017. *Briefing for the Incoming Minister of Immigration.* Wellington: New Zealand Government.

Ministry of Business, Innovation and Employment. 2020. *Briefing for the Incoming Minister of Immigration.* Wellington: New Zealand Government.

Ministry of Social Development. 2020. *Benefit System Update—August 2020.* Wellington: New Zealand Government. Available from: www.msd.govt.nz/about-msd-and-our-work/publications-resources/statistics/covid-19/benefit-system-update-august-2020.html.

Nash, S., and K. Faafoi. 2021. 'Immigration Reset: Setting the Scene.' Speech, 17 May. Wellington: New Zealand Government. Available from: www.beehive.govt.nz/speech/immigration-reset-setting-scene.

Neureiter, M. 2021. 'The Effect of Immigrant Integration Policies on Public Immigration Attitudes: Evidence from a Survey Experiment in the United Kingdom.' *The International Migration Review* 56(4): 1040–68. doi.org/10.1177/01979183211063499.

New Zealand First. 2020. *Immigration.* Accessed from: www.nzfirst.nz/immigration [page discontinued].

New Zealand Labour Party. 2020. *Our Manifesto to Keep New Zealand Moving: Labour 2020.* 13 October. Wellington: Labour. Available from: www.labour.org.nz/news-labour_2020_manifesto.

New Zealand Treasury. 2018. *Screening of Residential Land: Questions and Answers.* Wellington: New Zealand Government. Available from: www.treasury.govt.nz/sites/default/files/2018-08/screening-res-land-qanda.pdf.

New Zealand Treasury. 2020. *Pre-Election Economic and Fiscal Update 2020.* Wellington: New Zealand Government. Available from: www.treasury.govt.nz/publications/efu/pre-election-economic-and-fiscal-update-2020-html#section-4.

Odmalm, P., and T. Bale. 2015. 'Immigration into the Mainstream: Conflicting Ideological Streams, Strategic Reasoning and Party Competition.' *Acta Publica* 50: 365–78. doi.org/10.1057/ap.2014.28.

Office of the Minister of Immigration. 2021. *Long-term Direction for the Immigration Portfolio: A Rebalance.* Cabinet Paper, July. Wellington: New Zealand Government.

Organisation for Economic Co-operation and Development (OECD). 2021. *International Migration Outlook.* Paris: OECD Publishing.

Pickup, M., E.A. de Rooij, C. van der Linden, and M.J. Goodwin. 2021. 'Brexit, COVID-19, and Attitudes Toward Immigration in Britain.' *Social Science Quarterly* 102(5): 2184–93. doi.org/10.1111/ssqu.13010.

Pryce, D.K. 2018. 'U.S. Citizens' Current Attitudes Toward Immigrants and Immigration: A Study from the General Social Survey.' *Social Science Quarterly* 99(4): 1467–83. doi.org/10.1111/ssqu.12514.

Radio New Zealand (RNZ). 2019a. 'Firearms Amendment Bill Passes Final Reading in Parliament.' *Radio New Zealand*, 10 April. Available from: www.rnz.co.nz/news/national/386778/firearms-amendment-bill-passes-final-reading-in-parliament.

Radio New Zealand (RNZ). 2019b. 'New Residents Down While Temporary Visas Up.' *Radio New Zealand*, 17 July. Available from: www.rnz.co.nz/news/national/394546/new-residents-down-while-temporary-visas-up.

Roy, E.A. 2019. '"Real Leaders Do Exist": Jacinda Ardern Uses Solace and Steel to Guide a Broken Nation.' *The Guardian*, 19 March. Available from: www.theguardian.com/world/2019/mar/19/real-leaders-do-exist-jacinda-ardern-uses-solace-and-steel-to-guide-a-broken-nation.

Satherley, N., K. Yogeeswaran, D. Osborne, S. Shanaah, and C.G. Sibley. 2021. 'Investigating the Effects of Right-Wing Terrorism on Government Satisfaction: A Time Course Analysis of the 2019 Christchurch Terror Attack.' Studies in Conflict & Terrorism. doi.org/10.1080/1057610X.2021.1913819.

Shanaah, S., K. Yogeeswaran, L. Greaves, J.A. Bulbulia, D. Osborne, M.U. Afzali, and C.G. Sibley. 2021. 'Hate Begets Warmth? The Impact of an Anti-Muslim Terrorist Attack on Public Attitudes toward Muslims.' Terrorism and Political Violence 35(1): 156–74. doi.org/10.1080/09546553.2021.1877673.

She, Z., K.-M. Ng, X. Hou, and J. Xi. 2022. 'COVID-19 Threat and Xenophobia: A Moderated Mediation Model of Empathic Responding and Negative Emotions.' *Journal of Social Issues* 78(1): 209–26. doi.org/10.1111/josi.12500.

StatsNZ. 2022. *Unemployment Rate*. Wellington: Statistics New Zealand. Available from: www.stats.govt.nz/indicators/unemployment-rate/.

StatsNZ. 2023. *International Migration: March 2023*. Wellington: Statistics New Zealand. Available from: www.stats.govt.nz/information-releases/international-migration-march-2023/.

Stockemer, D., A. Neimann, D. Unger, and J. Speyer. 2020. 'The "Refugee Crisis", Immigration Attitudes, and Euroscepticism.' *The International Migration Review* 54(3): 883–912. doi.org/10.1177/0197918319879926.

Tan, L. 2021. 'Covid 19 Coronavirus: Chinese Kiwis Fear for Safety As More Experience Discrimination Amid Pandemic.' *New Zealand Herald*, 17 February. Available from: www.nzherald.co.nz/kahu/covid-19-coronavirus-chinese-kiwis-fear-for-safety-as-more-experience-discrimination-amid-pandemic/TTFCG6Y YXVCSMLN2NRM3PV6OUU/.

Taylor, P. 2020. 'New Zealand House Prices Soar Despite Covid Recession, Worsening Affordability Crisis.' *The Guardian*, 29 October. Available from: www.the guardian.com/world/2020/oct/29/new-zealand-house-prices-soar-despite-covid-recession-worsening-affordability-crisis.

Victor, K. 2019. 'Public Opinion on Immigration.' *Oxford Bibliographies Online*. Oxford, UK: Oxford University Press. doi.org/10.1093/OBO/9780199756223-0280.

Vowles, J., F. Barker, M. Krewel, J. Hayward, J. Curtin, L. Greaves, and L. Oldfield. 2022a. *2020 New Zealand Election Study*. [Online]. ADA Dataverse, V3. doi.org/ 10.26193/BPAMYJ.

Vowles, J., S. Banducci, J. Karp, P. Aimer, and R. Miller. 2022b. *2002 New Zealand Election Study*. [Online]. ADA Dataverse, V6. doi.org/10.26193/9DE0X4.

Vowles, J., S. Banducci, J. Karp, R. Miller, and A. Sullivan. 2022c. *2005 New Zealand Election Study*. [Online]. ADA Dataverse, V3. doi.org/10.26193/WJ8DGC.

Vowles, J., H. Coffé, J. Curtin, and G. Cotterell. 2022d. *2014 New Zealand Election Study*. [Online]. ADA Dataverse, V3. doi.org/10.26193/MF9DNL.

Vowles, J., G. Cotterell, R. Miller, and J. Curtin. 2022e. *2011 New Zealand Election Study*. [Online]. ADA Dataverse, V3. doi.org/10.26193/YZDMF3.

Vowles, J., and J. Curtin (eds). 2020. *A Populist Exception? The 2017 New Zealand General Election*. Canberra: ANU Press. doi.org/10.22459/PE.2020.

Vowles, J., K. McMillan, F. Barker, J. Curtin, J. Hayward, L. Greaves, and C. Crothers. 2022f. *2017 New Zealand Election Study*. [Online]. ADA Dataverse, V3. doi.org/ 10.26193/28JJFB.

Wood, M. 2022. 'Government Steps Up Action to Plug Skills Gap.' Media release, 21 August. Wellington: New Zealand Government. Available from: www.beehive. govt.nz/release/government-steps-action-plug-skills-gaps.

Woodhouse, M. 2017. 'Speech Outlining the Government's Plan for Immigration.' Speech, 19 April. Wellington: New Zealand Government. Available from: www. beehive.govt.nz/speech/speech-outlining-government's-plan-immigration.

Woods, E.T., R. Schertzer, L. Greenfield, C. Hughes, and C. Miller-Idriss. 2020. 'Covid-19, Nationalism, and the Politics of Crisis: A Scholarly Exchange.' *Nations and Nationalism* 26(4): 807–25. doi.org/10.1111/nana.12644.

Appendix 6.1

Table A6.1 Logistic regression: Wanting level of immigration to decrease by SES, ethnicity, birthplace, and party vote*

	Model 1a Immigration	Model 1b Immigration	Model 1c Immigration	Model 1d Immigration
Age	0.004	0.007**	0.005	0.003
	(0.003)	(0.003)	(0.003)	(0.003)
Gender (male)	0.095	0.119	0.085	0.077
	(0.099)	(0.100)	(0.100)	(0.102)
Income	−0.001	−0.001	−0.001	−0.001
	(0.001)	(0.001)	(0.001)	(0.001)
Education (ref: no qualification)				
Level 1–3 qualification	−0.248	−0.176	−0.269	−0.226
	(0.166)	(0.170)	(0.168)	(0.169)
Level 4–7 qualification	−0.158	−0.095	−0.112	−0.156
	(0.173)	(0.176)	(0.174)	(0.176)
University degree	−0.861***	−0.724***	−0.775***	−0.845***
	(0.172)	(0.175)	(0.174)	(0.173)
Ethnicity (ref: NZ European)				
Māori		0.603***		
		(0.130)		
Pasifika		0.846***		
		(0.295)		
Chinese		−0.012		
		(0.281)		
Indian		0.281		
		(0.456)		
Other		−0.293*		
		(0.162)		
Country of birth (ref: New Zealand)				
Australia			−0.154	
			(0.345)	
Pacific Islands			−0.051	
			(0.383)	
Europe			−0.460**	
			(0.188)	
North-East Asia			−0.359	
			(0.348)	

	Model 1a Immigration	Model 1b Immigration	Model 1c Immigration	Model 1d Immigration
South Asia			0.417	
			(0.492)	
South-East Asia			−0.414	
			(0.381)	
America			−0.866	
			(0.548)	
Africa/Middle East			−0.402	
			(0.392)	
Party vote (ref: Labour)				
National				0.088
				(0.112)
Green				−0.579***
				(0.164)
New Zealand First				0.796**
				(0.340)
ACT				0.292*
				(0.168)
Māori Party				0.091
				(0.342)
TOP				−0.072
				(0.335)
New Conservatives				−0.346
				(0.442)
Other parties				1.320**
				(0.557)
Nonvote				0.086
				(0.192)
Constant	0.138	−0.192	0.171	0.132
	(0.248)	(0.270)	(0.250)	(0.249)
No.	3,410	3,384	3,344	3,321
Pseudo R^2	0.0239	0.0370	0.0296	0.0367

* $p < 0.10$
** $p < 0.05$
*** $p < 0.01$

Notes: Standard errors in parentheses; NZES sampling weights applied.
Source: Vowles et al. (2022a).

7

Gendering Leadership and Policy during Covid-19: Jacinda Ardern and the women's vote

Jennifer Curtin, V.K.G. Woodman, and Lara Greaves

Introduction

During the first six months of 2020, international media focussed on whether women political leaders were more effective than their male counterparts at managing the Covid-19 crisis. New Zealand Prime Minister Jacinda Ardern was front and centre of many of these analyses. Her inclusive and reassuring communication style accompanied comparatively extreme measures towards elimination, including international border closures, national lockdowns, and mandatory quarantine for New Zealanders returning to the country.

The 2020 election was one in which women leaders featured across the political spectrum. Judith Collins had taken the helm of National a little less than two months before the scheduled election date of 19 September, in part because the party was struggling in the polls.[1] In addition, of the three minor parties that entered parliament in 2020, two—Te Pāti Māori (the Māori Party) and the Green Party—had a woman co-leader. Alongside this, the 2020 result saw the largest number of women candidates (48 per cent) elected to parliament.

---

1   On 17 August, the election was rescheduled to 17 October 2020. Collins became leader on 12 July 2020.

In this chapter, we explore the extent to which New Zealand voters' views reflected the international awe of Ardern's leadership, and whether women's opinions on key policy issues shed light on whether women felt sufficiently included in the 'Team of Five Million'. Drawing on the NZES, we explore the responses of women and men of different ages to questions of women's leadership, as well as to leadership attributes of trust, competence, and likeability. We also investigate voters' perceptions of issues and government policy responses in relation to women's and men's policy preferences, with a particular focus on health, given the prominence and impact of the pandemic, with an exploration of differences among women.[2]

As such, we examine the extent to which the descriptive and symbolic representations of women as political leaders are connected to the substantive representation of policy issues in the 2020 New Zealand election. While this election featured two high-profile women major-party leaders, there was little campaigning by them on gender-related topics, which was largely left to the Greens. In its glowing endorsement of Prime Minister Ardern, the international media missed the fact that the government's pandemic economic recovery policies had focussed largely on traditionally male jobs with limited investment in the care economy and marginal support for those on benefits.

We find that New Zealand women voters continue to be more supportive than their male counterparts of increasing expenditure on social policy and health. And, despite its lack of a gender-specific policy lens on key issues relating to Covid-19, Labour was not penalised for this absence. Indeed, women returned to Labour in larger numbers than ever. The party also won its largest share of the male vote since the advent of the MMP electoral system in 1996. However, the gender gaps in vote choice are not stagnant over time, meaning these wins for Labour cannot be taken for granted.

---

2   The full sample (before standard sample weighting for gender, age, and Māori descent was applied) contained responses from 2,112 women (56.6 per cent of the sample), 1,563 men (41.9 per cent), and 15 participants who identified as 'gender diverse' (0.4 per cent). Further work could explore the voter preferences of gender-diverse voters (see, for example, Worthen 2020), however, we excluded this group from the analyses due to their small sample size.

Bringing a gender lens to pandemic political leadership

Crisis events heighten people's anxiety and their expectations of political leaders and, in response, political leaders must provide rapid and comprehensive policy and political solutions that rhetorically and substantively straddle political divides. As such, crisis leadership differs from routine political leadership. The risks are much higher, the public is more attentive, and the decision-making is more urgent (Ansell et al. 2014). With the advent of Covid-19 and the resulting cross-national variations in policy responses, there has been increased interest in gender and crisis leadership (Politics and Gender 2020). The challenge for such research is that there is a very limited pool of women leaders globally to test whether this descriptive representation impacts on policy outcomes or voters' interpretation thereof.

In New Zealand, women political leaders are not new. The 2020 election is the second general election in which both the Labour and the National parties were led by women and Ardern was New Zealand's third woman prime minister. Given this, we could expect both men and women to be comfortable with the idea of women's political leadership, irrespective of the pandemic.

To investigate this, the NZES asked respondents whether, overall, men make better leaders than women. Answers are indicated on a scale of one (strongly disagree) to five (strongly agree), with three being neutral (see Figure 7.1). We found statistically significant differences between groups' opinions of gendered fitness for leadership ($p < 0.001$), with men's average score of 1.83, higher than the 1.52 of women. However, in both groups, the mean rating is low (and lower than in 2017), indicating a low average level of agreement with the statement (Curtin and Greaves 2020, 193).

We also examined these results according to the combination of gender and party vote and found statistically significant differences between combinations of gender and party vote in their average rating of the statement ($p < 0.001$) (Figure 7.2). Men voting ACT and National scored highest on agreement. However, the average for ACT-voting men is still lower than the midpoint of the scale. This indicates that, across the board, people tend to disagree with this statement, regardless of their gender and party vote combination. The biggest difference between men and women within the same party was found for ACT voters, with a difference of 0.59 of a point between genders. The differences were similar for National and Labour at 0.28 each, while Green Party voters had the smallest gender difference. Overall, this shows a low level of general agreement with the notion that men make better political leaders than women, with some patterns of difference depending on gender and party vote.

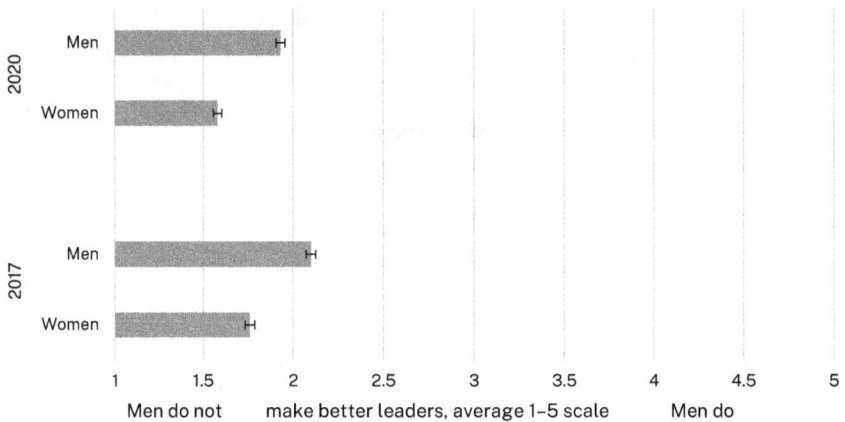

Figure 7.1 Do men make better leaders than women? 2017–2020
Source: Vowles et al. (2022).

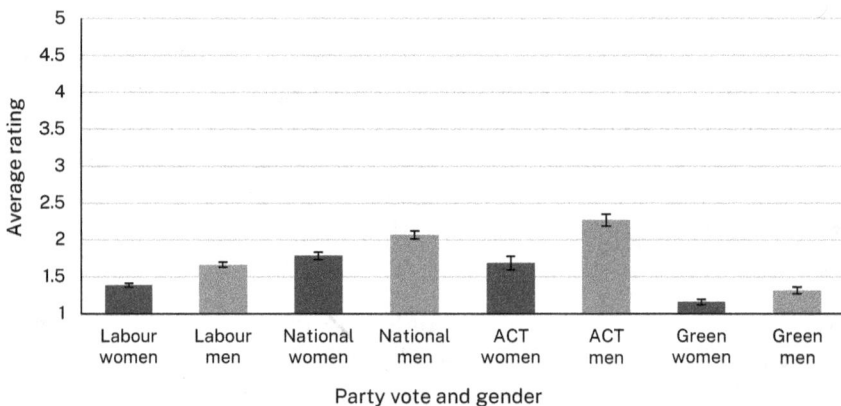

Figure 7.2 Do men make better leaders than women? Gender and party vote
Source: Vowles et al. (2022).

We found that when organised according to gender and generation, there were statistically significant differences between groups ($p < 0.001$) in their average rating of the statement (see Figure 7.3). Again, these responses all fall below the scale midpoint of three, indicating general disagreement with the statement across generation and gender. Comparing genders within the same generation, women of all generations were less likely to agree with the statement than men from their cohort.

However, the gender dimensions of the generational groupings suggest more analysis is required. Specifically, we see different patterns among men across generations.[3] The highest mean agreement was from men of the interwar generation, but the second-highest mean agreement was for men from Generation Z (those born after 1996). This suggests that while women become increasingly accepting of women's fitness for political leadership over time, this may not be the case for men. Future research will need to monitor the attitudes of younger men specifically to explore whether this is a real effect (that is, not based on a small subsample size). However, the universally low level of agreement with the statement, and the small downward shift over time, could indicate that women's leadership is viewed as increasingly normal over time.

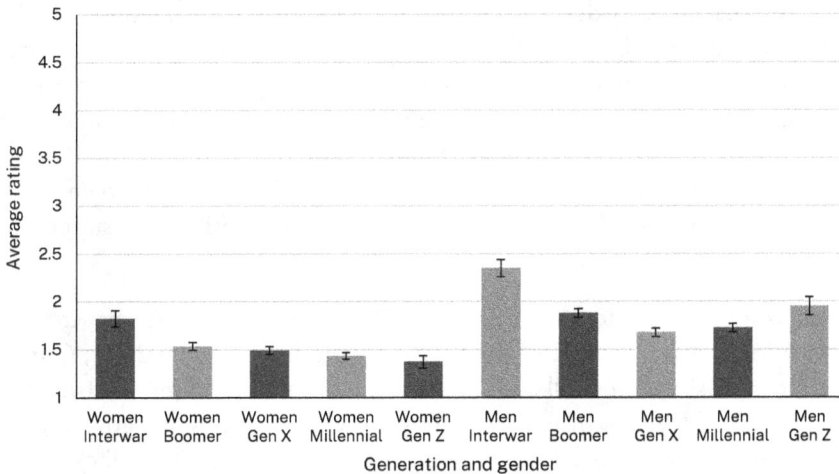

Figure 7.3 Do men make better leaders than women? Generation and gender

Source: Vowles et al. (2022).

---

3   The age categories are as follows: War and interwar: born 1945 or earlier; Baby Boomers: born 1946–64; Generation X: born 1965–79; Millennials: born 1980–96; and Generation Z: born after 1996.

Despite these gender gaps in attitudes to who is best suited to political leadership, Jacinda Ardern's leadership style garnered much attention before and during the pandemic (Anderson 2020; Curtin 2020c; Curtin and Greaves 2020; Friedman 2020; Taub 2020). In the 2017 election campaign, Ardern's political rhetoric emphasised kindness, inclusion, and hope, and frequently elicited a transformative policy agenda that would address poverty, inequality, and climate change.

Analysis of the 2017 NZES showed that this discursive approach was inclusive and convincing enough to prevent divisive or extreme populist politics from taking hold (Curtin and Greaves 2020). Once elected, Ardern's references to kindness and her inclusive, 'embracing' political rhetoric became a recurring theme of her first prime ministerial term. In her statement to the UN General Assembly in 2018, Ardern said:

> Be it domestic, or international, we are operating in challenging times … Perhaps then it is time to step back from the chaos and ask what we want. It is in that space that we'll find simplicity. The simplicity of peace, of prosperity, of fairness. If I could distil it down into one concept that we are pursuing in New Zealand it is simple and it is this. Kindness. (Ardern 2018)

Six months later, Ardern again invoked 'kindness' in response to the 15 March 2019 Christchurch terrorist attack, in which 51 people were killed. At press conferences and in subsequent statements, Ardern spoke of inclusion and compassion. Her embracing positioning of those who were affected gained substantial popular currency (Ardern 2019). Her government also acted rapidly to reform New Zealand's gun ownership laws, with the *Arms Act* amendment passing on 10 April 2019, supported by all but one MP.

This compassion and determined resolve became features of Ardern's leadership from the outset of the Covid-19 pandemic (Craig 2021; Curtin 2020a; Johnson and Williams 2020; Pullen and Vachhani 2020). In a response that deviated from that in most OECD countries, her government closed the international border and imposed strict domestic lockdowns to suppress viral transmission. New Zealand's geographic isolation 'at the bottom of the South Pacific'—a feature to which Ardern had drawn attention in her UN speech two years earlier—facilitated this response. The public health and economic policy measures that accompanied it were not unlike those seen elsewhere, but such restrictive policies were nonetheless not without political risk (Curtin and O'Sullivan 2023). However, Ardern's pre-existing emphasis on kindness and mutual care, in both state and society, ensured the Team of Five Million became an accepted part of her Covid-19 communication strategy (Beattie and Priestley 2021).

More generally, Ardern's use of mainstream and social media and her style of communication helped build support for her government's Covid-19 response. As the pandemic took hold, it became 'a matter of routine for many New Zealanders to have the prime minister in their homes', whether through the daily press conferences or Ardern's tendency to develop a 'personal-connection approach' through her use of social media (Bickerton 2021, 174). This was not a new strategy for the prime minister: in 2018, she announced her pregnancy on Instagram and, six months later, she announced a new family assistance package on Facebook Live as she cradled her newborn daughter.

Facebook was Ardern's preferred medium. There she exuded a comfortable conversational style, which—in the face of uncertainty, fear, misinformation, and some citizen scepticism—served as an important means to allay anxieties during the pandemic and the 2020 election campaign. It also enabled Ardern to supplement the traditional manicured style of television appearances and daily press conferences. Like traditional media, however, Ardern's online communications remained largely monodirectional, giving her 'tighter control' over her message while largely preserving the feeling of personal connection (Bickerton 2021, 176). The approach seemingly worked. In 2020, *PRovoke Media*'s global survey of public relations experts ranked Ardern as the most impressive leader for Covid-19 communications (Sudhaman 2020). A 2020 Scottish study argued that her warm, informal use of Facebook Live helped convey vital Covid-19 messages in a clear, relatable, and authentic way (McGuire et al. 2020).

National opposition leader Judith Collins' leadership style differed markedly from Ardern's. In her memoir *Pulling No Punches*, Collins reveals her scepticism of centrism, which she views as an excuse to do nothing and stand for nothing. In contrast to National Party Prime Minister John Key (2008–16), Collins' preference was to appeal to National's conservative base in a way that was reminiscent of the approach of National's earlier leader Don Brash (2003–06) to economics and 'separatist politics' (Curtin 2020b). Collins' maiden speech and her memoir demonstrate a disdain for what she calls the 'lazy gene' and a welfare system that 'funded women to have multiple children' (Collins 2002). Her direct and combative rhetoric differentiated her from Ardern. Collins was rewarded for this with positive verdicts after the first two televised leaders' debates. It was not evident, however, that this endeared Collins to the wider electorate.

While the NZES does not ask participants about perceived kindness or hostility in political rhetoric, it does include questions about three leadership attributes: trustworthiness, competence, and likeability. Given Collins' and Ardern's divergent leadership styles, we were particularly interested in whether there were gender gaps among participants on these three attributes. We found that Ardern scored significantly higher than Collins among both women and men on measures of trustworthiness and competence (see Figure 7.4). In addition, there were larger differences between men's and women's perceptions of Ardern's competence and trustworthiness than there were for Collins.

Unsurprisingly, perceptions of Ardern's and Collins' competence and trustworthiness were related to party vote (see Figure 7.5). Both Labour and Green-voting men and women perceived Ardern as more competent and trustworthy than Collins, although women scored Ardern higher than did men on both attributes. Collins, on average, scored below the midpoint of the scale on both attributes among Labour and Green-voting men and women, although men in this left bloc rated Collins higher on average than did women.

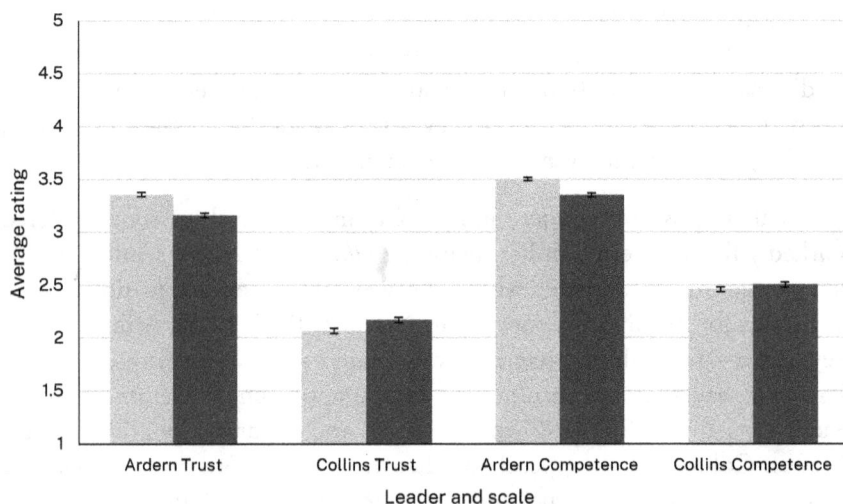

Figure 7.4 Ratings of Ardern's and Collins' trustworthiness and competence

Source: Vowles et al. (2022).

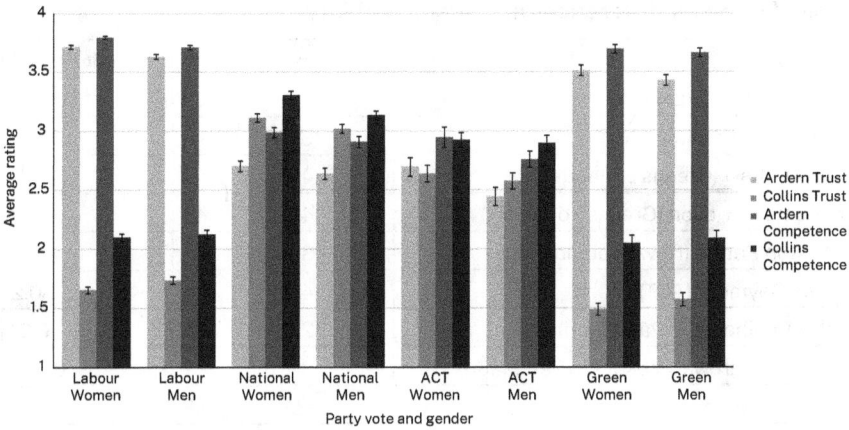

Figure 7.5 Ratings of Ardern and Collins by party and gender
Note: The maximum rating was four.
Source: Vowles et al. (2022).

By contrast, National-voting men and women were less favourable of Ardern and demonstrated the highest average ratings of Collins' competence and trustworthiness. However, the average ratings across both attributes were often relatively close between men and women who voted for the same party, but with clear left and right blocs evident. For example, there were only marginal differences between Labour women's average ratings of both Ardern's and Collins' competence and trustworthiness and those of Labour men. This was also the case for men and women who voted Green. In addition, Ardern's average ratings on all attributes sat much closer to Collins' among men and women National and ACT voters. Both Ardern's and Collins' competence was rated higher than their trustworthiness among all party vote–gender blocs. Nevertheless, as demonstrated by Jack Vowles in this volume, trust in Ardern was significant in explaining Labour's landslide victory in 2020.

The third attribute we explored was likeability, which was rated by respondents on a scale from zero to ten. Ardern scored high among both women and men, and her likeability increased from 2017.[4] We also found a statistically significant gender gap, with women liking Ardern more than did men. Collins, by contrast, did not score high on likeability.

---

4   Ardern increased her likeability score from 2017, with a one-point increase among women and a 0.8-point increase among men.

Table 7.1 Gender differences in leader likeability

Leader	Women	Men	Gender gap
Jacinda Ardern (Labour)	7.9	7.1	0.8***
Judith Collins (National)	3.7	3.8	–0.2
James Shaw (Greens co-leader)	4.9	4.3	0.6***
Marama Davidson (Greens co-leader)	4.9	4.1	0.8***
Winston Peters (New Zealand First)	3.3	3.4	0.0
David Seymour (ACT)	4.3	4.5	–0.2
John Tamihere (Te Pāti Māori)	2.8	2.6	0.2*
Debbie Ngarewa-Packer (Te Pāti Māori)	3.2	2.7	0.5***
Leighton Baker (New Conservatives)	2.1	1.8	0.3*
Geoff Simmons (TOP)	2.5	2.5	0.0
Billy Te Kahika (Advance NZ)	1.4	1.1	0.3*

* $p < 0.05$

** $p < 0.01$

*** $p < 0.001$

Notes: Results of t-tests between men and women on the 0–10-point liking rating scale. Positive values indicate a leader was liked more by women than by men.[5] Women tend to like leaders more than do men (a difference of an average of 0.2 overall); they are also far more likely to rate leaders with 'don't know' than are men (who express an opinion more often); women represent 57–62 per cent of the 'don't know' responses across leaders.

Source: Vowles et al. (2022).

There was also a statistically significant difference between male and female likeability preferences for both Greens co-leaders, with women more than men preferring both James Shaw and Marama Davidson. This was also true for several smaller party leaders, including the New Conservatives and Advance NZ as well as Te Pāti Māori co-leader John Tamihere. The gender gap in leader likeability was highly significant for Debbie Ngarewa-Packer. That Davidson and Ngarewa-Packer were rated as more likeable by women than men reflects findings from previous NZES analyses, which show that Māori women leaders tend to be liked less by men relative to women.[6]

---

5   Interacting comparative income (1–5 scale) and participant occupational groups with gender finds either a flat line or a tendency for people on higher incomes to like Ardern less. As we did not undertake modelling on the intersection of 'class' and gender, we assume this finding represents partisan bias.

6   These findings are yet to be published; contact the authors for more information.

Gender gaps in vote choice and policy preferences

International literature on the gender gap has suggested that women have always been more likely than men to care more about social than economic issues and to favour maintaining spending on health and welfare over tax cuts and market deregulation (Inglehart and Norris 2000; Gidengil et al. 2003). Various reasons explain this gender gap. In the postwar period, structural and cultural explanations were commonplace. Women's religiosity was one reason, as was the fact that women, as primary caregivers, were more likely to rely on the state for income and welfare support. For many years, conservative parties were seen as most likely to garner support from women (Curtin 2014).

In the late twentieth century, with changes in labour market participation, the rise of social movements, and shifting gender roles came evidence that greater numbers of women were voting for left-leaning parties. This did not reflect the fact that women voters were less interested in their family and domestic caregiving roles, but that they had become providers of care in both the private and the public spheres. Women's choice to vote left was posited to be connected to both an ethics of care and rational choice—because health, welfare, and education policies mattered to women's families' wellbeing and to women's financial wellbeing as public sector employees (Campbell 2006).

The 1980s saw the advent of large-scale labour market deregulation, public sector retrenchment, and cuts to social expenditure across many high-income democracies. This did not, however, always result in increased support from women for parties on the left. This can be explained by the fact that, historically, the industrial wings of left-leaning parliamentary parties and trade unions, were typically slow to recognise women as more than a supply of temporary labour (Curtin 1999). Furthermore, some countries bucked women voters' left realignment trend (Campbell and Shorrocks 2021; Shorrocks and Grasso 2020). In summary, the gender voting gap is not static, nor is it predictable in its direction of change, reminding us that women are not a monolithic voting bloc (Campbell 2006; Everitt 1998; Kellstedt et al. 2010; Shorrocks and Grasso 2020).

In line with international trends, early New Zealand election surveys found that women were more likely to vote for the right than the left (Vowles 1993). However, despite the activism of women's groups and the gender divisions associated with the 1981 Springbok Tour of New Zealand, there is little evidence of a consistent realignment of women voters to the left in the 30 years after the 1981 election (Vowles 1993; Coffé 2013). The available survey data show that between 1963 and 1993, women made up between 45 per cent and 51 per cent of National's support and 36 per cent and 43 per cent of Labour's support.

Table 7.2 reveals that women's votes for Labour and National have fluctuated under MMP. The columns, by party, display women's and men's votes, as well as the gender party vote gap (percentage of men, subtracting the percentage of women, with a positive value indicating more women than men preferring the respective party). In every election but 2002, 2011, and 2014 there was a statistically significant difference between genders across the major parties. In 2020, there was effectively no gender gap for National voters, with men and women equally likely to vote for that party. In addition, the gender voting gap for National has been more stable over time than for Labour. In Labour's case, there is a broader gender voting gap between men and women. The gap widened in 2020, suggesting that more women than men switched their vote to Labour that year. Overall, there is typically more gender variation between men and women on the left than on the right—evident both in 2020 and over time.

Table 7.2 Gender gap in party vote: National/Labour parties, 1996–2020

Year	National			Labour		
	Women	Men	Gap	Women	Men	Gap
1996***	33	35	-2	32	24	8
1999***	31	30	1	43	34	9
2002 n.s.	19	18	1	44	39	5
2005***	32	38	-6	41	33	7
2008***	36	40	-4	37	30	7
2011 n.s.	41	40	1	29	25	4
2014 n.s.	34	37	-3	21	18	3
2017**	35	33	-2	33	24	9
2020***	24	24	0	55	42	13

*** $p < 0.001$

** $p < 0.05$

* $p < 0.10$

n.s. = not significant

Note: Significance on basis of 2 x 2 tables (National and Labour voters only).

Sources: Curtin and Greaves (2020, 197); Vowles et al. (2022).

Table 7.3 presents gender voting gaps for non-major parties in 2020. There are statistically significant vote choice differences evident between women and men Green, ACT, and TOP voters. While the number of participants who gave their votes to TOP was small, the results for the Greens and ACT serve as a reminder that gender gaps are about men's voting choice as well as women's (Campbell and Shorrocks 2021; Hill 2006). Our data indicate that while both women and men deserted National, women appeared to go to Labour in greater numbers than did men; indeed, Labour's women's vote was its highest ever under MMP. Although men's vote for Labour in 2020 was its highest since 2002, men may have shared their discontent with National more widely than did women. Although further analysis is required before we can claim evidence of the realignment of women to the left, these gendered variations suggest it is important to look at women's attitudes to the government's responses to Covid-19. This is especially important given the presence of women leaders and comparative evidence that social and health policies are typically more important election issues for women than for men (Campbell 2006; Gidengil et al. 2003).

Table 7.3 Voting choice for all parties by gender

Party	Women (%)	Men (%)	Gender difference (women–men)	
Labour	**45.4**	**35.5**	**9.9**	***
National	20.9	20.8	0.1	
Green	**5.4**	**7.3**	**–1.9**	*
New Zealand First	1.6	2.7	–1.1	
ACT	**4.4**	**8.3**	**–3.9**	***
Māori Party	0.9	1.0	–0.1	
TOP	**0.5**	**2.0**	**–1.5**	***
New Conservatives	0.8	0.9	–0.1	
Others	1.4	3.1	–1.7	
Did not vote	18.7	18.4	0.3	

* p < 0.05

** p < 0.01

*** p < 0.001

Note: For Pearson Chi-square tests conducted across genders for party vote.[7]

Source: Vowles et al. (2022).

---

7   While #MeToo achieved a global profile in terms of drawing attention to gendered patterns of behaviour, we have not tested whether this movement impacted on the gender gap. However, as noted in Chapter 8 of this volume, those supporting minor and microparties on the right were impacted by their negative perceptions of Ardern.

Connecting women's leadership and policy responsiveness

Feminist political scientists are interested in the way that descriptive representation of women translates into the substantive representation of women, including questions about whether women's legislative presence influences policy agendas (Celis and Childs 2012; Curtin 2008; Forman-Rabinovici and Sommer 2019; Lowande et al. 2019; Phillips 1995; Sawer et al. 2006; Sawer 2012; Wängnerud 2009).[8] What is apparent is that women legislators have distinct policy priorities and are typically more assertive than men in advocating for social welfare and women's rights issues in legislative committees and debates, and in the sponsorship of bills (Swers 2016; see also Childs and Krook 2009; Grey 2006).

Research from other disciplines comes to similar conclusions about women politicians' role in advancing health policy specifically. For example, the percentage of women in both legislatures and governments is found to have an impact on mortality rates over time. Declining rates of mortality are evident net of alternative explanations and irrespective of the party in government in both single-country and large cross-national studies (Cunial 2021; Hessel et al. 2020; Macmillan et al. 2018; Ng and Muntaner 2019). Underpinning these findings is the hypothesis that women parliamentarians and government members are more likely than men to raise health issues and are more likely to advocate for, or support, increased healthcare spending.

More recently, others have explored the relationship between women political leaders and Covid-19 policy and management. First, women political leaders were found to react more rapidly and decisively than their male counterparts in the initial stages of the pandemic, implementing border closures and lockdowns to reduce fatalities and cases. Several possible explanations have been offered (Aldrich and Lotito 2020; Garikipati and Kambhampati 2021). Experimental research indicates that women leaders are likely to be more risk-averse than men, especially in the face of outcome uncertainty (Purkayastha et al. 2020; Garikipati and Kambhampati 2021). Such uncertainty during the Covid-19 pandemic could have led women leaders to prioritise precautionary measures over those that focussed on the economy.

---

8   A Google Scholar search of the term 'substantive representation of women' reveals almost 20,000 results between 2018 and 2022.

Second, women leaders were found to be more open to seeking public health experts' advice and were more relational and communicative with affected communities (Vroman and Danko 2020).[9] Third, most of the women-led countries had a historical propensity towards both social equality and comparatively robust and accessible healthcare systems—both factors that facilitate a public health–focussed response. However, some caution is necessary when seeking to infer a strong connection between women's leadership and pandemic management from cross-national comparisons because the number of women leaders is small and the diversity among dependent variables is substantial (Piscopo 2020).

This is not to say that gender and partisanship are irrelevant to gendered policy agendas. Swers (2016) shows that in the United States, championing health care, for example, is likely to provide rewards for Democrat women because the Democrats have issue ownership of this domain. Republican women may still champion health and welfare, but with different framing: while Democrat women usually pursue expanded spending or coverage of care, Republican women instead usually emphasise controlling costs and targeted spending to demonstrate fiscal responsibility (Swers 2016, 251–53). In the next section, we explore whether there are gender gaps in opinions on the key policy issues of the 2020 election, drawing on the NZES. We supplement descriptive statistics with qualitative material from the Gender Justice Project's election scorecard research.

Gender and Covid-19, economic and social policies

Applying this to New Zealand, we might expect that, because the Labour Party occupies the healthcare policy domain, voters are likely to find cognitive harmony in a Labour-led government adopting a public health approach to the pandemic. In contrast, Judith Collins committed a National government to tax cuts without concomitant cuts to health, education, and social services. Expenditure instead tended to focus on changing behaviour to improve health outcomes in the longer term—an approach reminiscent of previous 'social investment' programs (Cooke 2020). Collins also pledged to convene a public health summit to review alert level settings and 'to work

---

9   Although in New Zealand the government was slow to respond to expert advice from Māori health scientists.

out how our economy can flourish when it's clear COVID-19 will be with us for some time', with Collins further noting that '[w]e need to balance the social and economic costs, while ensuring the best possible health response' (Collins 2020).

In Figure 7.6, we see that the government received high levels of support for its Covid-19 response from Labour and Green voters of both genders. Overall, women were slightly more positive towards the government's response than were men—a gap that reflects the differences among ACT and, to a lesser extent, National voters. The result also mirrors international literature that included New Zealand, which found that there were significant gender differences in agreement and compliance with pandemic restraint measures including the closure of schools, nonessential businesses, and institutions, election postponement, travel, border, and quarantine restrictions, social meeting restrictions, and masking requirements. New Zealand respondents had comparatively high percentages of restriction measure agreement, at between 55 and 65 per cent. In addition, women were more likely than men to comply with the measures (Galasso et al. 2020).

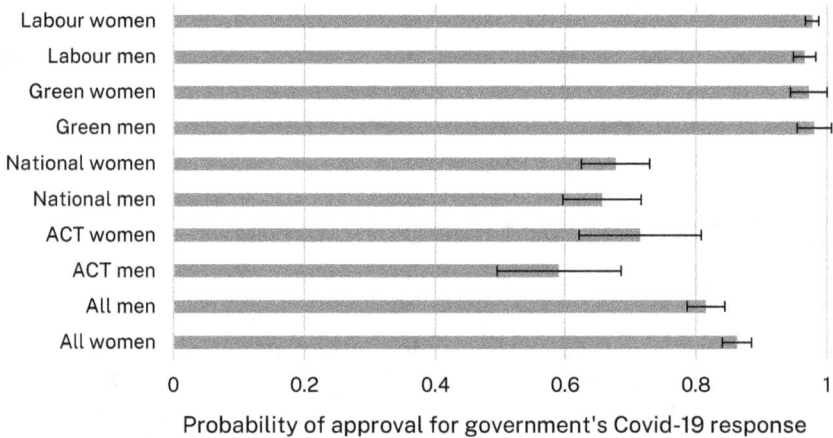

Figure 7.6 Support for the government's Covid-19 response by gender and party vote
Source: Vowles et al. (2022).

This is despite there being some disquiet with Labour's approach to social and health policy in the leadup to the 2020 election. Criticism was directed at the minimal implementation of the welfare reforms, particularly with respect to the material wellbeing of sole parents (CPAG 2021). Alongside this, the government's Covid-19 economic response policies were deemed to have done little for women in vulnerable sectors or for the women who made up a considerable component of essential workers, while also shouldering much of the increased weight of unpaid care work (Waddell et al. 2021).

Documents released under the *Official Information Act* revealed that the Ministry for Women in early April 2020 provided minister Julie Anne Genter with prospective gender analyses of the likely negative impacts of Covid-19 on different groups of women. A further summary document was sent to Finance Minister Grant Robertson at the end of April. An analysis of possible mitigating actions was completed in May, but there is little evidence that the 2020 budget reflected these findings (Curtin et al. 2020).

In mid-2020, the Gender Justice Collective (GJC) formed over the concern that political parties were not addressing the inequalities facing, and needs of, diverse groups of women. The GJC developed the #YouChoose2020 survey, an online, self-selecting questionnaire distributed to women nationwide between 30 July and 4 September through women's networks and community organisations. More than 3,500 people completed the survey: 96 per cent identified as women and 3 per cent as nonbinary; 82 per cent were Pākehā, 10 per cent Māori, and 4 per cent Pasifika. The academic advisory team used the survey results to identify women's policy priorities and analysed the policies of eight political parties against these priorities. The resulting #WeChoose2020 Election Scorecard collated this analysis, with the Green Party scoring the highest overall.[10]

Care responsibilities, health, and financial wellbeing were among the policy priorities YouChoose2020 survey respondents identified (New Zealand Herald 2020). These are also longstanding policy priorities for women NZES participants. Aimer's (1993) analysis of the 1990 NZES found that gender differences were only significant in attitudes towards five of 12 policy issues surveyed: health, welfare, education, environment, and defence. The greatest difference was in health, with 15 percentage points separating men's and women's ratings of this issue as 'extremely important'. Women were also significantly more likely than men to support increased government health and education expenditure. Aimer argued that the size of gender gaps depended partly on the salience of these issues during elections. For example, by 1990, New Zealand had experienced six years of retrenchment and economic

---

10 Available from: d3n8a8pro7vhmx.cloudfront.net/genderjustice/pages/25/attachments/original/1602401390/GJC_Matrix_A4_Landscape_v3.6.pdf?1602401390.

reform, which had impacted on health and education (Castles et al. 1995). The NewLabour Party formed in 1989 to oppose Labour's ideological shift to the economic right, and Aimer (1993, 119–21) found that women made up 63 per cent of these 'new left' voters in the 1990 election survey. Since 1990, we have seen that women are significantly less likely than men to vote for the smaller right-wing parties (Vowles et al. 2017).

With the advent of Covid-19, we might expect a gender gap in attitudes about the importance of health, care work, and financial wellbeing in the 2020 election. International comparative research completed in mid-2020— which included New Zealand in the pooled analysis—found that women were more likely than men to perceive the pandemic as a very serious health problem, despite men having a higher mortality risk globally. New Zealand studies found that pandemic job losses were unequally distributed between men and women, with women more likely than men to lose work (Galasso et al. 2020). Women also performed more domestic labour than men before the pandemic, even in households where both genders had outside employment (Sibley et al. 2021). These inequities continued during 2020 (Waddell et al. 2021), despite lockdowns providing more opportunities for men and women to share housework and parenting.

NZES data indicate that women were concerned about issues of economic security, health expenditure, and welfare. We asked NZES participants to indicate their emotional responses to a range of issues and situations: participants could choose multiple responses from a mix of positive emotions (for example, happy, hopeful, proud) and negative ones (such as angry, disgusted, afraid). Specifically, we asked participants to react to 'New Zealand's economic situation' and added the eight emotional reactions together, with each positive scoring one, and minus one for a negative. Figure 7.7 reveals that, across all parties, women felt less positive about the economic situation than did men but, overall, there was not a significant gender difference, indicating that party vote or partisan views, not gender, were the main driver of emotional responses to the economic situation.

The government did spend up large in its response to Covid-19 in 2020, although much of the focus was on wage subsidies and employment packages. This was in part possible because fiscal stimulus could be provided without undue long-term risk to the government budget. The budget surplus for the half-year to December 2019 was NZ$500 million higher than forecast, and the budget surpluses over the previous two years were $12 billion (Robertson 2020). Government debt was also comparatively low.

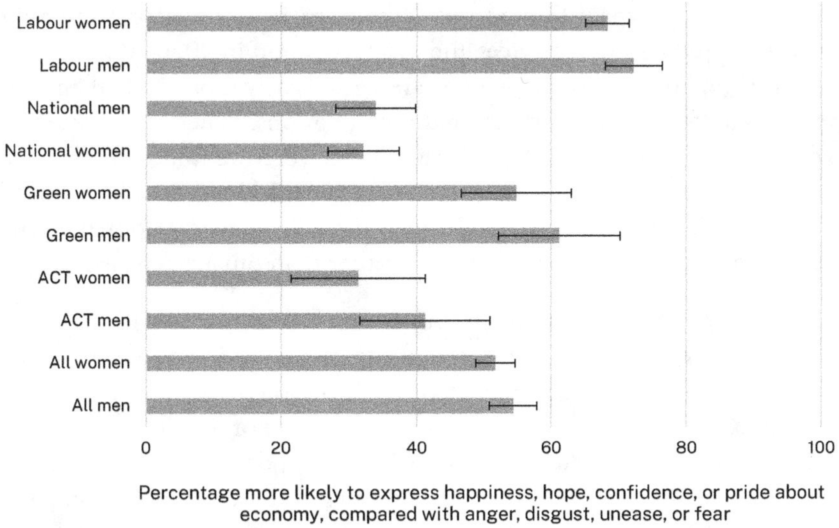

Percentage more likely to express happiness, hope, confidence, or pride about economy, compared with anger, disgust, unease, or fear

Figure 7.7 Positive emotional responses to economic situation by gender and party vote

Source: Vowles et al. (2022).

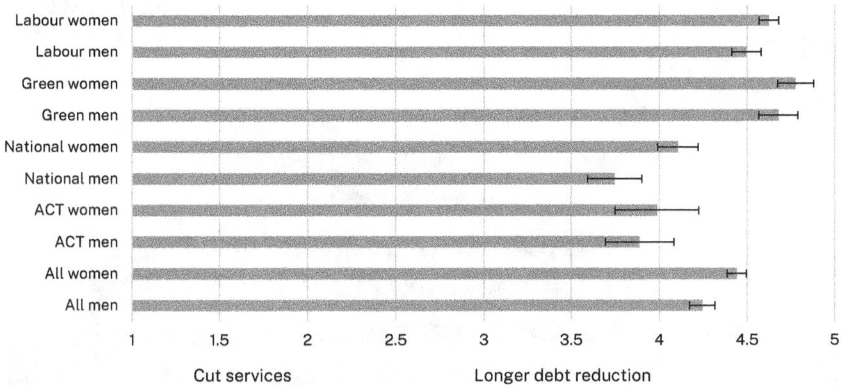

Figure 7.8 Gender attitudes to cutting social services and debt reduction by party

Source: Vowles et al. (2022).

Thus, we might expect limited public concern in terms of the trade-off between supplying social services and debt reduction in 2020. What we see in Figure 7.9, however, is that women are significantly more likely than men to express a desire to hold off debt reduction options. When examining this trade-off by combinations of gender and party vote, we find that left-wing voters are more likely to want to wait than right-bloc voters. Moreover, National-voting women were significantly more likely than National-voting men to want to maintain social services rather than pursue debt reduction.

We also undertook a descriptive examination of the extent to which age and gender mattered to the question of cutting social services versus reducing debt. Deckman et al. (2020) argue that consideration of the views of younger generations is increasingly necessary given the range of political protests led by young voters in recent years, including in response to climate change, BlackLivesMatter, and #MeToo. Recognising that the economic impacts of Covid-19 are likely to significantly impact Gen Z voters, Deckman et al. (2020) explored the gender differences in this cohort's health and economic concerns in the United States. While partisanship erases most of the gender gaps, they found young women were significantly more likely to be concerned about job security and young men were more likely to be concerned about their personal health.

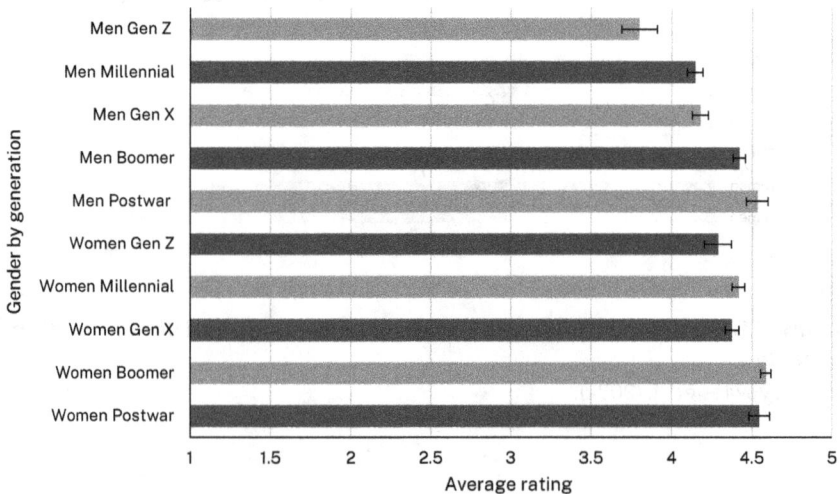

Figure 7.9 Ratings by gender and generation on cutting social services (1) versus taking longer to reduce debt (5)

Source: Vowles et al. (2022).

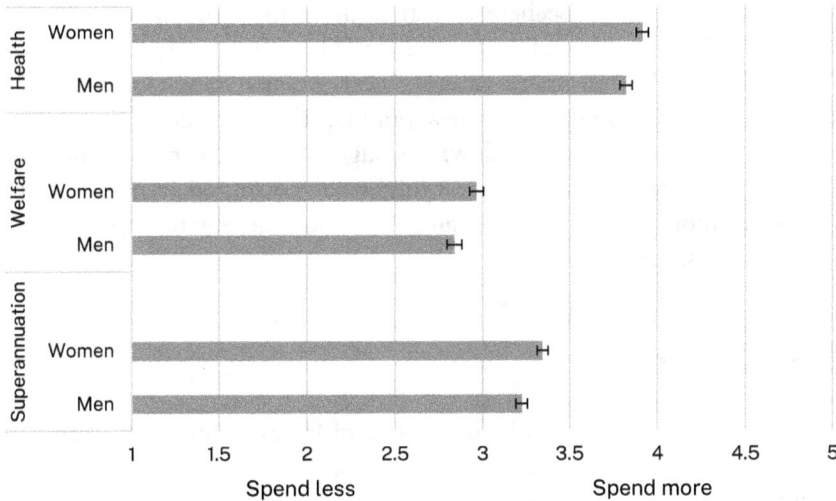

Figure 7.10 Gender differences in support for further spending across health, welfare, and superannuation
Source: Vowles et al. (2022).

Our NZES health and social services questions were not sufficiently alike to allow for a direct comparison with Deckman et al. (2020). However, we did test to see how different age groups viewed the trade-off between cutting social services and reducing debt. Figure 7.10 shows that Generation Z men were far more likely than Gen Z women to want to cut social services, rather than take longer to reduce debt (a mean of 3.8 versus 4.3). In fact, significance tests confirm that Gen Z men were more likely than every other group to want to cut social services. Moreover, except for a difference between Gen X and Millennials, variation between the other cohorts of men was also statistically significant. These results suggest that the trade-off between social services and debt reduction varies considerably across men by age cohort, but not for women. This could mean that men become less concerned about reducing debt or more concerned about social service provision as they age (or it could be a cohort effect).

Despite these differences in responses, we find that, in 2020, both men and women NZES participants were supportive of increased spending on health. In asking this question, respondents were reminded that 'more' or 'much more' spending could require a tax increase (Figure 7.8). This reflects findings by Lloyd (2022) that, over time, health spending matters to both women and men. That said, there remains a clear gender gap on each of the social policy issues, with women wanting more spending than men. Perhaps the surprise here is that both women and men show less support for increased spending on welfare. This result underscores earlier findings by Louise Humpage (2014), who revealed that targeted social policy expenditure tends to be less popular than universal allowances. However, given Covid-19 lockdowns brought with them predictions that unemployment rates would rise, we might have expected welfare benefits to become more widely accessed and thus more acceptable. Our NZES analysis suggests otherwise.

Conclusions

The 2020 election was notable for a range of factors relevant to gender in politics: first, for the substantial international media attention on Jacinda Ardern and her political style. Second, for the presence of women party leaders during the campaign and the number of women parliamentarians and parliamentary party leaders who were elected. Third, for the emergence of Covid-19 and the gendered impacts of the government's policy response.

In this chapter, we investigated these factors using descriptive statistical analysis to draw a picture of gender gaps in attitudes and results. We found differences in the way women feel and respond to questions on a range of policy issues. For example, women were on average less likely than men of the same party to feel positive about the economic situation and were more likely to support increased government spending on a range of social items including health, if the alternative was reducing debt more rapidly. Women were also more positive about the government's Covid-19 response although there was variation across parties.

More generally, women voters rewarded the Labour government in the 2020 election to an extent not seen in previous elections in New Zealand. The party also won back a share of male voters (albeit not to the same extent as women, nor to its pre-MMP levels of support). Before the arrival of Jacinda Ardern, the centre-right National Party had successfully wooed women away from Labour while the latter was in opposition and led by a series of less-than-inspiring men. This is not to suggest that women leaders drive Labour's support among women, but in this election, our analysis indicates voters, both women and men, found Ardern competent, likeable, and trustworthy as a leader. In conclusion, New Zealand voters may not have shared the international media's glowing opinions of Ardern, but in 2020 their vote choice suggested otherwise.

References

Aimer, P. 1993. 'Was There a Gender Gap in New Zealand in 1990?' *Political Science* 45(1): 112–21. doi.org/10.1177/003231879304500108.

Aldrich, A., and N. Lotito. 2020. 'Pandemic Performance: Women Leaders in the COVID-19 Crisis.' *Politics & Gender* 16(4): 960–67. doi.org/10.1017/S1743923X20000549.

Anderson, C. 2020. 'Why Do Women Make Such Good Leaders during COVID-19?' *Forbes*, 19 April. Available from: www.forbes.com/sites/camianderson1/2020/04/19/why-do-women-make-such-good-leaders-during-covid-19/?sh=633273942fc7.

Ansell, C., A. Boin, and P. 't Hart. 2014. 'Political Leadership in Times of Crisis.' In *The Oxford Handbook of Political Leadership*, edited by R. Rhodes and P. 't Hart, 418–34. Oxford: Oxford University Press. doi.org/10.1093/oxfordhb/9780199653881.013.035.

Ardern, J. 2018. 'New Zealand National Statement to United Nations General Assembly.' Speech, 28 September. Wellington: New Zealand Government. Available from: www.beehive.govt.nz/speech/new-zealand-national-statement-united-nations-general-assembly.

Ardern, J. 2019. 'Ministerial Statements: Mosque Terror Attacks—Christchurch.' *Hansard (Debates)*, 19 March. Wellington: New Zealand Parliament. Available from: www.parliament.nz/en/pb/hansard-debates/rhr/combined/HansDeb_20190319_20190319_08.

Beattie, A., and R. Priestley. 2021. 'Fighting COVID-19 with the Team of 5 Million: Aotearoa New Zealand Government Communication during the 2020 Lockdown.' *Social Sciences & Humanities Open*. Available at: ssrn.com/abstract=3844944. doi.org/10.2139/ssrn.3844944.

Bickerton, S.H. 2021. 'Social Media, Online Politics and the 2020 Election.' In *Politics in a Pandemic: Jacinda Ardern and New Zealand's 2020 Election*, edited by S. Levine, 170–79. Wellington: Te Herenga Waka University Press.

Campbell, R. 2006. *Gender and the Vote in Britain*. Colchester: ECPR Press.

Campbell, R., and R. Shorrocks. 2021. 'Finally Rising With the Tide? Gender and the Vote in the 2019 British Elections.' *Journal of Elections, Public Opinion and Parties* 31(4): 488–507. doi.org/10.1080/17457289.2021.1968412.

Castles, F., R. Gerritsen, and J. Vowles (eds). 1995. *The Great Experiment: Labour Parties and Public Policy Transformation in Australia and New Zealand*. Sydney: Allen & Unwin.

Celis, K., and S. Childs. 2012. 'The Substantive Representation of Women: What to Do With Conservative Claims?' *Political Studies* 60(1): 213–25. doi.org/10.1111/j.1467-9248.2011.00904.x.

Child Poverty Action Group (CPAG). 2021. 'Government Yet to Fully Implement a Single Key WEAG Recommendation Nearly Three Years On: New Research.' Media release, 8 December. Auckland: Child Poverty Action Group. Available from: www.cpag.org.nz/media-releases/govt-yet-to-fully-implement-a-single-key.

Childs, S., and M.L. Krook. 2009. 'Analysing Women's Substantive Representation: From Critical Mass to Critical Actors.' *Government and Opposition* 44(2): 125–45. doi.org/10.1111/j.1477-7053.2009.01279.x.

Coffé, H. 2013. 'Gender and Party Choice at the 2011 New Zealand General Election.' *Political Science* 65(1): 25–45. doi.org/10.1177/0032318713485346.

Collins, J. 2002. 'Address in Reply.' *New Zealand Parliamentary Debates*, Vol. 602, 29 August: 160–62.

Collins, J. 2020. 'Call for Public Health Summit.' Press release, 24 August. Wellington: National. Available from: www.national.org.nz/call-for-public-health-summit.

Cooke, H. 2020. 'Election 2020: Judith Collins and David Seymour Battle for the Right Wing.' *Stuff*, [Wellington], 16 September. Available from: www.stuff.co.nz/national/politics/300108237/election-2020-judith-collins-and-david-seymour-battle-for-the-right-wing.

Craig, G. 2021. 'Kindness and Control: The Political Leadership of Jacinda Ardern in the Aotearoa New Zealand COVID-19 Media Conferences.' Journalism and Media 2(2): 288–304. doi.org/10.3390/journalmedia2020017.

Cunial, S.L. 2021. 'Do More Female Politicians Translate into Better Health Outcomes? Gender Representation and Infant Mortality in Argentine Provinces.' *World Medical & Health Policy* 13(2): 349–72. doi.org/10.1002/wmh3.411.

Curtin, J. 1999. *Women and Trade Unions: A Comparative Perspective*. Aldershot: Ashgate Publishing.

Curtin, J. 2008. 'Women, Political Leadership and Substantive Representation: The Case of New Zealand.' *Parliamentary Affairs* 61(3): 490–504. doi.org/10.1093/pa/gsn014.

Curtin, J. 2014. 'Conservative Women and Executive Office in Australia and New Zealand.' In *Gender, Conservatism and Political Representation*, edited by K. Celis and S. Childs, 141–60. Colchester: ECPR Press

Curtin, J. 2020a. 'Jacinda Ardern's Renown is Great But She Must Do More for Women.' *The Guardian*, 21 May. Available from: www.theguardian.com/world/commentisfree/2020/may/21/jacinda-arderns-global-renown-is-great-but-she-must-do-more-for-women.

Curtin, J. 2020b. 'NZ Election 2020: As the Ultimate Political Survivor Judith Collins Prepares for Her Ultimate Test.' *The Conversation*, 13 October. Available from: theconversation.com/nz-election-2020-as-the-ultimate-political-survivor-judith-collins-prepares-for-her-ultimate-test-144488.

Curtin, J. 2020c. *Home for Progressive Politics: An Analysis of Labour's Success in New Zealand*. December. Bonn: Friedrich Ebert Stiftung. Available from: library.fes.de/pdf-files/id/ipa/17207.pdf.

Curtin, J., and L. Greaves. 2020. 'Gender, Populism and Jacinda Ardern.' In *A Populist Exception? The 2017 New Zealand General Election*, edited by J. Vowles and J. Curtin, 179–212. Canberra: ANU Press. doi.org/10.22459/PE.2020.06.

Curtin, J., S. Morrisey, and S. Bickerton. 2020. 'What the Budget Means for Women.' *Newsroom*, [Auckland], 15 May, [Updated 20 May]. Available from: www.newsroom.co.nz/ideasroom/what-the-budget-means-for-women.

Curtin, J., and D. O'Sullivan. 2023. 'Closing the Borders to COVID19: Democracy, Politics and Resilience in Australia and New Zealand.' In *Democracy, State Capacity and the Governance of COVID-19 in Asia-Oceania*, edited by A. Croissant and O. Hellmann. New York, NY: Routledge.

Deckman, M., J. McDonald, S. Rouse, and M. Kromer. 2020. 'Gen Z, Gender, and COVID-19.' *Politics and Gender* 16(4): 1019–27. doi.org/10.1017/S1743923X20000434.

Everitt, J. 1998. 'The Gender Gap in Canada: Now You See It Now You Don't.' *Canadian Review of Sociology and Anthropology* 35(2): 191–219. doi.org/10.1111/j.1755-618X.1998.tb00228.x.

Forman-Rabinovici, A., and U. Sommer. 2019. 'Can the Descriptive-Substantive Link Survive Beyond Democracy? The Policy Impact of Women Representatives.' *Democratization* 26(8): 1513–33. doi.org/10.1080/13510347.2019.1661993.

Friedman, U. 2020. 'New Zealand's Prime Minister May Be the Most Effective Leader on the Planet.' *The Atlantic*, 19 April. Available from: www.theatlantic.com/politics/archive/2020/04/jacinda-ardern-new-zealand-leadership-coronavirus/610237/.

Galasso, V., V. Pons, P. Profeta, M. Becher, S. Brouard, and M. Foucault. 2020. 'Gender Differences in COVID-19 Attitudes and Behavior: Panel Evidence from Eight Countries.' *PNAS* 117(44): 27285–91. doi.org/10.1073/pnas.2012520117.

Garikipati, S., and U. Kambhampati. 2021. 'Leading the Fight Against the Pandemic: Does Gender Really Matter?' *Feminist Economics* 27(1–2): 401–18. doi.org/10.1080/13545701.2021.1874614.

Gidengil, E., A. Blais, R. Nadeau, and N. Nevitte. 2003. 'Women to the Left? Gender Differences in Political Beliefs and Policy Preferences.' In *Women and Electoral Politics in Canada*, edited by M. Tremblay and L. Trimble. New York, NY: Oxford University Press.

Grey. S. 2006. 'The "New World"? The Substantive Representation of Women in New Zealand.' In *Representing Women in Parliament: A Comparative Study*, edited by M. Sawer, M. Tremblay, and L. Trimble, 134–51. Abingdon: Routledge.

Hessel, P., M.J.G. Jaramillo, D. Rasella, A.C. Duran, and O.C. Sarmiento. 2020. 'Increases in Women's Political Representation Associated with Reductions in Child Mortality in Brazil.' *Health Affairs* 39(7): 1166–74. doi.org/10.1377/hlthaff.2019.01125.

Hill, L. 2006. 'Women's Interests and Political Orientations: The Gender Voting Gap in Three Industrialized Settings.' In *The Politics of Women's Interests: New Comparative Perspectives*, edited by L. Chappell and L. Hill, 66–92. Abingdon: Routledge.

Humpage, L. 2014. *Policy Change, Public Attitudes and Social Citizenship: Does Neoliberalism Matter?* Bristol: Bristol University Press. doi.org/10.1332/policypress/9781847429650.001.0001.

Inglehart, R., and P. Norris. 2000. 'The Developmental Theory of the Gender Gap: Women's and Men's Voting Behaviour in Global Perspective.' *International Political Science Review* 21(4): 441–63. doi.org/10.1177/0192512100214007.

Johnson, C., and B. Williams. 2020. 'Gender and Political Leadership in a Time of COVID.' *Politics & Gender* 16(4): 943–50. doi.org/10.1017/S1743923X2000029X.

Junn, J., and N. Masuoka. 2020. 'The Gender Gap is a Race Gap: Women Voters in US Presidential Elections.' *Perspectives on Politics* 18(4): 1135–45. doi.org/10.1017/S1537592719003876.

Kellstedt, P.M., D.A.M. Peterson, and M.D. Ramirez. 2010. 'The Macro Politics of a Gender Gap.' *Public Opinion Quarterly* 74(3): 477–98. doi.org/10.1093/poq/nfq003.

Krook, M.L. 2009. *Quotas for Women in Politics: Gender and Candidate Selection Reform Worldwide.* New York, NY: Oxford University Press.

Lloyd, R. 2022. 'Is There Evidence of a Gender Gap? Attitudes Towards Health Policy from 1996 to 2020.' Unpublished dissertation, University of Auckland, New Zealand.

Lowande, K., M. Ritchie, and E. Lauterbach. 2019. 'Descriptive and Substantive Representation in Congress: Evidence from 80,000 Congressional Inquiries.' *American Journal of Political Science* 63(3): 644–59. doi.org/10.1111/ajps.12443.

Macmillan, R., N. Shofia, and W. Sigle. 2018. 'Gender and the Politics of Death: Female Representation, Political and Developmental Context, and Population Health in a Cross-National Panel.' *Demography* 55: 1905–34. doi.org/10.1007/s13524-018-0697-0.

McGuire, D., J.E.A. Cunningham, K. Reynolds, and G. Matthews-Smith. 2020. 'Beating the Virus: An Examination of the Crisis Communication Approach Taken by New Zealand Prime Minister Jacinda Ardern during the Covid-19 Pandemic.' *Human Resource Development International* 23(4): 361–79. doi.org/10.1080/13678868.2020.1779543.

New Zealand Herald. 2020. 'Election 2020: Gender Justice Collective Scores Parties on Equity, Greens Top Results.' *New Zealand Herald*, 12 October. Available from: www.nzherald.co.nz/nz/election-2020-gender-justice-collective-scores-parties-on-equity-greens-top-results/GCDHLC6DQJZYUSDWHWQBK6DCMU/.

Ng, E., and C. Muntaner. 2019. 'The More Women in Government, the Healthier a Population.' *The Conversation*, 10 January. Available from: theconversation.com/the-more-women-in-government-the-healthier-a-population-107075.

Phillips, A. 1995. *The Politics of Presence.* Oxford: Clarendon Press.

Piscopo, J.M. 2020. 'Women Leaders and Pandemic Performance: A Spurious Correlation.' *Politics and Gender* 16(4): 951–59. doi.org/10.1017/S1743923X20000525.

Politics and Gender. 2020. 'Gender Politics and the Global Pandemic.' *Politics and Gender* 16(4)(SI). Available from: www.cambridge.org/core/journals/politics-and-gender/virtual-special-issues/gender-politics-and-the-global-pandemic.

Pullen, A., and S.J. Vachhani. 2020. 'Feminist Ethics and Women Leaders: From Difference to Intercorporeality.' *Journal of Business Ethics* 173: 233–43. doi.org/10.1007/s10551-020-04526-0.

Purkayastha, S., M. Salvatore, and B. Mukherjee. 2020. 'Are Women Leaders Significantly Better at Controlling the Contagion during the COVID-19 Pandemic?' *Journal of Health and Social Sciences* 5(2): 231–40. doi.org/10.1101/2020.06.06.20124487.

Robertson, G. 2020. 'Budget Speech 2020.' 14 May, New Zealand Parliament, Wellington. Available from: www.treasury.govt.nz/publications/budget-speech/budget-speech-2020.

Sawer, M. 2012. 'What Makes the Substantive Representation of Women Possible in a Westminster Parliament? The Story of RU486 in Australia.' *International Political Science Review* 33(3): 320–35. doi.org/10.1177/0192512111435369.

Sawer, M., M. Tremblay, and L. Trimble (eds). 2006. *Representing Women in Parliament: A Comparative Study*. Abingdon: Routledge. doi.org/10.4324/9780203965672.

Shorrocks, R., and M. Grasso. 2020. 'The Attitudinal Gender Gap Across Generations: Support for Redistribution and Government Spending in Contexts of High and Low Welfare Provision.' *European Political Science Review* 12(3): 289–306. doi.org/10.1017/S1755773920000120.

Sibley, C.G., N.C. Overall, D. Osborne, and N. Satherley. 2021. *Social, Psychosocial and Employment Impacts of COVID-19 in New Zealand: Insights from the New Zealand Attitudes and Values Study 2020/2021*. Report prepared for the Ministry of Social Development. January. Auckland: University of Auckland. Available from: www.msd.govt.nz/documents/about-msd-and-our-work/publications-resources/research/impacts-of-covid-19-insights-from-the-nz-attitudes-and-values-study/nzavs-report-on-covid-19-outcomes.pdf.

Sudhaman, A. 2020. 'Jacinda Ardern's Covid-19 Comms Most Impressive, Say PR Leaders.' *PRovoke Media*, [New York], 16 September. Available from: www.provokemedia.com/latest/article/jacinda-ardern's-COVID-19-comms-most-impressive-say-pr-leaders.

Swers, M. 2016. 'Pursuing Women's Interests in Partisan Times: Explaining Gender Differences in Legislative Activity on Health, Education, and Women's Health Issues.' *Journal of Women, Politics & Policy* 37(3): 249–73. doi.org/10.1080/1554477X.2016.1188599.

Taub, A. 2020. 'Why Are Women-Led Nations Doing Better with Covid-19?' *The New York Times*, 15 May. Available from: www.nytimes.com/2020/05/15/world/coronavirus-women-leaders.html.

Vowles, J. 1993. 'Gender and Electoral Behaviour in New Zealand: Findings from the Present and the Past.' *Political Science* 45(1): 122–35. doi.org/10.1177/003231879304500109.

Vowles, J., F. Barker, M. Krewel, J. Hayward, J. Curtin, L. Greaves, and L. Oldfield. 2022. *2020 New Zealand Election Study*. ADA Dataverse, V3. doi.org/10.26193/BPAMYJ.

Vowles, J., H. Coffé, and J. Curtin. 2017. *A Bark But No Bite: Inequality and the 2014 New Zealand General Election*. Canberra: ANU Press. doi.org/10.22459/BBNB.08.2017.

Vroman, S.R., and T. Danko. 2020. 'Against What Model? Evaluating Women as Leaders in the Pandemic Era.' *Gender, Work & Organization* 27(5): 860–67. doi.org/10.1111/gwao.12488.

Waddell, N., N.C. Overall, V.T. Chang, and M.D. Hammond. 2021. 'Gendered Division of Labor during a Nationwide COVID-19 Lockdown: Implications for Relationship Problems and Satisfaction.' *Journal of Social and Personal Relationships* 38(6): 1759–81. Available from: doi.org/10.1177/02654075 21996476.

Walls, J. 2020. 'Election 2020: Judith Collins Promises "Massive" Temporary Tax Cuts in National's Economic Plan.' *New Zealand Herald*, 18 September. Available from: www.nzherald.co.nz/nz/election-2020-judith-collins-promises-massive-temporary-tax-cuts-in-nationals-economic-plan/GEGYH6APGBWR Z2WUT3GIH7MP74/.

Wängnerud, L. 2009. 'Women in Parliaments: Descriptive and Substantive Representation.' *Annual Review of Political Science* 12: 51–69. doi.org/10.1146/annurev.polisci.11.053106.123839.

Worthen, M.G. 2020. 'A Rainbow Wave? LGBTQ Liberal Political Perspectives during Trump's Presidency: An Exploration of Sexual, Gender, and Queer Identity Gaps.' *Sexuality Research and Social Policy* 17(2): 263–84. doi.org/10.1007/s13178-019-00393-1.

Appendix 7.1

Gender Justice Collective Scorecard | Election 2020

In the lead up to the 2020 New Zealand Election, we conducted the YouChoose2020 survey. Over 3,500 people responded. Thank you! You told us what you want and need from your elected representatives. We have taken the top three issues from each of the sections of the survey and analysed the election manifestos and policies of each of the political parties to see how they stack up. Here are the results:

CARING RESPONSIBILITIES	ACT	Green	Labour	National	NZ FIRST	Māori	TOP	NZ CONSERVATIVE
Paid parental leave	✗	✓	✓	✓	✗	✗	◐	◐
Childcare funding	✗	✓	✗	◐	✗	✓	✓	✗
Elder care funding	✗	✓	✗	✗	✗	✗	✗	✓

HEALTH AND WELLBEING	ACT	Green	Labour	National	NZ FIRST	Māori	TOP	NZ CONSERVATIVE
Specialist violence healthcare providers	✗	✓	✓	✗	✗	✗	◐	◐
Free GP visits for children	✗	◐	✓	✗	✗	✗	✗	✗
Accessible public places	✗	✓	✗	✗	✗	◐	◐	✗

GJC Gender Justice Collective

WeChoose 2020

Figure A7.1 Gender Justice Collective Scorecard: Election 2020

Source: d3n8a8pro7vhmx.cloudfront.net/genderjustice/pages/25/attachments/original/1602401390/GJC_Matrix_A4_Landscape_v3.6.pdf?1602401390.

8

Boycotting the 'Team of Five Million'

Josh Van Veen and Luke Oldfield

Introduction

In a self-published book, National MP Chris Penk wrote of a country that was under existential threat, not from a pathogen but from 'compulsory kindness' (Penk 2020, 149). Penk believed that lockdown restrictions were well-meaning but ill-conceived and disproportionate to the threat of Covid-19. The success of the Ardern government's elimination strategy was attributed to luck rather than leadership. Penk was speaking for a faction on the political right by claiming that the suspension of personal and economic freedoms did much greater harm than any virus could. It was a belief that few New Zealanders shared in 2020. As an independent review of the National Party's campaign later found, MPs 'neither responded well' to Covid-19 'nor conducted themselves in a way to gain the public's confidence', and failed to connect with large parts of society (Vance 2022, 219). Penk's opposition to the elimination strategy, then, can be understood as existing outside the mainstream politics of the Labour and National parties.

This chapter takes a closer look at the politicians and their parties who were electioneering outside the mainstream. It notes that a ragtag collection of small parties opposing Covid-19 lockdowns, and largely mischaracterised as being on the 'far right', were ineffectual in gaining a sufficient level of public support. At the same time, confused messaging from National Party MPs opened the door for the smaller ACT New Zealand (ACT) to substantially increase its share of the vote.

While it is a truism that elections are fought and won in the 'centre', pandemic politics exposed National on a new front: it also found itself in competition with the ideological right. Formed in 1994 to carry forward a neoliberal agenda, ACT, after initial success in electing a handful of MPs, fell on hard times following the 2008 election. One ACT MP was elected in 2011 but only because of a tacit electorate deal with the National Party. But in 2020 a rejuvenated ACT presented the biggest challenge on the right to support for the National Party. Its leader and sole MP, David Seymour, garnered considerable attention for his provocative style, leading some to compare him to populist Winston Peters. Advance NZ, established just two months before election day, was led by disgraced former National MP Jami-Lee Ross and musician turned conspiracy theorist Billy Te Kahika, Jr. Despite a very large following on social media, prompted by anti-vaccine messaging and opposition to lockdowns, Advance NZ captured only 1 per cent of the vote, prompting Te Kahika to adopt the mantle of New Zealand's Donald Trump and claim the election result was fraudulent. The New Conservative Party, led by Christchurch businessman Leighton Barker, also opposed lockdowns but did not fare much better, though its vote count increased significantly from 6,253 in 2017 to 42,615 at the 2020 election.

In this chapter, we use data from the 2020 NZES to explore the intersection between hostility to the government's Covid-19 response and support for right-wing parties. To provide further context, we begin the chapter with a brief history of the National Party's decline and the rise in support for minor parties during 2020. The chapter then analyses the subset of NZES participants who objected to the government's Covid-19 response. We find that religiosity and right-wing ideological traits are the strongest predictors of whether a person disapproved of the way the Ardern government responded to Covid-19. Having established this relationship between ideology and Covid-19, we then turn our attention to the three right-wing parties in competition with National. First, we explore the demographic correlates between supporting the two Covid-sceptic parties, Advance NZ and the New Conservatives. We then consider whether these parties can appropriately be classified as 'radical right' using a comparative framework (Donovan 2020). Finally, we use data from the NZES to investigate the rivalry between ACT and National.

'Cindy's kindy': The decline and fall of National[1]

Throughout the early stages of the pandemic, it was common for both local and international media to cast lockdown measures as a trade-off between public health and economic wellbeing. Signalling an ideological preference for prioritising the economy, the Conservative government in the United Kingdom initially sought to ride out the crisis without introducing comprehensive restrictions on the movement of people (Smith 2021). In the United States, a Republican president and Republican-led state governments were at odds with Democrat-led state governments, which had opted to prioritise a public health response to the crisis (Baccini and Brodeur 2021; Yamey and Gonsalves 2020). As the virus spread across the United States, lockdowns and associated public health measures became partisan issues that led to nationwide protests beginning in April 2020.

In New Zealand, a health-centred response had bipartisan support. There was virtually no opposition to the first lockdown, in March–April 2020, and very little opposition to the second, in August–September 2020, while police reported high levels of compliance across the country. With the encouragement of former prime ministers from both Labour and National, the 'Team of Five Million' heeded the prime minister's call to 'stay home, save lives'. This bipartisan consensus helped ensure that the first nationwide lockdown was a remarkable success. Despite the bipartisan support for the first lockdown, opinion polls recorded a dramatic swing in voting intention from National to Labour. As findings from the New Zealand Attitudes and Values Survey (Sibley et al. 2020) suggest, the success of the first lockdown correlated with a heightened sense of community and national pride while trust and confidence in the government increased significantly.

The government had successfully cultivated a perception among voters of competency during times of crisis, presenting difficulties for the opposition. It was a frustration expressed by former National Party president Michelle Boag when she bemoaned 'Cindy's kindy', thus evoking a sexist trope of female leadership (Ensor 2020). To scrutinise government decision-making in the absence of parliament operating as it usually would, National Party leader Simon Bridges chaired an Epidemic Response Committee

---

1   'Cindy's kindy' was a pejorative reference to Prime Minister Jacinda Ardern and her leadership during Covid-19 lockdowns.

(ERC). However, balancing support for the government's health-centred response while also criticising the government's preparedness proved to be a difficult task. Bridges himself faced scrutiny for travelling to Wellington to participate in the ERC during the lockdown (RNZ 2020). Moves to replace Bridges as leader were precipitated by his own widely pilloried Facebook post criticising the government for taking a cautious approach to reopening. Bridges's eventual successor, Bay of Plenty MP Todd Muller, would last only 57 days in the role before resigning as leader. Muller was also impacted by pandemic politics, with one of his MPs forced to quit after leaking confidential information about persons with Covid-19. Following Muller's resignation, long-serving National Party MP Judith Collins filled the leadership vacuum, taking the party into the 2020 election.

Leadership issues were not the only problem faced by the country's main opposition party. A lack of cohesive response from its MPs to the threat posed by the pandemic could also have undermined its credibility among voters. In June 2020, National MP Simon O'Connor drew ridicule for a speech he gave to parliament that suggested 'Keep left' road signs were part of a broad sweep of government propaganda that extended from an appeal to kindness by the Ardern government. During the second Covid-19 outbreak in August, O'Connor wrote a now-deleted blog on his electorate Facebook page suggesting that loosened Covid-19 restrictions were preferable to a return to hard lockdown—a position at odds with his party's commitment to an elimination strategy. Deputy party leader Gerry Brownlee also attracted criticism for his comments after the start of the second lockdown, implying that the government had known of an impending outbreak and had been withholding information from the public. Brownlee said on talkback radio that he 'just found it interesting' that the government had, in the preceding weeks, visibly ramped up the nation's preparedness for a second outbreak, but he later walked back his remarks after being branded a conspiracy theorist (Wade 2020).

National was unable to capitalise on the government's failure to prevent a second outbreak and won only 25.6 per cent of the party vote on election night—barely half that of the Labour Party. As discussed in Chapter 2 of this volume, 84 per cent of NZES participants approved of the government's Covid-19 response and only 6 per cent disapproved. When asked how the government's Covid-19 response made them feel, only 10 per cent of participants were 'uneasy', 2.4 per cent were 'angry', 2.3 per cent were 'afraid', and 1.4 per cent were 'disgusted'. These emotions were well outweighed by positive emotions, with 35 per cent saying they felt 'proud'.

Such overwhelming support for the government's health-centred response suggests a miscalculation on the part of some high-profile National MPs who had been sceptical of or hostile to the government's pandemic response.

Covid-19 and anti-government sentiment

As described in Chapter 1, public opinion polls in 2020 recorded a dramatic swing in voting intention from National to Labour. Alleged mishandling of the public health response and failure to prevent a second outbreak in August 2020 had no discernible effect on support for the Ardern government. Of those New Zealanders who opted out of the Team of Five Million, it seems they did not belong to one ideologically homogeneous group. Instead, opposition to the Covid-19 response can be best explained through an explicit distrust of Prime Minister Ardern.

While the number of NZES participants who disapproved of the Covid-19 response was indeed small, they are still an important part of the story. Several political parties gave expression to those who were sceptical or downright hostile to public health measures. At times, this even included the centre-right National Party. But it was a broad spectrum of minor parties ranging from the libertarian ACT to the Christian fundamentalist ONE Party that made the most explicit appeal to boycott the Team of Five Million.

Chapter 2 discussed the impact of Covid-19 on public opinion and electoral outcomes. A key finding of that chapter was the relationship between trust in Jacinda Ardern, approval of the Covid-19 response, and change in the Labour Party vote between 2017 and 2020. In contrast to Chapter 2's analysis, which included 'prior bias' as a control, we have used a simple binary logistic regression to investigate the relationship between certain social structural variables and disapproval of the pandemic response. We have done this to construct a demographic profile. We report our findings in terms of odds ratios (see the first column of Appendix Table A8.2).[2] With an odds ratio of 0.569, our baseline analysis finds that women were a little more than half as likely to disapprove of the government's Covid-19 response as men—that is, their odds of disapproving were 0.569 to one. Disapproval also correlated highly with farming and self-employment on

---

2   An odds ratio of one would mean there is no difference in the effect on the outcome variable of the value or values or category or categories compared. An odds ratio of less than one designates a negative relationship with the outcome variable, and more than one, a positive relationship.

a household basis (odds ratios of 2.8 to 1 and 1.8 to 1, respectively). In an alternative exploratory model, we found no significant relationship between disapproval and education. In our baseline model, appraisal of household finances was another significant predictor. Those who reported their household finances had worsened over the past year were 2.4 times more likely to disapprove of the Covid-19 response than those who reported they were doing better. However, the model explains only 9.2 per cent of the variance between disapproval and approval. It is important to also consider the role of ideology.

There is an emerging literature on ideological responses to Covid-19. Recent studies in other jurisdictions have established a relationship between right-wing ideology and scepticism of Covid-19 (Calvillo et al. 2020; Choma et al. 2021; Latkin et al. 2021; Murphy et al. 2021). These studies make use of two attitudinal dimensions to measure ideology: right-wing authoritarianism (RWA) and social dominance orientation (SDO). While RWA measures deference to authority and tradition, SDO is used to measure support for group-based hierarchies. It is generally accepted that those who score highly for RWA and SDO are more sensitive than the general population to perceived threats against society. However, research by Onraet et al. (2013) found that right-wing individuals are less sensitive to threats of a personal nature such as mental distress. Clarke et al. (2021) have theorised that this dual nature could explain why RWA and SDO appear to predict scepticism of Covid-19 and opposition to public health restrictions. In other words, right-wing individuals may perceive loss of personal freedom as a greater threat to society than the virus.

In broader terms, authoritarianism can be understood as 'a cluster of values prioritising collective security for the group at the expense of liberal autonomy for the individual' (Norris and Inglehart 2019, 9). There has been extensive research on authoritarianism in New Zealand focussed on understanding the relationship between ideology and prejudice against minorities (Brune et al. 2016; Duckitt and Sibley 2016; Satherley and Sibley 2018; Sibley et al. 2019). The effects of authoritarianism on voting behaviour have also been subject to investigation (Greaves and Vowles 2020, 85–87). The NZES uses a scale to estimate authoritarian attitudes based on three questions about leadership, interpersonal trust, and discipline. Further, the 2020 NZES also included a set of questions asking the respondent which of two qualities are more important in children. It has been established that people who value qualities such as obedience and respect for elders are predisposed to authoritarianism (Feldman 2003; Feldman and Stenner 1997; Stenner 2005).

The claim that authoritarianism could predict opposition to public health restrictions intended to prevent mass death sits uncomfortably with Norris and Inglehart's (2019) conceptualisation of authoritarianism. Ironically, the Covid-19 pandemic has seen right-wing authoritarians champion negative freedom and personal choice over state control. Vowles (2022) suggests the answer to this paradox could lie in the emphasis placed on submission rather than dominance in conventional measures of authoritarianism. It is therefore instructive to consider the role specific traits may play. Clarke et al. (2021) found that opposition and reactance to government restrictions in Australia were associated with traditionalism. However, a preference for in-group dominance appeared to be a stronger predictor. While a direct comparison might not be possible, the relationship is worth exploring further with the data available to us in the 2020 NZES.

To rule out the effect of authoritarianism as conventionally measured in the NZES, we included a three-item authoritarian time-series scale in our regression model that has been used in the NZES from its beginning.[3] We found the expected relationship between placement on the NZES authoritarian scale and disapproval of the government's Covid-19 response when controlling for social structural variables. This added a further 2 per cent to the explanation of the variance between approval and disapproval. The person most disposed to authoritarianism was just over eight times more likely to oppose the government's response than someone least disposed. We also tested the Child-Rearing Values Scale (Feldman and Stenner 1997; Vowles 2022). Substituting this variable for the NZES authoritarian scale, we found that authoritarian disposition also had a significant but weaker effect, with an odds ratio of 2.7 between its authoritarian and non-authoritarian extremes, adding much less to the variance explained.

What about specific traits? To explore the possible relationship between traditionalism, in-group dominance, and Covid-19, we used a question on whether minorities 'should adapt to the customs and traditions of the majority' to operationalise these sentiments. Those who strongly agreed

---

3   The questions are in a five-point agree/disagree format. They are: 'Most people would try to take advantage of others if they had the chance'; 'A few strong leaders could make this country better than all the laws and talk'; and 'What young people need most is strict discipline from their parents'. The scale is based on addition of these responses, transformed to run between zero and one.

with the statement were a little less than twice as likely to disapprove of the Covid-19 response than those who strongly disagreed but this fell short of statistical significance and added almost nothing to the variance explained. Authoritarian attitudes add something to the explanation of disapproving of the government's Covid-19 policies, but a combination of social structural variables and concern about the economy explain much more. A large part of this effect was age: people aged 61 and above were about one-third less likely to disapprove than those in the 18–31 age group. It was those aged 41–60 who were the most likely to disapprove.

Authoritarianism could also manifest in attitudes to the Treaty of Waitangi and the constitutional status of Māori. This reflects the fact that New Zealand is a colonial–settler society, in which Pākehā are the ethnic majority. It follows that those who have a strong psychological need for conformity feel threatened by diversity and are therefore much less inclined to support notions of co-governance. To measure anti-Māori sentiment, we constructed a scale from three questions in the NZES. The first two of these asked participants the extent to which they agreed or disagreed with the following statements: 'Reference to the Treaty of Waitangi should be removed from law' and 'Māori should have more say in all government decisions'. The third question asked: 'Do you think the Treaty settlement process has gone too far, far enough, or not far enough?' Those who agreed with the first statement, disagreed with the second statement, and believed that the Treaty settlement process had gone 'too far' represented 5.2 per cent of the sample. Including this new variable in our model, we found a strong relationship between scoring high for anti-Māori sentiment and disapproval of the government's Covid-19 response. Those most opposed to policies to advance the interests of Māori were just over seven times more likely to disapprove of the government's Covid-19 response. Including this variable added another 2 per cent to the explanatory power of the model—about the same effect as that of authoritarianism.

However, consistent with the findings in Chapter 2, we found that distrust of Jacinda Ardern had the most explanatory power when it came to disapproval of the government's Covid-19 response. Those with the lowest degree of trust in Ardern were about 95 times more likely to disapprove than those with the highest trust.[4] Including this variable in our model increased its explanatory power by 24 per cent, to 38 per cent. In other words, this combination

---

4   'How well do you feel the following descriptions apply to Jacinda Ardern: A competent leader; a trustworthy leader?' Five-point scales.

of social structure, ideology, and leadership accounts for more than one-third of the variance. Perhaps unsurprisingly, it was voters' perception of Ardern herself that had the greatest impact on whether someone chose to boycott the Team of Five Million. In the end, a small minority reacted negatively to Ardern's appeal for kindness and solidarity.

Party support: Sceptics and opportunists?

While these voters represent a theoretically significant bloc, the fragmentation of party support undermined any electoral strength this bloc might have had. About 46 per cent of those who disapproved of the government's Covid-19 response gave their party vote to National, while 16 per cent voted for ACT, and a further 11 per cent voted for minor parties of the right (n = 208).[5] The last category included Advance NZ and the New Conservatives but also the Christian fundamentalist ONE Party, Vision New Zealand, and the Outdoors Party. These five 'Covid-sceptical' parties received a combined 86,662 votes (about 3 per cent of the total). Thus, National lost the election, but won the anti-lockdown vote and, in so doing, could have suppressed a more extreme reaction from the authoritarian right.

To investigate the relationship between party support and Covid-19 further, we analysed support for Advance NZ and the New Conservatives. The two parties received 1.5 per cent and 1 per cent of the vote, respectively, making them the most significant of the Covid-sceptical parties. However, given the small number of Advance NZ and New Conservative voters in our sample, it is inappropriate to make generalisations. To overcome the small sample size, we measured party support in terms of 'likeability' rather than party vote, which was defined as a score of six or more on a zero–10 scale. On this measure, about 3 per cent (n = 109) of NZES participants were favourable to Advance NZ and 4.8 per cent (n = 178) to the New Conservatives. Likeability is a reasonable indication of potential support in the electorate (Vowles et al. 2017). Using a similar social structural model to that discussed in the previous section, we investigated the demographic and ideological correlates of party support.

---

5   Seventeen per cent did not vote, with most of the remainder voting Labour, Green, and New Zealand First.

Appendix Table A8.3 shows that religiosity, measured by church attendance, was the most significant factor in liking or disliking the New Conservatives. Those attending church at least once a month were about six times more likely to support the New Conservatives. When it came to Advance NZ, religiosity had a much smaller effect, with regular churchgoers only twice as likely to indicate support. There was no relationship between ethnicity and support for the New Conservatives; however, Māori were just over twice as likely to support Advance NZ as those in the residual European/other category of ethnicity. The almost equal strength of religion and ethnicity in predicting support for Advance NZ is consistent with the profile of co-leader Te Kahika and his belief in Christian End Times theology (Galbraith 2020).

We found a positive relationship between liking Advance NZ or the New Conservatives and living in a household in which at least one person was employed in a manual or service occupation; in the case of Advance NZ, it was not statistically significant, but for the New Conservatives, it met that test at the 90 per cent level (in nine of 10 possible samples). In the case of the New Conservatives, such a person was 1.5 times more likely than someone living in a non–working-class household to indicate support. There is a vast literature on the 'proletarianisation' of the radical right in Europe (Oesch 2008; Bornschier and Kriesi 2012). Our finding could be interpreted as evidence that a segment of the New Zealand working-class electorate was galvanised by right-wing opposition to the Ardern government during 2020. However, while class could have been a factor, the weight of evidence suggests that anti-government sentiment with respect to Covid-19 is better explained by personal values or psychological traits than by economic inequality.

What about ideology? Adding the minorities variable to our model, we found that this had a positive effect on support for the New Conservatives significant at the 90 per cent level and a non-significant negative effect for liking Advance NZ. As for anti-Māori sentiment, we found the same non-significant effects on liking or not liking each party, although removing the minorities must adapt variable from the model generated a significant effect for the New Conservatives. This could reflect different voter bases. The New Conservatives appealed to a segment of the Pākehā electorate with its 'one law for all' stance. Advance NZ, as previously mentioned, received greater support from Māori than from Pākehā, yet both parties tapped into the same wellspring of support among those who opposed lockdowns and were inclined to believe conspiracy theories about the origin of Covid-19.

This intersection between anti-government sentiment and conspiracism was on full display at public demonstrations held around New Zealand in the lead-up to election day (Palmer 2020). These gatherings were in breach of social distancing rules and attracted mainstream media coverage for their defiance.

At one such gathering on 29 August, New Conservative Party deputy leader Elliot Ikilei and Advance NZ co-leader Jami-Lee Ross addressed a crowd of several hundred in Auckland's Aotea Square. Paranoia about the UN Sustainable Development Goals program, known as 'Agenda 2030', was a recurring theme among protestors (1News 2020). Te Kahika himself believed the New Zealand Government was complicit in a UN 'plandemic' (Peters 2020). According to Te Kahika, global elites manufactured the virus as a bioweapon for population control. It is unclear how prevalent such beliefs are in New Zealand; however, research from the United States has found that religiosity and belief in the supernatural are the most powerful predictors of conspiracism (Oliver and Wood 2014, 2018). This suggests an underlying predisposition to believe in hidden forces. Oliver and Wood (2018) found that such cognitive tendencies can lead to magical thinking whereby a person attributes an event to unobservable phenomena despite evidence to the contrary. Te Kahika and his followers exemplified magical thinking in New Zealand during 2020.

The relationship between Covid scepticism and conspiracy theories originating in 'alt-right' cyberspace led New Zealand commentators to portray Advance NZ and, to a lesser extent, the New Conservatives as being analogous to the radical right of North America. According to Ngata (2020), Māori were particularly susceptible to the Trump-inspired 'Q-Anon' narrative of elite corruption and state illegitimacy. Our findings suggest that this apparent convergence between Māori nationalism and symbols associated with white supremacy can be understood in the context of religious fundamentalism. But where do Advance NZ and the New Conservatives fit within a comparative framework? Donovan (2020) has proposed five criteria for categorising a party as 'radical right': 1) intersection of populist style and antipathy towards immigration; 2) cultural authoritarianism; 3) political authoritarianism; 4) supporters in the electorate identify as right-wing; and 5) the electorate views the party as right-wing (Donovan 2020, 60). We applied these criteria to our models on liking or not liking Advance NZ and the New Conservatives.

Attitudes to immigration are measured by a range of questions in the NZES (for further discussion, see Chapter 6, this volume). For this study, we have used a question about the number of immigrants who should be allowed into New Zealand when the border reopened. Those who said the number should be reduced 'a lot' or 'a little' are considered to have an antipathy to immigration. For cultural authoritarianism, two questions are applied, the first of which asks how important the country's customs and traditions are to one's identity as 'a true New Zealander'. As discussed by Barker and Vowles (2020), it is difficult to identify a homogeneous nation in the New Zealand context given the legacy of biculturalism. Nevertheless, the question about traditionalism is useful for exploratory purposes. A second question measuring cultural authoritarianism comes from the Child-Rearing Values Scale. The trait of 'obedience' has been established as having particular significance to cultural authoritarians (Hetherington et al. 2009). Again, following Donovan (2020), we used the question about strong leadership and rule-bending to operationalise political authoritarianism. Finally, we analysed where Advance NZ and New Conservatives supporters placed themselves on the left–right scale compared with where the electorate located those parties.

Appendix Table A8.4 replicates Donovan's (2020) model. This included a variable measuring perceptions of the country's economic performance (which was non-significant). The control variables were age, education, and gender. We found a relationship between Advance NZ and antipathy to immigration; however, there was no relationship between Advance NZ and three of the other four criteria. The model was more effective at predicting support for the New Conservatives, with 'obedience' and ideological self-placement both strong predictors. Yet, despite evidence of cultural authoritarianism, the model found a negative relationship between preference for rule-bending leaders and support for the New Conservatives. When it came to the ideological placement of the parties, NZES participants gave Advance NZ a mean score of 9.6 and the New Conservatives a mean score of 9.4 on the left–right scale (0–10), placing both on the extreme right. Taken together, these findings suggest that, while voters perceive Advance NZ and the New Conservatives as being to the right of mainstream parties, they do not represent the exclusionary populism of authoritarians in Europe and North America. Indeed, cultural and institutional differences often make such analogies fraught. While the rise of a homegrown radical right should not be dismissed, it is likely to manifest in a way that defies international stereotyping (see also Oldfield and Van Veen 2023).

A new ACT?

Despite their emotional resonance with Covid-sceptics, Advance NZ and the New Conservatives were rejected even by those outside the Team of Five Million. In fact, most gravitated to the mainstream centre-right. While a plurality who opposed the government's pandemic response gave their support to National, Her Majesty's loyal opposition had a strong rival in ACT. Both parties aggressively campaigned against what they perceived as bureaucratic incompetence and political mismanagement of the crisis; however, neither proposed to abandon the elimination strategy. They promised to accelerate technological improvements that would reduce the need for lockdowns and allow for international travel. National would establish a border protection agency to provide 'world-class defence' against the virus (Moir 2020). ACT leader David Seymour told party faithful in a major speech on 11 July of his vision for 'smart borders that people and money can come through, but not COVID-19' (Robson 2020). Such policies were consistent with the belief that New Zealand's geographical isolation made it a 'Shangri-la' (Cheng 2021). From Seymour's perspective, only the government stood in the way of this Covid-free, high-tech utopia.

An explanation for National's and ACT's approaches to Covid-19 lies in the 'valence' or performance model of electoral choice (Stokes 1963; Clarke et al. 2011). According to Whiteley et al. (2013, 1–2), 'voters make choices primarily on the basis of rival parties' perceived abilities to deliver policy outcomes on salient issues involving broad consensus about what governments should do'. In 2020, the overwhelming majority of New Zealanders supported the Ardern government's elimination strategy and regarded the Level 4 nationwide lockdown as a success. While some elites argued for a 'herd immunity' approach on utilitarian grounds, claiming the economic and social costs of lockdown outweighed the infection fatality rate (Chaudhuri 2020; Hooton 2020), this was rejected by National. In August, during a second outbreak of Covid-19, opposition leader Judith Collins disagreed with the suggestion that New Zealanders should 'learn to live with the virus' (Small 2020). Seymour, while sceptical about the efficacy of lockdowns, distanced ACT from the herd immunity approach and argued for New Zealand to follow the example of Taiwan, which relied on extensive contact tracing (McCulloch 2020). Thus, the mainstream centre-right attempted to present itself as more agile and sophisticated than Labour when it came to pandemic politics.

About one-quarter of NZES participants nominated Covid-19 as the most important issue for them in 2020. Of these, 80 per cent believed that Labour was the best party to deal with Covid-19 issues. These numbers reinforce the view that National made a strategic blunder in emphasising the minor differences between itself and Labour on Covid-19. National and ACT may have won the anti-lockdown vote, but the opposition misjudged the electorate. Collins and her strategists appeared to be suffering from a false consensus effect (Ross et al. 1977) in believing that anti-government sentiment was popular. For National, the result was devastating. ACT, however, had good reason to celebrate on election night: it was arguably the most successful of the minor parties. With 7.6 per cent of the vote, ACT went from having a sole MP to a caucus of 10, reaching parity with the Greens. What explains this remarkable success? About 60 per cent of ACT voters in our sample reported voting for National in 2017.

We analysed the demographic correlates of ACT support and a range of other variables to explore why someone might have voted for ACT. Seymour remarked in his speech at the triennial post-election conference that market research leading into the election had suggested the party could appeal to two archetypal voters: a male business owner named 'Ken' and a middle-aged professional woman named 'Angela'. However, the gender gap in ACT support was the largest of any mainstream party in our sample, with males representing 64 per cent of ACT voters. The analysis in the first two columns of Appendix Table A8.5 finds that controlling for other social structural variables, a man was about twice as likely as a woman to vote for ACT (a female–male odds ratio of 0.577). All ethnic groups other than those in the residual European/other category were significantly less likely to vote ACT. However, living in a household in which at least one person was self-employed or owned a business did not correlate with voting for ACT. Nor was there any relationship between occupation and voting ACT. From the available data in the NZES, the existence of 'Ken' is somewhat plausible but that of 'Angela' is less so. ACT support was strongest in rural areas and weakest in the suburbs of large cities. ACT voters were three times more likely to have a very high income than non-ACT voters, but no greater number of assets, and were unlikely to be a union member or live in a household with one.

What about the rivalry for the centre-right vote between ACT and National? In Columns 3 and 4 of Appendix Table A8.5, we compared the two voter bases. ACT voters were twice as likely to be men and more likely than National voters to live at a rural address. National voters had a higher number of assets than ACT voters. Adding the five variables from Donovan (2020), those who preferred the trait of obedience in children were more likely to vote for National, while those who self-identified as right-wing were more likely to vote for ACT.

Conclusion

In 2020, right-wing opposition to the Ardern government was characterised by Covid-scepticism and hostility to public health measures. While the prime minister succeeded in uniting most New Zealanders against Covid-19, a significant minority reacted negatively to her appeal for kindness and solidarity during the pandemic. Those voters found representation in both the mainstream centre-right National Party and a host of right-wing parties. Most of these parties were electorally inconsequential, fulminating around the edges of the 2020 campaign, and falling well short of either the 5 per cent party vote or one electorate seat threshold. ACT was the exception, increasing its caucus from one MP to 10 after winning a historic 7.6 per cent of the party vote.

According to the 2020 NZES, most of ACT's support in the 2020 election came from voters who abandoned National under the leadership of Judith Collins. Adding the NZES authoritarianism scale to an alternative version of the ACT versus National model (without the Donovan variables) indicates that ACT voters were somewhat less authoritarian than National voters. While the trend of opinion polling following the 2020 election suggested ACT was on course to maintain its share of the vote in 2023 (Malpass 2022), the party was struggling to broaden its appeal among women, Māori, and urban voters. Yet these three groups remained well represented in the ACT caucus both before and after the 2023 election. Indeed, the party has performed well with Seymour's archetypal male voter 'Ken', but less so with 'Angela'. The relative success of ACT also prompted questions about whether Seymour has displaced New Zealand First leader Winston Peters as the nation's pre-eminent populist (for a more thorough discussion of this topic, see Oldfield and Van Veen 2023). While it could be true in the performative sense, it was less evident in responses to the NZES. Only 12 per cent of those who reported voting for New Zealand First in 2017 said they voted for ACT in 2020.

None of the Covid-sceptic parties was successful in gaining parliamentary representation; however, many of the individuals aligned with parties such as Advance NZ and the New Conservatives have since coalesced around the anti-vaccine movement. In February 2022, during the peak of the Omicron outbreak, several thousand protestors occupied the grounds of Parliament House and Molesworth Street in central Wellington to demand the government revoke vaccine mandates. While many of the participants disavowed violence, the occupation was marred by extreme rhetoric and violent confrontations with police. The Wellington protests have led some commentators to speculate that the post-2020 electoral landscape is fertile ground for the 'far right' (Manhire 2022). However, our findings suggest a lack of ideological conformity among those who voted for right-wing parties in 2020. New Conservative Party supporters, for example, were anti-Treaty and intolerant of minority differences but there was no relationship between supporting the New Conservatives and hostility to immigration. Advance NZ supporters, on the other hand, were no more authoritarian than any other set of voters or supporters. Indeed, neither party fits the typology of a radical right populist movement. While there was some evidence of a class dimension, leaving open the possibility for a right-wing populist leader to mobilise those 'left behind' in future, opposition to the Ardern government's Covid-19 response was better explained by personal values or psychological traits than by economic inequality and traditional ideology. In other words, while the voters supporting these fringe parties were ideologically amorphous, the parties representing them were equally broad. These divergent interests make the consolidation of support behind a single party or coalition of parties unlikely.

While this subgroup of voters was indeed diverse, an overall profile did emerge. Religiosity was a significant factor, as were certain aspects of right-wing authoritarianism. The latter were teased out by comparing support for the government's Covid-19 response with attitudes to the assimilation of minorities or whether the Treaty of Waitangi should feature in government legislation. However, one factor stood out as the most likely predictor in the NZES of participant disproval of the Covid-19 response and that was a specific dislike of Prime Minister Jacinda Ardern. In the end, perhaps, disapproval of the government's handling of the pandemic, or an outright rejection of the health-oriented response, was evident among a small minority, who, much like Chris Penk, were reacting negatively to Ardern's appeal for kindness and solidarity.

References

1News. 2020. 'Hundreds Protest Against Lockdowns, Vaccines While Unmasked in Auckland.' *1News*, [Auckland], 29 August. Available from: www.1news.co.nz/2020/08/29/hundreds-protest-against-lockdowns-vaccines-while-unmasked-in-auckland/.

Baccini, L., and A. Brodeur. 2021. 'Explaining Governors' Response to the COVID-19 Pandemic in the United States.' *American Politics Research* 49(2): 215–20. doi.org/10.1177/1532673x20973453.

Barker, F., and J. Vowles. 2020. 'Populism and Electoral Politics in New Zealand.' In *A Populist Exception? The 2017 New Zealand General Election*, edited by J. Vowles and J. Curtin, 9–34. Canberra: ANU Press. doi.org/10.22459/PE.2020.01.

Bayer, K. 2020. 'Covid 19 Coronavirus: Hundreds Turn Out for Anti-Lockdown Protests.' *New Zealand Herald*, 5 September. Available from: www.nzherald.co.nz/nz/covid-19-coronavirus-hundreds-turn-out-for-anti-lockdown-protests/AHE2NJJY3VMTTXLAUHLWIJOODY/.

Bornschier, S., and H. Kriesi. 2012. 'The Populist Right, the Working Class, and the Changing Face of Class Politics.' In *Class Politics and the Radical Right*, edited by J. Rydgren. London: Routledge. doi.org/10.4324/9780203079546.

Brune, A., F. Asbrock, and C.G. Sibley. 2016. 'Meet Your Neighbours: Authoritarians Engage in Intergroup Contact When They Have the Opportunity.' *Journal of Community & Applied Social Psychology* 26(6): 567–80. doi.org/10.1002/casp.2289.

Calvillo, D.P., B.J. Ross, R.J.B. Garcia, T.J. Smelter, and A.M. Rutchick. 2020. 'Political Ideology Predicts Perceptions of the Threat of COVID-19 (and Susceptibility to Fake News About It).' *Social Psychological and Personality Science* 11(8): 1119–28. doi.org/10.1177/1948550620940539.

Chaudhuri, A. 2020. 'A Different Perspective on Covid-19.' *Newsroom*, [Auckland], 7 April, [Updated 29 July]. newsroom.co.nz/2020/04/07/a-different-perspective-on-covid-19/

Cheng, D. 2021. 'Covid 19 Delta Outbreak: Sir David Skegg Warned About a Delta Outbreak.' *New Zealand Herald*, 25 October. Available from: www.nzherald.co.nz/nz/politics/covid-19-delta-outbreak-sir-david-skegg-warned-about-a-delta-outbreak/QPJIXOCMV45RDGQ66YUZNWXMNI/.

Choma, B.L., G. Hodson, D. Sumantry, Y. Hanoch, and M. Gummerum. 2021. 'Ideological and Psychological Predictors of COVID-19–Related Collective Action, Opinions, and Health Compliance Across Three Nations.' *Journal of Social and Political Psychology* 9(1): 123–43. doi.org/10.5964/jspp.5585.

Clarke, E.J.R., A. Klas, and E. Dyos. 2021. 'The Role of Ideological Attitudes in Responses to COVID-19 Threat and Government Restrictions in Australia.' *Personality and Individual Differences* 175: 110734. doi.org/10.1016/j.paid. 2021.110734.

Clarke, H., D. Sanders, M. Stewart, and P. Whiteley. 2011. 'Valence Politics and Electoral Choice in Britain, 2010.' *Journal of Elections, Public Opinion and Parties* 21(2): 237–53. doi.org/10.1080/17457289.2011.562614.

Daalder, M. 2022. '"Splintered Realities": How NZ Convoy Lost Its Way.' *Newsroom*, [Auckland], 12 February, [Updated 12 January 2023]. Available from: www.newsroom.co.nz/hijacked-the-inside-story-of-how-nzs-convoy-lost-its-rudder.

Donovan, T. 2020. 'Misclassifying Parties as Radical Right/Right Wing Populist: A Comparative Analysis of New Zealand First.' *Political Science* 72(1): 58–76. doi.org/10.1080/00323187.2020.1855992.

Duckitt, J., and C. Sibley. 2016. 'The Dual Process Motivational Model of Ideology and Prejudice.' In *The Cambridge Handbook of the Psychology of Prejudice* (Cambridge Handbooks in Psychology), edited by C. Sibley and F. Barlow, 188–221. Cambridge, UK: Cambridge University Press. doi.org/10.1017/97813 16161579.009.

Ensor, J. 2020. '"End is Nigh" for Simon Bridges Who May Have Just Two Weeks Left as Leader: Tova O'Brien, Michelle Boag.' *Newshub*, [Auckland], 19 May. Available from: www.newshub.co.nz/home/politics/2020/05/end-is-nigh-for-simon-bridges-who-may-have-just-two-weeks-left-as-leader-tova-o-brien-michelle -boag.html.

Feldman, S. 2003. 'Enforcing Social Conformity: A Theory of Authoritarianism.' *Political Psychology* 24(1): 41–74. doi.org/10.1111/0162-895X.00316.

Feldman, S., and K. Stenner. 1997. 'Perceived Threat and Authoritarianism.' *Political Psychology* 18(4): 741–70. doi.org/10.1111/0162-895X.00077.

Galbraith, D. 2020. 'How Billy TK is Using the Far Right.' *Newsroom*, [Auckland], 24 November. Available from: www.newsroom.co.nz/ideasroom/how-billy-tk-is-using-the-far-right.

Geana, M.V., N. Rabb, and S. Sloman. 2021. 'Walking the Party Line: The Growing Role of Political Ideology in Shaping Health Behavior in the United States.' *SSM—Population Health* 16: 100950. doi.org/10.1016/j.ssmph.2021.100950.

Greaves, L., and J. Vowles. 2020. 'Measuring Populism in New Zealand.' In *A Populist Exception? The 2017 New Zealand General Election*. Canberra: ANU Press. doi.org/10.22459/PE.2020.

Hetherington, M.J., J.D. Weiler, and P.J.D. Weiler. 2009. *Authoritarianism and Polarization in American Politics*. Cambridge: Cambridge University Press. doi.org/10.1017/CBO9780511802331.

Hooton, M. 2020. 'Covid 19 Coronavirus: Matthew Hooton—Save Lives, But at Any Cost? That's Jacinda Ardern's Awful Dilemma.' *New Zealand Herald*, 3 April. Available from: www.nzherald.co.nz/business/covid-19-coronavirus-matthew-hooton-save-lives-but-at-any-cost-thats-jacinda-arderns-awful-dilemma/QGQK XQRILLN2LKESGUUSCEUYBU/.

Latkin, C.A., L. Dayton, M. Moran, J.C. Strickland, and K. Collins. 2021. 'Behavioral and Psychosocial Factors Associated With COVID-19 Skepticism in the United States.' *Current Psychology* 41: 7918–26. doi.org/10.1007/s12144-020-01211-3.

Malpass, L. 2022. 'Polls Diverge On Voter Direction as Left and Right Blocs Neck and Neck.' *Stuff*, [Wellington], 22 June. Available from: www.stuff.co.nz/national/politics/129051542/polls-diverge-on-voter-direction-as-left-and-right-blocs-neck-and-neck.

Manhire, T. 2022. 'Divided? Splintered? What the Parliament Occupation Says About New Zealand Now.' *The Spinoff*, [Auckland], 23 February. Available from: thespinoff.co.nz/politics/23-02-2022/divided-splintered-what-the-parliament-occupation-says-about-nz-now.

McCulloch, C. 2020. 'Covid-19: ACT Says NZ Should Model Its Covid Approach on Taiwan.' *Radio New Zealand*, 20 August. Available from: www.rnz.co.nz/news/political/424035/covid-19-act-says-nz-should-model-its-covid-approach-on-taiwan.

Moir, J. 2020. 'Judith Collins Unveils National's Border Security Policy.' *Radio New Zealand*, 20 August. Available from: www.rnz.co.nz/news/political/423980/judith-collins-unveils-national-s-border-security-policy.

Murphy, J., F. Vallières, R.P. Bentall, M. Shevlin, O. McBride, T.K. Hartman, R. McKay, K. Bennett, L. Mason, J. Gibson-Miller, L. Levita, A.P. Martinez, T.V.A. Stocks, T. Karatzias, and P. Hyland. 2021. 'Psychological Characteristics Associated With COVID-19 Vaccine Hesitancy and Resistance in Ireland and the United Kingdom.' *Nature Communications* 12(1): 29. doi.org/10.1038/s41467-020-20226-9.

Murphy, T. 2020. 'I Saw You Praying in the Chapel.' *Newsroom*, [Auckland], 8 October, [Updated 12 October]. Available from: www.newsroom.co.nz/i-saw-you-praying-in-the-chapel.

Ngata, T. 2020. 'The Rise of Māori MAGA.' *e-Tangata*, 9 August. Available from: e-tangata.co.nz/comment-and-analysis/the-rise-of-maori-maga/.

Norris, P., and R. Inglehart. 2019. *Cultural Backlash: Trump, Brexit, and Authoritarian Populism*. Cambridge: Cambridge University Press. doi.org/10.1017/9781108595841.

O'Connor, S. 2020. 'Budget Debate.' *Hansard (Debates)*, 3 June. Wellington: New Zealand Parliament. Available from: www.parliament.nz/en/pb/hansard-debates/rhr/document/HansS_20200603_051480000/oconnor-simon.

Oesch, D. 2008. 'Explaining Workers' Support for Right-Wing Populist Parties in Western Europe: Evidence from Austria, Belgium, France, Norway, and Switzerland.' *International Political Science Review* 29(3): 349–73. doi.org/10.1177/0192512107088390.

Oldfield, L.D., and J. Van Veen. 2023. 'Man Alone: Winston Peters and the Populist Tendency in New Zealand Politics.' In *Routledge Handbook on Populism in the Asia Pacific*, edited by D.B. Subedi, H. Brasted, K. von Strokirch, and A. Scott. London: Routledge.

Oliver, J.E., and T.J. Wood. 2014. 'Conspiracy Theories and the Paranoid Style(s) of Mass Opinion.' *American Journal of Political Science* 58(4): 952–66. doi.org/10.1111/ajps.12084.

Oliver, J.E., and T.J. Wood. 2018. *Enchanted America: How Intuition and Reason Divide Our Politics*. Chicago, IL: University of Chicago Press. Available from: press.uchicago.edu/ucp/books/book/chicago/E/bo28752049.html. doi.org/10.7208/chicago/9780226578644.001.0001.

Onraet, E., A. Van Hiel, K. Dhont, and S. Pattyn. 2013. 'Internal and External Threat in Relationship with Right-Wing Attitudes.' *Journal of Personality* 81(3): 233–48. doi.org/10.1111/jopy.12011.

Palmer, S. 2020. 'Anti-Lockdown Protestors Take Over Auckland's Aotea Square in "Rally for Freedom".' *Newshub*, [Auckland], 12 September. Available from: www.newshub.co.nz/home/new-zealand/2020/09/anti-lockdown-protestors-take-over-auckland-s-aotea-square-in-rally-for-freedom.html.

Penk, C. 2020. *Flattening the Country: The Real Story Behind Labour's Lockdown*. Self-published.

Peters, M. 2020. 'Global "Plandemic": Ardern, Bloomfield, Labour Party All Part of the Communist Coronavirus Conspiracy—NZ Public Party.' *The Gisborne Herald*, [NZ], 8 July. Available from: static.ew.ghe.navigacloud.com/wp-content/uploads/sites/2/2020/07/09001011/200708GH.pdf.

Radio New Zealand (RNZ). 2020. 'Simon Bridges Will Continue Commute to Chair Epidemic Response Committee.' *Radio New Zealand*, 8 April, Available from: www.rnz.co.nz/news/political/413731/simon-bridges-will-continue-commute-to-chair-epidemic-response-committee.

Raymond, C.D. 2017. 'Religious Voters and the Religious–Secular Cleavage Since 1990.' *Political Science* 69(1): 71–86. doi.org/10.1080/00323187.2017.1313687.

Robson, S. 2020. 'ACT Leader Uses Campaign Launch to Slate Government's Covid-19 Response.' *Radio New Zealand*, 12 July. Available from: www.rnz.co.nz/news/political/421055/act-leader-uses-campaign-launch-to-slate-government-s-covid-19-response.

Ross, L., D. Greene, and P. House. 1977. 'The "False Consensus Effect": An Egocentric Bias in Social Perception and Attribution Processes.' *Journal of Experimental Social Psychology* 13(3): 279–301. doi.org/10.1016/0022-1031(77)90049-X.

Satherley, N., and C. Sibley. 2018. 'The Modern Racism Toward Maori Scale.' *New Zealand Journal of Psychology* 47(2): 4–13. doi.org/10.1037/t74859-000.

Sibley, C.G., R. Bergh, N. Satherley, D. Osborne, P. Milojev, L.M. Greaves, Y. Huang, C.S. Townrow, A. Faapoi, K. Yogeeswaran, D. Hawi, and J. Duckett. 2019. 'Profiling Authoritarian Leaders and Followers.' *TPM-Testing, Psychometrics, Methodology in Applied Psychology* 26(3): 401–17.

Sibley, C.G., L.M. Greaves, N. Satherley, M.S. Wilson, N.C. Overall, C.H.J. Lee, P. Milojev, J. Bulbulia, D. Osborne, T.L. Milfont, C.A. Houkamau, I.M. Duck, R. Vickers-Jones, and F.K. Barlow. 2020. 'Effects of the COVID-19 Pandemic and Nationwide Lockdown on Trust, Attitudes Toward Government, and Well-Being.' *American Psychologist* 75(5): 618–30. doi.org/10.1037/amp0000662.

Small, Z. 2020. 'Coronavirus: Judith Collins Not Keen on ACT Leader David Seymour's Call to Learn to Live with COVID-19.' *Newshub*, [Auckland], 17 August. Available from: www.newshub.co.nz/home/politics/2020/08/coronavirus-judith-collins-not-keen-on-act-leader-david-seymour-s-call-to-learn-to-live-with-covid-19.html.

Smith, J. 2021. 'COVID-19, Brexit and the United Kingdom: A Year of Uncertainty.' *The Round Table: The Commonwealth Journal of International Affairs* 110(1): 62–75. doi.org/10.1080/00358533.2021.1875686.

Stenner, K. 2005. *The Authoritarian Dynamic.* Cambridge: Cambridge University Press. doi.org/10.1017/CBO9780511614712.

Stokes, D. 1963. 'Spatial Models of Party Competition.' *The American Political Science Review* 57(2): 368–77. doi.org/10.2307/1952828.

The Spinoff. 2020. 'Gerry Brownlee Just Thinks It's Interesting.' *The Spinoff*, [Auckland], 12 August. Available from: www.youtube.com/watch?v=N2L9s_V4bWg.

Vance, A. 2022. *Blue Blood: The Inside Story of the National Party in Crisis.* Auckland: HarperCollins New Zealand.

Vowles, J. 2022. 'Authoritarianism and Mass Political Preferences in Times of COVID-19: The 2020 New Zealand General Election.' *Frontiers in Political Science* 4: 885299. doi.org/10.3389/fpos.2022.885299.

Vowles, J., F. Barker, M. Krewel, J. Hayward, J. Curtin, L. Greaves, and L. Oldfield. 2022. *2020 New Zealand Election Study.* [Online]. ADA Dataverse, V3. doi.org/10.26193/BPAMYJ.

Vowles, J., H. Coffé, and J. Curtin. 2017. *A Bark But No Bite: Inequality and the 2014 New Zealand General Election.* Canberra: ANU Press. doi.org/10.22459/bbnb.08.2017.

Wade, A. 2020. 'National's Gerry Brownlee: "I Totally Reject Any Idea That I'm A Conspiracy Theorist".' *New Zealand Herald*, 18 August. Available from: www.nzherald.co.nz/nz/nationals-gerry-brownlee-i-totally-reject-any-idea-that-im-a-conspiracy-theorist/W6FUF76DGEFNSTXZEMLJO3XRX4/.

Whiteley, P., H.D. Clarke, D. Sanders, and M.C. Stewart. 2013. *Affluence, Austerity and Electoral Change in Britain.* Cambridge: Cambridge University Press. doi.org/10.1017/cbo9781139162517.

Yamey, G., and G. Gonsalves. 2020. 'Donald Trump: A Political Determinant of Covid-19.' *BMJ* 369: m1643. doi.org/10.1136/bmj.m1643.

Appendix 8.1

Table A8.1 Disapproval of Covid-19 response by social structure, authoritarianism, cultural conservatism, and trust in Jacinda Ardern: Coefficients and robust standard errors

	(1)	(2)	(3)	(4)	(5)	(6)
Female (male)	−0.564**	−0.540**	−0.523**	−0.501**	−0.483**	−0.256
	(0.219)	(0.219)	(0.222)	(0.229)	(0.238)	(0.245)
Age 31–41	−0.164	−0.185	−0.199	−0.170	−0.240	−0.194
	(0.372)	(0.373)	(0.378)	(0.368)	(0.369)	(0.368)
Age 41–51	0.397	0.342	0.314	0.289	0.171	0.665*
	(0.317)	(0.323)	(0.321)	(0.312)	(0.315)	(0.370)

	(1)	(2)	(3)	(4)	(5)	(6)
Age 51–61	0.407	0.355	0.322	0.322	0.244	0.368
	(0.315)	(0.318)	(0.315)	(0.330)	(0.362)	(0.407)
Age 61–71	–1.033***	–1.074***	–1.115***	–1.167***	–1.296***	–0.881**
	(0.345)	(0.355)	(0.352)	(0.360)	(0.362)	(0.396)
Age 71+	–1.165***	–1.277***	–1.331***	–1.394***	–1.581***	–1.254***
	(0.376)	(0.384)	(0.393)	(0.376)	(0.373)	(0.402)
Asian	–0.671	–0.858**	–0.785*	–0.854**	–0.737*	–0.439
	(0.412)	(0.422)	(0.422)	(0.423)	(0.435)	(0.432)
Pasifika	0.916*	0.628	0.752	0.635	1.119**	1.565***
	(0.469)	(0.494)	(0.481)	(0.487)	(0.494)	(0.607)
Māori	–0.267	–0.441	–0.307	–0.413	0.091	–0.063
	(0.280)	(0.290)	(0.289)	(0.291)	(0.335)	(0.340)
Employer/self-employed	0.607*	0.670**	0.601*	0.687**	0.679*	–0.046
	(0.316)	(0.320)	(0.310)	(0.328)	(0.364)	(0.392)
Farming	1.045***	0.918***	0.942***	0.915**	0.842**	0.529
	(0.344)	(0.350)	(0.333)	(0.365)	(0.422)	(0.368)
Nonmanual	0.059	–0.052	0.041	–0.058	–0.086	–0.216
	(0.243)	(0.244)	(0.244)	(0.244)	(0.243)	(0.285)
Household economy same	0.200	0.201	0.168	0.224	0.270	0.080
	(0.397)	(0.396)	(0.393)	(0.405)	(0.417)	(0.427)
Household economy worse	0.877**	0.752*	0.820**	0.763*	0.759*	0.438
	(0.386)	(0.386)	(0.387)	(0.394)	(0.403)	(0.434)
Authoritarianism		2.112***		1.870***	1.548***	0.895
		(0.493)		(0.532)	(0.588)	(0.629)
CSV-authoritarian			1.007**			
			(0.428)			
Minorities adapt				0.626	0.175	0.169
				(0.446)	(0.425)	(0.438)
Anti-Māori					1.977***	0.850
					(0.765)	(0.601)
Trust in Ardern						–4.552***
						(0.349)
Constant	–3.097***	–4.138***	–3.438***	–4.292***	–5.029***	–1.492**
	(0.384)	(0.468)	(0.419)	(0.489)	(0.601)	(0.646)
Observations	3,650	3,650	3,650	3,650	3,650	3,582

	(1)	(2)	(3)	(4)	(5)	(6)
r^2_p	0.0915	0.114	0.0984	0.118	0.141	0.377
ll	–728.9	–710.9	–723.4	–707.6	–689.5	–494.5

*** $p < 0.01$

** $p < 0.05$

* $p < 0.1$

Note: Robust standard errors in parentheses.

Source: Vowles et al. (2022).

Table A8.2 Disapproval of Covid-19 response by social structure, authoritarianism, cultural conservatism, and trust in Jacinda Ardern: Odds ratios and adjusted robust standard errors

	(1)	(2)	(3)	(4)	(5)	(6)
Female (male)	0.569**	0.583**	0.592**	0.606**	0.617**	0.774
	(0.125)	(0.128)	(0.131)	(0.139)	(0.147)	(0.190)
Age 31–41	0.849	0.831	0.819	0.843	0.787	0.824
	(0.316)	(0.310)	(0.309)	(0.311)	(0.290)	(0.303)
Age 41–51	1.488	1.408	1.369	1.335	1.186	1.945*
	(0.471)	(0.454)	(0.439)	(0.417)	(0.374)	(0.719)
Age 51–61	1.503	1.427	1.380	1.380	1.276	1.445
	(0.473)	(0.454)	(0.435)	(0.456)	(0.461)	(0.587)
Age 61–71	0.356***	0.342***	0.328***	0.311***	0.274***	0.414**
	(0.123)	(0.121)	(0.116)	(0.112)	(0.0991)	(0.164)
Age 71+	0.312***	0.279***	0.264***	0.248***	0.206***	0.285***
	(0.117)	(0.107)	(0.104)	(0.0933)	(0.0768)	(0.115)
Asian	0.511	0.424**	0.456*	0.426**	0.479*	0.644
	(0.211)	(0.179)	(0.192)	(0.180)	(0.208)	(0.278)
Pasifika	2.500*	1.874	2.121	1.888	3.060**	4.785***
	(1.172)	(0.926)	(1.020)	(0.919)	(1.511)	(2.905)
Māori	0.765	0.643	0.736	0.662	1.095	0.939
	(0.214)	(0.187)	(0.213)	(0.192)	(0.367)	(0.319)
Employer/self-employed	1.835*	1.954**	1.823*	1.987**	1.973*	0.955
	(0.580)	(0.625)	(0.565)	(0.652)	(0.718)	(0.374)
Farming	2.843***	2.504***	2.565***	2.496**	2.322**	1.698
	(0.979)	(0.876)	(0.854)	(0.910)	(0.979)	(0.625)
Manual or service	1.061	0.950	1.042	0.943	0.918	0.806
	(0.258)	(0.231)	(0.254)	(0.230)	(0.223)	(0.230)
Household economy same	1.222	1.223	1.182	1.251	1.310	1.084
	(0.485)	(0.484)	(0.465)	(0.506)	(0.547)	(0.463)

	(1)	(2)	(3)	(4)	(5)	(6)
Household economy worse	2.404**	2.121*	2.271**	2.145*	2.137*	1.550
	(0.928)	(0.819)	(0.878)	(0.846)	(0.861)	(0.673)
Authoritarianism		8.268***		6.489***	4.703***	2.450
		(4.076)		(3.450)	(2.765)	(1.543)
CSV-authoritarian			2.736**			
			(1.171)			
Minorities adapt				1.871	1.192	1.184
				(0.835)	(0.507)	(0.518)
Anti-Māori					7.224***	2.341
					(5.524)	(1.407)
Trust in Ardern						0.0105***
						(0.00368)
Constant	0.0452***	0.0160***	0.0321***	0.0137***	0.00654***	0.225**
	(0.0174)	(0.00747)	(0.0135)	(0.00669)	(0.00393)	(0.145)
Observations	3,650	3,650	3,650	3,650	3,650	3,582

*** $p < 0.01$

** $p < 0.05$

* $p < 0.1$

Note: Robust standard errors in parentheses.

Source: Vowles et al. (2022).

Table A8.3 Social structure and right-wing populism? Liking of Advance NZ and the New Conservative Party

	Advance NZ		New Conservative Party	
Variables	Coeff.	Odds ratio	Coeff.	Odds ratio
Female (male)	−0.486*	0.615*	−0.514**	0.598**
	(0.264)	(0.162)	(0.207)	(0.124)
Age (18–70)	0.575	1.777	−0.125	0.882
	(0.472)	(0.839)	(0.418)	(0.369)
Asian	0.094	1.099	−0.467	0.627
	(0.482)	(0.530)	(0.385)	(0.242)
Pasifika	0.879	2.408	−0.671	0.511
	(0.827)	(1.992)	(0.763)	(0.390)
Māori	0.749**	2.115**	−0.238	0.789
	(0.299)	(0.633)	(0.263)	(0.207)
Church attendee	0.665*	1.944*	1.831***	6.241***
	(0.362)	(0.703)	(0.249)	(1.552)
Self-employed/employer	0.554	1.741	0.603	1.828
	(0.523)	(0.911)	(0.388)	(0.710)

	Advance NZ		New Conservative Party	
Variables	Coeff.	Odds ratio	Coeff.	Odds ratio
Farming	−0.801	0.449	−0.074	0.928
	(0.534)	(0.240)	(0.401)	(0.373)
Manual or service	0.409	1.506	0.432*	1.541*
	(0.303)	(0.457)	(0.230)	(0.354)
Household economy same	−0.398	0.672	−0.474	0.622
	(0.449)	(0.302)	(0.309)	(0.192)
Household economy worse	0.586	1.797	−0.026	0.974
	(0.446)	(0.801)	(0.330)	(0.322)
Minorities adapt	−0.322	0.725	0.723*	2.060*
	(0.445)	(0.323)	(0.383)	(0.788)
Anti-Māori	−0.170	0.844	0.665	1.945
	(0.700)	(0.591)	(0.486)	(0.945)
Constant	−3.946***		−3.894***	
	(0.590)	0.0193***	(0.420)	0.0204***
		(0.0114)		(0.00856)
Observations	3,601		3,601	
r²_p	0.0676		0.123	
Ll	−447.7		−601.5	

*** p < 0.01
** p < 0.05
* p < 0.1
Note: Robust standard errors in parentheses.
Source: Vowles et al. (2022).

Table A8.4 Testing the Donovan model

	Advance NZ		New Conservative Party	
Variables	Coeff.	Odds ratio	Coeff.	Odds ratio
Female (male)	−0.335	0.715	−0.428*	0.652*
	(0.292)	(0.209)	(0.236)	(0.154)
Age (18–70)	−0.038	0.963	0.305	1.357
	(0.451)	(0.435)	(0.339)	(0.460)
University degree	0.267	1.306	0.382	1.465
	(0.298)	(0.389)	(0.302)	(0.443)
Economy worse	0.623	1.865	0.313	1.367
	(0.906)	(1.690)	(0.601)	(0.821)
Anti-immigration	0.924***	2.520***	0.379	1.460
	(0.274)	(0.690)	(0.243)	(0.354)

Variables	Advance NZ		New Conservative Party	
	Coeff.	Odds ratio	Coeff.	Odds ratio
Observe customs	−0.090	0.914	−0.141	0.868
	(0.334)	(0.305)	(0.262)	(0.227)
Obedient	0.322	1.379	0.594**	1.812**
	(0.357)	(0.492)	(0.244)	(0.443)
Strong leader	−0.016	0.984	−0.009	0.992
	(0.013)	(0.0130)	(0.011)	(0.0105)
Right (6–10)	0.385	1.470	0.928***	2.530***
	(0.304)	(0.446)	(0.277)	(0.702)
Constant	−4.490***	0.0112***	−3.959***	0.0191***
	(0.841)	(0.00944)	(0.585)	(0.0112)
Observations	3,549		3,549	
r^2_p	0.0386		0.0572	
ll	−460.2		−646.7	

*** p < 0.01

** p < 0.05

* p < 0.1

Note: Robust standard errors in parentheses.

Source: Vowles et al. (2022).

Table A8.5 ACT, ACT versus National, and the Donovan model

Variables	ACT vs all		ACT vs National		ACT vs National	
	Coeff.	Odds ratio	Coeff.	Odds ratio	Coeff.	Odds ratio
Female (male)	−0.550***	0.577***	−0.630***	0.532***	−0.592***	0.553***
	(0.166)	(0.0961)	(0.185)	(0.0984)	(0.192)	(0.106)
Age (18–70)	0.228	1.256	−0.904**	0.405**	−0.973**	0.378**
	(0.331)	(0.416)	(0.396)	(0.160)	(0.418)	(0.158)
Asian (Euro–other)	−0.938**	0.391**	−0.928*	0.395*	−0.854	0.426
	(0.463)	(0.181)	(0.533)	(0.211)	(0.544)	(0.232)
Pasifika (Euro–other)	−0.639	0.528	0.325	1.384	0.066	1.068
	(0.749)	(0.395)	(0.873)	(1.208)	(0.903)	(0.965)
Māori (Euro–other)	−0.855***	0.425***	0.091	1.095	−0.003	0.997
	(0.256)	(0.109)	(0.282)	(0.309)	(0.281)	(0.280)
University degree	−0.488**	0.614**	−0.086	0.918	−0.196	0.822
	(0.194)	(0.119)	(0.216)	(0.198)	(0.219)	(0.180)
Self-employed/ employer	−0.172	0.842	−0.001	0.999	−0.006	0.994
	(0.278)	(0.234)	(0.287)	(0.287)	(0.291)	(0.290)

Variables	ACT vs all		ACT vs National		ACT vs National	
	Coeff.	Odds ratio	Coeff.	Odds ratio	Coeff.	Odds ratio
Farming (nonmanual)	0.201	1.223	−0.389	0.678	−0.379	0.684
	(0.289)	(0.353)	(0.314)	(0.213)	(0.309)	(0.211)
Manual or service (nonmanual)	0.030	1.030	0.042	1.043	0.059	1.061
	(0.178)	(0.183)	(0.204)	(0.213)	(0.211)	(0.224)
Town (rural)	−0.723***	0.485***	−0.342	0.710	−0.420	0.657
	(0.235)	(0.114)	(0.272)	(0.193)	(0.275)	(0.181)
City suburb (rural)	−1.600***	0.202***	−1.303***	0.272***	−1.415***	0.243***
	(0.331)	(0.0668)	(0.374)	(0.102)	(0.382)	(0.0928)
City (rural)	−0.975***	0.377***	−0.560**	0.571**	−0.672***	0.510***
	(0.223)	(0.0843)	(0.255)	(0.146)	(0.259)	(0.132)
Income	1.179***	3.251***	−0.165	0.847	−0.133	0.875
	(0.316)	(1.028)	(0.373)	(0.316)	(0.380)	(0.333)
Assets	0.043	1.044	−0.154**	0.857**	−0.177**	0.838**
	(0.064)	(0.066)	(0.070)	(0.0599)	(0.070)	(0.0589)
Union household	−0.653**	0.521**	−0.321	0.725	−0.372	0.689
	(0.264)	(0.137)	(0.291)	(0.211)	(0.293)	(0.202)
Church attendee	−0.435	0.647	−0.484	0.616	−0.363	0.695
	(0.289)	(0.187)	(0.295)	(0.182)	(0.301)	(0.209)
Anti-immigration					0.092	1.096
					(0.186)	(0.204)
Observe customs					0.349	1.418
					(0.254)	(0.361)
Obedient					−0.663***	0.515***
					(0.232)	(0.119)
Strong leader					−0.014	0.986
					(0.010)	(0.00950)
Right (6–10)					0.491**	1.635**
					(0.228)	(0.373)
Constant	−1.995***	0.136***	0.677	1.968	0.408	1.504
	(0.359)	(0.0488)	(0.464)	(0.914)	(0.540)	(0.813)
Observations	3,320	3,320	875	875	875	875
r^2_p	0.0862		0.0601		0.0851	
ll	−710.0		−452.2		−440.2	

*** $p < 0.01$

** $p < 0.05$

* $p < 0.1$

Note: Robust standard errors in parentheses.

Source: Vowles et al. (2022).

9

In the Shadow of Covid-19? Climate change and the 2020 election

Sam Crawley

Introduction

The effects of climate change are already being felt in New Zealand and around the world and will continue to worsen over the coming decades (IPCC 2021).[1] Urgent government action is needed to substantially reduce emissions and ensure that global warming does not exceed the internationally agreed maximum of 1.5°C by 2100 (DDPP 2015). For that action to occur, politicians will likely need to feel public pressure to act, particularly during elections when their jobs are on the line. However, as discussed in several of the previous chapters, the 2020 New Zealand election was clearly the 'Covid-19 election'. Unsurprisingly, the worst pandemic in a century occupied the minds of politicians and voters throughout the 2020 campaign.

This chapter therefore investigates two questions about public attitudes towards climate change during the 2020 New Zealand election. First, given the way in which Covid-19 dominated the election, was there any room for debate about climate change or was it 'crowded out' as an issue by Covid-19? There is finite space on the election agenda and certain topics can be pushed

---

1   I am grateful to Ralph Chapman for his comments on an earlier version of this chapter.

aside by high-salience issues such as Covid-19 in 2020 (Pralle 2009). Using data from the NZES, I show that, while climate change was not one of the major talking points of the 2020 election, this had more to do with it being perceived as a niche issue, rather than Covid-19 taking space away from debate about climate change.

Second, I ask to what extent does the 'Team of Five Million' slogan—used by the government to signify united public support of the country's Covid-19 response—apply to public opinion on climate change in New Zealand? As I will illustrate, some degree of consensus has been reached among politicians, with all the major parties accepting that climate change exists and almost all backing major climate legislation. However, the analysis of NZES data shows that, while all but a very small minority of New Zealanders believe that climate change is happening, there are partisan divides when it comes to the degree of support for government action.

In the next section, I briefly review recent progress on climate change mitigation policy in New Zealand and discuss the ways in which the main parties (and other actors) incorporated climate change into their campaigns. I then examine the results of a series of questions on climate change that were included in the 2020 NZES asking participants about their beliefs on the existence and causes of climate change, their perceptions of the likely harm climate change will cause, and their support for government action on climate change. I conclude by suggesting that the data indicate that we may not see a 'climate election' in New Zealand in the near future.

The politics of climate change in New Zealand

A renewed focus on climate policy

When taking power in 2017, the incoming Labour-led government promised a renewed focus on climate change (Hall 2020). This emphasis marked a contrast from the previous National-led government, which had received heavy criticism internationally for being a 'laggard' on climate policy (Barrett et al. 2015). Immediately before the 2017 election, Jacinda Ardern—in a frequently referenced quote—declared climate change as her 'generation's nuclear-free moment' (Bramwell 2017), alluding to the ban on nuclear weapons and nuclear marine vessel power instituted by the fourth

Labour government in the 1980s. Ardern's government enacted a range of policies to progress action on climate change, including significant changes to the Emissions Trading Scheme, a large-scale tree planting program, an end to new offshore oil exploration permits, and the creation of a green investment fund (Leining et al. 2020).

The centrepiece of Labour's climate strategy during the 2017–20 term was the *Climate Change Response (Zero Carbon) Amendment Act 2019* (known as the *Zero Carbon Act*). The Act was designed as a framework for further action and included several important features, such as a 2050 'net zero' emissions target enshrined in law and the requirement for the government to regularly set carbon budgets (Ministry for the Environment 2019). The Act also established the Climate Change Commission (CCC), which was modelled on a similar body that has operated in the United Kingdom since 2008 (Hall 2021). The CCC is designed to be an apolitical body that advises the government on climate policy and emissions targets. The *Zero Carbon Act* was supported by all parties in parliament at the time, except for ACT party's single MP, David Seymour (Bailey et al. 2021).

The government also took steps to ensure an understanding was reached with the important farming industry. In 2003, Helen Clark's fifth Labour government stumbled over this hurdle when trying to introduce a modest charge to finance research on methane emissions from livestock (Roper and Toledano 2005). After fierce opposition from farming industry groups and others, including protests on the steps of Parliament House, Clark's government was eventually forced to abandon the policy. Not wanting to repeat past mistakes, Ardern's government reached an agreement with Federated Farmers of New Zealand and other major farming groups to form a partnership between the government and primary industries aimed at reducing emissions from this sector (Malpass and Cooke 2019). The partnership, dubbed '*He Waka Eke Noa*' (lit. 'We're all in this together'), aims to find ways for producers to manufacture products sustainably or—as a backstop—to fold agricultural emissions into New Zealand's Emissions Trading Scheme.[2]

---

2   In 2022, He Waka Eke Noa produced a set of recommendations that includes pricing agricultural emissions outside the Emissions Trading Scheme. While the major farming groups now support pricing of farming emissions, there has been a backlash from some members of the farming community, who have organised under the name 'Groundswell' (McKenzie 2022).

Several steps forward on climate policy were thus made under Ardern. The question remains, however: how substantial is this action on climate change? While the *Zero Carbon Act* provides a robust framework to reduce New Zealand's emissions, the 'rubber has yet to meet the road'. One of the clearest signals that there is still much more to do is New Zealand's 2030 emissions target, which is set out in the Nationally Determined Contribution document that New Zealand is required to submit under the Paris Agreement. This target was initially set by John Key's National government in 2015 at 30 per cent below 2005 levels. Despite international criticism of this target, it was not improved on by the Labour-led government during the 2017–20 term (Corlett 2021). Monitoring body Climate Action Tracker has rated New Zealand's 2030 target—and the revised target set by the government in late 2021—as 'insufficient'. New Zealand's current emissions target is therefore incompatible with the internationally agreed goal of limiting warming to a maximum of 1.5°C (CAT 2021). Moreover, Climate Action Tracker assesses New Zealand's overall approach to climate change, including policy and action, as 'highly insufficient'.

Perhaps most tellingly, New Zealand's emissions have not declined over the past decade, as they have in many other developed countries (McLachlan 2020). Since 2008, New Zealand's carbon dioxide emissions trajectory has been relatively flat. In fact, in 2019, emissions increased by 2 per cent over 2018, largely due to decreased rainfall, meaning electricity generation relied less on hydro and more on coal (Ministry for the Environment 2021a). To be compatible with the 1.5°C pathway, emissions would have to peak very soon (Ministry for the Environment 2021b). Policies that have a more immediate effect on New Zealand's emissions are thus required.

Overall, then, the Labour-led government has made some progress towards enabling declines in emissions towards net zero by 2050 but has so far taken few substantive steps to realise these emissions reductions. In other words, there is a gap between New Zealand's climate ambition and its policy. It is likely that the focus of political debates about climate issues over the coming years will be on how quickly this gap should be closed.

Climate change during the 2020 election campaign

Climate change featured in several ways throughout the 2020 campaign, which—as discussed in Chapter 4—was substantially disrupted by a Covid-19 outbreak immediately before the start of the official campaign period. Climate change appeared in the policy platforms of all the main parties, in debates and media coverage of the campaign, and in more 'specialised' areas of campaigning, which catered to the small section of the public for whom climate change is a critical issue. Below, I briefly review some of these appearances.

Beginning with policies, the Labour, Green, and Māori party platforms covered a range of climate issues. The Greens made climate change a central pillar of their campaign, including policies on clean energy, transport, agriculture, and forestry. Labour promised to decarbonise the public transport fleet by 2035 and to introduce fuel-efficiency standards for imported vehicles. Green Party co-leader Marama Davidson, however, criticised Labour's climate policies and record since taking office, claiming the action it had taken would not lead to rapid cuts in emissions (Cheng 2020). The Māori Party also released a detailed climate policy, which included the withdrawal of permits for mining, oil, and gas extraction, and the establishment of a large fund for Māori-owned community energy projects.

National, ACT, and New Zealand First—while not making climate issues as central to their platforms as the Labour, Green, and Māori parties—all included climate policies in their campaign manifestos. National's climate policy centred on encouraging the uptake of electric vehicles but promised to roll back Labour's ban on new oil and gas exploration permits. Even the libertarian ACT party—which in the past has taken ambiguous positions on the existence of climate change (Cooke 2016; Vaughter 2012)—emphasised the need to reduce emissions, despite opposing the *Zero Carbon Act*.

Almost all the televised leaders' debates, which are viewed by a wide audience, covered climate change to some extent (Craig 2021). For example, the *Stuff* leaders debate between Jacinda Ardern and Judith Collins on 6 October included approximately 10 minutes dedicated to a discussion of electric vehicles and how uptake could be increased. During the *Newshub* debate between the two main leaders on 30 September, approximately eight minutes covered climate change—this time focussing on the oil and gas exploration ban and agricultural issues.

Climate issues came to the fore in a range of less 'mainstream' campaigning venues. For example, climate activist group Generation Zero ran a campaign during the 2020 election that included an online discussion dedicated to climate issues, featuring representatives from many of the parties. News website *Newsroom* invited party leaders to respond to questions, with climate change selected by readers as one of the top five issues to be addressed (Newsroom Staff 2020). One of the leaders of the School Strike 4 Climate NZ, Sophie Handford, was involved in a 'Vote Climate 2020' campaign, which posed climate questions asked by voters to candidates (McGlennon 2020).

Climate change was thus very much a part of the 2020 campaign but, for the most part, was confined to relatively brief appearances during the leaders' debates or to the more specialised venues described above. Assessing the campaign activity of the parties and media alone makes it difficult to say whether 2020 represents a change from previous elections in the prominence of climate change as a campaign issue. On the one hand, debate about climate change issues does seem to have become a regular feature of election campaigns and the coverage of environmental issues in the media has increased since 2014 (Mills et al. 2018). On the other hand, previous elections have also featured debates about and activities related to climate change. In 2014, for instance, several organisations—including Oxfam and Greenpeace—ran a 'Climate Voter' campaign, asking voters to pledge to vote with climate issues in mind, to which tens of thousands of people signed up. It is thus unclear whether 2020 represented a relatively 'normal' election for climate issues and policies or whether it was 'crowded out' by Covid-19. Examining the public opinion data on this topic, which I turn to in the next section, can help to provide more clarity here.

Public opinion on climate change in 2020

What the public thinks about climate change has been the focus of research in countries around the world for many years. We now understand that public opinion on climate change is complex and most people cannot easily be categorised as either a 'denier' or a 'believer' (Corry and Jørgensen 2015). For instance, among people who accept that climate change is happening, some do not support government policies to address it, some see it as an issue that does not require action for years or decades, and some are uncertain in their views (Crawley et al. 2020).

Researchers have also attempted to understand variation among deniers, identifying three main ways in which people deny climate change (Poortinga et al. 2019; Rahmstorf 2004). Not accepting that climate change is happening is the first type of denial and is found in only a small percentage of the population in most countries (Leiserowitz et al. 2022). The second type, which is usually more prevalent than the first, holds that climate change is happening but is primarily caused by natural processes, rather than almost entirely by humans as the science suggests. The third type of denial—which tends to be the most common—is that climate change will not cause any serious consequences and thus is not worth worrying about (Leiserowitz et al. 2022; Poortinga et al. 2019).

Levels of belief in climate change seem to be increasing in New Zealand. Research relying on data from 2010 or earlier suggested that New Zealand had relatively high levels of denial compared with most other developed countries—on par with countries such as Australia and the United States (Smith and Mayer 2019; Tranter and Booth 2015). More recent surveys have shown that few people in New Zealand do not believe climate change is happening at all (for example, Thaker 2021). For instance, data from the New Zealand Attitudes and Values Survey show that, in 2009, 14 per cent of people disagreed with the statement 'Climate change is real', but by 2018 this had dropped to 6 per cent (Milfont et al. 2021). This compares with the United States and Australia, where a survey in 2022 found that 11 per cent and 10 per cent of the population, respectively, did not believe that climate change is happening (Leiserowitz et al. 2022). The rise in belief could be related to better communication of the scientific consensus about climate change (Kerr and Wilson 2018) and to political debates that are less contentious in New Zealand than in the United States and Australia (Linde 2020).

One of the reasons researchers are interested in public opinion on climate change is that it can help us to understand the political response to the issue. Politicians are much more likely to act on climate change if they feel public pressure to do so, and public opinion has been shown to influence climate policy, at least in some circumstances (Drummond et al. 2018; Schaffer et al.

2021). For example, Vandeweerdt et al. (2016) found that representatives in the US Congress were more likely to support climate change legislation if their constituents had high levels of concern about the issue.

In New Zealand, as outlined above, there has been criticism that the government's climate policies do not go far enough (Corlett 2021). Taking a broad view of climate opinion can help us to understand the role that public opinion could be playing in the apparently slow government response to climate change. Moreover, there appears to be elite consensus on climate change, at least with respect to its existence and seriousness. No party currently in parliament openly denies that climate change is happening and all major parties have policies to address it, although there are disagreements about the course of action. Investigating public opinion on climate change in New Zealand can show us whether there is a corresponding (near) consensus among the public on climate change or what could be thought of as a 'climate team of five million'.

Using 2020 NZES data, several aspects of public opinion on climate change are examined.[3] First, I investigate the extent to which NZES participants felt climate change was the most important issue of the election. I then consider different elements of the New Zealand public's beliefs about the climate change phenomenon itself: whether it exists, what is causing it, how harmful it is, and how soon that harm is likely to be felt. Next, I examine people's perceptions of action on climate change, including the degree to which they believe action can be effective, and how much they support government action. Finally, I examine how demographic and ideological factors (such as political orientation and party choice) relate to people's opinions on climate change.

---

3   In most of the statistics below I include 'Don't know/No response' as a separate category. While such responses are often removed when presenting frequency data, they are important when it comes to climate opinion. This is because some climate change issues are complex, which could cause people to respond with 'Don't know'. Moreover, on some issues (such as the existence of climate change), 'Don't know' could indicate a form of denial, given most people have had the opportunity to form an opinion by now (Haltinner and Sarathchandra 2021). All statistics presented in this chapter (including those based on the regression models below) have had the NZES sample weighting variable applied.

Prominence of climate change in 2020

The NZES includes a question asking people to nominate their most important issue for the election. Participants are asked to write open-ended answers in the box provided. I use these data to investigate how prominent climate change was as an issue in the minds of voters in 2020, compared to the two previous elections. The prominence of climate change was measured by taking all responses to the most important issue question that mentioned either 'climate' or 'warming'. For comparison, I also include all responses that were classified by NZES coders as relating to the environment (which also include those relating to climate change).

Table 9.1 Percentage of responses to 'most important issue' question relating to climate change and the environment, 2014–2020

Year	Climate	Environment
2014	0.33% (9)	1.98% (56)
2017	0.83% (29)	5.30% (183)
2020	2.28% (84)	4.63% (172)

Note: Responses containing the word 'climate' or 'warming' were classified as relating to climate change. Responses that mentioned any environmental issue were classified as the environment, including those that mentioned climate change.

Source: Vowles et al. (2022).

Table 9.1 shows that climate change appears to be growing in importance as an election issue among the public. In 2017, just less than 1 per cent of participants mentioned climate or warming, while in 2020 the number had climbed to 2.3 per cent—a statistically significant increase.[4] However, the number of responses indicating that environmental issues were the most important dropped slightly between 2017 and 2020. These results indicate that while roughly the same number of people saw environmental issues as most important in 2020 as they did in 2017, of those people, more now saw climate as the main environmental issue about which to be worried.

If Covid-19 crowded out climate change during the 2020 election, we could expect to see a decline—or at least no change—in the importance of climate change among the public. The fact that we see the importance of climate change rising since 2020 suggests that Covid-19 may not have taken space away from it in 2020. It is obviously not possible to tell from these data whether the importance of climate change would have risen further

---

4   A chi-squared test resulted in a value of 32, p < 0.001.

if Covid-19 had not dominated. However, polling data from Ipsos suggest that the public importance of climate change in New Zealand has been stable over the past few years, only rising in February 2023 in response to Cyclone Gabrielle (Ipsos 2023).

Despite the increase in the importance of climate change between 2017 and 2020, it appears to be seen as a niche issue. Only 2.3 per cent of participants saw climate change as the most important issue in 2020, whereas 15 per cent saw the economy as the most important, and 8 per cent listed an issue relating to housing (see Appendix 1.1 for more details). In other words, while Covid-19 may not have crowded out climate, the NZES data—in line with that from Ipsos—suggest that few voters see climate change among the main issues that influence their vote choice in an election.

What does the New Zealand public believe about climate change?

The NZES included two questions about people's climate beliefs. The first asked participants, 'Do you believe that climate change is happening and, if so, why?' The results (Figure 9.1) show a majority (70 per cent, 2,538 responses) of New Zealanders accept that climate change is happening and that it is mostly caused by humans. Only 2 per cent (n = 77) of people do not think climate change is happening, while a further 18 per cent (n = 662) believe it is happening but is caused mostly by natural processes. Some 10 per cent (n = 370) of respondents either did not know what is causing climate change or did not give a response. This is a substantial number, given that scientific information about climate change has been available to the public for many years and this could indicate a high degree of latent denial among the public (Haltinner and Sarathchandra 2021).

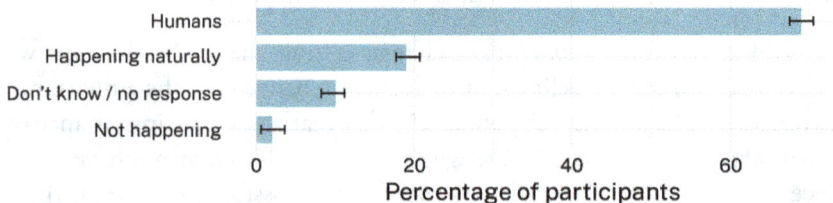

Figure 9.1 'Do you believe that climate change is happening and, if so, why?'
Note: Error bars indicate 95 per cent confidence intervals.
Source: Vowles et al. (2022).

Another dimension of climate opinion worth considering is people's perceptions of the risks of climate change. Previous international research has shown that even among people who accept that climate change is happening and is primarily caused by humans, some do not see it as a serious problem (van der Linden 2017). Low levels of concern about climate change can be driven by the belief that it simply will not cause much harm for humans (which can be considered a form of denial) or by the belief that society will take effective action to avoid the worst consequences of climate change (I return to these two explanations for low risk perception in the next section) (Lo and Chow 2015).

People's degree of climate risk perception, however, can be moderated by their perception of the immediacy of its effects. As mentioned, the effects of climate change are already being felt in New Zealand and elsewhere. It is highly likely these effects will worsen over the coming decades as the world experiences the results of warming that is already locked in by present-day emissions (IPCC 2021). Despite this, many people do not see the harm caused by climate change as being immediate, in part because the worst effects could be (perceived to be) some decades away (McDonald et al. 2015).

To gauge people's perceptions of the degree of harm climate change will cause, the NZES survey asked: 'Do you think climate change will harm you? And how much will it harm future generations of people?' Figure 9.2 shows the results of this question. Most people do not think climate change will harm them substantially. Only 15 per cent (n = 544) believe it will harm them 'a great deal', with a further 33 per cent (n = 1,189) believing it will harm them moderately. However, most people see climate change as a serious threat to the next generation already born, and particularly to future generations not yet born, whom 70 per cent of participants (n = 2,549) thought will be harmed 'a great deal'. These results could be driven in part by participant age, with older people perhaps expecting the worst effects of climate change will be beyond their lifetime. While older people were less likely than younger people to say climate change will harm them a great deal, older people were also less worried about harm to any generation. It seems, then, that while most New Zealanders see climate change as a serious threat, they perceive this threat as temporally distant, primarily affecting people not yet born.

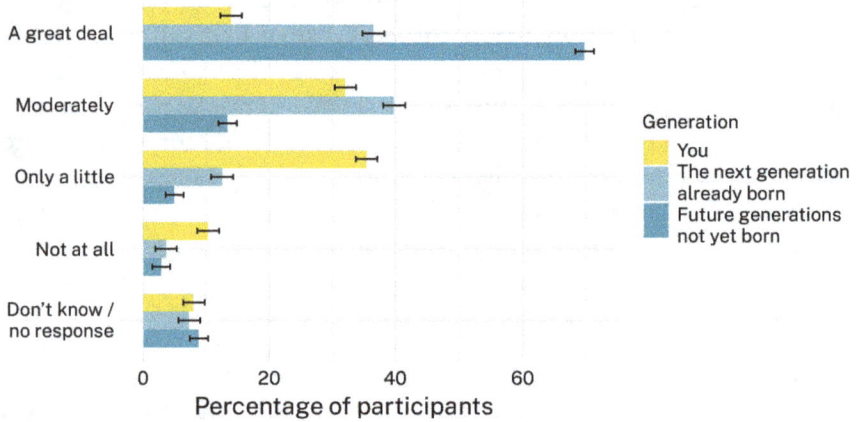

Figure 9.2 'Do you think climate change will harm you/future generations of people?'

Note: Error bars indicate 95 per cent confidence intervals.

Source: Vowles et al. (2022).

Perceptions of climate action

This section considers two NZES questions about people's perceptions of climate action. The first asked participants how effective they thought climate action is likely to be, and the second measured the degree to which people support government action on climate change.

People's level of 'response efficacy'—the degree to which they see action on climate change as likely to be effective—is an important indicator of how likely they are to support action on climate change and to take action themselves (Bostrom et al. 2018; Bradley et al. 2020). People who believe that not much can be done about climate change are, unsurprisingly, unlikely to believe action is worth taking.

Figure 9.3 presents the results for the question asking people how likely it is that action by governments, businesses, and people will significantly slow climate change. New Zealanders are evenly divided on this topic, with 47 per cent (n = 1,701) believing climate action is very or somewhat likely to be effective, while 43 per cent (n = 1,561) think it is somewhat or very unlikely that climate action will make a difference. Despite the high levels of belief in the reality of climate change illustrated in the previous section, many New Zealanders appear to be sceptical that emissions can be brought under control.

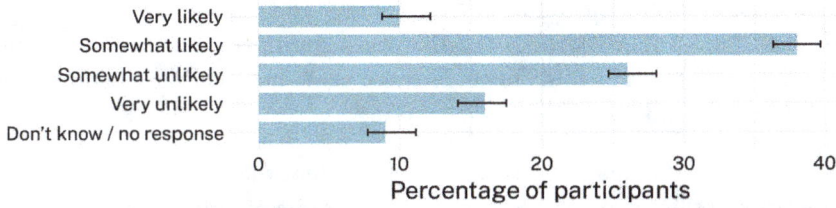

Figure 9.3 'In your opinion, over the next 20 years, how likely is it that action by governments, businesses, and people in general will significantly slow climate change?'

Note: Error bars indicate 95 per cent confidence intervals.

Source: Vowles et al. (2022).

The response efficacy data can also help to determine the extent to which people who do not see climate change as a serious risk are putting faith in climate action to curb emissions or are simply unaware of the likely effects of climate change in the coming decades. To test these possible explanations, correlations between perceptions of risk (Figure 9.2) and climate external efficacy (Figure 9.3) were examined. The results show a small but positive correlation between each of the three risk variables and the efficacy variable.[5] In other words, people who see climate change as likely to cause significant harm also tend to be more optimistic about the effectiveness of climate action. Conversely, people who do not see climate change as a significant risk are generally less likely to see climate action as effective. It appears that many people who do not see climate change as likely to cause harm to themselves or future generations believe this because they are sceptical about the risks suggested by the science.

Governments play a critical coordination role in addressing climate change (Aklin and Mildenberger 2020; Hepburn 2010). To reach emissions targets that are aimed at limiting warming to 1.5°C, emissions must be reduced rapidly across all industries. Reducing emissions cannot, therefore, be left to individuals and businesses, but requires government action, including a carbon price and additional measures such as investment, subsidies, and regulations (Tvinnereim and Mehling 2018). People who accept that climate change is happening and is a serious problem do not necessarily support

---

5   The correlations were calculated by coding the three harm variables as numeric, ranging from one (not at all) to four (a great deal), and the response efficacy variable to range from one (very unlikely) to four (very likely). The Spearman's rho rank coefficient was 0.17 for harm to 'you', 0.18 for harm to 'the next generation already born', and 0.17 for harm to 'future generations not yet born'. All correlations were significant at $p < 0.001$.

government action on climate change (Drews and van den Bergh 2016). Measuring the public's level of support for government action on climate change can therefore help us to understand how much public pressure the government is under to take climate action.

The 2020 NZES asked participants to what extent they supported stronger government policies to reduce emissions. The same question was also asked in 2017, and Figure 9.4 presents the results from both surveys. As can be seen, most New Zealanders support government action on climate change. In 2020, 61 per cent (n = 2,214) agreed that stronger government policies are needed to reduce emissions—a slight drop from 2017 when 65 per cent (n = 2,243) agreed with the same statement. Overall, the responses were very similar between 2017 and 2020, indicating that people tend to have stable opinions on climate change action and that the Covid-19 crisis did not substantially affect those opinions.

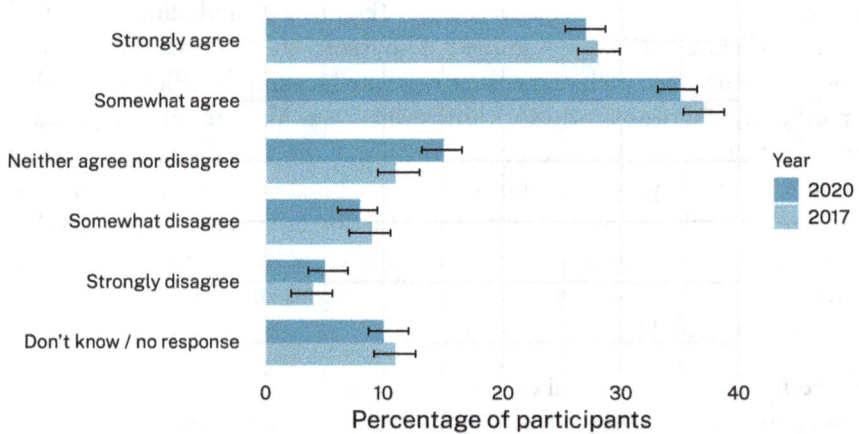

Figure 9.4 'How much do you agree or disagree with the statement: "To act against climate change, stronger government policies are needed to reduce carbon emissions"?'

Note: Error bars indicate 95 per cent confidence intervals.

Source: Vowles et al. (2022).

Demographic and ideological attributes and climate opinions

Investigating the relationships between demographic and ideological factors and public opinion on climate change can provide insight into why people hold certain climate views. Previous research has found several such factors have consistent relationships with climate opinion (Crawley 2021; Hornsey et al. 2016; van der Linden 2017). In particular, people's left–right political orientation is frequently found to relate to their climate views, with those on the right less likely than those on the left to accept that climate change is happening, is a serious problem, and requires government action to address it (McCright et al. 2016). Differences in demographics also seem to relate to climate opinion. Women, younger people, people in higher income brackets, and people with higher levels of education are, on average, more likely to accept the science of climate change and the need for government action than men, older people, people receiving lower incomes, and people with lower levels of education (Hornsey et al. 2016).

I investigated how these different attributes related to climate opinion in New Zealand using linear regression, with Figure 9.5 presenting the results. The outcome variable for this analysis is support for government action, for which participants were asked how much they agree that stronger government action is needed to address climate change.[6] This variable was coded as numeric, ranging from one (strongly disagree) to five (strongly agree), meaning three is the midpoint of the scale. Figure 9.5 shows the predicted means for each predictor variable on support for government action.[7] The dashed line indicates the overall sample mean.

---

6   Models using the other measures of climate opinion (existence/cause of climate change, perceptions of risk, external efficacy) as the dependent variable were also investigated. The results were similar to those presented below. All predictors were added to the model as categorical. The reference categories were: Labour (party vote), centre (left–right), 18–31 (age), men (gender), '$196,001 and over' (income), and not having a degree. All categories showed a statistically significant effect ($p <= 0.05$) versus the reference category, with the exceptions of gender diverse, Māori Party, TOP, 'No income', '$38,000 or less', and '$149,001 – $196,000' (income). Although left–right orientation and party choice had a medium correlation (Cramer's V = 0.43), models that omitted each of these variables produced similar predicted means to those presented in Figure 9.5.

7   Predicted means indicate the average degree of support for government action for a given predictor (for example, voting for Labour) while holding all other variables constant.

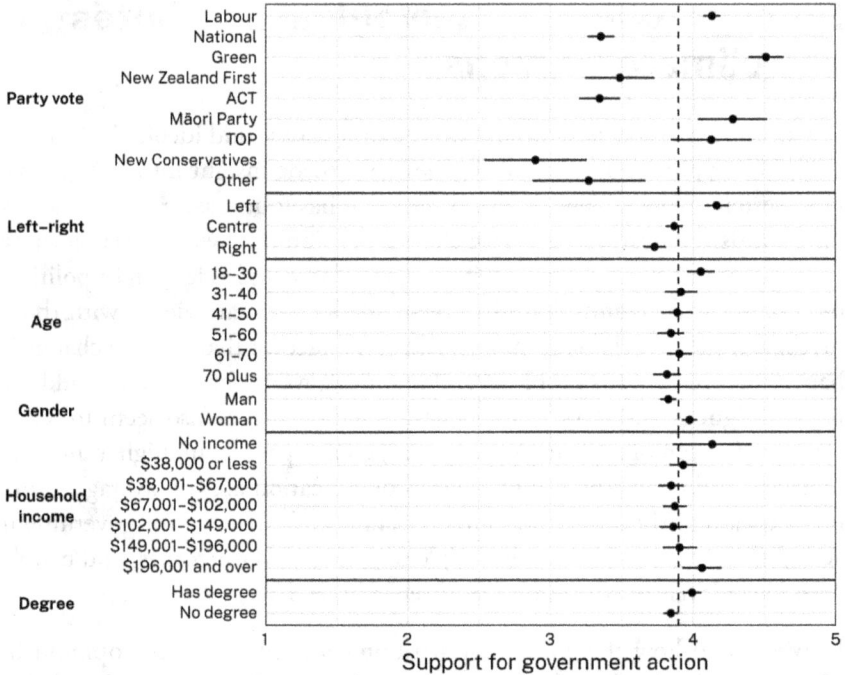

Figure 9.5 Support for government action according to demographic and ideological predictors

Source: Vowles et al. (2022).

The first predictor examined is the 2020 party vote. Unsurprisingly, on average, a person who reported voting for the Green Party is more likely to agree that stronger government action on climate change is necessary compared with a person voting for any other party. Labour, Māori Party, and TOP voters have means just over four (somewhat agree), while ACT, New Zealand First, and National voters all have roughly similar levels of support, which is below 3.5, for government action. New Conservative Party voters are, by far, the least supportive of government action on climate change, with a mean score (2.9) just below the midpoint of the agreement scale.

Turning to political orientation, participants were asked to place themselves on a scale, where zero indicates the far left of politics and 10 is the far right. A recoded variable—where zero to three was categorised as 'left', four to six as 'centre', and seven to 10 as 'right'—was used in the model. As can be seen in Figure 9.5—and aligning with most previous research on public opinion on climate change—people who were categorised as being on the left of politics were more likely to support government action than those in the centre or on the right.

All the demographic variables investigated had significant but small effects on supporting government action on climate change. As per previous studies in other Western countries, younger people, women, people on higher incomes, and people holding a university degree were all slightly more likely to support government action on climate change than older people, people on lower incomes, and people without a degree.[8] Although all these demographic variables had a statistically significant relationship with people's climate opinions, it is important to note the small size of the relationships. For instance, the difference in the predicted means of men and women was only 0.15 on the five-point scale. The differences for left–right political orientation and party vote were larger compared with the demographic variables. Thus, as the divisions over New Zealand's Covid-19 response discussed in Chapter 8, people's ideological outlook or partisanship tends to be a better predictor of their climate views than demographic factors.

The economic situation and climate opinion

The response to Covid-19 led to a severe economic downturn in 2020. While the worst fears of economic doom had been allayed by late 2020, worries about the economic outlook could influence people's climate opinions. Scruggs and Benegal (2012) showed that, after the 2008 GFC, a decline in public concern about climate change in the United States and Europe was most likely driven by feelings of economic insecurity. It is reasonable to expect that the same could happen with the economic problems caused by the pandemic, given that most people tend to have a 'finite pool of worry' (Weber 2010). If people are concerned about the economic situation caused by Covid-19 and therefore do not have the 'resources' to be worried about climate change, it could suggest that the pandemic reduced the space for climate change during the election.

To test this hypothesis, variables measuring people's perspectives on the status of the economy over the previous 12 months were investigated. The first question asked participants to rate the state of the New Zealand economy, while the second asked them to rate the financial situation of their household. The answers ranged from 'got a lot worse' to 'got a lot better'. These variables were included in the regression model described above, and Figure 9.6 presents the results.

---

8   Participants who identified as gender diverse were included in the regression models but are not reported on above due to the small number (n = 15).

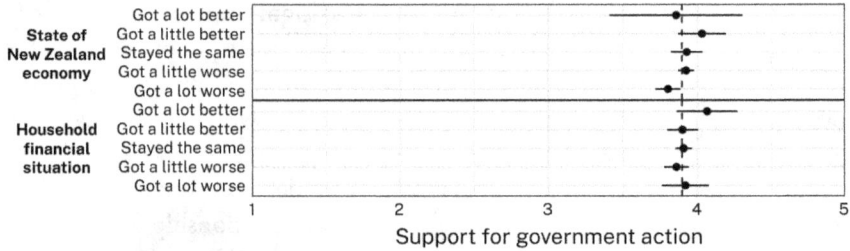

Figure 9.6 Support for government action according to economic outlook predictors

Source: Vowles et al. (2022).

Neither variable had a substantial impact on people's support for government action on climate change.[9] People who think the New Zealand economy 'got a lot worse' in the past 12 months were slightly less likely to support stronger climate policies compared with the other responses. There is no clear relationship between support for government action on climate change and people's perceptions of their household financial situation over the past 12 months. These results are therefore another piece of evidence suggesting that Covid-19 did not have a significant impact on people's climate views during the 2020 election. The perceived economic impacts of Covid-19 do not seem to relate substantially to support for government action on climate change, which contrasts with the effects of economic worry on climate concerns in some countries after the GFC.

Discussion and conclusion

Several years ago, some considered New Zealand to be among the countries with the highest levels of 'hard' climate denial (Tranter and Booth 2015). However, the results of the 2020 NZES coincide with other recent surveys showing that only a very small percentage of New Zealanders (2 per cent) do not believe that climate change is happening (Milfont et al. 2021; Thaker 2021). That said, a relatively large number of NZES participants (18 per cent) thought that climate change is mostly the result of natural causes.

9   The reference category in the regression model was 'stayed the same'. For the 'state of the New Zealand economy' variable, the only category with a statistically significant coefficient relative to the reference category was 'got a lot worse' (p = 0.02). None of the coefficients was statistically significant for the 'household financial situation' variable.

While most participants accepted that climate change will harm people 'a great deal', many thought this harm would apply mainly to future generations not yet born or to the 'next generation already born' rather than to themselves. Some 44 per cent ($n = 810$) of participants believe that climate change will affect them personally either only a little or not at all. Given that research shows extreme weather events such as flooding and droughts are likely to become substantially more frequent over the next 20 years (IPCC 2021), these findings suggest that many people are not fully aware of (or do not fully accept) how close significant climate consequences are.

Turning to people's perceptions of climate action, a large majority of the New Zealand public supports stronger government action on climate change. This degree of support did not wane substantially between 2017 and 2020, despite the visible activity by the government on climate during the 2017–20 parliamentary term. However, many New Zealanders who accept the existence and severity of climate change do not believe action on climate change is likely to be effective. Such low levels of response efficacy could create a problem for the country's climate response. People are less likely to support and engage in pro-environmental behaviour if they do not believe the overall response to climate change is likely to make a substantial dent in emissions (Bradley et al. 2020).

There are clear partisan divides in climate opinion, with Green, Labour, Māori Party, and to a lesser extent, TOP voters tending to have stronger support for climate policies and more concern about climate change than National, ACT, and New Zealand First voters. It is important to note that people who voted for the second group of parties in 2020 still, on average, support stronger government action on climate change. The mean level of support for climate policy among these voters is, however, lower than those of the more left-oriented parties. Overall, these partisan divides suggest that the New Zealand public is not as close to 'consensus' on climate change as the parties appear to be. There does not seem to be a 'team of five million' when it comes to climate change. We can thus expect cross-party support for policies relating to some of the more contentious climate issues (such as agriculture) to be very difficult to achieve.

What all these data suggest is that the dominance of Covid-19 as an issue in 2020 did not take away space from climate change; there is simply not much demand from New Zealand voters for more climate debate during an election campaign and the presence of Covid-19 did not seem to change this. As illustrated above, the electoral importance of climate change among voters rose between 2017 and 2020, while support for government action did not change much in the same period. There is also little evidence that the economic problems created by Covid-19 influenced people's climate opinions. This—admittedly, mostly indirect—evidence does not readily support the hypothesis that climate change struggled to find space on the electoral agenda due to the issues surrounding the pandemic.

Overall, while 2020 may have been a historic election for Labour, it does not seem to have been one for the issue of climate change. It remains a relatively niche issue in terms of salience, at the front of the minds of only a small section of voters. There is a small (and probably growing) section of the population who see climate change as their most important issue and who may take an interest—or be involved—in the kinds of climate-related campaign events discussed earlier in this chapter. However, it should be noted that the picture is complex. As already mentioned, most NZES participants agree that stronger government action is required on climate change, suggesting there is strong public demand for policies beyond the *Zero Carbon Act*.

Combating climate change will likely require far-reaching changes to society (O'Brien 2018). Politicians generally need a clear electoral mandate to build or confirm support for such changes. An election in which an issue takes centre stage during the campaign can help to create this mandate. The 2020 'Covid-19 election' was a good example of this, even though Covid-19 was not the only important campaign issue, as Chapter 1 illustrated. Labour won in a landslide during an election in which Covid-19 was the most important issue for a large part of the electorate, suggesting that (as discussed in Chapter 2) Labour was rewarded by voters for its management of Covid-19. Labour won a mandate to continue its elimination policy, at least for several months after the election.

A similar example was observed in the 2022 Australian federal election, in which climate change was seen by many as the defining issue of the campaign (Baker 2022). Voters were unhappy about the performance of Scott Morrison's government on climate change and handed a mandate to the Australian Labor Party to do more on the climate (Quiggin 2022). It is important to note the context in Australia is quite different to that in New Zealand. Climate policy in Australia had been lagging far behind most of the developed world for several years (Mann and Turnbull 2022), so Australian voters had strong reasons to make it an important election issue. The 2022 Australian election could reasonably be labelled a 'climate' election.

What, then, are the prospects of a climate election happening in New Zealand in the current decade? Based on the data presented above, the outlook is not promising. The low salience of climate change suggests that most voters and politicians are occupied with other issues during an election campaign. Public opinion does not always move in a straight line and it is entirely possible that the increased prominence in the news of climate change (and its effects) will lead to larger sections of the public viewing it as an important issue during future New Zealand election campaigns. However, those wishing to see the gap closing between climate ambition and substantive policy may benefit from reflecting on why so few of the New Zealand public view climate change as an important issue.

References

Aklin, M., and M. Mildenberger. 2020. 'Prisoners of the Wrong Dilemma: Why Distributive Conflict, Not Collective Action, Characterizes the Politics of Climate Change.' *Global Environmental Politics* 20(4): 4–27. doi.org/10.1162/glep_a_00578.

Bailey, I., O. Fitch-Roy, T.H.J. Inderberg, and D. Benson. 2021. 'Idealism, Pragmatism, and the Power of Compromise in the Negotiation of New Zealand's Zero Carbon Act.' *Climate Policy* 21(9): 1159–74. doi.org/10.1080/14693062.2020.1868393.

Baker, E. 2022. 'Vote Compass Data Shows Climate Change, Cost of Living and the Economy Are the Big Election Issues, But Voters Still Split Along Party Lines.' *ABC News*, 22 April. Available from: www.abc.net.au/news/2022-04-22/vote-compass-federal-election-issues-data-climate-change-economy/101002116.

Barrett, P., P. Kurian, and J. Wright. 2015. 'Environmental Security and the Contradictory Politics of New Zealand's Climate Change Policies in the Pacific.' In *Environmental Security in the Asia-Pacific*, edited by I. Watson and C.L. Pandey, 157–78. New York, NY: Palgrave Macmillan. doi.org/10.1057/9781137494122_6.

Bostrom, A., A.L. Hayes, and K.M. Crosman. 2018. 'Efficacy, Action, and Support for Reducing Climate Change Risks.' *Risk Analysis* 39(4): 805–28. doi.org/10.1111/risa.13210.

Bradley, G.L., Z. Babutsidze, A. Chai, and J.P. Reser. 2020. 'The Role of Climate Change Risk Perception, Response Efficacy, and Psychological Adaptation in Pro-Environmental Behavior: A Two Nation Study.' *Journal of Environmental Psychology* 68: 101410. doi.org/10.1016/j.jenvp.2020.101410.

Bramwell, C. 2017. 'Ardern Heads into Greens' Territory.' *Radio New Zealand*, 21 August. Available from: www.rnz.co.nz/news/political/337619/ardern-heads-into-greens-territory.

Cheng, D. 2020. 'Election 2020: Greens Say Labour's Climate Policy Not Good Enough.' *New Zealand Herald*, 7 October. Available from: www.nzherald.co.nz/nz/politics/election-2020-greens-say-labours-climate-policy-not-good-enough/27WXVCMZI6LKOP6ASHEKPDHQOU/.

Climate Action Tracker (CAT). 2021. *Country Summary: New Zealand*. 15 September. Berlin: Climate Action Tracker. Available from: climateactiontracker.org/countries/new-zealand/.

Cooke, H. 2016. 'ACT Deletes Climate Change Policy from Their Website.' *Stuff*, [Wellington], 26 February. Available from: www.stuff.co.nz/national/politics/77338800/act-delete-climate-change-policy-from-their-website.

Corlett, E. 2021. 'New Zealand Plan to Halve Greenhouse Gas Emissions Criticised as an "Accounting Trick".' *The Guardian*, 1 November. Available from: www.theguardian.com/world/2021/nov/01/new-zealand-plan-to-halve-greenhouse-gases-criticised-as-an-accounting-trick.

Corry, O., and D. Jørgensen. 2015. 'Beyond "Deniers" and "Believers": Towards a Map of the Politics of Climate Change.' *Global Environmental Change* 32: 165–74. doi.org/10.1016/j.gloenvcha.2015.01.006.

Craig, G. 2021. 'Performing Politics: Leaders' Debates in the 2020 Election.' In *Politics in a Pandemic: Jacinda Ardern and New Zealand's 2020 Election*, edited by S. Levine, 282–97. Wellington: Te Herenga Waka University Press.

Crawley, S. 2021. 'Disentangling the Relationships Between Conservative Economic and Social Attitudes and Support for Environmental Action.' *Journal of Political Ideologies* 28(2): 297–317. doi.org/10.1080/13569317.2021.1966939.

Crawley, S., H. Coffé, and R. Chapman. 2020. 'Public Opinion on Climate Change: Belief and Concern, Issue Salience and Support for Government Action.' *The British Journal of Politics and International Relations* 22(1): 102–21. doi.org/10.1177/1369148119888827.

Deep Decarbonization Pathways Project (DDPP). 2015. *Pathways to Deep Decarbonization: 2015 Report*. Paris: Sustainable Development Solutions Network & Institute for Sustainable Development and International Relations. Available from: www.iddri.org/sites/default/files/import/publications/ddpp_2015synthetis report.pdf.

Drews, S., and J.C.J.M. van den Bergh. 2016. 'What Explains Public Support for Climate Policies? A Review of Empirical and Experimental Studies.' *Climate Policy* 16(7): 855–76. doi.org/10.1080/14693062.2015.1058240.

Drummond, A., L.C. Hall, J.D. Sauer, and M.A. Palmer. 2018. 'Is Public Awareness and Perceived Threat of Climate Change Associated with Governmental Mitigation Targets?' *Climatic Change* 149: 159–71. doi.org/10.1007/s10584-018-2230-2.

Hall, D. 2020. 'Ardern's Government and Climate Policy: Despite a Zero-Carbon Law, Is New Zealand Merely a Follower Rather Than a Leader?' *The Conversation*, 5 October. Available from: theconversation.com/arderns-government-and-climate-policy-despite-a-zero-carbon-law-is-new-zealand-merely-a-follower-rather-than-a-leader-146402.

Hall, D. 2021. 'Expertise Within Democracy: The Case of New Zealand's Climate Change Commission.' *Political Science* 73(2): 103–22. doi.org/10.1080/00323187.2021.2022902.

Haltinner, K., and D. Sarathchandra. 2021. 'Considering Attitudinal Uncertainty in the Climate Change Skepticism Continuum.' *Global Environmental Change* 68: 102243. doi.org/10.1016/j.gloenvcha.2021.102243.

Hepburn, C. 2010. 'Environmental Policy, Government, and the Market.' *Oxford Review of Economic Policy* 26(2): 117–36. Available from: www.jstor.org/stable/43664556. doi.org/10.1093/oxrep/grq016.

Hornsey, M.J., E.A. Harris, P.G. Bain, and K.S. Fielding. 2016. 'Meta-Analyses of the Determinants and Outcomes of Belief in Climate Change.' *Nature Climate Change* 6(6): 622–26. doi.org/10.1038/nclimate2943.

Intergovernmental Panel on Climate Change (IPCC). 2021. '2021: Summary for Policymakers.' In *Climate Change 2021: The Physical Science Basis. Contribution of Working Group I to the Sixth Assessment Report of the Intergovernmental Panel on Climate Change*. Geneva: IPCC Secretariat. Available from: www.ipcc.ch/report/ar6/wg1/.

Ipsos. 2023. *19th Ipsos New Zealand Issues Monitor*. 26 February. Auckland: Ipsos. Available from: www.ipsos.com/en-nz/19th-ipsos-new-zealand-issues-monitor.

Kerr, J.R., and M.S. Wilson. 2018. 'Changes in Perceived Scientific Consensus Shift Beliefs About Climate Change and GM Food Safety.' *PLOS One* 13(7): e0200295. doi.org/10.1371/journal.pone.0200295.

Leining, C., S. Kerr, and B. Bruce-Brand. 2020. 'The New Zealand Emissions Trading Scheme: Critical Review and Future Outlook for Three Design Innovations.' *Climate Policy* 20(2): 246–64. doi.org/10.1080/14693062.2019. 1699773.

Leiserowitz, A., J. Carman, N. Buttermore, L. Neyens, S. Rosenthal, J. Marlon, J. Schneider, and K. Mulcahy. 2022. *International Public Opinion on Climate Change, 2022.* Report, 29 June. New Haven, CT: Yale Program on Climate Change Communication & Data for Good at Meta. Available from: climate communication.yale.edu/publications/international-public-opinion-on-climate-change-2022/.

Linde, S. 2020. 'The Politicization of Risk: Party Cues, Polarization, and Public Perceptions of Climate Change Risk.' *Risk Analysis* 40(10): 2002–18. doi.org/10.1111/risa.13530.

Lo, A.Y., and A.T. Chow. 2015. 'The Relationship Between Climate Change Concern and National Wealth.' *Climatic Change* 131(2): 335–48. doi.org/10.1007/s10584-015-1378-2.

Malpass, L., and H. Cooke. 2019. 'Government Sets Deadline for Farmer Emissions.' *Stuff*, [Wellington], 24 October. Available from: www.stuff.co.nz/national/politics/116816786/government-sets-deadline-for-farmer-emissions.

Mann, M., and M. Turnbull. 2022. 'How Australia's Electoral System Allowed Voters to Finally Impose a Ceasefire in the Climate Wars.' *The Guardian*, 28 May. Available from: www.theguardian.com/commentisfree/2022/may/28/how-australias-electoral-system-allowed-voters-to-finally-impose-a-ceasefire-in-the-climate-wars.

McCright, A.M., S.T. Marquart-Pyatt, R.L. Shwom, S.R. Brechin, and S. Allen. 2016. 'Ideology, Capitalism, and Climate: Explaining Public Views About Climate Change in the United States.' *Energy Research & Social Science* 21: 180–89. doi.org/10.1016/j.erss.2016.08.003.

McDonald, R.I., H.Y. Chai, and B.R. Newell. 2015. 'Personal Experience and the "Psychological Distance" of Climate Change: An Integrative Review.' *Journal of Environmental Psychology* 44: 109–18. doi.org/10.1016/j.jenvp.2015.10.003.

McGlennon. 2020. 'Meet the Young People Bringing Climate into Focus for the 2020 Election.' *Stuff*, [Wellington], 14 October. Available from: www.stuff.co.nz/environment/climate-news/123072530/meet-the-young-people-bringing-climate-into-focus-for-the-2020-election.

McKenzie, P. 2022. 'New Zealand's Once All-Powerful Farmers Split Amid Anger Over Ardern Climate Policy.' *The Guardian*, 30 May. Available from: www.the guardian.com/world/2022/may/30/new-zealands-once-all-powerful-farmers-split-amid-anger-over-ardern-climate-policy.

McLachlan, R. 2020. 'Climate Emergency Or Not, New Zealand Needs to Start Doing Its Fair Share of Climate Action.' *The Conversation*, 1 December. Available from: theconversation.com/climate-emergency-or-not-new-zealand-needs-to-start-doing-its-fair-share-of-climate-action-151083.

Milfont, T.L., E. Zubielevitch, P. Milojev, and C.G. Sibley. 2021. 'Ten-Year Panel Data Confirm Generation Gap but Climate Beliefs Increase at Similar Rates Across Ages.' *Nature Communications* 12: 4038. doi.org/10.1038/s41467-021-24245-y.

Mills, K., C. Berti, and V. Rupar. 2018. 'What Kind of Country We Want for Our Children: An Analysis of Media Coverage of the 2017 New Zealand General Election.' *Kōtuitui: New Zealand Journal of Social Sciences Online* 13(2): 161–76. doi.org/10.1080/1177083X.2018.1476390.

Ministry for the Environment. 2019. *Climate Change Response (Zero Carbon) Amendment Act 2019*. [Last updated 5 April 2021]. Wellington: New Zealand Government. Available from: environment.govt.nz/acts-and-regulations/acts/climate-change-response-amendment-act-2019/.

Ministry for the Environment. 2021a. *New Zealand's Greenhouse Gas Inventory 1990–2019*. 1 April. Wellington: New Zealand Government. Available from: environment.govt.nz/assets/Publications/New-Zealands-Greenhouse-Gas-Inventory-1990-2019-Volume-1-Chapters-1-15.pdf.

Ministry for the Environment. 2021b. *New Zealand's Projected Greenhouse Gas Emissions to 2050*. 30 August. Wellington: New Zealand Government. Available from: environment.govt.nz/what-government-is-doing/areas-of-work/climate-change/emissions-reduction-targets/new-zealands-projected-greenhouse-gas-emissions-to-2050/.

Newsroom Staff. 2020. 'Election 2020 and Climate Action: Leaders Answer Your Questions.' *Newsroom*, [Auckland], 28 September. Available from: www.newsroom.co.nz/page/election-2020-and-climate-action-leaders-answer-your-questions.

O'Brien, K. 2018. 'Is the 1.5°C Target Possible? Exploring the Three Spheres of Transformation.' *Current Opinion in Environmental Sustainability* 31: 153–60. doi.org/10.1016/j.cosust.2018.04.010.

Poortinga, W., L. Whitmarsh, L. Steg, G. Böhm, and S. Fisher. 2019. 'Climate Change Perceptions and Their Individual-Level Determinants: A Cross-European Analysis.' *Global Environmental Change* 55: 25–35. doi.org/10.1016/j.gloenvcha. 2019.01.007.

Pralle, S.B. 2009. 'Agenda-Setting and Climate Change.' *Environmental Politics* 18(5): 781–99. doi.org/10.1080/09644010903157115.

Quiggin, J. 2022. 'The Election Showed Australia's Huge Appetite for Stronger Climate Action. What Levers Can the New Government Pull?' *The Conversation*, 23 May. Available from: theconversation.com/the-election-showed-australias-huge-appetite-for-stronger-climate-action-what-levers-can-the-new-government-pull-183548.

Rahmstorf, S. 2004. 'The Climate Sceptics.' In *Weather Catastrophes and Climate Change: Is There Still Hope for Us?*, 76–83. Munich: Munich Re Group. Available from: www.pik-potsdam.de/~stefan/Publications/Other/rahmstorf_climate_sceptics_2004.pdf.

Roper, J., and M. Toledano. 2005. 'Taking in the View from the Edge: Issues Management Recontextualized.' *Public Relations Review* 31(4): 479–85. doi.org/10.1016/j.pubrev.2005.08.005.

Schaffer, L.M., B. Oehl, and T. Bernauer. 2021. 'Are Policymakers Responsive to Public Demand in Climate Politics?' *Journal of Public Policy* 42(1): 136–64. doi.org/10.1017/S0143814X21000088.

Scruggs, L., and S. Benegal. 2012. 'Declining Public Concern About Climate Change: Can We Blame the Great Recession?' *Global Environmental Change* 22(2): 505–15. doi.org/10.1016/j.gloenvcha.2012.01.002.

Smith, E.K., and A. Mayer. 2019. 'Anomalous Anglophones? Contours of Free Market Ideology, Political Polarization, and Climate Change Attitudes in English-Speaking Countries, Western European and Post-Communist States.' *Climatic Change* 152(1): 17–34. doi.org/10.1007/s10584-018-2332-x.

Thaker, J. 2021. *Climate Change in the Kiwi Mind: An Audience Segmentation Analysis*. Wellington: Massey University. Available from: www.researchgate.net/publication/354935732_Climate_Change_in_the_Kiwi_Mind_An_Audience_Segmentation_Analysis.

Tranter, B., and K. Booth. 2015. 'Scepticism in a Changing Climate: A Cross-National Study.' *Global Environmental Change* 33: 154–64. doi.org/10.1016/j.gloenvcha.2015.05.003.

Tvinnereim, E., and M. Mehling. 2018. 'Carbon Pricing and Deep Decarbonisation.' *Energy Policy* 121: 185–89. doi.org/10.1016/j.enpol.2018.06.020.

van der Linden, S. 2017. 'Determinants and Measurement of Climate Change Risk Perception, Worry, and Concern.' In *The Oxford Encyclopedia of Climate Change Communication*, edited by M.C. Nisbet, M. Schafer, E. Markowitz, S. Ho, S. O'Neill, and J. Thaker. Oxford: Oxford University Press. Available from: papers.ssrn.com/abstract=2953631. doi.org/10.1093/acrefore/9780190228620.013.318.

Vandeweerdt, C., B. Kerremans, and A. Cohn. 2016. 'Climate Voting in the US Congress: The Power of Public Concern.' *Environmental Politics* 25(2): 268–88. doi.org/10.1080/09644016.2016.1116651.

Vaughter, P.C.-D. 2012. 'The Role of Information Flow in Climate Change Policy Formation in New Zealand: A Social Analysis.' PhD dissertation, University of Minnesota, Minneapolis, MN. Available from: hdl.handle.net/11299/139740.

Vowles, J., F. Barker, M. Krewel, J. Hayward, J. Curtin, L. Greaves, and L. Oldfield. 2022. *2020 New Zealand Election Study*. [Online]. ADA Dataverse, V3. doi.org/10.26193/BPAMYJ.

Weber, E.U. 2010. 'What Shapes Perceptions of Climate Change?' *Wiley Interdisciplinary Reviews: Climate Change* 1(3): 332–42. doi.org/10.1002/wcc.41.

10

The Disappearing 'Team of Five Million'? The road to the 2023 election

Jack Vowles, Jennifer Curtin, and Lara Greaves

The idea of the 'Team of Five Million' epitomised Jacinda Ardern's ability to find the right words at the right time when her country needed steady and determined leadership. The metaphor represented the ideal of collective effort by all members of society, all working together. High levels of compliance with lockdowns and other restrictions confirmed its resonance. But to the side there were dissenters, and their number would steadily increase in the aftermath of the 2020 election. Indeed, on the day she announced the date of the 2023 election, Ardern also announced her resignation as prime minister and Member of Parliament. Here we conclude our analysis of the 2020 election by reviewing the findings of previous chapters and summarising events in the months before the 2023 election. We reassess the framing of New Zealand voters as 'a team' before discussing the longer-term implications.

Was the Team of Five Million more than a metaphor?

As explained in Chapter 1, the scale of Labour's victory in 2020 was momentous. In a historic net shift of votes, Labour acquired an unprecedented single-party majority under the MMP electoral system. Nearly 60 per cent of the votes were cast for parties of the left that supported the government's pandemic response with few if any qualifications. Age-eligible valid vote turnout hit a 20-year peak at 76.5 per cent. Nonetheless, the sociodemographic foundations of party voting did not appreciably change. There were more Labour votes in the provinces, but this simply reflected the national trend. Farmers, employers, and the self-employed still resisted Labour more than others, as did those with high incomes and numerous assets. While turnout among younger voters was up, they were still disproportionately represented among those who did not vote. Māori and Pasifika leaned toward Labour, but also towards not voting at all. The call for a collective response to an emergency could temporarily obscure but could not transcend ongoing social divisions.

Chapter 2 challenges analysts for whom the election outcome was more about the pandemic's emotional impact than a substantive appraisal of Labour's performance. Sceptics have argued that, in countries holding 'Covid' elections, voters opted for an incumbent government, for conservative parties willing to 'take charge', or just rallied around the flag. No one can deny the emotions brought out by Covid-19, particularly in those countries hardest hit. Yet, evidence from New Zealand and elsewhere suggests that if voters had the opportunity to go to the polls in the year or two after the crisis emerged, governments that kept cases under control and their people safe were more likely to be re-elected than those that could not. This was particularly the case if government leadership was competent and clear in its communications. In such situations, the quality of elites matters as much, if not more than, the quality of collective judgement among the public. The ability to inspire trust in the government's decisions was Jacinda Ardern's great contribution for which she will be long remembered. Not all were convinced, but when it most mattered they were a small minority.

The Labour Party was given a temporary reward: an unprecedented victory. But the high net shift of votes was boosted by increased turnout and otherwise based on very much the same proportion of changing votes as previous elections. In 2020, those shifts simply tended to go one way more than others. There was no sign of a fundamental policy preference shift among voters. Approval of the Covid-19 response and trust and confidence in Jacinda Arden were responsible for a strong shift among voters towards the Labour Party. As expected, those who changed were mainly median or 'centre-ground' voters that Labour would have no other reasons to retain on an ongoing basis. There was no sign of a realignment in 2020. Only if an expanded number of younger voters were to remain engaged with the electoral process would a longer-term shift emerge over time (van der Brug and Rekker 2021).

Chapter 3 documents the increasing focus on social media in the 2020 election campaign. Voter receipt of political party social media messaging was lower than many might have expected. Despite the pandemic, traditional campaign methods such as direct mail and person-to-person contact still dominated. A little less than 12 per cent reported party contact by social media although 80 per cent reported they used the internet for accessing political information. By its nature, social media has the potential to polarise by encouraging members of groups to reinforce their opinions in 'echo chambers'. During the campaign, the major political parties kept their Facebook messaging positive, relatively accurate, and targeted swinging voters. In the final week and perceiving its imminent defeat, National Party messaging became more negative and directed more strongly to retaining its core voters. Disinformation was almost entirely confined to the echo chambers of the very small parties opposing the government's pandemic response. The Māori Party provided a good example of how social media can be used effectively by a small party with limited resources. Jacinda Ardern's positive social media messaging was the most pervasive and influential.

Chapter 4 addresses the increase in turnout in 2020. New Zealand politics differs from that of other countries where some political parties actively seek to suppress turnout. In New Zealand, the institutional encouragement of turnout and inclusion are widely accepted norms and there are very few barriers to casting a vote. Voting rights even extend beyond citizens to those from other countries with permanent resident status. The New Zealand Electoral Commission makes strong efforts to maximise turnout, including advance voting and election day registration. In 2020, those efforts were redoubled. The election was delayed to ensure it could be held in the absence of community Covid cases thus making it possible for parties to campaign and voters to be protected. Nonetheless, contact between candidates and voters during the campaign was lower than at the two previous elections.

The 2020 election was held concurrently with two referendums: one on euthanasia and one on the legalisation of cannabis. At least some of the turnout increase in 2020 could have been generated by interest in the referendums rather than in the general election. An alternative explanation could be that generalised political trust and political efficacy had increased because of support for the government's pandemic response. But while generalised political trust is relatively high in New Zealand compared with other democracies, there was no such increase in either of those traditional correlates of turnout. This finding pours further cold water on the idea that the 2020 election will have long-lasting effects on political behaviour.

Chapter 5 discusses the return of the Māori Party to parliament. On the surface, this appears to indicate a loss of support for Labour among Māori, thus questioning the metaphor of the Team of Five Million. One potential reason for Māori disillusionment with Labour was the government's inability to resolve a *hapū* land claim at Ihumātao in South Auckland. But while those on the Māori roll were critical of the government in its handling of that matter, their overall rating of Labour remained high, and their support for the Māori Party did not increase. Voters for Labour and the Māori Party tended to be similarly aligned at the left of centre. Identification with Māori culture is a better predictor of Māori Party vote choice than left–right position. The new Māori Party leadership could not compete with the popularity of Jacinda Ardern. Nonetheless, the Māori Party held its ground at the 2020 election. Its capture of the Waiariki electorate provided the platform for its success in winning no less than six of the seven Māori electorates at the 2023 election.

Chapter 6 considers the implications of border closure and its impact on political attitudes about immigration. New Zealand is a society based on immigration and more than one-quarter of its population in 2020 was born elsewhere. Large parts of the economy rely on immigrant labour. As noted in Chapter 2, tourism normally generates very significant economic activity. Yet, the inclusive implications of the metaphor of the Team of Five Million are somewhat belied by the fact that half the electorate indicated they would prefer a lower level of immigration than that before the pandemic. This is consistent with data from previous elections in that public opinion about immigration has remained relatively stable over time. A declining number of people felt that immigration has negative economic or cultural consequences. However, there continues to be hostility towards those entering New Zealand as big investors or non-residents in the housing market. Immigrant access to welfare benefits for those on temporary work visas is also unpopular.

Chapter 7 analyses the significance of Jacinda Ardern's leadership and the gender gaps in voting behaviour and attitudes to social and health policy in the context of the pandemic. Ardern was widely known and appreciated for her policy rhetoric emphasising kindness, inclusion, hope, and a transformative policy agenda that would address poverty, inequality, and climate change. This rhetoric sat easily alongside the government's public health–first approach and came across as authentic and trustworthy.

In the end, women were significantly more likely to vote Labour in 2020 than men: indeed, under Ardern, Labour had more voting support among women than under any previous prime minister. Only a minority of people believed that men were better leaders than women. The positive experience of Ardern's leadership in a situation of crisis appears to have shifted attitudes to an even more positive appreciation of female leadership among both men and women. This is despite slow progress on several policy issues that were found to matter to New Zealand women. Only a small minority among both older and younger men tended to resist that trend. Post-election, many of these voices grew louder. Time will tell whether the new Labour leader, Chris Hipkins, can maintain Labour's appeal to women voters generated by Ardern.

Chapter 8 examines those who did not accept membership of the Team of Five Million. The National Party generally supported the government's pandemic response and occasional criticisms by its MPs were often off-message and failed to hit their marks. National's succession of leadership changes weakened the party's credibility. Those opposed to the government's policy response to Covid-19 tended to be male, aged between 41 and 60, farmers, self-employed, and those whose household incomes had declined over the previous year. In terms of ideology, authoritarians and those less sympathetic to the interests of Māori were more disposed to be against the government. A lack of trust in Jacinda Ardern had a very strong additional effect on people with those beliefs.

The two most prominent small parties opposing the pandemic response were the New Conservatives and Advance NZ. The New Conservatives drew more from religious Pākehā social conservatism; Advance NZ from Māori. The voters supporting these fringe parties were ideologically amorphous and the parties representing them were equally broad in their political positions. These divergent interests make the future consolidation of support behind a single party or coalition of parties unlikely.

At the 2020 election, the ACT party managed to re-establish its position in the party system on the neoliberal right. Like National, ACT supported the Covid-19 elimination strategy but criticised aspects of its implementation. Most of its votes came from previous National voters and disproportionately from men and people on high incomes and in rural areas. While authoritarianism is associated with both National and ACT voters, ACT voters were less authoritarian than those for National.

Chapter 9 considers the apparent eclipse of climate change in an election dominated by the pandemic. The reality of climate change is now accepted by most politicians and voters in New Zealand, but a 'team' approach is lacking on what and how much the government should do to address the problem. Under Labour since 2017, a combination of negotiation and legislation has created a framework for reducing carbon dioxide and methane emissions but there has been little real progress in its practical implementation. For most people, climate change is not perceived as an issue important enough to shape their voting choice. They accept it as a problem that will affect their children and grandchildren, but not so much themselves. About four in 10 are sceptical that collective action can reduce emissions, about half think it can, although six in 10 support government action to do so. It was unlikely that climate change would come back as an urgent issue in 2023 given the post-Covid focus on the cost of living. This intensified concern about economic issues is the main theme of the discussion that follows, following the path towards the 2023 election.

Post-pandemic politics

The temporary nature of Labour's election victory is borne out by trends in public polling since the 2020 election (see Figure 10.1). The downward movement of Labour polling is apparent from about April–May 2021. National vote intentions remained flat until November of that year, when former Air New Zealand CEO Christopher Luxon took over the party's leadership reins from Judith Collins. A polling shift to the right was apparent from at least August but ACT was the main beneficiary. Once put in charge, Luxon began to capture a bigger share for National. A further fall in Labour polling coincided with the number of Covid-19 cases exploding in March and April 2022.

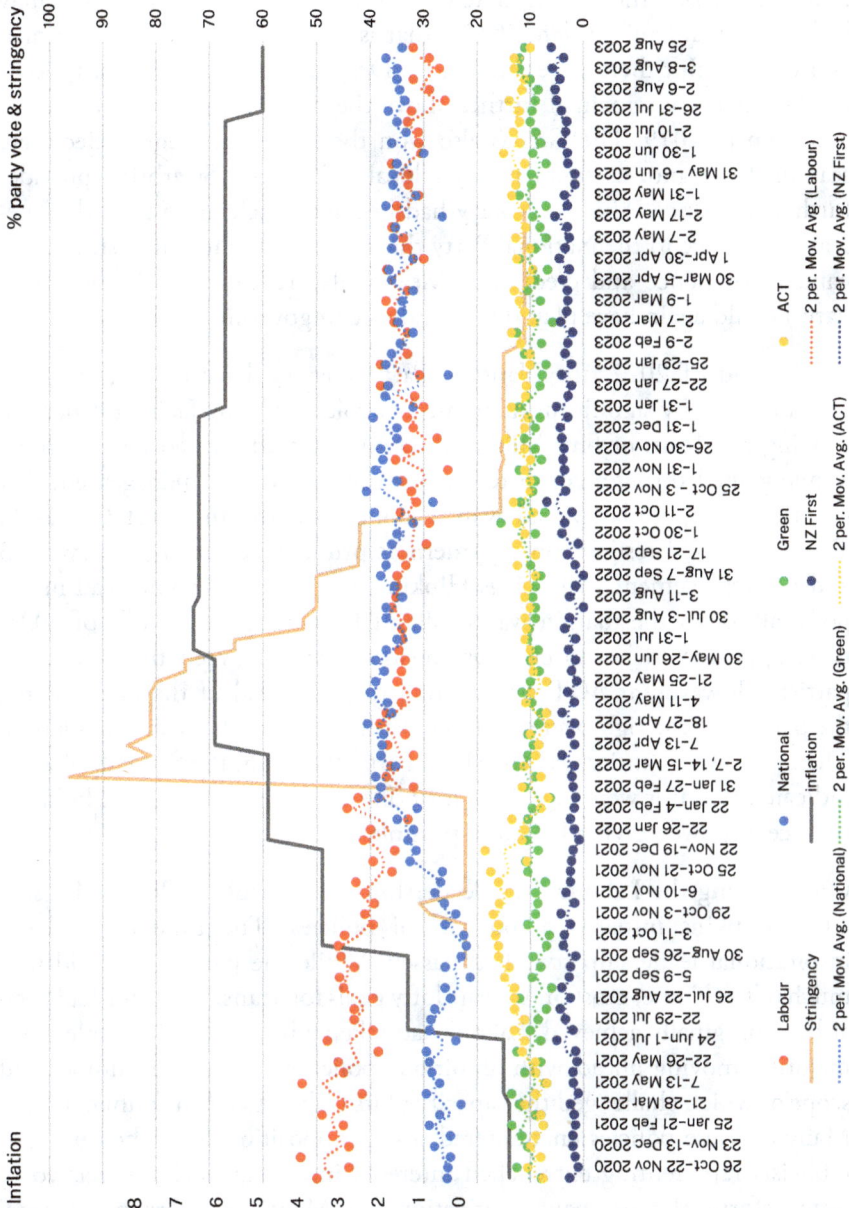

Figure 10.1 Political polls, inflation, and the stringency index, 2020–2023
Sources: Our World in Data (2022); StatsNZ (2023); Wikipedia (2023).

From mid-2022, the polling state of play was similar to that immediately before the pandemic in late 2019—that is, a tight race between National and Labour. But there were differences. Despite some internal disruptions, the Green Party remained further above the 5 per cent threshold than it had been in 2019. The Greens also won the Auckland Central electorate seat in 2020 and, as such, popular local MP Chlöe Swarbrick provides further insurance. The ACT party had become much more than the one-seat appendage to the National Party that it was in the recent past. Its MPs gained experience and credibility. Meanwhile, Te Pāti Māori (the Māori Party) could again have played a critical role in government formation.

By the end of 2022, the National Party was regularly polling ahead of Labour, often by significant margins. The role played by Jacinda Ardern in evoking the Team of Five Million to combat Covid-19 had lost its shine. While gained through competent and caring pandemic management, her government's popularity had waned along with the threat of Covid-19. The unexpected resignation of Ardern as prime minister in January 2023 and her replacement with Chris Hipkins recaptured a Labour lead in the polls, although the margin was small. At least until the middle of 2023, there appeared to be no clear or consistent gap between the two major parties. However, as ACT was tending to poll ahead of the Green Party, the parties on the right were seen as most likely to reach a winning margin. The unknown quantity was the Māori Party. Polling in the first half of 2023 indicated that if it were to hold at least one electorate seat it could hold the balance of power, giving Labour a possible edge.[1]

On assuming the Labour Party leadership and the job of Prime Minister, Chris Hipkins initiated a 'bonfire' of policies. The time for Ardern's inspirational leadership style had passed. While the pandemic could take much of the blame, most of Ardern's lofty goals for 'transformation' had been at best marginally achieved. Labour had taken advantage of its single-party majority, moving ahead with ambitious policy changes, the number and scope of which challenged the capacity of its Cabinet and the public service. Many of these policies encountered strong opposition from the public or lobbyists representing entrenched interests, including on issues related to water reform, climate change mitigation, and Māori co-governance. Several other policy options were dropped or set aside until after the 2023 election, including a contributory social insurance scheme, a merger of public radio

---

1   National ruled out working with Te Pāti Māori on 10 May 2023 (RNZ 2023a).

and television broadcasting, hate speech legislation, and legislation that would clarify the definition of contractors and employees. The government's attention turned towards addressing the effects of post-Covid inflation and its sometimes-devastating effects on real incomes. As Figure 10.1 shows, increasing inflation between mid-2021 and mid-2022 ran in tandem with Labour's declining support in the polls.

We can hypothesise that three factors lie behind the poll movements since the 2020 election: the rise of inflation, the leadership changes, and the diminishing salience of Covid-19, as measured by the Blavatnik School of Government's 'stringency index' (BSG 2020–23).[2] Inspecting Figure 10.1, inflation appears to have been the dominant factor behind Labour's decline from its 2020 election peak. The upward steps in the announced levels run in the opposite direction to Labour's downward polling. If we assume the announcement of the inflation rate over the previous quarter sparks the upward step, the parallel is clear.[3]

Data collected by Ipsos throughout 2022 and into 2023 confirm the effects of rising inflation on public perceptions (Ipsos 2022b, 2023). In February 2023, inflation/the cost of living was named by 65 per cent of those surveyed as one of the top three issues facing New Zealand. The economy in general was mentioned by 22 per cent. The Ipsos government approval rating on a zero–ten scale remained at an average of 5.4, just within positive territory, compared with 7.3 at the time of the 2020 election. The National Party was in the lead in assessments of parties' ability to manage three of the six top issues: inflation, law and order, and the economy. Labour ranked ahead on the second most salient issue, housing and its price, and on healthcare and hospitals, the issue ranked fourth.

Together with unemployment and growth, inflation forms one of the trinity of economic factors expected to play into public opinion and voting preferences. For the past 30 years, inflation has been relatively low. Economic growth has been the prime focus of analysis in New Zealand as elsewhere (Gardener 2016). When inflation has been discussed in the literature and

---

2   The measure that estimates the degree of Covid-19 restrictions. Systematic and robust statistical analysis of the polls would run foul of several unresolvable problems. This is particularly problematic for the possible effects of change in the economy. While many households and individuals feel the effects of inflation personally, its official estimate is indexed through a set of complex measurements and only reported quarterly. There are not enough measurements of inflation to correlate with the poll movements.
3   That is, the official release of the data rather than the real inflation experienced over the previous months is the trigger, reinforced by media coverage that reports and frames the information.

commentary, it has been set beside unemployment. It was believed there was an inevitable trade-off between the two, but that relationship is now understood to be much more complex (Gabriel et al. 2022). It was also assumed that inflation was most damaging to the political fortunes of centre-right parties and that unemployment was most damaging to those of the centre-left (Swank 1993; Carlsen 2000). Inflation tends to cut into the value of assets and the savings of those on high incomes, while the risk and reality of unemployment most affect those on low incomes.

In May 2022, Ipsos (2022a) reported marginally less concern about inflation among New Zealanders on low incomes, but the difference was not a big one. Inflation is less likely to affect those on low incomes where there are forms of social protection to compensate them, particularly if they are inflation-linked. Welfare benefits, low-income family financial support through the Working for Families program, and the minimum wage were increased in April 2022, partially cushioning the blow for the most vulnerable (Edmunds and Carroll 2022). A further one-off payment to low-income earners was also announced in May, extending to almost 40 per cent of the population. Tax on petrol was also temporarily cut to reduce the burden on drivers.

The Working for Families increase also penetrates further up the income ladder, but only for those with children. Those on middle incomes without children have been given less relief, providing a large residue of discontent although wage rises over the period of rising inflation have been significant, offering some relief (Dann 2022). While a range of benefits were increased with the potential to ameliorate political fallout (Park and Shin 2019), many doubt that New Zealand's social programs are sufficiently up to their task.

A focus on economic issues tends to shift the discursive advantage to parties of the centre-right. There is a form of popular wisdom that believes that because the National Party draws its ideas and support from business, its leaders must be more competent at managing the national economy. While running a business is not the same as running an entire economy, most people do not appreciate the differences (Krugman 2009).

As Chapter 2 explains, New Zealand's economic stimulus to meet the challenges of the Covid-19 pandemic in 2020 was one of the largest in the OECD, although several other countries were not far behind. Yet, as inflation peaked in mid-2022, the latest inflation rate for the second quarter of 7.1 per cent was in the lower half of the OECD countries—very close to levels in Sweden, Germany, and Canada. Sweden's Covid response was one of those with the lightest touch in the OECD, but it did not escape the high inflation of 2022. Indeed, comparing OECD countries, the growth of inflation in 2022 appears to have had very little relation to the size of the Covid-19 stimulus (Renney 2022). The baseline increase in inflation is driven predominantly by global trends. The flow-on effect of Russia's invasion of Ukraine has pushed up energy and food prices. China's efforts to eliminate Covid-19 cut its growth and disrupted trade supply chains. By early 2023, New Zealand's inflation rate was tracking only a little above the average among advanced economies (IMF 2023).

Most of the criticism of Labour's economic response centres on the Reserve Bank, which is responsible for setting base interest rates. The Reserve Bank is theoretically independent of day-to-day government control or influence, but in 2018, the bank's criteria for setting rates upward or downward were widened by Labour beyond inflation alone, adding the support of 'maximum sustainable employment'. With its emphasis on wage subsidies channelled through employers affected by lockdowns and other restrictions, the government's Covid-19 response also strongly reflected that concern. Almost all businesses that qualified accepted the subsidies. They were easily accessed and almost certainly made the government's Covid response far more palatable to businesses than any alternative means of delivery.

With the support of the government, the Reserve Bank also kept interest rates low and expanded the money supply. The bank's monetary expansion funded a large part of the government's own borrowing to pay for the wage subsidies and other measures. The Treasury issued new government bonds, which banks purchased and sold to the Reserve Bank, which paid for them using the money it created. Unemployment remained low. However, through their encouragement of bank lending, these policies had the effect of raising the prices of housing and other assets, benefiting asset-holders and thereby increasing asset inequality. New Zealand's house prices increased by almost one-third between the end of 2019 and the end of 2021—the second-highest growth in the OECD. Despite the availability of relatively low-interest mortgages, because of the rising prices, people on lower and middle incomes began finding it more and more difficult to buy a home. Economic stimulus kept economies from crashing; with the benefit of hindsight, many economists now argue that it went on for too long, not just in New Zealand but also around the world (Wilkinson and Wheeler 2022; but see Pullar-Strecker 2022). In combination with the war in Ukraine and supply chain disruption from China, inflation has been boosted by all these developments, both domestic and foreign. Meanwhile, the Reserve Bank has begun selling the bonds back to the Treasury, which then 'retires' them, gradually reducing the money supply.

The rise of inflation has had one more positive consequence: a fall in house prices. But that fall has been generated by rising interest rates. Seeking to bring inflation under control, the Reserve Bank has increased the base rate at which it will loan to commercial banks, thus obliging them to increase their rates to lenders. While houses are more affordable, the interest rates on loans to purchase them have increased. The housing market is more favourable to buyers, but not for the majority of those who require mortgages.

These were considerable political and economic challenges for Labour to face as the incumbent government leading into the 2023 election. There was residual discontent with the post-elimination Covid-19 response, including the vaccination rollout that began in 2021—later than in most comparable countries. Vulnerable older age groups were targeted first, which became a matter of controversy. Epidemiological research has shown that for a combination of reasons Māori and Pasifika populations were more vulnerable to Covid-19 than the majority Pākehā population (Steyn et al. 2020). This was soon borne out by data from cases as outbreaks began to take hold in the local population. Making matters worse, anti-vaccination messages originally sourced offshore were being targeted at these groups. Outreach efforts spearheaded by Māori and Pasifika organisations were required, and the official response was slower than what Māori and Pasifika health experts argued was needed.

As the more infectious Delta variant entered the community in August 2021, another lockdown was enforced briefly across the whole country, with Auckland and its immediate surroundings remaining in that condition until December. Criticism of the delay in the vaccine rollout when measured against other countries was widespread. In-depth polling detected increasing opinion that it was time to 'move on' and 'live with the virus' (Lord Ashcroft 2021). Figure 10.1 indicates the timing of the August–December lockdown by way of the stringency index (BSG 2020–23). Labour polling held up at first but began to fall back with the new inflation figures and as the lockdown continued in Auckland and its environs.

Early in 2022, the appearance of the greatly more infectious but less fatal Omicron variant of Covid-19 made it no longer feasible to contain the infection by contact tracing and public testing. The government had been restricting the use of do-it-yourself rapid antigen tests (RATs) not just because of their lower reliability but also to accurately monitor and control cases (Verrall 2021). Early in March, cases began to surge. Tracing and public testing became ineffective; RATs were made available. For a few weeks, despite likely underreporting, New Zealand had one of the world's highest case ratios, reflecting the country's very small number of cases until that point. The Covid-19 dam had been breached. But by then New Zealand had attained a high level of vaccination, limiting cases and, of much greater importance, greatly reducing the risk of serious illness and death.

Initially, the government had rejected the idea of wide use of mandates to make vaccination compulsory for people in jobs in which there was face-to-face contact with the public. To protect people and to encourage vaccination, mandates were gradually extended from border workers, health and care providers, police, and defence, through to fire service workers and teachers; all these groups were covered by November 2021. In January 2022, vaccination became required for people working in and entering hospitality and close-contact businesses: bars, restaurants, and all shops except food retailers and pharmacies. The main purpose was to incentivise vaccination among those hitherto casually reluctant. This strategy significantly steepened the upward curve of vaccinations (Ministry of Health 2022), but it also led to the mobilisation of anti-vaccination sentiments around an anti-mandate and anti-masking campaign that began to attract many people not opposed to vaccination itself. Over 24 days from early February 2022, against a background of increasing Covid-19 cases, up to 3,000 protesters occupied the grounds of Parliament House in Wellington. There were scenes of increasing violence. Protesters were eventually dispersed by forceful police action on 2 March.

While most New Zealanders opposed the parliamentary protest because of its violence and disregard of other people's rights, anti-mandate messages began to take hold. Polling in February 2022 estimated that 26 per cent of people wanted fewer restrictions, 24 per cent wanted them to be more robust, and support for the government response was down to 63 per cent from 83 per cent a year earlier (Manhire 2022). While the organisers of the protests were associated with the small anti-establishment political parties, none had ever gained parliamentary representation. New Zealand First leader Winston Peters visited the protest unmasked. On 23 March, after the vaccination rate had significantly improved, the government announced most vaccination mandates would cease to apply on 4 April. A second booster shot was made available to those eligible in July 2022, with further boosters made available later to the most vulnerable groups.

By the middle of 2022, the sense of unity represented by the idea of the Team of Five Million had not entirely disappeared, but the numbers opposed to it had grown. After two waves of Omicron infections, the relatively high level of vaccination was reducing vulnerability to illness, making it possible to establish a balance that could stretch hospital resources, but not break them.[4] This balance relied on the isolation of those infected and their household contacts and continued mask-wearing in most confined public places, although compliance began to wane (Coughlan 2022; DPMC 2022). The vaccine mandate almost certainly reduced Covid-19 incidence but there remains the possibility of negative effects on public trust and social cohesion, with increased political polarisation a real possibility (Bardosh et al. 2022). The 'team' metaphor no longer resonates in the public discourse.

Throughout 2022, the government's response to the Covid-19 pandemic remained a live issue, continuing to 'worry' 44 per cent of the public in May. However, New Zealanders remained divided between those who believed that all restrictions should be removed and those who preferred retention or strengthening of restrictions (DPMC 2022). While disagreement about the need for restrictions moved into the background of debate over time, it remained a potential source of polarisation that tends to track partisan preferences between centre-left and centre-right.

Indeed, polarisation was predicted to be a feature of the 2023 campaign and beyond. Indigenous rights in Aotearoa New Zealand and the place of Māori *iwi* (tribal council) and *hapū* (kinship group) in the political process have become a 'wedge' issue for several parties on the right. Commissioned as a background paper to lead to the implementation of the previous National government's signing of the UN Declaration of the Rights of Indigenous Peoples, the *He Puapua* report initiated by then Māori affairs minister Nanaia Mahuta recommended a range of options for a much greater role for Māori in government (Charters et al. 2020). The substantive, long-term options included creating a separate legal system and an upper house of

---

4   In August 2022, 3,982,068 people were fully vaccinated—78 per cent of the total population and 95 per cent of the Ministry of Health's defined target group of those aged 12 or more. Comparative analysis continued to confirm that New Zealand was one of the most successful countries in preventing deaths from Covid-19. Excess deaths remained in negative territory, even after two waves of the Omicron variant (Morton 2022).

Māori representatives. The report was not released to the Cabinet, which at the time included New Zealand First ministers who would have opposed it. *He Puapua* was not available to the public until early in 2021 after it was leaked to the National and ACT parties.

The prime minister quickly rejected the idea of a Māori upper house, but many of the discussion paper's other recommendations were taken up as part of policy work foreshadowed in Labour's 2017 and 2020 election policies. These included enabling the creation of additional Māori wards in local government, a Māori health authority, a school history curriculum with a strong focus on Māori history, greater use of the Māori language in mainstream media and public organisations, and *iwi* co-governance with local government representatives in four new regionally based 'entities' controlling water supply, stormwater, and wastewater: the 'Three Waters'.

Consultations on *He Puapua* took place with Māori *iwi* and opinion leaders, to be followed by a paper to the Cabinet and wider public consultation. But Minister of Māori Affairs Willie Jackson requested revisions, anticipating that the draft would not be accepted by Cabinet (Moir 2022). In the end, no revision acceptable to Jackson was submitted by the authors of *He Puapua* and the matter was shelved.

The Three Waters proposals became the biggest focus of public and local government criticism. Local government would continue to own and hold the debt of the consolidated assets while the authority structure would involve co-governance with Māori *iwi* representatives. Local government rights of control and ownership would be diluted by half and set several steps back from management, diminishing accountability (Ludbrook 2022). Thirty-one of the 76 local councils, including Auckland, came out in opposition.

An initial promise that these 'entities' would not be imposed was broken. When Three Waters came under review as part of the 'policy bonfire', after several weeks it was announced that the four entities would become ten. Their boundaries would be defined not by Māori *iwi* areas as in the original plan but by those of the regional government. The numbers appointed to the representative bodies would increase to include all local councils, but so, too, would those appointed by *iwi*, continuing to maintain the model of co-governance.

Meanwhile, the direct appointment of two Ngāi Tahu councillors to Canterbury's otherwise elected regional government, Environment Canterbury, was passed into law. A core democratic principle of one person, one vote of equal value was questioned by the Māori Party and some Labour MPs, including Jackson himself (Jackson 2022). Labour's Tāmati Coffey argued in parliament that 'there is nothing to preclude us being able to tweak democracy to make it work for us here in Aotearoa' (Coffey, cited in Edwards 2022). The idea of democracy itself was challenged (Satherley 2021), the criticism justified by its empowering a 'tyranny of the majority' and thus 'white majority rule' (Randerson 2022).

The danger of a damaging 'culture war' around these developments and the associated rhetoric was widely recognised. The National, ACT, and New Zealand First parties were strongly critical and called for more substantive debate, with ACT demanding a referendum (Seymour 2022). In response, National and ACT were often chastised for their statements that were frequently interpreted as 'racist' (for example, Cheng 2021) or as playing the 'race card' (Stuff 2021).

The implications in public opinion and political behaviour remained uncertain. In 2004, Pākehā opinion was strongly mobilised against Māori claims to title over the foreshore and seabed that had potentially been enabled by a ruling of the Court of Appeal (Palmer 2006, 199–204; Cullen 2021, 330–46). The National Party campaigned strongly for legislation to override the court and there was a massive increase in its polling support. Labour subsequently legislated in response to the court's decision to establish Crown ownership but was met with strong Māori opposition that led to the formation of the Māori Party.

Much of National's 2004 poll rise proved temporary, although the party kept many of its gains. The 2005 election was extremely close and fought partly on the issue. Labour edged ahead narrowly. Policy related to Māori was the most salient issue in the 2005 campaign, mentioned by 19 per cent of NZES respondents, followed by health on 17 per cent (Vowles et al. 2006). The majority opinion was strongly against Māori claims to the foreshore and seabed. In a confused and polarised debate, many people on both sides misunderstood the rights in question as being for exclusive freehold rather than for customary title—a matter all parties then in parliament agreed needed clarification. Later legislation by National in consultation with the Māori Party established that the foreshore and seabed would be owned by no one and claims of customary title would be determined through the legal process, and the issue has subsided. As Chapter 5 explains, bitterness remains among many Māori.

In 2022 and 2023, there was much less evidence of such strong Pākehā opinion. Ipsos issue salience polling put Māori-related policy issues at a very low level of interest. Depending on question phrasing, most polling on Three Waters showed majority opposition, but many people had no opinion, which is not surprising given the complexity of the proposals and a lack of incisive analysis in the mainstream media and free-access platforms.[5] The foreshore and seabed claim appeared to propose restrictions on people's access to the seashore; access to beaches is regarded as a fundamental right by many New Zealanders. Rights to control the nation's collective plumbing systems do not provoke the same emotions. Nonetheless, Three Waters continued to have traction, particularly in the provinces where local councils regard the policy as an effective confiscation of their assets.

Over the years public opinion has become more sympathetic to Māori issues and claims. As Figure 10.2 shows, opinion about the place of the Treaty of Waitangi in law has changed since 2005, from most against to most in favour. In the 2020 NZES, as a proxy for the principle of co-governance, agreement or disagreement with the statement 'Māori should have more say in all government decisions' showed 27 per cent in agreement and 42 per cent in opposition. Willie Jackson's caution in taking the first draft response to *He Puapua* to the Cabinet seemed justified. Among people of Māori descent, there was more support: 54 per cent agreed that Māori should have more say. But when asked about the idea of a Māori upper house, 25 per cent of people of Māori descent were in favour, with 42 per cent opposed. Whether it is a sleeping issue or one to be mobilised later, the idea of co-governance with Māori *iwi* and *hapū* remains in the background rather than to the fore. However, there was increasing concern about the danger of 'pernicious polarisation' driven from both sides of the debate (Salmond 2022). As the election drew near, growing support for the New Zealand First Party was putting it above the party vote threshold for parliamentary representation in some polls. Its conservative attitudes to the Treaty and so-called woke issues appeared to strike a chord in public opinion.

---

5   The *1News* Kantar poll of January 2022 put 40 per cent against and 26 per cent in favour (1News 2022). A Horizon Research poll in November 2021 put 48 per cent against and 24 per cent in favour (Horizon Research 2021). A summary of 10 polls is also available online (theFacts 2022).

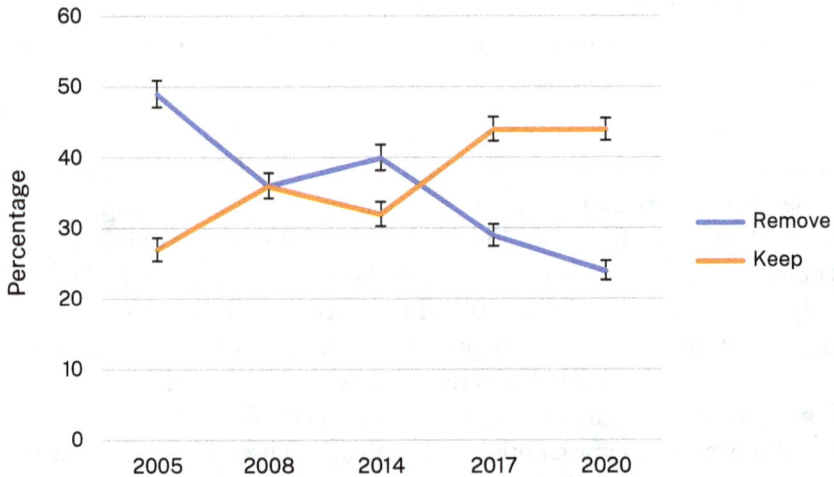

Figure 10.2 'Remove or keep Treaty in the law'

Note: The question was in agreement or disagreement with the statement: 'The Treaty of Waitangi should be removed from the law.'

Sources: Vowles et al. (2006, 2022a, 2022b, 2022c, 2022d, 2022f).

While 'culture war'–style politics was becoming more prominent as 2023 wore on, economic issues remained at the centre of public debate. The National Party's promise of tax cuts to address inflation—themselves likely to be inflationary—was revised after disparagement not only from Labour but also from ACT. By mid-2022, Luxon's performance as National Party leader was coming under increasing criticism. His stock responses in short interviews went down well among journalists, but in extended interviews, he often proved unwilling or unable to answer key questions in any detail (Hooton 2022; Trevett 2022). As Luxon's performance improved, it was still open to criticism as excessively cautious and scripted (Hooton 2023).

Meanwhile, Prime Minister Chris Hipkins was proving a more effective Labour leader than many had expected. His high public exposure during the height of the pandemic as the minister in charge of the response made him familiar to the public. His propensity for straight-talking made a sharp contrast to Ardern's inspirational rhetoric and was more in keeping with the times. Moreover, Hipkins and his new Cabinet gained good media coverage after the severe flooding in Auckland and elsewhere in late January 2023, followed by the devastation of Cyclone Gabrielle in February. As New Zealand's recent past has shown, natural disasters, terrorist attacks, and a pandemic can provide a politically valuable platform for a leader who can demonstrate competence and communicate in a way that builds both trust and likeability. However, by the onset of the election campaign, Chris Hipkins's lustre had begun to fade and his leadership ratings had fallen close to those of Christopher Luxon (RNZ 2023b). A month out from the election Luxon's approval ratings were holding firm while those of Hipkins had plummeted. There was to be no opportunity for Labour to recover lost votes before election day. While National was only able to reach 38 per cent share of the vote, Labour's result was just short of 27 per cent, close to halving the sitting government's share of both votes and seats. An analysis of whether this represents a new period of polarisation, or something else, will be the subject of the 2023 New Zealand Election Study.

References

1News. 2022. 'Poll: More Voters Against Three Waters Than Support.' *1News*, [Auckland], 29 January. Available from: www.1news.co.nz/2022/01/29/poll-more-voters-against-three-waters-than-support/.

Bardosh, K., A. de Figueiredo, R. Gur-Arei, E. Jamrozik, J. Doidge, T. Lemmens, S. Keshavjee, J.E. Graham, and S. Baral. 2022. 'The Unintended Consequences of COVID-19 Vaccine Policy: Why Mandates, Passports and Restrictions May Cause More Harm Than Good.' *BMJ Global Health* 7(5): e008684. doi.org/10.1136/bmjgh-2022-008684.

Blavatnik School of Government (BSG). 2020–23. *COVID-19 Government Response Tracker*. Research Project. Oxford, UK: Blavatnik School of Government, University of Oxford. Available from: www.bsg.ox.ac.uk/research/research-projects/covid-19-government-response-tracker.

Carlsen, F. 2000. 'Unemployment, Inflation and Government Popularity: Are There Partisan Effects?' *Electoral Studies* 19(2–3): 141–50. doi.org/10.1016/s0261-3794(99)00044-x.

Charters, C., K. Kingdon-Bebb, T. Olsen, W. Ormsby, E. Owen, J. Pryor, J. Rura, N. Solomon, and G. Williams. 2020. *He Puapua: Report of the Working Group on a Plan to Realise the UN Declaration on the Rights of Indigenous Peoples in Aotearoa, New Zealand*. 1 November. Wellington: Te Puni Kōkiri. Available from: ndha deliver.natlib.govt.nz/delivery/DeliveryManagerServlet?dps_pid=IE68578740.

Cheng, D. 2021. 'Green Co-Leaders Unleash Scathing Attack on National Party.' *New Zealand Herald*, 8 August. Available from: www.nzherald.co.nz/nz/green-co-leaders-unleash-scathing-attack-on-national-party/DM4GJQ37IQDHD HPVOIWTBILL7U/.

Coughlan, T. 2022. 'People Less Willing to Comply with Covid-19 Rules, or Listen to Prime Minister Jacinda Ardern According to Government Survey.' *New Zealand Herald*, 22 August. Available from: www.nzherald.co.nz/nz/politics/people-less-willing-to-comply-with-covid-19-rules-or-listen-to-prime-minister-jacinda-ardern-according-to-government-survey/XC42SWUJNPNG 6PXSKW5HSPPO7I/.

Cullen, M. 2021. *Labour Saving: A Memoir*. Sydney: Allen & Unwin.

Dann, L. 2022. 'Wage Growth Soars as Unemployment Holds Steady at Record Low.' *New Zealand Herald*, 4 May. Available from: www.nzherald.co.nz/business/wage-growth-soars-as-unemployment-holds-steady-at-record-low/4R23BXB7 QZJBHITMTA4OB2TTX4/.

Department of the Prime Minister and Cabinet (DPMC). 2022. *Behaviour & Sentiment May 22 Update*. Wellington: New Zealand Government. Available from: covid19.govt.nz/assets/Proactive-Releases/Research/19-August-2022/Behaviour-and-Sentiment-Report-May-22-Update.pdf.

Edmunds, S., and M. Carroll. 2022. 'Inflation May Absorb Impact of New Zealand's Minimum Wage, Benefit Rises.' *Stuff*, [Wellington], 1 April. Available from: www.stuff.co.nz/business/industries/300556386/inflation-may-absorb-impact-of-nzs-minimum-wage-benefit-rises.

Edwards, B. 2022. 'Bryce Edwards: A Polarising Co-Governance Decision for Parliament.' *Political Roundup*, 21 April. Victoria University of Wellington. Available from: democracyproject.nz/2022/04/21/bryce-edwards-political-roundup-a-polarising-co-governance-decision-for-parliament/

Forbes, S. 2023. 'Former Labour MP Louisa Wall Could Stand for Te Pāti Māori in Manurewa.' *Radio New Zealand*, 17 April. Available from: www.rnz.co.nz/news/political/488115/former-labour-mp-louisa-wall-could-stand-for-te-pati-maori-in-manurewa.

Gabriel, V., Y.B. Kim, L. Martins, and P. Middleditch. 2022. 'A Relação entre Inflação e Desemprego: Considerações Empíricas e uma Comparação Simples entre EUA e Zona Euro [The Inflation–Unemployment Trade-Off: Empirical Considerations and a Simple US–Euro Area Comparison].' *Notas Económicas* 2022(54). doi.org/10.14195/2183-203X_54_1.

Gardener, L. 2016. 'The Economic Vote in New Zealand: An Analysis of How Macroeconomic Conditions and Perceptions of the Economy Affect Voter Behaviour.' MA thesis, University of Otago, Dunedin, NZ. Available from: ourarchive.otago.ac.nz/esploro/.

Hooton, M. 2022. 'Matthew Hooton: Peak Christopher Luxon Now Firmly in the Past.' *New Zealand Herald*, 5 August. Available from: www.nzherald.co.nz/business/matthew-hooton-peak-christopher-luxon-now-firmly-in-the-past/PFMJENYZFU7KOP35LA4OP3N76M/.

Hooton, M. 2023. 'Don't Rule Out National Leadership Change Before the Next Election.' *Patreon*, [Blog], 23 January. Available from: www.patreon.com/posts/dont-rule-out-77593479.

Horizon Research. 2021. 'Major Survey: Kiwis Demand Consultation on Three Waters.' 5–12 November. Auckland: Democracy Action. Available from: www.democracyaction.org.nz/major_survey_kiwis_demand_consultation_on_three_waters.

International Monetary Fund (IMF). 2023. 'New Zealand.' *Inflation Rate, Average Consumer Prices*. Washington, DC: International Monetary Fund. Available from: www.imf.org/external/datamapper/PCPIPCH@WEO/ADVEC/NZL.

Ipsos. 2022a. *The Ipsos New Zealand Issues Monitor: An Ipsos Survey—May 2022*. Auckland: Ipsos NZ. Available from: www.ipsos.com/en-nz/17th-ipsos-nz-issues-monitor-june-2022.

Ipsos. 2022b. *The Ipsos New Zealand Issues Monitor: An Ipsos Survey—September 2022*. Auckland: Ipsos NZ. Available from: www.ipsos.com/en-nz/18th-ipsos-new-zealand-issues-monitor-sept-2022.

Ipsos. 2023. *The Ipsos New Zealand Issues Monitor: An Ipsos Survey—February 2023*. Auckland: Ipsos NZ. Available from: www.ipsos.com/en-nz/19th-ipsos-new-zealand-issues-monitor.

Jackson, W. 2022. 'Māori Development Minister Willie Jackson Slams "One Person, One Vote" Outrage.' *New Zealand Herald*, 8 August. Available from: www.nzherald.co.nz/kahu/maori-development-minister-willie-jackson-slams-one-person-one-vote-outrage/PWAXX3ZYL6RZJZL5DBBAAHGZIM/.

Krugman, P. 2009. *A Country Is Not a Company*. Cambridge, MA: Harvard Business Publishing.

Lord Ashcroft. 2021. 'Living the Kiwi Dream? Politics and Public Opinion in New Zealand.' *Lord Ashcroft Polls*, [London], 31 October. Available from: lordashcroftpolls.com/2021/10/living-the-kiwi-dream-politics-and-public-opinion-in-new-zealand/.

Ludbrook, J. 2022. 'Three Waters Co-Governance: More of the Same or Different?' *BusinessDesk*, [Auckland], 2 August. Available from: businessdesk.co.nz/article/opinion/three-waters-co-governance-more-of-the-same-or-different.

Manhire, T. 2022. 'One in Four Say NZ Covid Restrictions Too Harsh, One in Four Say Too Weak—Poll.' *The Spinoff*, [Auckland], 20 February. Available from: thespinoff.co.nz/politics/20-02-2022/one-in-four-say-nz-covid-restrictions-too-harsh-one-in-four-say-too-weak-poll.

Ministry of Health. 2022. *COVID Vaccine Data*. Wellington: New Zealand Government. Available from: www.health.govt.nz/covid-19-novel-coronavirus/covid-19-data-and-statistics/covid-19-vaccine-data.

Moir, J. 2022. 'Jackson Not "Comfortable" With Co-Governance Draft.' *Newsroom*, [Auckland], 30 June, [Updated 2 July]. Available from: www.newsroom.co.nz/jackson-not-comfortable-with-co-governance-draft.

Morton, J. 2022. 'Covid 19: How Many Lives Did NZ's Pandemic Response Save?' *New Zealand Herald*, 24 August. Available from: www.nzherald.co.nz/nz/covid-19-how-many-lives-did-nzs-pandemic-response-save/6CL6PXKC226OWDYWEZCNRGCOOU/.

Our World in Data. 2023. *Covid-19 Stringency Index*. Global Change Data Lab, University of Oxford. Available from: ourworldindata.org/explorers/coronavirus-data-explorer?uniformYAxis=0&country=~NZL&hideControls=true&Metric=Stringency+index&Interval=7-day+rolling+average&Relative+to+Population=true&Color+by+test+positivity=false.

Palmer, M. 2006. 'Resolving the Foreshore and Seabed Dispute.' In *Political Leadership in New Zealand*, edited by R. Miller and M. Mintrom, 197–214. Auckland: Auckland University Press.

Park, B.B., and J. Shin. 2019. 'Do the Welfare Benefits Weaken the Economic Vote? A Cross-National Analysis of the Welfare State and Economic Voting.' *International Political Science Review* 40(1): 108–25. doi.org/10.1177/0192512117716169.

Pullar-Strecker, T. 2022. 'So Far, Reserve Bank Governor Adrian Orr Deserves a Second Term.' *Stuff*, [Wellington], 3 August. Available from www.stuff.co.nz/business/opinion-analysis/129441935/so-far-reserve-bank-governor-adrian-orr-deserves-a-second-term.

Radio New Zealand (RNZ). 2023a. 'Christopher Luxon Rules Out Working with Te Pāti Māori Post-Election.' *Radio New Zealand*, 10 May. Available from: www.rnz.co.nz/news/political/489609/christopher-luxon-rules-out-working-with-te-pati-maori-post-election.

Radio New Zealand (RNZ). 2023b. 'Labour Support Drops Again; Hipkins, Luxon Neck and Neck, According to Latest 1News-Verian Poll.' *Radio New Zealand*, 21 August. Available from: www.rnz.co.nz/news/top/496283/labour-support-drops-again-hipkins-luxon-neck-and-neck-according-to-latest-1news-verian-poll.

Randerson, R. 2022. 'He Puapua: A Fair Go for Māori.' *Anglicantaonga*, [Auckland], 1 April. Available from: www.anglicantaonga.org.nz/features/social_justice/bprr_hepuapua.

Renney, C. 2022. 'CTU Economist Questions How Government Spending Is Supposedly Lifting Prices When Countries That Have Spent Less Than NZ Are Also Experiencing High Inflation.' *Interest.co.nz*, [Auckland], 20 April. Available from: www.interest.co.nz/public-policy/115436/ctu-economist-questions-how-government-spending-supposedly-lifting-prices-when.

Salmond, A. 2022. 'Anne Salmond: Injustice Is Like a Whale.' *Newsroom*, [Auckland], 23 August, [Updated 27 August]. Available from: www.newsroom.co.nz/anne-salmond-injustice-is-like-a-whale.

Satherley, D. 2021. '"Not in a Democracy": Māori Party Co-Leader Rawiri Waititi Outlines His Vision for a "Tiriti-Centric Aotearoa" Where the Majority Doesn't Rule Over Māori.' *Newshub*, [Auckland], 3 July. Available from www.newshub.co.nz/home/politics/2021/07/not-in-a-democracy-m-ori-party-co-leader-rawiri-waititi-outlines-his-vision-for-a-tiriti-centric-aotearoa-where-the-majority-doesn-t-rule-over-m-ori.html.

Seymour, D. 2022. 'Lift the Veil on He Puapua.' Press release, 14 June. Auckland: ACT. Available from: www.act.org.nz/lift-the-veil-on-he-puapua.

StatsNZ. 2023. 'Annual Inflation at 6.0 Per Cent.' *News*, 19 July. Wellington: New Zealand Government. Available from: www.stats.govt.nz/news/annual-inflation-at-6-0-percent/.

Steyn, N., R.N. Binny, K. Hannah, S.C. Hendy, A. James, T. Kukutai, A. Lustig, M. McLeod, M.J. Plank, K. Ridings, and A. Sporle. 2020. 'Estimated Inequities in COVID-19 Infection Fatality Rates by Ethnicity for Aotearoa New Zealand.' *New Zealand Medical Journal* 133(1520): 28–39. Available from: pubmed.ncbi.nlm.nih.gov/32994635/.

Stuff. 2021. 'When Playing the Race Card Doesn't Work.' [Editorial], *Stuff*, [Wellington], 20 May. Available from: www.stuff.co.nz/national/politics/opinion/125177908/when-playing-the-race-card-doesnt-work.

Swank, O.H. 1993. 'Popularity Functions Based on the Partisan Theory.' *Public Choice* 75: 339–56. doi.org/10.1007/bf01053443.

theFacts. 2022. 'Summary of 10 Three Waters Polls.' *theFacts*, 26 July. Available from: thefacts.nz/environment/summary-of-10-three-waters-polls/.

Trevett, C. 2022. 'Claire Trevett: Cost of Living and National's Tax On, Tax Off Wobbles End a Bad Week for Both Labour and National.' *New Zealand Herald*, 6 August. Available from: www.nzherald.co.nz/nz/claire-trevett-cost-of-living-and-nationals-tax-on-tax-off-wobbles-end-a-bad-week-for-both-labour-and-national/AZG6TCAPIGQPLEANHUA4WFVTZI/.

van der Brug, W., and R. Rekker. 2021. 'Dealignment, Realignment and Generational Differences in the Netherlands.' *West European Politics* 44(4): 776–801. doi.org/10.1080/01402382.2020.1774203.

Verrall, A. 2021. 'COVID-19 Protection Framework Supported by New Testing and Contact Tracing Strategy.' Press release, 25 November. Wellington: New Zealand Government. Available from: www.beehive.govt.nz/release/covid-19-protection-framework-supported-new-testing-and-contact-tracing-strategy.

Vowles, J., S. Banducci, J. Karp, R. Miller, and A. Sullivan. 2022a. *2005 New Zealand Election Study*. [Online]. ADA Dataverse, V3. doi.org/10.26193/WJ8DGC.

Vowles, J., S. Banducci, J. Karp, R. Miller, A. Sullivan, and J. Curtin. 2022b. *2008 New Zealand Election Study*. [Online]. ADA Dataverse, V3. doi.org/10.26193/6CVEYM.

Vowles, J., F. Barker, M. Krewel, J. Hayward, J. Curtin, L. Greaves, and L. Oldfield. 2022c. *2020 New Zealand Election Study*. [Online]. ADA Dataverse, V3. doi.org/10.26193/BPAMYJ.

Vowles, J., H. Coffé, J. Curtin, and G. Cotterell. 2022d. *2014 New Zealand Election Study*. [Online]. ADA Dataverse, V3. doi.org/10.26193/MF9DNL.

Vowles, J., G. Cotterell, R. Miller, and J. Curtin. 2022e. *2011 New Zealand Election Study*. ADA Dataverse, V3. doi.org/10.26193/YZDMF3.

Vowles, J., K. McMillan, F. Barker, J. Curtin, J. Hayward, L. Greaves, and C. Crothers. 2022f. *2017 New Zealand Election Study*. ADA Dataverse, V3. doi.org/10.26193/28JJFB.

Wikipedia. 2023. 'Opinion Polling for the 2023 New Zealand General Election.' *Wikipedia*. Available from: en.wikipedia.org/wiki/Opinion_polling_for_the_2023_New_Zealand_general_election.

Wilkinson, B., and G. Wheeler. 2022. *How Central Bank Mistakes After 2019 Led to Inflation*. Research Note, 26 July. Wellington: The New Zealand Initiative. Available from: www.nzinitiative.org.nz/reports-and-media/reports/how-central-bank-mistakes-after-2019-led-to-inflation/.

Appendix: The 2020 New Zealand Election Study

The 2020 New Zealand Election Study (NZES) was run after the 2020 general election on 17 October, which had been delayed due to a Covid-19 lockdown in Auckland. Data collection was run through the Public Policy Institute at the University of Auckland. Participants were sent a $20 grocery voucher as thanks for their efforts. The 2020 NZES was funded by Victoria University of Wellington, the New Zealand Electoral Commission, the University of Auckland, and Otago University. The 2020 NZES frequency tables, weighted by Māori/general electorates, age, gender, highest educational qualification, party vote, and turnout, are available from: www.jackvowles.com/2020Frequencies.html.

A new sample was taken from the electoral rolls that contained the names of 94.1 per cent of those eligible to vote by age according to Statistics New Zealand, less about 0.6 per cent whose names were on the confidential roll. The writ day roll as of one month before the election was first sampled. Several additional names were sampled from the final roll from those who had been added during the campaign. The text of the questionnaire can be found at: bpb-ap-se2.wpmucdn.com/blogs.auckland.ac.nz/dist/e/716/files/2021/12/NZES-2020-Final.pdf.

The new sample was segmented into those of Māori and non-Māori descent, and between those aged 18–31 and those aged 31 and above using the five-year age bands provided in the electronic roll. Both those of Māori descent and those aged 18–29 were oversampled. Those of Māori descent were oversampled to deliver a sufficiently large sample for separate analysis. Those aged 18–31 were oversampled to compensate for an expected lower response rate from that group.

Participants in 2017 who had agreed to be recontacted to participate in 2020 were also matched to the new roll and formed part of the 2020 sample.

All prospective participants were sent a hardcopy questionnaire by mail, except 500 non-Māori from the new sample who were encouraged to participate online only. If they had not responded after three weeks, they were sent a hardcopy questionnaire like other participants, who also received a second questionnaire at the same time. This 'push to web' experiment had the effect of slightly reducing the response rate among those aged 31 and over, but there was no difference among those aged 18–31 between being pushed to the web and not pushed to the web. The questionnaire was available online in English, te reo Māori, and Chinese.

Those of Māori descent were split, with half receiving an additional information letter in te reo Māori and the other half only the English version. Those receiving the te reo version had a slightly higher response rate, but the difference was not statistically significant.

The response rate for the 2020–17 panellists was 62 per cent. Weighting the component group response rates by their proportions of the sample, the overall response rate for the new sample was 32.3 per cent. The total sample was 3,730, including 1,246 of Māori descent, some of whom came from the 2017 panel. For most analyses, a sampling weight was applied to correct for the oversampling, adjusting first for age, gender, and Māori descent to match the distribution in the roll, and then for party vote/ nonvote and education, the latter by iterative weights on the party vote and education margins.

www.ingramcontent.com/pod-product-compliance
Lightning Source LLC
Chambersburg PA
CBHW050628280326
41932CB00015B/2568